A History of

EUROPEAN FOLK MUSIC

A History of

EUROPEAN FOLK MUSIC

Jan Ling

Professor of Musicology
Göteborg University

Translated from the Swedish
by Linda and Robert Schenck

Ⓡ UNIVERSITY OF ROCHESTER PRESS

First Published in Swedish by Akademiförlaget, 1988
First published in English by University of Rochester Press in 1997

University of Rochester Press
34–36 Administration Building
University of Rochester
Rochester, NY 14627   USA

and at P.O. Box 9
Woodbridge, Suffolk IP12 3DF
United Kingdom

ISBN 1–878822–77–2

Library of Congress Cataloging-in-Publication Data
Ling, Jan. 1934–
    [Europas musikhistoria. English]
    A history of European folk music / Jan Ling ; translated from the
Swedish by Linda and Robert Schenck.
        p.   cm.
    Includes bibliographical references (p. 225) and index.
    ISBN 1-878822-77-2 (alk. paper)
    1. Folk music–Europe–History.
ML3580.L5613 1997
    781.62'0094–dc21   97–1136
                                                                 CIP
                                                                 MN

British Library Cataloguing-in-Publication Data
A catalogue record for this book is
available from the British Library

Designed and typeset by Cornerstone Composition Services
Printed in the United States of America
This publication is printed on acid-free paper

CONTENTS

INTRODUCTION: WHAT DO WE MEAN BY
FOLK, *FOLK SONG*, AND *FOLK MUSIC*?   1
European Folk Music:
  The Music of Rural Areas   1

1   IN SEARCH OF "THE SONGS OF
   THE PEOPLE"   15
Discovering that the Hills Were Alive   15

2   MUSIC AT WORK   22
Rural Soundscapes of the Past   22
Herding Calls   23
Songs of Work   35
Outdoor Music for Pile-driving, Loading,
  Pulling, etc.   39
Songs of Domestic Labor   41

3   MELODIES MARKING THE PEN-
   DULUM OF LIFE AND THE
   CHANGING SEASONS   45
Concepts of Time in the Past and Today   45
Music throughout the Life Cycle   45
Instrumental Music and Songs about
  Love and Weddings   49
Music Around the Calendar   65

4   "BURSTING INTO SONG" (I): THE
   JOJK, NARRATIVE SONG, AND
   BALLAD   75
The Saami *Jojk*   75
Narrative Songs from the East   78
Narrative Song in the Balkans   86
Narrative Song in the West   90
Similarities, Relationships, and Origins
  in the Heroic Song Tradition   93
Ballads in East and West   94

5   "BURSTING INTO SONG" (II): THE
   LYRIC SONG AND THE HYMN   103
Lyric Songs, Spiritual Songs, and Hymns   103
Popular Hymns   114
Singing Folk Music   116

6   THE PLAYING OF FOLK MUSIC (I):
   SPONTANEOUS SOUND MAKERS,
   ACOUSTIC WORKING
   EQUIPMENT   123
What Do Musical Instruments Tell Us?   123
What is a Folk Instrument?   123

7   THE PLAYING OF FOLK MUSIC (II):
   THE TRANSFORMATION OF
   MUSICAL INSTRUMENTS   134
Medieval Instruments in Popular Music
  Cultures   134

8   THE PLAYING OF FOLK MUSIC (III):
   MUSICAL INSTRUMENTS FOR THE
   PEOPLE   154
Fiddles, Violins, and Books of
  Fiddlers' Tunes   154

9   FOLK MUSIC ENSEMBLES   167
Forms of Ensemble Playing   167

10   MOVEMENT AND DANCE, SONG
   AND INSTRUMENTAL MUSIC   179
Background   179
Line and Ring Dances   180
From Line and Ring to Two by Two   186

11   FOLK MUSIC BETWEEN TOWN
   AND COUNTRY   199
Folk Music as Art Music and Popular
  Music   199
Folk Music Transormed to the Composer's
  Personal Style   206

12   EUROPEAN FOLK MUSIC:
   A UNIFORM DIVERSITY   220
Concluding Remarks   220

BIBLIOGRAPHY   225

INDEX   253

Figure I.1. The author discussing folk music with three fiddler-philosophers, Ale Möller, Leif Stinnerbom, and Owe Ronström, at a public lecture at the Falun folk music festival in 1987. Photo: Per-Ulf Allmo.

Introduction

What Do We Mean by *Folk, Folk Song,* and *Folk Music?*

EUROPEAN FOLK MUSIC: THE MUSIC OF RURAL AREAS

Today, all over Europe, people are busy with something called *folk music*. The summer months are packed with "folk music festivals," and there are endless numbers of "folk music groups" and "folk dance groups." It is possible to be a "folk music" or "folk dance" scholar at many different conservatories, schools of dance, archives, and universities. Every self-respecting radio station will have its "folk music" shows. This book describes some of the roots of this music, beginning mainly in the eighteenth century, when systematic collection of rural songs, tunes, and dances began. It was also the time when the terms *folk song* and *folk music* (and their equivalents in other languages) were coined by collectors and scholars. Their twentieth-century counterparts did not begin to apply the terms to their own work, however, until *folk music* and *folk songs* had become acknowledged as genres and regarded as part of European cultural heritage.

However, it is difficult if not impossible to isolate of folk music as a genre. Both tunes and instruments associated with folk music can also be found in classical music, jazz, pop, rock, and Muzak®. Different kinds of music interweave and overlap, and trying to isolate a genre tends to amputate it. Although the foundation of this work is European folk music (i.e., the music of traditional peasant society, rooted in work and in fixed customs), the reader will also realize that such music is constantly being intermingled with urban, popular and art music, and is an ongoing melting pot.

When I use the terms *folk music, folk songs,* and *folk dances*, I primarily mean rural music taught, without being written down, by one generation to the next. Although other authors sometimes use these same terms to refer to the urban music played for entertainment that came into being in the eighteenth and nineteenth centuries, I refer to such music as *popular music*, and only mention it when it is directly related to rural music.

In one or two places, however, I have incorporated some aspects of urban music culture into this book. These are cases of what may be referred to as *city music folklore* (i.e., developments parallel to rural song, dance, and instrumental music with regard to both style and function, often closely associated with their rural parallels).

Big Bill Broonzy is said to have claimed, "I guess every song is a *folk* song—at least I never heard a horse sing 'em!" It is certainly true that it has proven to be extraordinarily difficult to define and delineate folk music. I agree with the words of Albert Lloyd, the British folk music scholar, who described folk music as one branch of an enormous tree of music: "Deep at the root, there is no essential difference between folk music and art music; they are varied blossoms from the same stock, grown to serve a similar purpose, if destined for different tables. Originally they spring from the same area of man's mind; their divergence is a matter of history, of social and cultural stratification" (Lloyd 1967, p. 17).

Music Labels

Labels such as *folk music, popular music,* and *art music* were invented to *distinguish* different kinds of music from one another. They may be appropriate, even essential, as key words for retrieval when look-

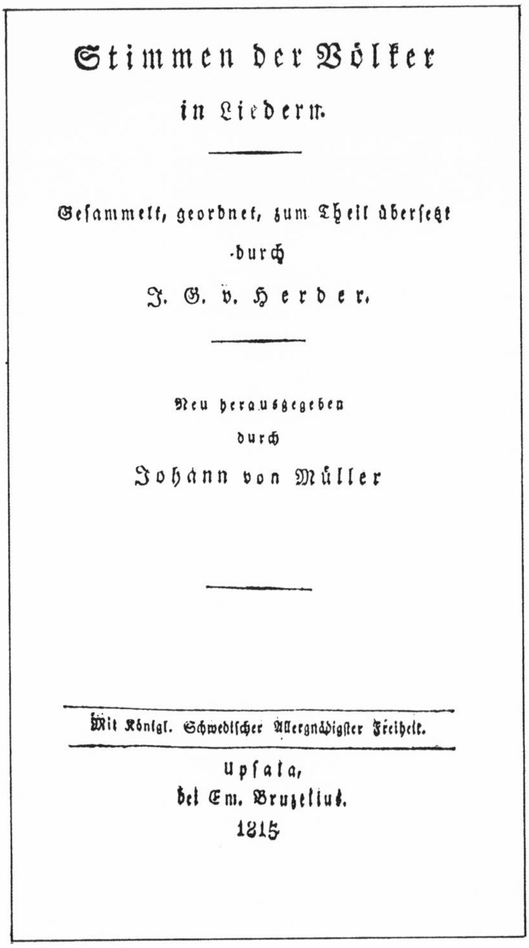

Stimmen der Völker

in Liedern.

Gesammelt, georbnet, zum Theil überfest

·durch

J. G. v. Herder,

Neu herausgegeben
durch
Johann von Müller

Mit Königl. Schwedischer Allergnädigster Freibeit.

Upsala,
bei Em. Brupellut.
1815

Figure I.2. The title page from Herder's *Stimmen der Völker in Liedern*, published as part of the series *Bibliothek der Deutschen Classiker*, Uppsala, 1815.

ing for a piece of music on disk or in a library database. But the preconceptions and myths that develop around these music labels may be a liability and not always the best way of encouraging dynamism in the world of music. Music scholars love to stress differences and to put up fences around their own musical territories, sometimes simply for ideological reasons in the absence of empirical knowledge about the people who listen to the music or about what it means to listen.

Folk

The term *folk* came into use in diverse contexts in late-eighteenth-century Europe, in conjunction with some trends in political ideology (Rehnberg 1977, Ronström 1987). Johann Gottfried von Herder, for example, called the songs he encountered among the rural population *Volkslieder* (1774, 1778-1779). One very important contribution he made was to claim that these folk songs were an expression of something both generalizable and universal, and restricted–reflecting the history, landscape, and unique national features of the country from which they came (Figure I.2).

> Germany, great nation, nation of ten peoples! You have no Shakespeare, but do you also lack great songs of your forefathers to swoon over? . . .
>
> People of strong tradition, noble virtue and language, are there no traces of your soul in times past? No doubt! There have been and still are perhaps, but they may be concealed, unknown, despised. (Herder 1777, quotes after Frey/Siniveer 1987, p. 116.)

Folk Music and Written Musical Notation

Folk music, both sung and played, is traditionally learned by ear and has been closely associated with work, tradition, and ceremony. Although folk music has been notated so that it would not have to be memorized, and to preserve it for posterity, newly created folk music has not traditionally been presented in written form.

Since written notation is not the traditional medium of folk music, it is not surprising to find that only a fraction of all the songs traditionally sung as lullabies, or while cooking, spinning, or weaving, the songs played for dancing, and the shouts and rhymes of sailors, lumberjacks, mountain shepherds, and farmers have been preserved. Still, there is such a wealth of material preserved that no single human life would suffice to read and listen to the contents of existing folk music volumes and archives.

There are only sporadic sources available on the period prior to the eighteenth century, but the flow picks up considerably as that century rolls on. From isolated, random "pieces of evidence" early in the 1800s, there were, by the end of the century, increasingly systematic collections which provided the backbone for the folk music archives that can be found in nearly every country in Europe and that contain recordings of all kinds of folk music dating from the early twentieth century onwards.

Who Decided What a *Folk Song* and *Folk Music* Are?

As mentioned above, the terms *folk song, folk music,* and *folk culture* were coined by literary and historical collectors as early as the late eighteenth century, but not until relatively modern times did fiddlers and singers begin to call their tunes and songs *folk music* and *folk songs*. Farmers and peasants did not even tend to think of their shouts or ceremonial melodies as *music* at all, nor did the majority of people who were considered experts on music. Connoisseurs of music were barely able to keep a straight face when confronted with yodelling, and reacted to laments with either distaste or laughter:

> Karl Spaizier, the north German music critic, made the following observations about yodelling in 1790: 'Any musician would have to work hard to suppress a sarcastic smile.' (Salmen 1980, p. 69.)
> Elias Lönnrot regarded laments as 'painful to listen to.' (Kuusi/Honko, 1983, p. 80.) (See Fig. I.3.)
> Goethe described the singing he heard in Verona in 1786 as a mixture of screaming, singing, and general noise. (Schmidt 1980, p. 58.)

Work shouts and peasant dances and songs were also familiar outside their own musical environment among musicians and intellectuals. Peasant melodies found their way into polyphonic art music as early as the fifteenth century and also appear in sixteenth and seventeenth-century instrumental books as curiosities, along with classical or exotic instruments (see Ling 1983, pp. 295f. and 414f.). Not until the eighteenth and early nineteenth century, however, were folk songs, dances, and tunes cultivated as a specific, independent category. The fact that this happened in various European countries at about the same time is not a coincidence. Such music provided a counterbalance to the highly specialized functions and aesthetic regulations of art music. Many people regarded folk music as an antidote to the "artificialization" of music, that could be used to build bridges, closing the gap between highly disparate musical environments.

Unfortunately, there are very few extant indications of what the musicians, dancers, singers, and audiences from the rural environments actually thought about what we now call folk music. What we do know for certain, however, is that there were extremely highly developed concepts of what such songs, tunes, and dances should be and when, where, and how they were to be performed. It must be borne in mind, however, that such information often reaches us via collectors and scholars whose point of departure is firmly fixed in theories of art music, and that these sources, therefore, are biased.

Folk Music: Music in Constant Flux

There is one misconception that must be rectified before this voyage into folk music begins: rural music has not been static, nor has it remained unchanged throughout the centuries. Radical transformations of society, such as wars, the industrial revolution, the introduction of compulsory schooling, new means of transportation such as trains and road vehicles, have facilitated cultural migration and hastened the pace of change. This has had a highly innovative effect on ceremonial songs, melodies, and dances. In some places, cultures have remained more isolated, and these are the places where more traditional music has remained unaffected, passed down from one generation to the next (by people with good memories), until the present day, when recordings have allowed them to take a place of honor in archives and on disk. This isolation is reflected both in how the music is performed and in its structure.

Studying song, dance, and melody from recordings poses special problems. It is important to remember that more recent recordings cannot be taken at face value as real examples of how music noted down in early times was actually performed, since every period has its own style of performance of both songs and instrumental music.

Aims of This Book

The primary aim of this book is to increase the reader's understanding of the fascinating art of folk music, and to keep it alive as a dynamic, changing art form, not merely a part of sentimental cultural history.

The questions I hope we will be able to answer after our encounters with different kinds of music and different national and cultural environments include:

- What similarities and differences can be found when comparing the different kinds of rural music from all over Europe? What links can be found between rural music and popular and art music?
- Can we elucidate the connections among and the development of contemporary folk music from different parts of Europe by (a) examining the ways in which scholars from different periods and with different ideological and artistic ambitions have collected various kinds of music? (b) describing the interfaces between folk music and art and popular music?

- Is it possible to distinguish, today, anything special about the contents or function of the musical material we refer to as folk music, or is folk music simply a mythological guise we impose on certain sound structures in order to avoid the restrictions imposed by the official education system and status of other kinds of music, such as art music and commercial popular music?

Structure of This Book

Chapter 1 introduces some of the collectors from different parts of Europe, with a view to illuminating the ideological nature of the source material. What do the sources actually tell us of the soundscape of the rural areas in the eighteenth and nineteenth centuries, and how should we interpret it? What is "behind" the notation of a melody or the description of a dance performance in words or images?

Chapter 2 deals with shouts and calls used at work, and working tools that were also used to make music, highlighting the fact that what we call folk music is primarily music from rural and maritime areas.

Chapter 3 describes songs of the life cycle and the cycle of the year in order to provide insight into a cyclic time perspective, with song as the lodestar.

Chapters 4 and 5, Parts I and II, present songs from evenings by the fireside, hiking songs, songs of prayer, and songs from other occasions when it was used to gild the atmosphere without infringing on the other activities at hand.

Chapters 6–9 deal with musical instruments and instrumental ensembles. This leads directly into Chapter 10, on dance, since the vast majority of all rural instrumental music was music for dancing.

Chapter 11 is intended to provide insight into different kinds of interplay between composers, singers, and fiddlers, as well as how composers took inspiration from folk melodies that, among other things, provided their works with a patriotic substance. This chapter also discusses the encounter between rural folk music and urban popular music.

Chapter 12 provides a summary and draws some conclusions about folk music.

Literature

The articles on individual countries in the *New Grove Dictionary of Music and Musicians* provide a good overview of the positions of the experts and scholars of the folk music of their own countries.

Figure I.3. Elias Lönnrot (1802-1884), one of the most prominent European gatherers of material on popular cultures, on one of his journeys in the Finnish countryside. (Caricature by A.W. Linsén, 1847.)

For a more theoretical discussion of the term *folk music,* an excellent overview of the Nordic countries may be found in Dal (1956). Many attempts, mostly fruitless, have been made to standardize what is meant by folk music. Maud Karpele's short 1954 article on efforts to define folk music provides a very useful perspective. Regarding the concept of folk music in Sweden, I can refer to *Folkmusikboken* (1981), and to an article by myself from 1979 in Swedish, "The melting pot of folk music," *Folk* (1977) by Mats Rehnberg, is a survey of words relating to the concept of *folk.* An article on "European Folk Music" (unpublished ms. 1987, in Swedish), by Owe Ronström is an attempt to examine various problems associated with the words *Europe, folk,* and *music.*

There is a lively, ongoing debate all over Europe on what these terms mean within the folk music revival movement in journals such as the Swedish *Spelmannen* and *Hembygden,* as well as elsewhere in the media.

There are also tensions between a "purist" folk music strategy and a more "open" one, in which the former attempts to be historically correct according to traditional concepts while the latter tends to regard folk music as a symbiosis between various kinds of popular music (see also Chapter 11).

One

In Search of "the Songs of the People"

DISCOVERING THAT THE HILLS WERE ALIVE

The second half of the eighteenth century and the early nineteenth century saw the real "discovery" of Europe by artists and authors. Above all, they were enticed by the more exotic places—the wild, barren mountain regions or idyllic peasant villages, in contrast to cultured, bourgeois civilization. Artists and authors had patrons, members of the nobility and the bourgeoisie, whose wanderlust could be vicariously satisfied through gazing at works of art and reading more or less imaginative eyewitness accounts. The wealth of letters available from this time also testifies to the obligatory dramatic descriptions of the landscape. However, travelling for education and pleasure was restricted to the educated upper classes.

Putting the Hills into Music

It was only natural for travelers to discover that strange landscapes and cultures also had music of their own. This discovery often took the shape of a sudden, overwhelming moment of beauty, not unlike the feeling a mountain climber would have when coming upon an exquisite view.

There are many extant descriptions of travelers' spontaneous experiences of singing, dancing, and instrumental music. Some of these were simply transitory "snapshots" from musical journeys, while others left lasting impressions. These experiences provided a foundation for what was to be known as European folk music. This took place in at least three different ways:

1. The travelers wrote down the music they heard and presented it at a later date in musical and literary salons, as a sort of musical travelog.
2. They intellectualized their musical experience, incorporating it into the history of peoples and nations.
3. They used the music they experienced as a source of inspiration for their own musical compositions, citing from memory and mixing these quotations with their own creative efforts.

While the first of these methods increased general interest in folk music among the educated élite, the second was the prerequisite for the scholarly collection and analysis of folk music that began during the nineteenth century, and the third laid the foundation for the kind of nationalistic composition that largely came to dominate nineteenth-century music.

This chapter follows the trends emanating from points 1 and 2 above, while point 3, the relationship between the composer and folk music, is discussed in Chapter 11.

The description given here cannot, of course, be an exhaustive one. The reader wanting to know more about the growing interest in folk music as a literary phenomenon is referred to the various national and regional surveys, some of them mentioned in the bibliography. This chapter provides examples of the thoughts of those whose early writings describe folk music about the music they encountered. The transcriptions as such are, and will remain, like "dried flowers in a collection," to quote a collector from the early nineteenth century. Using them along with our own voices or instruments, in combination with listening to similar vocal and instrumental music and learning about different musical environments, gives us some idea of the musical scent of such dried flowers. Sketches and paintings of dancing and literary descriptions of different musical events are also useful in giving us a feel for the environment.

Discovering Music of the People

What actually happened when a painter or an author approached "the people"? In his memoirs, painter Wilhelm Tischbein describes an occasion on which he was travelling through Switzerland in 1780 and asked the people at an inn at the foot of Mount Saint Gotthard to dance. The girls were immediately pleased to do as he requested; "however, they made such a dreadful clapping with their heavy wooden shoes that I was relieved when they stopped. They went on to sing yet another Kuhreihen" [on the Kuhreihen see p. 32] (Schmidt 1980, p. 58). Although Tischbein did not appreciate popular entertainment, he had contemporaries who did, and who thus described it in more glowing terms. Take, for example, Baron Karl Eherbert, a popular educator from Salzburg, who found himself in a wooden shack on a rainy evening in 1784:

> There we sat round the hearth in a pitch dark kitchen, nearly suffocating from the smoke—the hunter, his faithful wife, his shepherd and my bearer. It would have been quite miserable to spend the evening in such company if the honourable shepherd had not passed the time displaying his musical gifts. He would whisper an allemand on his Jew's harp, fiddle a couple of lovely minuets or folk tunes on his violin, or play the great lover singing a heart-rending aria. (Quotes after Schmidt 1980, p. 58.)

The people these first explorers of folk songs and music encountered in the eighteenth and early nineteenth centuries appear to have been happy to sing, dance, and play for strangers. It was not even necessary to ask rural people to perform. Song, dance, and music were part of their everyday lives and not displays that had to be sought out. They were part of the soundscape to be experienced by any traveler who had ears prepared to listen to music as a new experience, even if their

view point was of the normative structure of classical music. George Sand, the French novelist, described the singing of cattle-drivers from Berry, France:

> Male voices . . . intoning their grave, melancholy song, passed down by ancient tradition in the region not, of course, equally to all peasants, but only to those most skilled at driving the cattle and encouraging them at their work. This song, which might once have been thought to be spiritual in origin and to which mythical powers were attributed, is still thought to be able to cheer the animals, ease their woes, and distract them from their tiresome toil. It is really a sort of recitative, arbitrarily interrupted and recommenced. Its irregularities in form and intonation, which are often disharmonic when regarded as music, make it impossible to describe. At any rate it is a wondrously beautiful song, so well suited to the nature of the attendant labour, the pace of the oxen, the harmony of the countryside and the simplicity of the song, that it could never have been invented by anyone unacquainted with rural life, nor sung by anyone other than a hardworking peasant from these tracts. . . .The last note in each phrase, held in a tremolo of astonishing length and volume, rises a quarter tone in well-calculated disharmony. It is a wild song, but it has an indescribable charm. (George Sand, *La mare au Diable*, from the province of Berry.)

Composers from Frédéric Chopin to Igor Stravinsky could sit for hours trying to transcribe these songs onto paper, exactly as a landscape artist might spend days working to capture a rural scene. Sand also wrote: "I have seen Chopin, one of the greatest musicians of our times and Madame Pauline Viardot, spending hours transcribing some melodic phrases from our singers and our bagpipe players." (Hollinger, Roland *Les Musiques a Bourdons. Vielles a roue et cornemuse.* Paris 1982, p. 192.)

Although George Sand's description of the ox-drivers' singing is musically observant, such descriptions are often of music in a social context. Carl Gustav Carus, a physician, artist, and a childhood friend of Johann Wolfgang Von Goethe, describes a journey in an open carriage from Dresden to Lauback in 1839:

> Then I heard a peculiar sharptone from afar—it was a straw fiddle [German *Strohfiddel* = a xylophone with wooden bars laid across a bed of straw]. By the roadside there was a man, sitting or rather crouching, half clad in rags, playing his instrument on the ground. Nearby there was a little carriage with simple

household goods, a child, and a woman marked by long suffering. At her side was tied a small pig. (Schmidt 1980, p. 62.)

This description could well be the caption to many earlier sketches and paintings of wandering musicians who begged for alms. There are any number of pieces of circumstantial evidence. An earlier example consists of notes made by Empress Anna of Russia in 1739. She heard the commander-in-chief in Moscow sing a song, and was so enchanted by it, she commanded that a dance be choreographed to it and that it be noted down. (Zemtsovsky 1967, p. 12.) But let us now abandon these more or less incidental sources and approach the more systematically oriented collections.

Toward the Systematic Collection of Folk Song

The painters and travelers sought characteristic scenes to satisfy the tremendous and fashionable desire to experience, at least indirectly, savage nature and its primitive inhabitants.

The title page of Linnaeus's *Flora Lapponica* of 1737, (Figure 1.1) illustrates the romantic, beautiful, and exotic wildness and proximity to nature that recurs in eighteenth- and nineteenth-century travelogs and letters. This was the very beginning of the infatuation with nature that evolved first into rural sentimentality and then tourism. The artist has included various attributes: the reindeer, the Lapp tent, the skis, and two Lapp drums, one being played by a Saami, the other lying on the skis. Near them is a drum-beater.

But even scientists who, in the spirit of the Enlightenment, strove for sober descriptions had their limits. Italian envoy J. Acerbi and his Swedish guide A. F. Skjöldebrand provide examples of "the dreadful" and "the acceptable" in music from their journeys to study the Saami and the Finns in 1798–99:

> I tried on several occasions, using both coins and spirits to wield my power, to encourage the herde-lapparna (the herding Lapps) to perform their melodies which, if possible, would give me some idea of their music: but the most I could achieve was to make them utter terrible shouts, during the course of which I sometimes had to put my fingers in my ears. It is hardly credible, but entirely true, that mountain Lapps and nomadic Lapps have no sense of harmony whatsoever, and that they are entirely incompetent

VIRO NOBILISSIMO ET CONSULTISSIMO D. GEORGIO CLIFFORTIO J. V. D.

Figure 1.1. Title page from Linnaeus's *Flora Lapponica*, 1737. (Copperplate print by Adolf van der Lann, Amsterdam, after a sketch by Martin Hoffman.)

> to experience the pleasure which, to my knowledge, mother nature has not withheld from any other tribe or nation access. Serious music appears to be entirely banned from these godforsaken and isolated areas. (Acerbi 1802: II, pp. 66f.)

It is not surprising that historians of music who read Acerbi's accounts thought of the Saami as the only people unable to sing. Acerbi was considerably more understanding in his encounter with runic song in Finland (see p. 78), which was less wild and alien.

> *Runa* is an example of the most ancient Finnish melody, maintained by this people and adapted to their national instrument, known as the *harpu* (*kantele*), probably the forerunner of our harp, or a copy of the ancient Greek kithara. Most certainly, the inhabitants of Finland have a real sensitivity to both music and poetry. These two art forms seem to merge, but the Finns have made less progress in music than in poetry, as may be seen in the limita-

tions of their national instrument, and the respect and devotion with which they maintain it. The harpu has five strings, which gives us some idea of the primitive level of their art. They have not considered equipping it with more strings than they have fingers on one hand. (Acerbi 1802: II, pp. 283f.)

The runic song was, then, instrumentally accompanied on the kantele, and this may be regarded as a first step in the direction of an art form. Later in their journey, when the two explorers heard more ordinary folk singing they were enthusiastic, probably because of the similarities to the kind of music to which they were accustomed.

The Balkans were another "wild" area. The extremely exotic heroic melodies from this area were appreciated early, despite the fact that both the melodies and the accompaniment on the *gusle* (see p. 87, 139) were clearly very different from the norms applying to art music of the time. There were a couple of intermediate phases leading to the appreciation of this music.

The first was the translation, and adaptation of folk songs. In connection with the interest in folk music triggered by Herder, German musicians became interested in explorers' descriptions of the Balkan Peninsula as the quintessence of a dramatic landscape inhabited by a wild, freedom-loving people.

The second was the composition of "Slavic melodies" inspired by the text of the folk songs but with no connection whatsoever with their melodies. Such "Slavic melodies" were composed by Goethe's nephew Walter Wolfgang (1818–1885) and others. In *Slawische Bilder für eine Singstimme mit Pianofortebegleitung* the composer tried to establish the appropriate tone for the folk songs, a project in perfect accord with his renowned uncle's intentions. This prepared the ground for Smetana, Dvorák and others who later presented exotic music from the east in the concert halls of central Europe. Their music became "Slavic nationalist," an idea completely foreign to the people whose poetry served as the composers' source of inspiration.

After these phases the way had been paved for scholarly notation of the song themselves. This, in turn, triggered an interest in the original, sources, and so began scholarly collection (see also the preface of *Serbische Volkslieder* 1980).

This view of the Balkans as a wild, romantic place may also be found in a series of illustrations. Vuk himself was an incarnation of romantic na-

tionalism, the inventor of written Serbo-Croatian, and a participant in the revolt against the Turks in 1804. Inspired by Herder and Arnim/Bretano he began to note down the heroic poems and songs (see also *Serbische Volkslieder* 1980, pp. 240 ff. and 109).

Of the innumerable extant compositions of Serbian folk poetry, the example given here is the second of Antonín Dvorák's four songs set to Serbian texts (Figure 1.2).

This is one of many successful efforts to harness the wild and the exotic and transform it into music for entertainment in the salons. But, of course, it was not the heroic songs of the men but the lyrical songs of the women that were used in this manner.

The New Home of Folk Song: Salon and Concert Hall

That collectors were primarily interested in folk song lyrics is quite clear from the two cases described above: 1) presentations of folk music for musicians, music lovers, and the bourgeoisie: 2) ideological declarations of the songs as belonging to the people (i.e. folk songs, national songs, or what came to be referred to as cultural heritage or traditional music).

Let us examine examples of presentations to the bourgeoisie from two Swedish environments illustrating the introduction of the folk song in private salons and public concert halls.

Arvid August Afzelius (1785–1871), later a pastor, was in his youth one of numerous fanciful romantics all over Europe who performed the folk songs he had collected and noted down. He spent one summer in the 1810s journeying in the spirit of Linnaeus, collecting herbs in western Sweden, and increasing:

not only my collection of herbs but also of folk songs. In the evenings when I took shelter with a crofter or a peasant and sang one or two of the old songs of chivalry for the young people of the house, the farm hands would often take me into their confidence and the daughters of the house would always donate a new song to my collection. I would listen and note it down at once, and would also note down the melody with the help of a little pipe. In the end, I had a large collection of folk songs and traditional tales. (Jonsson 1967, p. 402.)

A couple of years later Afzelius performed these folk songs in Stockholm, at the home of General Field Marshall Helvig:

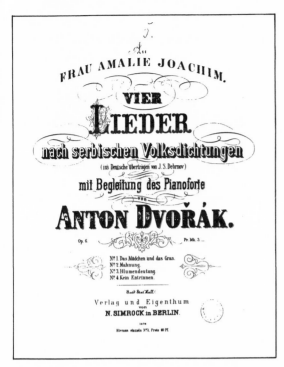

Figure 1.2. Title page and first page of the second of Antonin Dvorák's four songs set to Serbian folk poems from 1872, published in Berlin in 1879.

After a couple of hours' conversation on scholarly subjects, a simple evening repast was served, always consisting of chops and a glass of well-aged Malaga. Then my time had come, and the General shouted: 'Afzelius, do give us the pleasure of a folk song!' I would sing one of the old folk songs, such as 'Spellbound,' 'A maiden on her way to morning mass,' 'Hillebrand served on the King's estate,' 'I want to travel to the east' or another song of my choice from the Middle Ages. I knew all these songs by heart, and would have to sing one from beginning to end, as it was the words everyone wanted to hear, and they could never be properly understood without their melody. (Jonsson 1967, p. 402.)

The songs performed by Afzelius at Helvig's home were later published in his collection of folk songs (Figure 1.3) "Hillebrand Served on the King's Estate" was first written down by Sven Magnus Liedzén (1783–1850). According to later information "he often described the difficulty of figuring out the melody, since the old woman who sang the song did not sing in tune." (See also Jonsson 1967, pp. 408f. and *Sveriges medeltida ballader,* vol. 1, 1983 pp. 158f.). Thus an "uncertain" melody became a stable folk tune once it was written down.

In addition to this way of presenting folk songs in the salons, there was also the option of public performance. Originally this mainly meant professional artists singing arrangements of folk songs and melodies. Richard Dybeck, antiquities researcher, organized this type of folk music evening in Stockholm in the 1840s. After attending one such concert, Amanda Kerfstedt, described her experience:

It was to take place in the large concert hall at the Kirstein Building. The tickets were sold out in advance, as his case was a touching one. [Dybeck had recently suffered a stroke.] There were rumours of a newly-notated folk song, the melody of which had been somewhat revised by the man who organized the concert, who had also written a text. Many of the most prominent Stockholm music personalities were present.

In one corner of the stage, near the wall, was an armchair, and sitting in it a man wrapped in a wolfskin coat. It was he. It had been impossible to keep him away. His own beloved music was to be performed for the élite of the music connoisseurs of the capital. The performers were amateurs of the highest calibre.

Figure 1.3. "Hillebrand served on the King's estate," no. 2 in the Geijer-Afzelii edition of Swedish folk songs 1814–1814, arranged by Johann Christian Friedrick Hæffner.

They performed song after song for a cheering audience, and at last it was time for the new one. I no longer recall the name of the performer, who sang solo, but the silence was audible when he began:

'Thou ancient thou freeborn, thou mountainous North,

In beauty and peace our hearts beguiling!'

And when it was time for the refrain after the second verse, something happened.

The man in the armchair stood up, threw off his wolfskin coat and stood tall and solemn in his black evening coat and his pale beauty. And when his lovely bass voice filled the room and joined in rapture with:

'Oh, I would live and I would die in Sweden!'

The applause was so loud that the building could have burst, and very few eyes were dry. This was the first public performance of what was to become the Swedish national anthem. (See figure 1.4)

But members of the bourgeoisie were not the only ones to perform folk songs and melodies in concert form. Troubadours and fiddlers were taken for granted on the staff of many Swedish rural estates. In her very detailed diary from the late eighteenth and early nineteenth centuries *Årstafruns dagbok* (The Diary of a Homemaker from Årsta,) Märta Helena Reenstierna testifies to the mixture of peasant fiddlers and serious musicians "When the screen was set up, a noisy peasant *polska* was played on two keyed fiddles. This divine music enticed the guests into the concert hall. They stopped to gaze at the painting, and the keyed fiddles quietened, to be replaced by two violins, playing a quadrille. I danced three quadrilles before I had to help lay the tables" (Quote after Ling 1967, p. 211). The extent to which folk songs and melodies made their way to the salons of the nobility and the bourgeoisie was very different in different countries, depending on how much rural peasant music resembled the serious music that dominated the salons and how much class conflict there was. If the two worlds were very different from one another, there was no contact at all. For example, we may recall Franz Liszt's renowned judgement of Hungarian peasant music: "The

Figure 1.4. A version of what is now the Swedish national anthem taken from *Svenska visor*, vol. 1, 1847–48. In the introduction, Dybeck describes its first performance at an evening entertainment in Stockholm on 18 November 1844, saying that he was the author of the lyrics. The accompaniment was of the bombastic type associated with songs like "God Save the King," with strong choral harmonies and the feeling of a men's choir.

Hungarian songs we encounter in our villages, and the melodies so simply performed on the above-mentioned instruments [flute and bagpipe], are poor and incomplete and cannot win general respect." (Sárosi 1986, p. 16)

Liszt's Hungarian "national" rhapsodies are based on the branch of familiar gypsy music greatly influenced by the popular music of the upper classes and not on Hungarian peasant music. The latter did not correspond to Liszt's view of the aesthetics of national music. The vocal and instrumental music known only to the gypsies themselves, not hybridized with the tonalities of classical music from Vienna, would have been still farther from Liszt's musical preferences. Even today, the gypsy people's own music is relatively little known.

Collections of Folk Songs for Present Use and for Posterity

Let us now abandon these isolated incidents of "spontaneous" transcriptions of melodies and descriptions of musical events, and devote ourselves to the publishers and followers of humanism who set out purposefully to collect folk songs for posterity and thus to make an impact on the culture of humanity.

Large numbers of folk songs were published with piano accompaniment in almost all European countries. These, along with all kinds of arrangements for keyboard, harp, guitar, and various ensembles, were central to the wide dissemination of folk music at the time. They included everything from

Drei Reiter am Thor

Es rit = ten drey Rei = ter zum Thor hin=aus, a = de!
Feins Lieb = chen guck = te zum Fenſter hin=aus, a = de!
Und foll es denn ge = ſchie = den ſeyn, ſo

gieb mir dein gol = de = nes Rin = ge = lein, a = de, a = de, a = de! Ja ſchei = den und mei = den thut weh.

Figure 1. 5. (a) A song from *Des Knaben Wunderhorn* in an old-fashioned edition from the German Democratic Republic in 1958. Note the German typeface. (b) Title page from the collection of children's songs in Achim von Arnim and Clemens Brentano's *Des Knaben Wunderhorn*, 1808. (Illustration by Brentano with etching by Ludwig Emil Grimm.)

arrangements of transcribed melodies to pastiches "in a folk tone," in "folk style," etc., which often makes the origins of this music difficult to appraise.

These interpretations were not always appreciated by their creators' contemporaries. Ludvig Matthias Lindeman (1812–1887), a prominent Norwegian folk music collector and interpreter, could read the following judgment of his work in a review of *Norske Fjeldmelodier* (Norwegian Mountain Tunes) in the Oslo morning paper on 7 February 1842: "he may have applied substantially too much wit and wisdom to these simple offsprings of nature" (Sandvik 1950, p. 11).

Many other collections of folk songs were published as only texts without music, to the deep dismay of reviewers. Even those mainly interested in the literary aspects of the lyrics realised the value of the melodies. Achim von Arnim (1781–1831), one of the authors of *Des Knaben Wunderhorn* (1806–1808), wrote in a letter that he found it extremely unfortunate that he and his colleague Clemens Brentano (1778–1842) knew too little about music to be able to note down the melodies, although they could sing them (Stockmann 1958, p. 7). Figure 1.5 shows one of the songs from *Des Knaben Wunderhorn*.

Arnim and Brentano also provide a good example of the folk song enthusiasts who created a romantic and nostalgic mythology around the folk songs in the spirit of Johann Gottfried von Herder. This was important not only for introducing wider segments of the population to folk songs, but also for establishing a scholarly interest in them. Arnim and Brentano's collection of seven hundred songs was also regarded as a German response to collections of English and Scottish folk songs, a kind of manifestation of nationalism. This, however, was

in no way the original intention of the collectors. Their idea had been to render the inherent living art of the people, their faith, their emotions about life and death, and "their songs, legends, proverbs, stories, prophecies and melodies" (Stockmann 1958, p. 8). They also intended to help stave off the general decline of the folk song. In this respect, however, voices of objection were raised against their pragmatic view, including the voice of Jacob Grimm, who accused the authors of ignoring historical studies: "They do not allow what is old to remain so. Instead, they want to entirely transpose it to our times, where it does not belong. Only amateurs will be briefly attentive to it, and even they will soon tire" (Quotes from Stockmann 1958, p. 5).

What these two "wunderhornists" actually wanted to achieve was primarily to bridge the gap between popular and erudite poetry, but they underestimated the value of the melodies as a factor in dissemination. In his review of volume I, Goethe stated that this volume of lyrics should be placed in the hands of a music lover or master composer, and the texts of the songs supplied "either with well-known melodies they could note down or new ones that would become valuable" (Stockmann 1958, p. 6).

The aspiration of the collectors to trigger a new kind of folk music among the peasants and craftsmen was not fulfilled. Instead, *Des Knaben Wunderhorn* was integrated into the history of Romantic poets and composers for whom it served as an inexhaustible source of inspiration (for instance, Gustav Mahler's arrangements of the *Wunderhorn* texts for voice and piano or orchestra, and his use of these melodies in his second and fourth symphonies).

Publishing Folk Songs for the Edification of the People

As described above, the melodies were necessary because the *primary* aim of the publication had been to reawaken the old folk melodies and make them living songs. The scholarly ambitions stand out as a *secondary* aim, in relation to the discussions about how folk songs were actually to be published. This zeal for popular enlightenment lived on long into the nineteenth century, and folk songs were seen as a means of staving off the onslaught of a cultural eclipse. Levin Christian Wiede (1804–1822), a minister and collector of folk songs said, in a letter from 1844:

> I am preoccupied with an idea, and am asking those who are in the know about such things their opinion—whether it might in fact be possible to publish, instead of the rubbish of which popular literature consists today, a neater, more well-ordered series of folk songs with their melodies. These could be prepared individually and printed by a publishing company, and well enough made to interest even "educated" people, who might be expected to purchase a certain part of every edition. (Ling 1965, p. 24.)

Figure 1.6 displays Wiede's notation of a song, *Herr Olof och älvorna* (Herr Olof and the elves), as

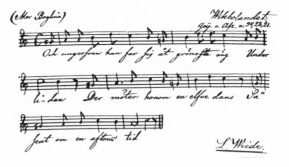

Figure 1.6. Levin Christian Wiede's notation of the song about Herr Olof and the elves as rendered by Madame Boglina at Vikbolandet, prepared for individual printing.

an example of how he worked. It was performed by Madame Boglina at Vikbolandet. This song was proposed for individual printing. Madame Boglina, as he calls her, was Brita Cajsa Carlsdotter, born in 1796 and married to Johan Peter Boglina, a sexton. In the 1840s she lived in the poorhouse at Östra Stenby in the province of Östergötland, and it was there Wiede found her and noted down her songs, probably in conjunction with a parish catechetical meeting.

In Denmark, The nineteenth-century monthly journal *Maanedsskriftet Iris* had been promoting the re-publication in broadsheet form of "good folk music," adapted to the taste, knowledge, and language of the peasantry (Dal 1956, p. 45).

The fact that folk music was experienced as having moral, ethical, and aesthetic value was more important than its mere admission to salons and concert halls. In 1848 Ludvig Matthias Lindeman applied for funding to journey to Valdres to collect popular chorales on which to base new congregational hymns for the churches.

But how on earth did they imagine that the songs they collected could be spread without their melodies? Indeed, just as Goethe suggested in his review, they recommended that the reader contact an amateur musician or master composer who could either render the correct melody or a suitable one, or even write a new more exciting one.

The Approach of Collectors to Texts and Melodies

Those who noted down folk songs never aimed to record the texts and melodies exactly; they considered it as necessary to tame and improve them in order to make them edifying to the singer or reader, and they also had to resist the "gutter slush" (*Geijer*) of broadsheets and other popular music emanating from increasing urbanization. However, hearing the songs in their natural environment, often did away with the desire to improve them, giving them, instead, a real incentive to copy down a version that reflected as faithfully as possible what they heard. Oskar Kolberg (1814–1890), a Polish composer and pianist, was one of those who was fascinated by the songs, stories, customs, and traditions he encountered in rural Poland. He sketched individuals and environments, and noted down texts and melodies, with a view to publishing a volume on popular culture and history. Despite this comprehensive aim, he found himself swept away by the beauty of the simple songs, and stated that arrangements could not possibly mean improvements.

"I render the melody in its untainted simplicity . . . exactly as it sprang forth from the mouth of the people. I am convinced that the very best thing about it is its unspoilt purity–precisely as if inspired by nature" (Sobieska 1975, p. 1.)

There was one aim all the collectors shared: to preserve something that was about to be lost, and certainly would have been without their efforts. They attempted to rescue folk songs, a genre for which there was no natural place in general nineteenth century literature and in a rapidly urbanizing society. In addition, there was another underlying ideology that has already been mentioned: nationalism–the idea that a national culture could be created on the basis of voices from the past and of the people.

The ambition of making a singable song was sometimes more important than the obligation of presenting scholarly work:

This is a book to sing from. To make the songs singable, the editorial hand has been used where necessary. We assure our readers that the melodies have not been doctored, but are as the collector took them from the traditional singer. With the words, the case is rather different. Music is a matter of emotion, words of logic. If a bad singer mars a tune, we either keep it as it is, or leave it out; in no case do we alter it. However, if a forgetful singer omits verses or lines, or knows the song only in imperfect form, we do not hesitate, in compiling a book for popular use, to complete the song from other traditional sources. (Albert Lloyd, Vaughan Williams, *English Folksong*, 1958, preface p. 8.)

Folk Music and Nationalism

In the latter half of the eighteenth and throughout the nineteenth century, the ground for a national culture was laid in several European countries. National canons of poetry and literature were created, inspired by popular legends, songs, and stories. Foresighted individuals now discovered the folk song as raw material for national, religious, or popular enlightenment. Chapter 11 discusses how composers, too, began at the time, to use popular melodies to give expression to their nationalism. When Erik Gustav Geijer (1783–1847) moaned about the general indifference toward Swedish popular poetry, he was comparing the Swedish situation with international literary models, not musical ones. It was too early (the 1810s) for there to have been any real models for the collection of historical musical artifacts:

However, of all the peoples who have had any impact on the destiny and development of Europe, the Swedes are nearly the only one who have not made an active effort to rescue from total oblivion and transience the remnants of an older, artless poetry which is still alive in the memory and bloodstream of the people. Only considering our own kin, who among us has shouldered task undertaken by Percy, Pinkerton, Walter Scott and Jamieson for the English and Scots, or by Herder, Evert Eschenburg and more recently Büsching, von der Hagen, Achim von Arnim, Berntano and others for German popular poetry? (Geijer & Afzelius 1880 p. XVI.)

Selection of Songs

The collectors tended to favor what was oldest, and carried the scent of ancient times or the Middle Ages. Thus they came to focus on different types of epic tales, including Nordic ballads, the Finnish-Estonian *Kalevala* cycle, Russian *bilinï*, and Balkan heroic songs. One very good example of such a collector was Elias Lönnrot (1802–1884), a Finnish physician who was inspired to collect songs in the surge of nationalism following the 1809 war. In this way, the *Kalevala* cycle became a national epic. Like his predecessors since the days of the Gilgamesh epic, he collected and collated existing songs, in this case runic songs, into a whole, writing the transitional pieces himself.

Two Estonian physicians, Friedrich Faelmann and Friedrich Kreutzwald, worked in the same way to save the Estonian epic corresponding to the

Kalevala, the *Kalevigoeg*. They regarded this epic tradition as a shed in a state of collapse that they restored with the aid of timber from the Estonian forest of folk melodies (*Kalevigoeg*, 1951, pp. 319ff.).

The Russian heroic songs, the *bilini*, were also "discovered" in collaboration between literary and historical scholars who shared an interest in the origins of peoples and their simple traditions. The first evidence of the *bilini* appears in inspired proclamations in eighteenth-century scholarly works on literature and other disciplines relating to the Russian language. But it would be erroneous to believe that the main driving force of the collectors was a political-ideological one: they constantly emphasized the artistic experience itself as primary. The following testimony was given by Russian folk song collector Rubnikov when, at Lake Onega, he encountered the *bilini*. (See also p. 83.)

Warmed by the fire, I gradually dozed off. I was awakened by extraordinary sounds. By this point I had heard many songs and religious poems, but never songs like these. Lively, fantastic, cheerful, sometimes fast and sometimes slower, these melodies reminded me of something ancient, forgotten by our generation. I wished not to wake up for a very long time, and I listened to every word of the songs—I was so delighted to stay, entirely overwhelmed by this new experience. (Entwistle 1939, p. I.)

In the late nineteenth century the *bilini* were documented by A. D. Grigorjev, who collected and published them much like Lönnrot had done with the *Kalevala*.

The nineteenth century also saw the development of impressive collections of Balkan heroic songs. The tradition of heroic songs in the Balkan countries is documented as early as the Middle Ages. However, not until the eighteenth century were these songs incorporated into the world of written literature. Beginning in 1820, collections were published in large numbers. This phenomenon culminated with the publication between 1891 and 1902 of the nine volumes known as the Vuc Karadzi collection. Unlike the *Iliad*, the *Odyssey,* or the *Kalevala*, these songs were not integrated into long epic poems. The collector does not appear to have had such vast literary ambitions.

Interest in the actual tunes was never as great as in the words. This may have been because the style in which they were performed was so very special, and did not consist of melodies in the strict sense of the word (see also p. 88). The Irish Finn cycle, the *Fianaíocht*, has been retained virtually only in its literary form, despite the fact that it remained a living form of musical narrative as late as in the early nineteenth century. In a description from Ireland in 1873, O'Curry describes how these medieval tales were performed in his childhood:

I have heard my father sing these Ossianic poems, and remember distinctly the air and manner of their singing; and I have heard that there was, about the time that I was born, and of course beyond my recollection, a man named Anthony O'Brien, a schoolmaster, who spent much of his time in my father's house, and who was the best singer of Oisn's poems that his contemporaries had ever heard. He had a rich and powerful voice, and often, on a calm summer day, he used to go with a party into a boat on the Lower Shannon, at my native place, where the river is eight miles wide, and having rowed to the middle of the river, they used to lie on their oars there to uncork their whiskey jar and make themselves happy, on which occasions Anthony O'Brien was always prepared to sing his choicest pieces, among which were no greater favourites than Oisín's poems. So powerful was the singer's voice that it often reached the shores at either side of the boat in Clare and Kerry, and often called the labouring men and women from the neighbouring fields at both sides down to the water's edge to enjoy the strains of such music. . . . (Quoted from Breathnach 1971, p. 25.)

Folk Music as a National Issue

In the nineteenth century, collecting folk songs became an issue of national importance in many European countries. The objective was to strengthen national identity and maintain freedom and independence, or to assert the strength of the nation and its ability to suppress others. Folk music collectors, especially in smaller countries, were seized by extremely strong nationalistic sentiment, as well as the desire to make the voice of their country heard above the din of the cultures of larger nations. Readers of the Hungarian journal *Magyar Hirondo* were invited to collect and submit old songs "since nothing will be considered suitable until examples have been presented in more cultivated European nations" (Sárosi 1986, p. 12).

Later more official regulations were also laid down. Count Frans Anton Lolowrat-Liebsteinsky, who took the initiative of collecting folk songs in Czechoslovakia-Moravia, and who was a cultural patron and Austrian minister, presented a set of stipulations in 1819 regulating submission of Czech-Moravian folk songs to the national museums. Of course such official interventions also had an impact on the selection process. What was collected were the especially beautiful and unique works of music that might do as decoration for the national-cultural coat of arms. This often prevented the collection of genuine peasant songs in favor of many other popular songs of different kinds. Perhaps what we now consider truly unique and what interests folk music connoisseurs today was not even considered worth collecting at the time.

In eighteenth-century France, the folk song was hotly debated by various schools of ideology, represented for example by Mme. de Sévigné, Voltaire, and Rousseau. Curiosity about folk songs continued to grow in the nineteenth century, and in 1852 Louis Napoleon ordered a government commission to study a collection of songs from Brittany and determine their authenticity. From about 1860 collections were being actively organized in virtually every province in France. Unfortunately, the feeling that there were insurmountable obstacles to noting down melodies prevailed for far too long.

When Tiersot (1889) published his classical *Histoire de la chanson populaire en France* he used this material, but the most valuable sources were the ones he found from tracing his travels to several provinces, where he found the folk song still alive: La Bresse, Bretagne, le Morvan, la Piaccardie, la Lorraine, la Franche-Comté, la Bourgogne, le Pauphiné, and also Paris, where he found several living musical documents from "la bouche de provinciaux authentiques" (see preface p. VIII). His aim, to present "une idée exacte et complète de nos chansons populaire," was extremely ambitious and forward-looking.

In countries such as Italy, Spain, and Portugal, collection began even later, toward the end of the nineteenth century. Ideas of basing a sense of national unity on such collections of folk songs or instrumental folk music never gained a real foothold in these countries. In Italy, for example, it was the music of operatic composer Giuseppe Verdi that became the national symbol.

Regional cultural profiles were and still are so strong in countries such as Italy, Poland, and Spain that it would have been quite impossible to attempt to organize them into a comprehensive national style, as was being done elsewhere in Europe. This would have meant falling into the same trap as did nineteenth-century ideologists of folk music in countries such as Russia, France, Germany, and Sweden, where theories about "national folk music" developed, sometimes with the support of the central government. These theories had virtually no substance in fact, as there is certainly nothing nationally genetic about music. Yet it was generally accepted that music indeed had a national character, although this proved difficult to define and delimit.

In the early nineteenth century Carl Envallson, a member of the Swedish Academy of Arts and Letters, wrote an article for the *Swedish Dictionary of Music* entitled "National Music." He described a dilemma that must have been recognized by any serious observer at the time, no matter how strong a spirit of patriotism prevailed:

> NATIONAL MUSIC. A type of music or songs, known to the general public of a nation and associated with its character and spirit. . . . Thus a distinction must be made between Provincial melodies and national music. The songs sung by the men of Dalacarlia (*Darkarls-Wisan*) belong to the former category and, like the music characteristic of several other provinces, are in a minor key. It is nevertheless difficult to deny that genuinely Swedish national music tends to be in the major. And if one is at all familiar with the area around Sigtuna and Uppsala, the home of the 'Ups'-song (*upsvisorna*), it will be clear that most of the melodies and dances tend to be in major keys. (*Swedish Dictionary of Music* 1802, p. 215f.)

The scope and intensity of national currents were, then, reflected in the collections of folk music.

The Scots attempted to retain their unique culture and identity by collecting, singing, and playing Scottish songs and melodies during the period of oppression by the English in the eighteenth century. These songs were tidied up and redone to suit conventional harmonies, and sometimes the texts were given new melodies "in the Scottish style," as the phrase had it, throughout Europe. There was plenty of enthusiasm:

> The object of this Publication is to simplify and reduce the Pipe Music to such a system, as not only to facilitate the attempts of Students of the Great Highland Bag-Pipe, but to accommodate its Music to almost all other instruments–such as the Organ, Pi-

ano-Forte, Violin, and German Flute. In the progress of this undertaking, the Publisher has been encouraged by a Prize from the Highland Society of Scotland, as being the first who had succeeded in setting the *Piobaireachd* to Music, in a way to suit all the above instruments.

To accomplish this Work, the Publisher has sacrificed the leisure moments of the last fifteen years, and now, encouraged as above, and by the countenance of many enlightened individuals, he presumes to submit to the Public a portion of the result of his labours; and he entertains a humble confidence, that, whatever the learned and the critical may say in other respects, every lover of the wild Melodies of his wilder Country will thank him for making familiar to the more fashionable instruments of the day, those strains hitherto confined to the Bag-Pipe, and so worthy of being made universal. . . .

In conclusion, the Publisher has only to add to the general voice, his heart-felt wish, that this Society may continue to be cheered in the progress of their unwearied labours, by the increasing prosperity of their Country, and the consciousness of their having already done so much to promote it; and to say how proud he is, at once, to grace his undertaking with such a name, and to subscribe himself,

Gentlemen,

Your humble and grateful Servant,

Donald MacDonald

(Preface to a collection of Highland Vocal Airs, 1784.)

Donald MacDonald prepared his manuscript while in service in India and Persia. Scottish musicians attempted to combine this "national style" with the new musical forms popular on the continent, including the violin sonata (see p. 158, Fig. 8.5).

By the time it made its way into print, much European folk music had become a combination of traditional forms of music and text with an international art music style. This, of course, impacted on how folk music was interpreted and performed, and this is even more true today. For example, not long ago, in Nicaragua and El Salvador, efforts were being made to shape a kind of national music by integrating local folk music traditions with the style of international popular music.

Folk music has been used as a tool in shaping a comprehensive national identity to counter external oppression. This movement began as early as the seventeenth century in Scotland, where it culminated in the eighteenth century when bookseller Allan Ramsay published enormous editions of collections including *Scots Songs* (1719) and *The Tea-Table Miscellany* (1724) (see Harker 1985, pp. 9ff.). Scotland, where the solo bagpipe playing of different clans is still considered to be folk music today (see p. 144), was only one of the countries where the movement took place. In Russia there has never been a very large gap between popular and art cultures nor between rural and urban ones. The courts of the tsars and the nobility of St. Petersburg displayed an interest in folk songs and pastiches of folk music in the late eighteenth century, and themes and variations on Russian folk melodies for harp or keyboard were extremely popular. Chamber Vasiliy F. Trutovsky (1740–1810) did not need to travel into the countryside to collect Russian folk songs or gather inspiration for his own pastiches. The music was to be found in the city as well, performed by drivers, ferrymen, and women. His collection from 1776 was not meant for that audience, however, but for the elite for use in the salons (Figure 11.5). However, even in Russia it was difficult for the upper class to appreciate these songs in their original state, so they were modified considerably.

We may observe another variant of the development of national folk music if we look to Ireland. Even the title of John and William Neal's 1724 work, *A Collection of the Celebrated Irish Tunes Proper for the Violin, German Flute or Hautboy*, shows that their intention was to present the Irish melodies in a way that made them useful to a large, general audience. The melodies themselves are a mixture of the popular songs of the time, some older traditional transcriptions and compositions by one of the last bards in the employ of an Irish clan, harpist Turlough Carolan (1679–1738), and others. Today, the Irish harp is considered to be a folk instrument and the music written for it dance music, but until the end of the eighteenth century it was the musical symbol of the clan chiefs. Harp music was regarded as highly sophisticated, as was the playing technique. The transition took place at a competition in Belfast in 1792, when the last of the older generation of harpists, many of them between the ages of 80 and 100 at the time, gathered to compete. On that occasion, Edward Bunting (1773–1843) transcribed a large number of melodies and then published them with the melodies and rhythms adapted to the prevailing norms of art music, with continuo accompaniment.

A century later Francis O'Neill, a policeman from Chicago, made a great contribution to Irish folk music when he published several collections, including *The Music of Ireland* in 1903 and *The Dance of Ireland* in 1907, with a total of nearly three thousand melodies (Figure 1.7). His informants were Irish immigrants. In Dublin today, a mixture of regional music traditions from all over Ireland can be heard, including eighteenth-century harp tunes and interpretations of various Irish dances such as the reel and jig, influenced by twentieth-century American fiddlers. Thus Irish national music contains strong elements of art music and international popular music. Such a melting pot is a true sign of a living musical culture, and is significant for folk music revivals in all countries.

Collection Work Professionalized

Let us return to the mid-nineteenth century and follow the changes in and orientation of collection work and the ideology associated with it. More and more musicians, educators, and composers began to collect and publish folk music. For example, collections of German folk music made by Ludwig Christian Erk (1807–1883), including *Singvöglein* (1812–48) and *Deutscher Liederhort* (1856), were widely disseminated and had a major impact. Erk's work also marked the true beginning of criticism of sources, with scholarly and educational goals. His aim was to make a comprehensive collection. His huge files, including his own discoveries and those of his many fellow workers, later provided a basis for the Deutsches Volksliederarchiv in Freiburg im Breisgau, founded in 1914. However, the final volume of *Deutscher Liederhort*, published ten years after the death of Erk by F. M. Böhme, was met with disapproval by Johannes Brahms and others. According to Brahms, Böhme was not sufficiently selective. Brahms wrote to music scholar Philip Spitta in 1894, "Can it [the volume] give anyone (especially anyone from a foreign country) the slightest idea of what our folk music is? Is it really such a scholarly necessity to spread the droppings as thickly along the road as Böhme does?" (Schmidt 1983, p. 134)

This triggered the debate on "true" and "false" folk music that has preoccupied researchers and folk music collectors until the present (note the title of Walter Wora's 1950 essay, "Das echte Volkslied"). A recurrent theme in all autobiographical testimony from the collectors, even those who became the outstanding scholars in the field, describes the transitory nature of the personal experience of folk music. Cecil Sharp (1859–1924), an outstanding English collector, had his own "folk music epiphany" in Oxford in 1899, when he experienced the Morris dance in the Headington tradition. This was his impetus to begin exploring a dying culture, and he contributed to its eventual survival. Swedish painter Anders Zorn and rural court judge Nils Andersson also "discovered" phenomena that were threatened with extinction. The former took the initiative to the first of the Swedish fiddlers' meetings that led to the survival of the fiddling tradition. The latter planned and collected most of the material for the monumental *Svenska låtar* (1922–1940), which still, despite its scholarly shortcomings, remains the most important printed source of Swedish folk music today.

As mentioned above, more and more composers began to collect folk music in the nineteenth century. Their ability to render musical expression, and their sensitivity to what made this music unique and artistic, were important aspects of collection work. In Russia a number of prominent composers transcribed folk songs for us as raw material for their own compositions: Mikhail Glinka (1804–1857), Aleksandr Dargomyzhsky (1813–1869) Mili Balakirev (1837–1910), Nikolai Rimsky-Korsakov (1844–1908), Modest Mussorgsky (1839–1881), Peter Tchaikovsky (1840–1893), and others. Ukrainian composer Niukolai W. Lissenko (1842–1912) was another collector, as was Czech composer Leos Janácek 1854–1928) who worked with collections and presentations of Ukrainian and Moravian folk music, and who established national schools of music. Initially, Janácek was better known as a collector than as a composer. He also paved the way for scholarly research on Moravian folk music. Janácek, in turn, has a great deal in common with his Hungarian counterparts Zoltán Kodály (1882–1967) and Béla Bartók (1881–1945).

These and many other composers, not only collected and studied folk music, they also endowed it with an independent artistic status, putting it on a par with art music. They aimed to assess folk music on the basis of its own unique features, and to acknowledge the special aesthetic laws prevailing in music passed down by ear from generation to generation. They also realized that there was a special value associated with the unique *functions* of folk music.

The composers were trying to get away from the pan-European folk music style (described in greater detail in Chapter 11) that was developing, with different nuances in different countries. Instead, they sought the unique artistic features of each individual vocalist or fiddler:

> In the prevailing musical climate in Hungary, it was not easy to get at the folk music. The air was full of the harvest of songs gathered in from the 50s and 90s. This was the folk music of educated circles, but much of it was also taken over by the people, and it would have been very easy for anyone at all to fall for the optical illusion that this was folk music. (Ujfalussy 1981, p. 26)

In his autobiography (1923), Béla Bartók describes his first discoveries of a new musical world (quoted from Ujfalussy 1981, p.57):

> I also found that the Hungarian melodies erroneously thought of to be folk songs, but in reality more or less trivial popular songs in a more serious vein, have very little of interest to offer. For this reason I got to work in 1905 in a serious way, tracing what was then unknown Hungarian peasant music. . . . (Ujfalussy 1981, p. 57)

We will be discussing Bartók, in his capacity as composer inspired by folk music, in Chapter 11. Bartók came from a very different social and musical world than that of the peasant music. Despite this background, Bartók possessed the ability to create close musical and human contact with people from environments not his own, and in many ways he was unique in his time. Yet even a humanist like Bartók held values we consider obsolete today. He tended to idealize the "good old days," and to consider the illiteracy and isolation of his subjects as nothing but an advantage from the narrow perspective of the preservation of folk music.

New Research Orientations and Older Ones

The study of non-European music that began in the late nineteenth century triggered insights and ideas about music that impacted on studies of European folk music as well. The first archives of recordings came into being at the turn of the century in Vienna and Berlin. Erich Moritz von Hornbostel introduced the concept of comparative musicology (see also Hornbostel 1986). His intent was to explain similarities and differences in the music of non-European countries from the perspective of development and dissemination. As theoretical issues gained ground, and music began to be studied from a more analytic perspective, an interest arose in quantifying melodic, rhythmic, and tonal qualities, and in seeing music in its sociological-functional context.

The twentieth century saw an increasing emphasis on the old idea of rescuing the remains of the ancient, "dying" folk music. This led to the establishment of a large number of archives, as well as other efforts. The hunt for folk music now concentrated on what was considered to be the oldest music, which was given priority in collections. Even the earliest collectors had this idea, as we have seen, but in the twentieth century it was transformed into academic dogma, which led to efforts to preserve the old and distinguish it from the new. Folk music was turned into a musical genre, and efforts were made to provide it with a history. This book is, to some extent, part of that tradition.

Today, folk music is the object of a great deal of academic attention, and is a full-fledged research subject. There are international associations of scholars and research institutes, the most important of which include the International Council for Traditional Music (ICTM) and the Society for Ethnomusicology, in which European folk music and non-European music are regarded as one huge research field. The ICTM has special publications for "Interests and Projects," providing a network for contact among researchers with similar interests. The directories of members of these societies also provide the names and addresses of the many archives, museums, and university departments where folk music collection and research take place.

"Long Live Folk Music!": Vocalists and Musicians Reclaim Their Rights

In the first half of the twentieth century, most folk music was collected under the auspices of official archives and by scholars, but this has now changed. After the 1950s, an interest in playing, singing, and dancing to this music began to spread among

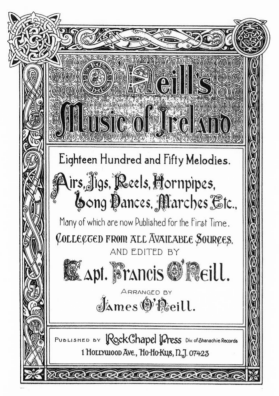

Figure 1.7. The cover of Francis O'Neill's collection of 1,850 Irish melodies from 1903, gathered by him and his associates in Chicago between 1890 and 1900. Emigrants and people moving from rural to urban areas have often made sure that they did not lose touch with their musical roots.

young intellectuals as wave after wave of old music washed across Europe. They collected melodies and songs, learned old dances in order to perform them, and sought their cultural identities in a world where the mass media was filled to overflowing with music of all kinds. In some respects, a conflict arose between these hands-on users of folk music and scholars in terms of retaining traditions. The existing societies for the promotion of local and regional traditional cultures were sometimes upset. They saw folk music as a part of history, to be presented in accordance with the established rules. In Sweden, for example, the following criteria applied to folk music if it was to be labeled truly Swedish national music:

1. The music was to have been a part of a peasant ceremony or peasant dance.
2. The dance melodies had to be *polskas* or waltzes, while the *schottisch*, the one-step and the two-step were regarded as "new." (This was despite the fact that many of them were older than many of the new *polskas* and waltzes being composed.)
3. The true folk music instruments were the violin, the clarinet, the bagpipes, and the horn. (The accordion, the guitar, and the harmonium were banned as not belonging to the tradition.)
4. Folk music was to be learned by ear and not from printed music.
5. Folk music was to have a territorial identity and was to be passed down among the local population. (A kind of "genetic" thinking arose which made it a matter of suspicion when people who came from anywhere but Uppland played the Uppland keyed fiddle, not to mention if the people in question were non-Swedes or non-white.)

Similar rules applied to Swiss yodelling societies, and reflect their ideology:

1. Upbeat, jazzy versions of songs damage the cause of folk music and must be eliminated.
2. A real folk melody is a reflection of the soul of the people.
3. It requires special talent to write a folk song, and folk songs must only be written in the service of the local culture and the fatherland.
4. It requires a knowledge of music theory to arrange a folk melody.
5. Folk melodies and folk songs are parts of the national heritage. They reflect the soul of the people, the lives of the people, and free Swiss thinking. (Baumann 1976, p. 238)

Revival Groups

The new groups that began to make use of both the recordings in the archives and their own transcriptions of folk music were not only seeking a new musical identity, they were also trying to create new areas in which music could fill a social function outside the concert hall and the media. Playing in the home became popular again. These new interpretations of folk music soon made their way to the stage, and today they are an important element of public music performances all over Europe in concert halls and on radio and television. Folk music is also being spread primarily on disc and tape.

Henceforth in this book, the new folk music

will be classified as a revival movement, since it consisted of a return of folk music after a period of relative stagnation and existence mostly in archives and with few performers. The revival movement meant new forms and contexts for the performance of folk music, covering an entire spectrum:

1. One trend was historical (i.e., it followed the regulations for older performances and "purity of style in folk music" as established as the norm and ideal in scholarly research).
2. Another trend made efforts to be creative, making new interpretations. Instead of following the historical trend, which was similar to playing classical music on ancient or original instruments (as is done in the 1990s), adherents of this second trend initiated what composers like Glinka, Grieg, and Chopin did in their day. They were musicians who allowed folk music to inspire them to create new music.
3. A third trend is the revival of folk music as "tourist music." This trend is mostly a continuation of the nineteenth-century national encapsulation of folk music.

Today, the "national heritage" as reflected in folk music has become a commodity of mass tourism, taking the shape of tapes, discs, or pieces on concert programs. This folk music is taken to be the "voice of the nation" in international ceremonies, trade fairs, and conferences.

Folk Music–Inexhaustible?

Thus we have observed how the external social guise of folk music has radically changed over time, and how different it is in different environments. Folk songs have been used in varying contexts, and sometimes we wonder whether the people who originally sang them would even recognize them written in their present contexts. However, similar rules seem to apply to these songs, tunes, and dances as to all "good" music: it appears to be inexhaustible, indestructible, and eternal, because of some artistic quality that can transcend. It gives us, today, the very same basic experience it gave the first collectors. Beyond that, we are free to incorporate it into those contexts where we feel it belongs.

At the time of writing, there are interesting trends in music. The boundaries between studies of classical, popular, and even folk music appear to be dissolving. The realization that music does not allow itself to be tied down to ideologies or scholarly norms but follows laws of its own, has led to studies of the overlap between the genres. In a way, this means that we may now go on to ask new questions about music rather than simply occupying ourselves with labelling it.

Literature

It is likely that there is no all-encompassing study of collections of European folk music. This means that it can only be examined by genre. For example, through studies of the ballad, or by nation, as in the work of Moberg (1951) (Sweden), Dal (1956) (Scandinavia), and Zemtsovsky (1967) (Russia). A Ph.D. dissertation by Bengt Jonsson (1967) provides a very good example of a study in source criticism of the early collectors of Swedish folk music (with an English summary). In *Fakesong* Dave Harker (1985) describes what he refers to as the mediators. His subtitle is *The Manufacture of British "Folksong," 1700 to the Present Day*, and his aim is to expose the bourgeois ideologies and class perspective underlying various collections. Although it contains a great deal of important information, this study also applies an anachronistic view and is more judgmental than explanatory.

La musique folk des peuples de France by Roland Pécout (1979) gives a historical-sociological overview, reflecting another variant of the leftist ideology of the 1970s.

There are often excellent surveys of existing in general national works on folk music. For example, Sandvik (1950), Suppan (1984), Sárosi (1986), catalogue of Hungarian Folksong types (1992). In this context *New Grove* is also worthy of recommendation, as many of the articles on the different countries begin with a survey. I have used these *Grove* summaries as points of departure in several places. My main sources with regard to my discussion of the concepts of folk, culture, etc., are Burke (1983) and Rehnberg (1977).

Philip V. Bohlman's *The Study of Folk Music in the Modern World* (1988) is a cross-cultural perspective of folk music, which I recommend as complementary reading.

Two

Music at Work

RURAL SOUNDSCAPES OF THE PAST

The soundscapes of rural areas have changed radically over the past century. Today, the sounds of machinery compete constantly with the sounds of silence, in the country as well as the city. In the past, it was possible to distinguish between weekday noise and Sunday tranquillity, and also different songs of work in different seasons.

In the late nineteenth century, German political scientist Karl Bücher produced his renowned *Arbeit und Rhythmus* (1896), in which he describes the rhythms of the work of different crafts and occupations, both male and female. He regarded each job as having its own "tone rhythm," with an impact on the intensity with which the job was done. For example, the rhythm used by the blacksmith to pound the steel at his forge was a kind of "ostinato of work," while the rhythmic sound of the flail against the timber floor when the grain was being threshed signaled the rhythmic tone of autumn or winter work. He also described a softer kind of music at work, a sort of *musica bassa* of labor: for example, in the milking of domesticated animals, the sound of a stream of milk hitting the bottom of the pail, or the sound of the scythes harvesting hay or grain, or the sounds of spinning, carding, flax-making, and the washing-board. Many of these rhythmic sounds of work bear a relation to the beat of the human pulse. Bücher regarded the sounds and rhythms of work as endowing different environments with their identities.

Bücher's ideas are still alive today. In *Biomusicology*, published in 1991, Nils L. Wallin pre-

sents different biorhythmic couplings to the listener. According to Wallin, music might have an ethnological and ecological significance similar and parallel to that of sleep, dreams, and voluntarily evoked changes of consciousness (Wallin 1991, p. 291). Music can also have a regenerative effect of a cathartic nature. "The tribal dance, rock and beat performances, and symphony concert are, from this viewpoint, dynamic aspects of the society whose aim is to demonstrate group stability under pressure of the social cognitive imperative" (Wallin 1991, p. 291).

Tools and Utensils as Instruments: The Voice, the Whip, and the Ratchet

The human voice and implements such as animal or man-made horns, whips, ratchets, and drums were important components of labor. The human voice was used for interpersonal communication as well as communication with animals, the whip was used to give orders to oxen and horses, horns to herd the grazing animals, ratchets for hunting, and the drum to call people to village meetings, (further details on instruments are in Chapter 6).

The whip was used by both coachmen and shepherds, but the strap of the coachman's whip was much shorter than that of the shepherd. In Slovakia the coachman's whip was only about one meter long, while that of the shepherd could be up to six meters long. Whip handles were often richly ornamented. In earlier times coachmen and shepherds made their own whips. Later, whip-making became a specialized craft. Whips had a special status because they could be used to produce snapping sounds which were associated with the sound of a gun or rifle shot. In Slovakia there is an expression, "shooting your whip." Handling a whip requires strength, skill, and perseverance. This explains why it was often the young, assistant shepherds who used whips, while the head shepherd would usually use a rattle-stick. Sometimes whips also replaced bark horns as a signaling instrument between shepherd and master in the mornings when it was time to herd the animals into the village street and then on to the pastures, or to replace the *Kuhreihen* (herdsman's song) when the cows were moved to the mountain pastures in the Alps (Bachmann-Geiser 1981). According to Elschek, the whip "primarily filled magical functions": it was cracked on May Day when the herd was taken out for the summer, to ward off evil spirits, disease, and misfortune. The whip was also sounded to signal the end of the grazing season in the autumn. It was also used at weddings, alongside rifle shoots, and at various festivities of the season and on other occasions for celebration. Slovakian shepherds cracked their whips on their way to court the maidens whose approval they sought by competing in whip-wielding skills. In Switzerland whips were also used to mark festivities (Bachmann-Geiser 1981). In contemporary Slovakia and Hungary, folk dancers still use their whips to mark rhythms, and it is even possible to "play" a folk song on the whip (Elschek 1983).

The ratchet has been used in hunting, to entice the animals into the open. Ratchets have also been used to frighten birds out of gardens or vineyards, and guards have also used them to communicate with one another. Similar instruments have long been in use by vagabonds to intimidate the miserly into acts of charity (see Habenicht 1985). Peddlers and postmen used it to announce their arrival, and today, in Britain (and elsewhere), it is used by football spectators.

As Georg Sand so lyrically described (see p. 7), work signals were sometimes used with creative aspirations, and thus were pleasant to listen to. Figure 2.1 illustrates examples of ox-drivers' songs, the very same calls described in the novel of Georg Sand cited above, as noted down in the nineteenth century by Mme. Pauline Viardot.

The songs, calls, and instrumental melodies on the shepherds' horn and fife are probably the best-documented songs of work, followed by calls associated with harvesting. There are, in addition, rhymes for work, and songs for pile-driving, loading, sailing, fishing, driving, rowing, spinning, weaving, and sizing cloth. Sailors also had a complete battery of calls and songs, as well as instrumental melodies for different aspects of their work.

Let us make a journey through this music of labor, beginning with a visit to some shepherds and shepherdesses. We will then look in on some autumnal harvesters, construction workers, and road workers. We will visit sailors and fisherman, too, and conclude with the more intimate domestic working music heard in the kitchen and by the hearth. What musical structures will we find? Was there once a sense of magic associated with shouts and calls? What was the original association between work and entertainment? What happens when the labor-related function of a certain kind of music dies out? Does the music die with it, or find a new form?

HERDING CALLS

All European pastoral cultures had, and, to some extent, still have, a highly refined signaling system. The signals had both a communicative function for work and a decorative, aesthetic function. The grazing fields, the mountains, and the forests used to be an exciting soundscape of calls, music, barking, mooing, and bleating. Shepherds and shepherdesses in this environment developed a music of their own, both meaningful and beautiful to listen to. It came into being both through the influence of contact with other nearby cultures and during long periods of time in complete isolation.

Often, arbitrary external factors have determined whether the music of any particular pastoral culture has been brought to wider attention and preserved. For example, the Alpine *Kuhreihen*, yodelling, and bell-ringing became the object of widespread attention and admiration during the expansive period of tourism in the nineteenth century. The reputation of the shepherd as a sort of freedom fighter also paved the way for the popularity of their dances, instruments, and songs in eastern Europe (see also Chapter 3). Another example is that of the evening entertainment provided by Richard Dybeck, with shepherds' songs for voice and piano or for French horn and piano, without which the music of Swedish shepherds would probably never have come to be incorporated into Swedish romances and operas. In regions where external conditions were not conducive to bringing the

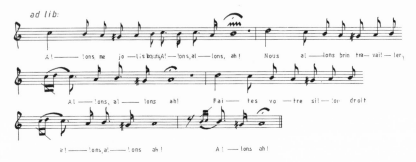

Figure 2.1. An ox-driver's call. (Tiersot 1889/1978, p. 158.)

music of the shepherds to light, it simply continued to have its own placid, functional existence, and it continues as such today in the places were there are still grazing, domestic animals.

However, not everyone appreciated the virtues of herding calls and music. Many diarists of journeys in the nineteenth century have described such music as simply dreadful. A German traveler made the following description when in Spain:

> Owing to their whinging intonation and monotonous accompaniment (on the guitar), I took the first Spaniards I heard to be quite mad.
>
> I found the shepherds' songs, heard over long distances and lasting some half an hour, to be particularly trying. To me they often sounded like the screams of some unfortunate soul who had fallen into the hands of highway robbers. As I came closer to the pitiful wailing singer, I discovered him lying on a hillside, and not with a highway robber but rather with a herd of peacefully grazing lambs, wandering about amongst the rosemary. The singer himself seemed to think that he was in the Elysian fields. All this in contrast to the music of the "enlightened Spaniard."
> (*Allgemeine musikalische Zeitung*, March 1799, pp. 391f)

The most complex shepherds' songs in Europe and a diversified use of shepherds' instruments can be found in the mountain regions of Europe, including the Pyrenees, Alps, Carpathians, and mountain areas of Scandinavia (see also Helmer 1975).

What do the various herding songs from all over Europe have in common? Helmer describes the type of syllabic sound used to call goats in Norway, Sweden, and Switzerland as being very similar: *kri, ki,* and *gi.* He claims, not unpredictably, that the various words for "Come, cow" plus the name of the cow tend to be used to call them. Of course, the function of the call is the same everywhere, to call the animals back to the herd or keep the herd to-

gether. This probably explains the basic agreement in sound structure and performance technique.

Herding music was sometimes solely a working signal. This applied, for example, when horns were blown or shouted to frighten off wild animals. These detested beasts could be both scared away by sharp sounds and enticed by sweet tones. The wolf says:

> Gather the reed pipes and the goat-horns
> These please my ears to hear,
> But the big long wooden horns and the horns
>   of the bucks
> Cause my feet to bleed.
> (From Grangärde, Dalacarlia, Sweden quoted in Moberg 1955, p. 57.)

Music to gather domestic animals, rather than to repel wild ones, could almost always be counted on to contain an "aesthetic" element, as could the music used to communicate with other shepherds.

Let us now take German musicologist Christian Kaden as our guide, and pay a visit to the shepherds of Harz and Thuringia. Kaden has made a unique effort to try to understand the signal system from inside, by making detailed analyses of apparently simple sound structures, and by scrutinizing the experience of both the signalers and the recipients of signals.

Interaction between Function and Aesthetics in Harz and Thuringia

In the mornings, the shepherds from Harz and Thuringia strolled down the village street signaling with their horns that it was time for the farmers to send out their animals to the shepherds, who would convey them to the meadows to graze. The first to arrive each morning were the cowherds, followed by those who herded the sheep. However, the cowherds only worked in the summer months, while the sheep were taken to pasture until the end of December, and began again after just a couple of months (for the annual farming cycle, see Chapter 3). At some points in the year, there were a whole series of shepherds arriving throughout the day. This kind of scheduled shepherding, with separate herders for cattle, sheep, and swine, began as early as the Middle Ages. There was also a social difference between a village shepherd and a shepherd who worked for a particular feudal lord. During the winter, the shepherds worked as carpenters, teachers, or night watchmen or had other positions of responsibility. This fact also had its impact on the way their herding signals took shape.

Various models of communication have been drawn up to describe the signaling of the shepherds and how their signals reached and affected other people and animals. A shepherd or shepherdess signaled to the flock, the sheep dog, the owner of the herd, as well as to other shepherds and shepherdesses, the people of the village, and outsiders. Sound signals were also transmitted back. There signals were of different kinds: some primarily functional, others more or less ornamental. They could also have very different natures; when a shepherd feared for his flock he might use the whip to attract the attention of the owner, but if all was well he might yodel. There were special signals for negligent owners who arrived late with their herds. Usually, the shepherd's instrument was an animal horn made of bone or wood or a metal pipe, but herding instruments included valve horns, bugles, French horns, flutes, and pipes, as well as the whip (the musical properties of which were described above), staves with rattles, and clapboard instruments. Signaling instruments were also often used in combination, with the shepherds determining the functions of various signals. As a result, every working group had its own set of signals, intelligible only to the members of the group but not to outsiders. This made herding signals different from the signals of soldiers and hunters.

The shepherds were able to endow their signals with new meaning by altering their aesthetic elements, thus "aiming" them at a different category of recipient. Sometimes signals gained added meaning when they were performed to a melody with a familiar text. In this way a single signal could encode more than one message. Familiar melodies used as signals were thus restructured to fulfill a more practical function.

Typically, shepherds' signals contained short themes with frequent interruptions, were constructed asymmetrically, and consisted of musical phrases in varying combinations (see also pp. 31 and 32 on Swedish herding calls and the Alpine *Kuhreihen* and yodelling). There was interplay between functional and aesthetic elements. Kaden illustrates this with a model consisting of five cases of melodies on a scale from functional to aesthetic. Kaden illustrates case 4 (see below and Figure 2.2) with a shepherding signal blown by Erick Hanf, a cowherd in Zella-Mehlis in Thuringia. It is based on the melody of the folk tune "Lazy Little Greta," a familiar song to shepherds. The shepherd only plays part of the melody. He adds brief cadences and excludes the repeats from the folk song version. His cadences serve to conclude one signal or the melody itself, making it possible for the shepherd to use part of a song as a signal without destroying its aesthetic value.

This is where the personal inclinations of the shepherd come into play as regards enriching the signals with unrelated sounds. Such additions may be jokes, love songs, and dances. In practice, shepherds and shepherdesses have been doing this since time immemorial. Kaden shows how this musical language has several levels.

Case 1: The structure of the signals basically follows the demands with regard to functional communication (based on elementary structures).

Case 2: The structure of the signals disintegrates into sequences consisting of easily distinguishable, functional, and aesthetic segments.

Case 3: The structure of the whole is marked by fixed functional and aesthetic characteristics.

Case 4: The functional and aesthetic aspects conflict here, making one another "fluctuate."

Case 5: The functional nature of the signals is entirely overshadowed.

The Transformation of Herding Music: From Cow-calls and *Kuhreihen* to Tourist Traps and Tyrolean Dancing

The shepherds of Harz and Thuringia may be taken to represent all the signaling European shepherds of past and present, from Finland, the Baltic

Figure 2.2. Shepherds' signals ranging from working to esthetic functions. (Kaden 1977:2, pp. 54ff.)

states, and Russia in the north to the Balkans in the south and Spain and France in the west (see Tiersot 1889/R1978, p. 152f.). Chapter 6, contains more about instruments and music from herding cultures, including its uses for dancing and entertainment.

Herding music has a history of its own, from its discovery until the present, when we find it as an element of tourism and folk music festivals and in the mass media. Let us examine this history in two different environments, the Swedish and the Swiss.

Before examining the work of Swedish traditional researcher, Richard Dybeck (1811–1877), let us look at what this music is variously called, by looking at studies made by Carl-Allan Moberg (1896–1978) in Uppsala. He takes the Swedish terms *kula, köka,* and *lulla,* used in different dialects, as his example:

Most of the words used to describe the musical techniques used by the shepherds appear to be onomatopoetic constructions, interjections bearing a resemblance to imitative sounds, and used to call the animals or to communicate with other shepherds. . . . Terms like 'kuja,' 'kula' and 'kulua' naturally fall into place as designations for songs used to call the cows, containing constant repetitions of the dialect word for 'cow.' . . . Other expressions, such as *lulla,* etc. are probably related to familiar sounds from lullabies, and are intended to settle the animals in. (Moberg 1955, pp. 64f.)

Let us now go along to the pasture lands with Richard Dybeck.

Once spring has arrived and the cattle have grazed for about a fortnight here at Bolby (Dalacarlia), they are taken to the mountain pastures, where the land is now ready for grazing. When the procession departs, the herd is driven before the shepherds in the right direction but without paths to follow. One person marches ahead of the herd, enticing the cattle to follow, while the others go behind, driving them on. And all the time (despite the sweat and toil of the journey of many miles) the sound rings out from mountain top to mountain top, with the singing of the cheerful duct flute (*Spälapipan*) and the wondrous fingerhorn. . . . Upon arrival at the pasture site we either find a cottage, with a hearth and windows, or a timbered shack with a roof of pine bark, in the middle of which there is a large hole to allow the smoke from the open fire to escape. At five in the morning, six in some places, the shepherds are out with the cattle. By noon, when the animals have eaten their fill, they are gathered to a resting place to sleep and chew their cud. . . . There is nothing lovelier than the evening signals in the pasture land! . . . I have an idea that these tunes, known to all, gave rise to what I refer to as horn songs, which were the building blocks of shepherds' songs and dances which, in turn, gave rise to all types of Swedish folk music. . . . It is remarkable that even dumb creatures listen to and seem able to distinguish among these signals, of which there are many more than those I have noted down here, each with its own meaning. . . . But how can words suffice to describe the performance of these songs? At least I can say that they cannot possibly be given full expression on paper. All means available must be used. . . . However, I comfort myself that I am not describing phenomena that are ancient history. Our pasture lands are still full of singers of herding songs and players of signal horns. So I would encourage each and every reader to go there, rather than to try to imagine them from this little book. (Dybeck 1846, pp. VI–VII)

Dybeck also states where he heard every signal and song he noted down (Figure 2.3).

In his travelog from 1798, Johann Gottfried Ebel described alpine herding songs, some fifty years prior to Dybeck:

The cows in the Alps are gathered together by the songs of the shepherds, known as "calls" in Appenzell. Different calls are used to gather the cows, the sheep and the swine. It is clear how well the cows know the voice of their own shepherd, because as soon as the shepherd raises his voice in a *Kuhreihen* or *rugusa* [sung gathering call] his own herd rushes to him from afar. [Baumann 1976, p. 140]

The *Kuhreihen*, sung by the Swiss mountain shepherds and duly famous (it is known in French as

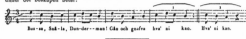

Figure 2.3. The different working functions of the herding call according to Dybeck 1846/R1974, p. 41f.)

the *Ranz des Vaches*), is often sung in Innerrhoden. This type of song is never sung in words. Its tones are mostly made in the aperture between the vocal chords, without the help of the larynx. This is why those who perform these songs cannot be seen to be moving their jaws or jaw muscles perceptibly, and it is what makes this music so different from what we are accustomed to hearing the human mouth utter. It sounds more like it is coming from a wind instrument, especially as the breathing is also quite imperceptible: some mountain men can sing for a whole minute without drawing a breath. It is extremely difficult to note down the melody of a *Kuhreihen*, particularly of those from Appenzell. For although they are always sung to the same rhythms, the same song may be produced very differently by different singers. This is attributable not only to the emotions and personality of the singers, but also to their methods. Their movements are sometimes slow and melancholy, sometimes quick and cheerful: and these shifts are unpredictable. Sometimes a *Kuhreihen* from Appenzell may last for half an hour, and change constantly. Nowhere else does one hear them sung by two or three singers, with one or two holding out a drone, accompanying the melody of the first singer. No one who had not mastered the song entirely would perform it in company. The final note of a *Kuhreihen* is always different from what one would expect of a traditional melody—it is a characteristic of these songs. I have noted that the final notes of every *Kuhreihen*, and I have heard them sung or blown all over Switzerland 'from the heights of the Alps to the Jura mountains' are special in this way, although they are not identical but suited to the theme and structure of the song. (Quoted from Baumann 1976, pp. 131f., 140; see Figure 2.4.)

Ebel concludes by explaining the word *Kuhreihen*:

"When all the cows from a herd that have been grazing in a certain area move towards the song of the shepherd, they form a line and walk one behind the other. I take this to explain the name of the song used to call and gather the cows: Kühreihen, Kuhreihen" (Quoted from Baumann 1976, pp. 140f. Ebel 1798 p. 155).

There is general agreement between the findings of Dybeck and Ebel, although Dybeck writes in a romantic, nostalgic style, while Ebel's writing is in the style of the enlightenment, uplifting and factual. Each author emphasizes function and sees the art form as a national or possibly regional one, and each tries in his own way to describe what makes this style of singing unique, although Ebel's description is far superior. Both also realize how difficult it is to put this peculiar kind of calling song on paper. Dybeck even recommends that the reader abandon his book for a visit to the pasture.

According to Dybeck, the music of his time was penetrating the pastures, but he does not imply that the calling songs were affected by it. Ebel also described the technique of the *Kuhreihen* as extremely stable and well developed.

The notion that some sounds have a magic power can also be found in both places. Dybeck writes:

The date on which the cattle are taken out to graze for the first time usually falls early in the month of May. The occasion is fraught with superstition and

Figure 2.4. The vignette on the title page of a collection of Swiss *Kuhreihen* and folk songs published in Bern, 1818. The picture is of a yodeller in Appenzell, a *ruguser*.

magical traditions. Even today in some distant places these superstitions prevail. The festive bonfires of Valpurgis Eve which burn on mountain and hilltops are believed to prevent wild beasts from harming the cattle throughout the summer. Over the next few days horns sound time and again, intended to safeguard the herds for the summer and ward off wild animals. (Dybeck 1846, p. IV; cf. Kjellström 1976, p. 35)

There is an "alpine blessing" meant to fill the same function, with recitative-like melodies intoned to pray to the Virgin Mary and various patron saints for protection. Special wooden megaphones are used on these occasions. (Figure 2.5). The pastures were safe from danger as far as the sound could be heard, thanks to the protection of the saints (see also Baumann 1976, p. 204).

However, the descriptions also indicate that there were considerable differences between the music of the Swedish pastures and the Swiss Alps. First, women performed it in Sweden and men in Switzerland. This was attributable to the different social systems: in countries such as Sweden, it was the women who were considered most dispensable and who could thus be sent to the pastures, while in Switzerland it was the men (see Moberg 1955, pp. 21ff., Johnson 1986, pp. 147ff.). Second, there were clear stylistic differences regarding the length and performance of the music.

Sweden Then and Now

Let us now leap forward 140 years in time, to Sweden in the 1970s, and see what the pastures

Figure 2.5. An alpine call to protect the fields from wild beasts. (Woodcut by Joseph Balmer from *Schweizerisches Kunst-Album* [1862].)

are like. When Dybeck made his nineteenth-century journey, there were pastures only in certain parts of Sweden: "If we wish to see the real life of the shepherds, we must make our way to the mountain pastures, which can only be found in the northern part of the country, and never south of Dalacarlia. But what wondrous sights they are to see! A whole way of life! . . . I will only describe what I have seen as the finest, in Westerbotten, Jemtland and Dalacarlia" (Dybeck 1846, p. VI).

The participants from an excursion to the southern part of the province of Jemtland wrote in 1977, "Today the music of the pasture lands may still be found in a few places in Sweden, mainly in northwestern Dalacarlia, Herjedalen and southern Jämtland" (*Fäbodmusik i förvandling* (Pasture Music in Transition) 1978, p. 6). This implies that we should still take Dybeck at his word and visit the pastures to hear the songs rather than read about them. However, the research group also registered the permeation of alien elements in 1977:

In stark contrast to this pastoral tradition [a farming family with one of the adults a professional teacher, and where the animals are still taken out to the mountain pastures in the spring] there are "pastoral cottages" where cows are kept but which are also cafés selling waffles and jam to attract tourists, which have grown up along the major thoroughfares and which give the transient visitor a false, romanticized view of the real pastoral culture. The village of Klövsjö, Jämtland needs the tourist trade to survive, and the villagers have adapted to the prevailing needs. Many of the "pasture lasses" are accustomed to having their mountain cottages visited almost daily by tourists who want to feed the goats and buy real goat cheese. Tourism has also affected the music. Once a week all summer, Gölin Morlind receives a busload of tourists from the nearby mountain resorts, and demonstrates how she calls her cows. 'My calls are really mostly for people and tourists nowadays.' (*Fäbodmusik i förvandling* (Pasture Music in Transition)1978, pp. 6f.)

However, despite this transformation, much of the material recorded by the 1977 research group corresponds well to Dybeck's description of the herding songs:

1. The calls are constructed of alternately short and long phrases, often distinctly rounded off and clearly distinguished from one another (Dybeck: "between each melodic period there is a long pause").
2. For functional reasons, there are vocal variations including pure speech-song, calling-to-attention, and melismatic song in a high register (see. Dybeck, musical example p. 43 no. 12, p. 44 no. 15, p. 34 no. 31).

In both collections of examples, from Dybeck's day and from our own (Figures 2.6, and 2.7), the calling songs are structured in alternately long and short phrases, often clearly rounded off, and distinctly separated from one another by rests for breathing. The phrases are added to one another functionally and from segments of varying length. The music must be extremely flexible in construction in order to function well in a wide variety of different working situations. The mountain lass uses speech-song when the cows are nearby. The calling phrases, on the other hand, feature the calling-to-attention characteristics, with loud attacks in a high register, described above. There is an excellent contemporary example of this sharp, loud

12.

Öster–Dalarna. — Med denna "blåses till hvila på *Sofvaholm*" (hvilostället. Se Ordförkl.) — På detta hviloställe, som vanligen är en öppen, grön plats i skogen med upphöjdt läge, tändes vid middagstiden en eld, och vallhjonen med kreaturen uppehålla sig der en stund.

Till Vallkullorna.

Lyster du li-ka-så, kommer du strax hit till mig; Middag är det län-ge-se'n,

ritard.   *Till boskapen.*

qväller är det rätt---nu. Kom nu straxt hit till mig. Si rö-, si rö-keu!

Kom hit och hvi-len er! Hvi-len e-der! hvi-len e-der! Si rö-, si rö-ken!

15.

Westmanlands skogsbygd. — Vanlig Lock-låt om qvällarna; af samma art som föregående.

Lis-se ko! Lis-se ko! Ko-na mi-na stac-ka-re, kom!

31.

Lima socken i Dalarna.

Upptecknaren, Kyrkoherden L. R., yttrar i bref af den första November 1844 (se Brefsaml. T. 2, s. 311) följande, rörande visan: "Då solen börjar sjunka i vestern, hemvända fäbokullorna med hjorden. Från alla väderstreck närma sig vallkullor fabostället, under det de sorgfritt tralla denna sång, den de kalla *Korla*, eller *Kôla*. Bergen genljuda, och i djupa skogen lyssnar — älskaren — den arbetströtte fästmannen. — — Ord finnas väl till sången, men om någon nu har dem i minnet, är denne att söka bland de urgamla".

Figure 2.6. Herding calls from Dybeck. (1846/R1974, pp. 43f, p. 34 no. 31.)

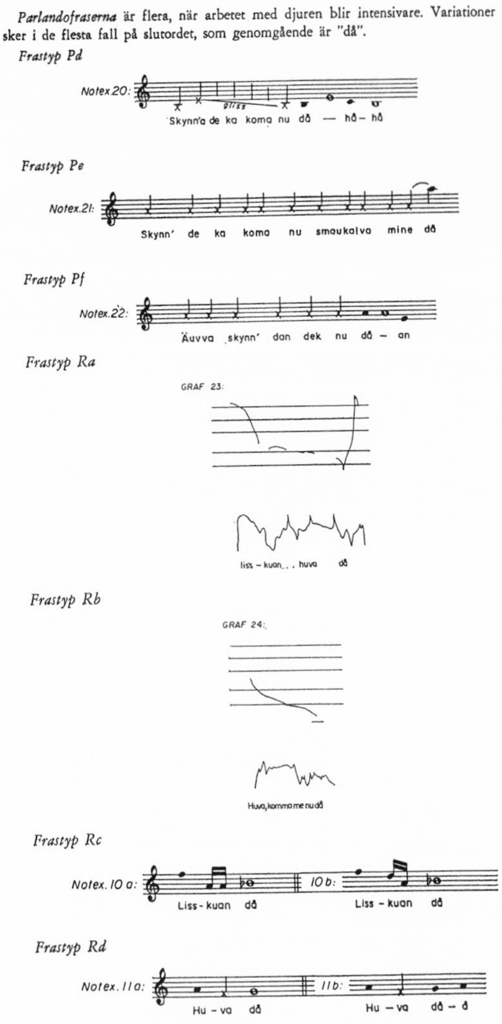

Parlandofraserna är flera, när arbetet med djuren blir intensivare. Variationer sker i de flesta fall på slutordet, som genomgående är "då".

Frastyp Pd

Notex.20:   Skynn'a de ka koma nu då — — hå — hå

Frastyp Pe

Notex.21:   Skynn' de ka koma nu smaukalva mine då

Frastyp Pf

Notex.22:   Äuvva skynn' dan dek nu då — an

Frastyp Ra

GRAF 23:

liss – kuan, . . huva   då

Frastyp Rb

GRAF 24:

Huva,kommamerudå

Frastyp Rc

Notex.10 a: Liss – kuan   då   *10 b:*   Liss – kuan   då

Frastyp Rd

Notex.11 a: Hu – va   då   *11 b:*   Hu – va   då – å

Figure 2.7. Herding calls from *Fäbodmusik i förvandling*, 1978.

attack followed by a glissando into speech-song transcribed using MONA, the sound analysis equipment in Uppsala, (For MONA, see Bengtsson et al., 1969). The first glissando begins somewhat after the opening of the phrase, while the second one appears at the very beginning. In addition, there are "melismatic phrases and forceful attacks with no vibrato at all in an extremely high register." Beckmann and Johnson provide an interesting systematization of the calling phrases in the 1977. The call is basically a descending one, with thirds as the main interval, often connected by passing notes. The end is marked by what the report describes as a "cut-off attack in a low parlando register." If one examines older transcriptions and applies the principles developed by these researchers to them, it appears possible to "decode" them correspondingly into melismatic phrases over a given structure of intervals, with some phrases more like calling, some parlando, some more ordinary folk song melodies, and some spoken text.

Those who have their animals in mountain pastures today, 140 years after Dybeck's description, may travel by automobile between their homes and their pasture cottages. In the cottages with waffle cafés tape-recorded, "real folk music" is used as background, but many old features remain the same. Thanks to their own memories and the stories of the older generation of mountain lasses the pasture women of today are historical bridge-builders. Take, for example, Matilda Nord (b. 1898) in the village of Ytterhogdal in the province of Jämtland:

When you herd the cows, you talk with them, but if there are cows missing in the evening, you have to call them loudly, so that they can hear you from so far away. We have a special call for that, the "distance call" I call it. . . . I was thirteen when I first went to the pastures in Lillhärdal. . . . You had to get ready in the mornings and take the cows out, and not lose them and bring them home later. They were long days, especially if you were alone. And there were bears in those parts. . . . In Lillhärdal the animals were taken to pasture before midsummer and kept there until Michaelmas, so we herded them all summer long. We were paid one krona a day . . . and we could help ourselves to the farmers' goat cheese, butter, and milk. You were supposed to get cloth for a dress, wool for a pair of stockings, and a scarf when you got home in the autumn. In those days we thought that was good wages. That was in 1932, . . . and times were hard then. . . . (*Fäbodmusik i förvandling* 1978, p.11 f.)

Had Dybeck taken the time to interview and describe the destiny of one of his mountain lasses, her life might not have been very different from that of Matilda Nord.

Today, the researcher armed with a video camera, a tape recorder, and sound analysis equipment can register and describe many kinds of herding calls far more simply than could Dybeck, whose frustration over having only pen and paper almost led him to a sense of resignation.

In various studies (the latest in 1986), Anna Johnson describes Swedish herding calls with the aid of various physiological measurements, and draws the following conclusions:

> The larynx is raised, the opening of the jaws extended, the opening between the lips is widened, the corners of the mouth pulled back, the tongue-bone lifted upwards and forward towards the jawbone, the epiglottis is raised in the direction of the back of the tongue, and the shape of the tongue changes so that the root of the tongue and the back of the tongue are raised while the point of the tongue is dropped. (Johnson 1986, p. 252)

Such analyses are of value even beyond scholarly circles, as they make it possible to better understand the techniques of calling songs and thus teach them to new generations of singers, even outside the traditional environment (see also p. 34). This, in turn, contributes to the fulfillment of Dybeck's objective: keeping the herding songs alive for the future.

The melodic material of herding calls seems to display a time-restricted factor, while the technique is more or less constant over time.

"Thus the melodic material used for the many herding songs probably always changed with the fashion over the course of the centuries, while the melismatic variation techniques are traditional" (Moberg 1959, p. 50). Here, as always in relation to cultural phenomena, the main question is the intentions of the individual singer, who chooses his or her melodic material freely and personally, from any era.

This applies to the calling techniques as well. In the 1960s, I met pasture women who thought shouting for the calls was so ugly that they modified their voices and harmonies for the tourists and folk music scholars, making it correspond more to the ideals of hymn singing. Today, the penetrating sound of cow calls is considered one of its aesthetic qualities, and it is regarded as being in symbiosis with a kind of older music found in the mountain-pasture culture. Cow calls have now become a defined style, a folk music genre.

Cattle Calling as a Musical Style

Carl-Allan Moberg made a study of cow calling in 1959, and Anna Johnson is currently conducting another, based on new analytic techniques (see also Johnson 1973). Moberg highlights the dynamic nature of the melodies of the calls, the mechanical expansion of calling phrases, and the structurally important interval which, in his opinion, stems from the descending tetrachord (e'–b') with a' as the final note. There are also a number of standardized phrases with a falling melodic movement. Moberg regards tendencies toward a return of the melodic movement to its original form as "signs of the influence of the cultivated landscape on the melodies of cattle calls" (p. 21). The "minor key-character" of the calls is also noted, as is their wealth of ornamentation. There is no actual principle of formal structure. Moberg also notes that the text loses meaning when the aesthetic elements gain the upper hand (p. 46). Techniques of melismatic variation are also characteristic. It is also interesting to note how, directly and indirectly as his work is used in popular presentations, Moberg has contributed to the general view of the music of the pastures.

Today, more and more artists are performing a sort of distillation of the musical heritage of the pastures, just as a prominent interpreter of Baroque music might present us with the organ compositions of Bach. It is not that the artist in question has necessarily herded a cow or been in Leipzig, but that he or she is able to maintain and artistically reinterpret an art and to give its esthetic potential an image on a new functional basis.

Thus it appears as if Swedish herding music—despite its detours via the tourist trade—has been salvaged more or less intact. It will survive thanks to the fact that the women who herd the cows today are also teachers, and have realized that music, no matter how good it is, cannot survive on nostalgia.

Switzerland then and Now

The Swiss have two different categories of herding music, the *Kuhreihen* and yodelling (Figure 2.8). The *Kuhreihen* is distinguished from yodelling in that it incorporates the names of the cows and does not make use of falsetto. The melodies of the *Kuhreihen* have a fixed structure, accompanied on special occasions with bell-ringing or drones played by the shepherds.

In the late eighteenth century, the *Kuhreihen* began to be regarded as a kind of national music. Nationalistic, educational texts were set to them. Many remarkable changes occur when music makes the transition from being functional to becoming a kind of national folk music. For example, the *Kuhreihen* were banned from performance in the area around St. Gallen, because they were causing the cows to break through the fences and go down into the village. Swiss recruits performed them over a beer, for their own entertainment and that of others (1756). It is even said that a Swiss man stood up and sang a *Kuhreihen* at the Paris opera:

> One of these people had come to Paris and was taken to the opera where he was so carried away by the trills of the castrato that he was rude enough to state that this song was far too feminine. He put his fingers into his ears, raised his voice in a Kuhreihen and soon out-shouted the opera singer entirely. Louis the Great and his court were greatly moved by all the intricacies of this song, and asked the singer to perform in the royal garden, but the Swiss man refused, claiming that he was a free man, the equal of the King, and only sang when the spirit moved him. (Quotes after Baumann 1976, p. 143.)

When the annual shepherds' festivals began to be held in Switzerland in 1805 (compare the Swedish fiddlers' festivals 100 years later), increasing em-

phasis was placed on the nationalistic and moralistic elements of the music.

Yodelling

According to Swiss scholar Max Baumann, the kind of yodelling we encounter in the various source materials is a rather young phenomenon. He regards it as having first become widespread around 1800, and bases this assumption on the fact that it features conventional tonal harmonic structure, based in major or minor keys. They are thus also easy to put on paper with traditional notation, except for the calls.

Baumann distinguishes among four basic types of yodelling-calling melodies:

1. a recited melody based on spoken inflection;
2. ascending movement;
3. descending movement;
4. a mixed form he refers to as a "hovering" call melody.

(Compare these with the categories of the Swedish research group on Herding Music in transition' above). Baumann defines yodelling as "melodies sung on a vowel with a larger or smaller number of spontaneous falsetto tones." There are a number of recurring formal structures, not consciously architectonic but resembling instead the kind of parallelism characterizing the medieval sequence, which switches from open to closed phrase endings. The vast majority of the melodies have a distinct major tonality, which Baumann refers to as the *fa* mode (i.e., a major scale with a raised fourth degree). Uneven rhythms dominate (Figure 2.9).

The touring Tyrolean choirs of the early nineteenth century were the most important contributors to the increasing familiarity and popularity of yodelling. Yodelling was also incorporated into popular music, and it is said that nearly all local songs from Vienna beginning in the 1820s included yodelling.

Yodelling has also attracted a great deal of scholarly interest. As early as 1942 there was a study of timber in yodelling made by Richard Luchsinger, in which he described the difference between yodelling and ordinary singing (see Baumann 1976, pp. 92f.). Active yodelling clubs have existed for many years. As a result, experienced yodellers have developed practical, descriptive models of their methods (Baumann 1976, pp. 94f.).

Figure 2.8. Peasant family at Giessbachfallen near Bern entertaining a city family with yodelling and horn blowing. (Part of a colored etching by J. M. Friedrich, ca. 1825. Schweizerisches Landesbibliotek.)

Baumann describes yodelling as sounding like a shawm, often sung with a treble or nasal voice. The voice of the unschooled yodeller often sounds forced. Yodelling shifts between full sounds from the chest and flute-like falsetto tones. The notes are interconnected to form whole slurred or portamento phrases (for further details, see Baumann 1976, p. 96).

Theories and Speculations about the Origins of Animal Calls

As indicated, there are many parallels between Swed- ish animal calls and the alpine *Kuhreihen* and yodel- ling. This has led scholars to speculate as to whether they might have originated in the same place.

Hypothesis #1:
In light of the circumstances described above, it appears feasible that, in both the Alps and Scandinavia, calling songs and herding songs in forced, unnatural voice, with or without mega-phonic techniques or mirliton, nasal sound, may bear some relation to dying traditions from the Germanic–early Norse–*galder* songs. They might be a popularized version of a more elitist "style," or at least as a related technique (Moberg 1955, p. 71).

Hypothesis #2:
Austrian musicologist Walter Graf has studied the capacity of the human voice to carry over long distances at certain frequencies and using certain techniques of singing (see Baumann 1976, p. 114f.). This could be the key to the origin of calling songs.

Hypothesis #3:
The explanation might be that sounds that attracted the cattle were given priority in practical herding work, and that the working process was fundamentally the same irrespective of whether it was carried out in Sweden or Switzerland.

I would like to mention one or two other hypotheses as examples of how musicologists speculate. Let us return to the name *Kuhreihen*. On the journey up to the alpine pastures the shepherd led the way, followed by the best-looking cow, who wore the largest bell and was followed in turn by other cows with bells. Thus the origin of the word *Kuhreihen* quite clearly seems to be "a row of cows." However, some scholars, including Alfred Tobler in 1890 (and quoted in Baumann 1976 and Moberg 1955) have referred to the word *Kühreigen*, to be interpreted as having to do with some kind of dance. Tobler claims that the shepherds did a sort of dance. Standing in a ring and facing the center, they repeated the word *lobe-lobela* over and over again. There was one soloist, and the others sang a drone accompaniment. Moberg used this "dance" to solve the problem of the name, regarding the old story of the cows marching in line as obsolete.

In such a context, the name Kuhreigen, which has given rise to some puzzlement, becomes easily ex-

Figure 2.9. The characteristic direction of movement of a yodel, irrespective of the melody type. (Baumann 1976, p. 153, ex. 27.)

plained—it means "the cow dance"—i.e., not a dance performed by cows but by their herders, danced in a ring, as a magical incantation.

From that point it is easy to associate this dance with the Lobetanz that is found in late medieval sources. (Moberg 1955, p. 78)

Baumann, however, is extremely skeptical of the *Lobetanz* theories, stating that there is no evidence the two are related. He regards the *Kuhreihen* and its eighteenth- and nineteenth-century predecessors as songs meant to gather the cattle, just like other herding songs.

Moberg appears convinced of the heathen origins of the *Kuhreihen* and of its use in semi-magical, semi-religious contexts. He sees it as a "Christianization of an ancient magic formula" (Moberg 1955, p. 77). We saw this earlier in the warding-off of wild beasts in the Alps. In a study from 1985, Ernst Emsheimer describes a kind of "cattle communion" to gather spiritual forces and promote growth, held in both heathen and Christian times, (see also p. 132). Cowbells played an important role in these contexts.

More Recent Explanatory Models

These kinds of magical explanations were once much more common in research, but in recent decades they have been replaced by theories emphasizing the functional, work-related aspects of this music. Perhaps, in fact, it would be appropriate to apply different explanatory models to dif-ferent epochs, depending on the world-view of the people living in each era. Prior to the nineteenth century, explanations of the world were often what we might classify as "irrational," although they were actually no less rational than the myths we use to explain things ourselves. In those times, the cow call may have been regarded primarily as magical, despite the fact that it had a practical function as well. Today, we may be prone to overemphasize the practical function when cow calls actually have very little but sentimental meaning or are merely a tourist attraction. To some extent, yodelling, the *Kuhreihen*, and cow calling have all survived as sort of musical picture postcards or as national symbols. At that time they also began to change and to take on new forms and functions. This process of transformation, as mentioned above, is based on myth. The music symbolizes the beauty of the Swedish mountains or the Swiss Alps, the dream of the virile yodeller, or the lonely, pining Swedish mountain maiden. One of the main aims of the cow-calling songs today may be to give the reveler nostalgia for a nonexistent reality to lessen the burdens of everyday life. If so, then the bargain has to include the occasional extreme, such as the dancing and yodelling Tyrolean man who stored his shirt in the stables so that it would have the appropriate odor for the female tourists.

Herding Calls in the Future

The musical future of the mountain-pasture areas of Sweden and Switzerland has at least three trends.

First, there will always be a handful of enthusiasts wanting to live by the old ways and to maintain both traditional herding and its cultural superstructure. This means that this music will exist as if in a mu- seum, performed actively but functioning as background music for tourists. Second, herding music will be performed at local fetes and national and international festivities, in concert halls, and on television and radio, as a musical symbol. It will then take a more artistic and esthetic form. Third, there will be new creations, compositions based on or taking their inspiration from the special sound and structure of the herding calls (such as Ingvar Lindholm's ballet music *Riter* (Rites), 1960). This trend will result from the great interest exhibited in herding calls as an art form by so many young people today.

Even now it is possible for students at institutes or colleges of music to study folk songs. Courses are held in herding calls in Sweden today, and eventually there will probably be some kind of textbooks or teaching materials on the subject. Herding calls are among the most original vocal forms in the rural soundscape, and thus they will probably retain a unique status.

SONGS OF WORK

Singing when planting, harvesting, working indoors, and walking to and from work provides us with another type of working music. Such songs came into being long before industrialization and the consequent total separation of work and leisure time and long before our workplaces became so noisy that it became impossible to hear singing or shouting at all. In those days, singing served to bridge the gap between work and leisure time.

Harvest Songs and Musical Entertainment at Harvest Festivals

The most well-documented harvest songs are those from Eastern Europe and the Iberian peninsula. Like herding music, many of these songs were purely communicative, with shouted formulas and loudly pitched notes to keep farm laborers in contact with one another despite the distance between the fields. The texts sometimes describe the different aspects and phases of harvest work, but some were love songs, warnings that the master was approach-

ing, or laments over the laborious work. Some harvest songs are related to laments (see p. 57), epic songs (see p. 78), or calendar songs (see p. 65).

As opposed to many songs of work that belong to no special category but which were sung throughout the farming season, built on repeated, varied melodic phrases with highly differing textual structures, some harvest songs have enough unique stylistic traits to merit separate scrutiny.

Many parts of Spain exhibit a wealth of harvest songs varying greatly in style and spanning the spectrum from calls to lyrical folk songs. They are often richly melismatic and rhythmically free, like flocks of swallows in flight.

In his *Cancionero del campo* (1966), Bonifacio Gil presents a selection of Spanish songs of work ranging from grape cultivation to olive harvesting (Figure 2.10). In a classic work, *Musica popular Española*, first published in 1927, Eduardo López Chavarri describes how the various songs broke the silence of the endless fields (p. 96). He saw these songs as substantially influenced by the Orient. He also attributed the free form of these folk songs, a sort of *ad libitum vocalis,* as corresponding to the human pulse beat, with ♩ = 66. Inserted calls to human or animal work mates characterize this sort of folk song. *Vocalises*, wordless songs performed using vowels only, are generally sung using the vowel sound *a.* Some of these working songs are very similar to the Scandinavian and alpine herding calls described earlier. However, there are also examples of laments and songs influenced by sacred song.

Typical Andalusian harvest songs are melismatic and highly dramatic, with sharp dynamic shifts. A calling form is characteristic of many of the melodies.

There is evidence from Germany that songs of work were considered so important that day workers were paid better wages if they could lead the singing (Frey/Siniveer 1987, p. 60).

In a manuscript study from 1985, Polish ethnomusicologist Anna Czekanowska provides a detailed analysis of harvest songs from the Slavic language area. Her objective was to identify unifying stylistic traits. Her conclusions include the following:

1. the melodies seldom span more than a few notes;
2. they are performed collectively, by at least two or three singers;
3. an identical melodic structure is repeated and varied by adding pedal points, melodic ornaments, falsetto screams and imitative effects.

Figure 2.10. Songs for work from Seville. (Bonifacio Gil 1966, p. 80.)

Such harvest songs have been used by virtually all the Slavic peoples, as well as in most of the Mediterranean cultures, and have been retained with varying degrees of authenticity. The southern Slavic regions, including Serbia, Macedonia, and Bulgaria, as well as the border regions of the Ukraine and Belarus, display the widest range of performance techniques for harvest songs.

Interviews with singers of these songs indicate that there was not a particularly strong relationship between the repertoire sung and the task at hand. Rather, it was up to the female singers to give the ritually conducted harvest work a brighter side. There were far more harvest songs than any other type of work songs, and they were more varied. Later they were more professionally performed, but they retained symbolic tonal qualities, as well as specific signaling elements.

The texts vary from short calls with a sexual message to long lyrical love songs, used to mark the different aspects of the working day. The texts are a sort of code, sometimes performed in dialog, with underlying layers of symbols. A special technique is used to achieve onomatopoetic effects, for example contrasting frontal and rear vowels, special i and u sounds in the calls, and the kind of consonants that can be found in whispering, stammering, or clucking. All these characteristics of harvest songs distinguish them from other Slavic ritual songs, which may also contain calls and invocations, but often in the form of special words.

Czekanowska formulates a system of norms on the basis of the "intensity" of various intervals, in which the second and the seventh are of particular importance, the second forming the axis around which the main core of musical material shifts, melodically and harmonically, while the seventh is the force that gathers and consolidates the whole. Fifths and fourths appear to have more punctuating functions, underlining and ornamenting the narrative. Heterophony and melismas operate in musical complement and are used interchangeably.

Czekanowska characterizes women's harvest songs as a highly specialized genre of folk music, related to certain activities but primarily with a magical function. Such songs were always sung collectively, and each singer had a particular assignment, such as to sing a pedal-point, provide ornamentation, be prepared to respond, shout, or add illustrative effects.

According to Czekanowska, change of register is an important stylistic instrument used to achieve either a harmony or a heterophony of consonants. Different groups and regions also seem to have different aesthetic ideals. It is possible to "model" the fixed and variable elements of the harvest song (cf. p. 69, Zemtsovsky). Czekanowska's conclusion is that the magical and esthetic functions dominate over the signaling function in the harvest songs.

The musicologist Radmila Petrović indicates in her analysis (1970) of Serbian songs, including harvest songs (1970) that the music and the text were not regarded as separate units: the word *poem* in Serbian means a text and its melody. By analyzing the formal structures both of the melodies and of verse stanzas, she attempts to reveal their inter-

Figure 2.11. Serbian folk songs, including harvest songs and hay-making songs. (Petrović 1970, p. 64 (a), p. 66 (b), p. 67 (c) and (d).)

relationship. She finds that the melodies of Serbian songs consist of a series of small, very meaningful melodic phrases, referred to by Petrović after Bartók (1951) as "melodic stanzas," repeated until the text has been sung in its entirety (Figure 2.11). Serbian rural melodies are characterized by a kind of free verse text, with lines varying from six to fourteen syllables, a ten-syllable line being the most common. (See also Bartók/Lord 1951, p. 39, which contains a survey of the different metric structures, as well as p. 109).

In the first example only one melodic phrase, a "melo-stanza," is repeated (a). Petrović now uses various examples to show how different musical forms appear to take shape. The phrases are concluded with proliferating cadenzas, and each individual phrase is formulated as a separate "variation" (b). The phrases in the two lines of verse often form a sort of question-and-answer. Example c has a descending melody line, and concludes, as is often the case, with a leap of a fifth (usually sung as a falsetto shout). In d a melodic motif has been added to the repeated line of text. It has very little in common with the original motif. When the melodic phrases are formulated according to the metric structure of the text, different formal structures arise.

This continual tension-relaxation in which melodic phrases and lines of text work together and then counteract one another is the prerequisite for the constant creation of new models. The models follow two different stylistic trends, referred to as glas, one older and one more contemporary. There are various types of the older glas. One is the extended glas, which is usually a melody with a free

rhythm, and another is the short glas, with a markedly rhythmic beat. The new glas has a fixed rhythmic structure, and contains several lines of text and melody composed according to standards and repeated so as to give rise to regular melodic forms. The old-fashioned types of glas were classified according to their function in the harvest or wedding. However, this type of association between melodic version and function appears to be quite unusual.

Lord writes:

The singers themselves—at least in the regions covered by our work—do not seem to recognize any categories other than a few rough and indeterminate ones. There are songs that are sung at weddings, and there are lullabies; there are songs for dancing, and there are a few children's game songs. When questioned about songs sung on any given occasion or under particular circumstances, as, for example, songs for dancing or reaping or weddings, the singers are likely to think of songs about weddings or reaping rather than songs sung at those times. Most of the songs are general love songs and can be sung on any occasion. (Bartók/Lord 1951, p. 253)

However, this may be attributable to the fact that the singers whose songs were noted down here were not harvesting, nor were they at weddings; rather, they were the leaders of the local mosques. In older published collections (see Bartók/Lord 1951, p. 82 for references) there are highly detailed lists of songs performed on special occasions including when working in the fields, (at harvest time, in the vineyards or maize fields going to and from, work, doing domestic chores such as carding wool, weaving rugs, spinning, churning butter, and working late in the evenings (known as *sedeljka*).

Songs, Instrumental Songs, and Migrant Workers

The music of Bulgaria and Serbia are so closely related both stylistically and functionally that in 1951 Bartók characterized them as one and the same musical culture. As in Russian and Ukrainian harvest songs, the verses are often concluded with a shouted leap, (usually a minor seventh). The vocal sound is penetrating, metallic, and perhaps somewhat sharper in Bulgaria than in other nearby nations (Figure 2.12a).

How can this stylistic correspondence be explained? Is it related to ways of singing from the past with magical intent, or to the function of the song? We must keep in mind that the spread of the style over such a large area need not be an indication of its age. The spread may have occurred in recent centuries, owing to the migrant harvest workers .

All over Europe, day work was a common phenomenon. In countries like Bulgaria, Romania, and Serbia, moreover, it was also very common for tasks like house-building, harvesting, plowing, corn-hilling, plum- and grape-picking, spinning, and weaving, to be done collectively. The boys, girls, and young women from the area would gather to volunteer their services, bringing in the sheaves, dressed in their best finery, because once the work was completed, everyone was invited to a huge celebration.

Migrant harvest workers, large groups of men and women, travelled in packs and worked for payment. They had one or two leaders who negotiated their terms with the masters, and who also distributed the tasks among them. As they walked from one estate to another, sometimes singing to bagpipe accompaniment, and when they stopped along the roadsides the girls would sometimes dance circle dances to liven up the dull routine. (Figure 2.12b) (See also Büchner 1896, who cites older travelers' descriptions.)

Harvest time was often a very festive period, and the wealthy estate owners or farmers might even hire an orchestra to play.

> The musicians sit in the shade of a huge willow tree, making lovely music on their viols, cymbals and pan flutes. And in the fields the scythes fly through the corn, sparkling. As if the rhythm had given their brown arms wings, they dance up and down to the beat. There is also singing—fragile lamentations and wild fiery songs, both strangely monotonous and with a wealth of ornamented figures the western ear can never memorize. (From an illustrated women's magazine quoted in Bücher 1896, p. 293.)

However, there are other less idyllic descriptions indicating that the musicians were not always hired strictly as entertainment. One Estonian manor lord made special use of the bagpipe player he hired at harvest time:

> It was a strange sight to see the squadrons flattening the grain, moving continually forward with the bagpiper as their field musician, and with their sergeants [the foremen] commanding them with their sticks in hand. The harvesters took it as a shameful criticism of themselves if the bagpiper began to play fast tunes, as this was a sign that they were working too slowly. Thus their work continued to the beat, with no interruptions, as long as the bagpipe was played. If the Bagpipe grew silent work stopped, and the scythe each worker held in his hand appeared to drop The day after the harvest was all in, there was a great celebration, known as 'Talkus' in Estonian. This is one of the happiest days of the year for poor Estonian farmers. Usually the day workers were also invited to a Talkus put on by the estate owner (Bücher 1896, p. 234.)

What Happened to Harvest Songs?

The special harvest songs with their sharp, biting sound were generally regarded as an ancient, heathen type of song. However, the texts of some, including the Spanish harvest songs, often include both heathen and Christian ideas. Like the herding songs, harvest songs are also multifaceted. There is a religious-magical level as well as a functional level to which the calls, the dialog structure, and the part-singing can be attributed. There is also an aesthetic, entertaining level which has come into being in contemporary times and has led to the development of new forms of harvest music.

The music of some countries displays no evidence of more ritualized uses of song, dance, or playing at harvest time, but all countries do have some music associated with harvesting. It was necessary to have some form of distraction from the hard work during the time of the year that provided employment.

Harvest work never had the same romantic sheen to it as herding, nor were the surroundings in which it was done equally exotic, wild, and pro-

Жъни, навалляй, невесто

Figure 2.12. (a) Bulgarian harvest songs with complex rhythms and with an oriental flavor. (*Naarodni pesni ot samokov* 1975, p. 23 no. 22, and p. 25, no. 27.)

Figure 2.12. (b) Line dance (*horo*) with bagpipe player. This drawing, by Bulgarian travelling scholar Felix Kanic is based on a photograph of his trip through Bulgaria from 1868–1874. It is blurred, with a balcony full of spectators in the background. Kanic has moved these dancers to the countryside, and made both the instrument and the dances very distinct. He has also portrayed the dancers in motion, while the photograph appears to show them standing still posing for the picture. (See also Atanassov 1976, p. 45 and Fig. 7.)

vocative as the mountains and the forests. Perhaps this is one of the reasons that the harsher harvest songs never received as much attention as the *Kuhreihen*, yodelling, and herding calls. Certainly the harvest songs are sufficiently beautiful and unique to deserve special attention and to be transplanted into environments such as the concert hall or the salons of the bourgeoisie, as the other songs have been. In recent years, in fact, harvest songs have experienced something of a revival. They were sung first by choirs in Eastern Europe and then elsewhere as well. Efforts are now being made by many choirs to reproduce the biting nasal sound that characterizes these harvest melodies.

OUTDOOR MUSIC FOR PILE-DRIVING, LOADING, PULLING, ETC.

Even more foreign to the salons were the calls and songs that accompanied heavy manual labor all over Europe. There was a highly refined system of different types of songs and methods of performing them, which might have interested curious musicians and amateurs. Some were sung with a leader and a choir, some as dialog between two groups, and they were characterized by complex rhythmic, melodic, and dynamic structures and dramatic shifts in harmony. Some such songs of work are still in use today, but they are becoming increasingly rare. Italian salt-bearers and Portuguese fishermen are two occupational groups that still integrate song with their work today, but in the 1890s, when Bücher was collecting material for his book, pile-drivers, blacksmiths, and loaders all over Europe still sang while they worked.

They [pile-driving songs] are typical songs of work in that improvisation is still a dynamic aspect of them, while it has disappeared from folk music. If the leader is creative, he will put all kinds of things in his song, including the news of the day, the building conditions, what's for dinner, how much the workers will be paid, and snide references to people listening. This last is a real contribution to lightening the heavy burden of the work at hand. (Bücher 1896, p. 248)

These songs often had a fixed form: first the number of shoves, lifts, or strokes was stated, then there was an interlude consisting of a short song, and then the next set of work tasks was described. (Figure 2.13)

Songs of work were powerful and seemed intimidating because they were sung in unison. Usually the melodies imitated well-known folk songs: Bücher describes one song criticizing a miserly employer to the melody of "O Tannenbaum." There were also special rhymes and songs used when pulling barges upstream, for example, on the Elbe or on the Volga (Figure 2.14).

Figure 2.13. Loading song from Norderney, an east Friesian island. (Bücher 1899, p. 164.)

The Songs and Calls of Sailors

Calls and songs of work at sea have existed since time immemorial, as long as crews have coordinated their efforts. Descriptions of fifteenth-century pilgrimages at sea contain descriptions of calls such as "Haul away! Hoist 'er up" or "Yo ho! Tail on the fall" (Hugill 1961, p. 2). Seventeenth- and eighteenth-century sailors at war hauled and lifted to the sounds of a fiddle or a fife. The only song the crew was allowed to sing was a "stamp-and-go" song for working in pairs.

On merchant vessels, shanty songs were sung. There were special melodies for pulling in the anchor, such as "Off She Goes" or "Drops of Brandy" (Hugill 1961, p. 7) (see also Figure 2.15).

Most of these were love songs, in which the pronoun *she* referred both to the vessel and to the girl the sailor had left behind—for example, "Pull away now, my Nancy O!" Black sailors had songs of their own. The following description is from Kingston, Jamaica, in 1811:

Our seamen having left the ship, the harbour work was performed by a gang of Negroes. These men will work the whole day at the capstan under a scorching sun with almost no intermission. They beguiled the time by one of them singing one line of an English song, or a prose sentence at the end of which all the rest join in a short chorus. The sentences which prevail with the gang we had aboard were as follows:

Two sisters courted one man,
Ch. Oh, huro my boys,

And they live in the mountains,
Ch. Oh, huro boys O.
And the second:
Grog time of day, boys
Grog time of day,
Ch. Huro, my jolly boys,
Grog time of day.
(Hugill 1961, p. 8)

Shanties may, in fact, even have been invented by black sailors.

There were many blacks on board these vessels because the plantation owners leased them out to the ship owners during the winter months instead of having to feed them while they were idle. Another source of the shanties was songs of entertainment by black minstrels. When Scottish, English, and Irish sailor-folk singers were in port, their songs mingled with American ones, and the shanties came into being. Ships' fiddlers also helped to spread the melodies.

It is said of shanties that "All kinds of fish get stuck in the sailors' nets." These "shanty-fish" include sixteenth-century English songs of work, ballads, and other folk songs, both instrumental and vocal dance melodies. Gradually they were joined by popular melodies from bourgeois dance music, operetta, and opera. The more exotic "fish" include Oriental songs, American plantation songs, West Indian, Latin American, and European folk songs, and, more recently, American and emigrant folk songs. The zenith of the shanty was in the mid-nineteenth century, and by the mid-1860s hardly any new ones were being written. For a few decades

Figure 2.14. "Song of the Volga Boatmen" containing the alternation between the call of work and the intermediate comments, here more lyrical than socio-critical. The painting by Repin has inspired many sentimental interpretations. This melody is famed as "Russian" in many parts of the world, and represents Russian folk music in many song books. (This particular version comes from Din don deine, *Lieder*.)

Figure 2.15. Shanty sung while baling out the boat. (Hugill 1961, pp. 48ff., 204.)

they remained very popular, as a kind of classic sentimental music during the time when the sailing boats were being replaced by steamships on which song was only seen as a disruptive element.

Today, shanties are a special feature of the folk music movement. The first International Shanty Festival, *Shanty '87*, was held in 1987 in Krakow, Poland, with Stan Hugill, the "godfather of the shanty," in attendance (see *Folk Roots*, September 1987, No. 51, "Hugill-Mania! Stan Hugill Godfather of the Shanty Mafia, Goes to Poland, p. 33ff.").

SONGS OF DOMESTIC LABOR

There were a wide variety of songs sung during domestic work, from lyrical songs to psalms to narrative tunes (see also chapters 4 and 5). There were also folk songs associated with certain domestic chores.

Early, Acerbi described the Finnish milling songs, sung to the endless task of grinding grain by hand. This was a job done all the year round with vocal accompaniment, in contrast to tasks such as flax-making, the songs of which were associated with a particular season. Flax-making also had a social function in that the young people of the village worked together, establishing the rhythmic beat of the cards with their song. Different

aspects of the task appear to have been associated with special songs. In Germany, for example, there were special flax-carding songs (see also Bücher 1896). Here are a couple of examples of songs associated with particular parts of tasks:

A Westphalian farmer encouraged his children and servants at their spinning by singing to them: 'As soon as I notice the wheel spinning less joyfully I suggest a cheerful song, and you should hear how fast the spinning wheel cheers up as well . . . (p. 85).' To encourage them to compete, the workers in the spinning cottages are enticed to spin a thread that does not break off until they have sung a certain verse to completion: 'The best of the spinners sing and spin long verses in the time it takes others to begin to spin their thread or to sing their first couplet. I must admit that it would be difficult to find a nobler yardstick by which to measure the skill of this handicraft.' (Bücher 1899, p. 91f.)

Songs were also sung when weaving, carrying water, washing, berry picking, rocking a cradle, etc. (p. 46). Most of these songs of work were intended to take the workers' minds off the domestic chore at hand. Probably their rhythms were not as important as the rhymes and songs sung during manual labor.

In Scotland there is a long tradition of songs of domestic work. The following description is from the eighteenth century:

Over all the Highlands and in the Isles there are various kinds of songs which are sung to airs suited to the nature of the subject. But on the western coast, from Lorne and in all the Hebrides, *luinneags* are most in request. These are in general very short and of a plaintive cast, analogous to their best poetry, and they are sung by women, not only at their diversions, but also during almost every kind of work where more than one person is employed, as milking cows and watching the folds, fulling of cloth, grinding of grain with the quern or hand mill, cutting down of corn, or peeling oak-bark, and haymaking. The men, too, have *iorrmas*, or songs for rowing, to which they keep time with their oars, as the women likewise do in their operations whenever their work admits of it. When the same airs are sung in their hours of relaxation, the time is marked by the motion of a napkin which all the performers lay hold of. In singing, one person leads the band, but in a certain part of the tune he stops to take breath, while the rest strike in and complete the air by pronouncing to it a chorus of words and syllables, generally of no signification.

These songs greatly animate every person present, and therefore, when labourers appear to flag, a *luinneag* is commonly called for, which makes them for a while forget their toil and work with redoubled ardour. In travelling through the remote Highlands in harvest, the sound of these little bands on every side, "warbling their native wood-notes wild," joined to a most romantic scenery, has a most pleasing effect on the mind of a stranger. (*Scotland and Scotsmen in the Eighteenth Century*, from the ms. of John Ramsay, esq. of Ochtertyre, edited by Alexander Allardyce, vol. II, p. 410)

Songs of Washerwomen

Even today, washerwomen sing as they work. In former times, washing and sizing newly woven cloth was both a heavy chore and unpleasant because the cloth was treated with urine. Songs helped to make anticipation of the task less distasteful. The women gathered, laid the tables with butter, cheesecake, barley bread, and whisky, and when the washing was done, the dancing began. Eighteenth-century travelogs describe the washing itself. The men were both ignorant about the task and intimidated by these singing female furies.

In *A Tour in Scotland* (1772), Thomas Pennat describes these remarkable songs, sung by a leader and a choir. They lived on very much unchanged into the twentieth century. (Figure 2.16):

On my return am entertained with a rehearsal, I may call it, of the *Luaghe* or, *walking of cloth*, a substitute for the fulling-mill: twelve or fourteen women, divided into two equal numbers, sit down on each side of a long board, ribbed lengthways, placing the

cloth on it: first they begin to work it backwards and forwards with their hands, singing at the same time as the *Quern*: when they have tired their hands, every female uses her feet for the same purpose, and six or seven pair of naked feet are in the most violent agitation, working one against the other: as by this time they grow very earnest in their labors, the fury of the song rises; at length it arrives to such a pitch, that without breach of charity you would imagine a troop of female demoniacs to have been assembled.

They sing in the same manner when they are cutting down the corn, when thirty or forty join in chorus, keeping time to the sound of a bagpipe, as the *Grecian* lasses were wont to do to that of a lyre during vintage in the days of *Homer* (Iliad, xviii, line 570). The subject of the songs at the *Luaghadh*, the *Quern*, and on this occasion, are sometimes love, sometimes panegyric, and often a rehearsal of the deeds of the ancient heroes, but commonly all the tunes slow and melancholy.

Singing at the *Quern* is now almost out of date since the introduction of water-mills. (Pennant, 1776, vol. 2, pp. 328–29)

The women began with a slow "warm-up"'song. Then the hostess would measure the cloth with her index finger, and after three songs she would measure once again. It generally took nine songs for the cloth to be ready. When it was the right thickness, it was rolled up, and a beating song was sung, usually with a very amusing text. In the past, there was a series of songs for the different parts of the task, apparently sung to syllables and words with no particular meaning or context. However, the texts that have been preserved are not generally about work. Instead, for example, they are love songs about young girls seduced by an aristocrat who is just looking for a temporary diversion. This was a very popular nineteenth-century theme and appears to have entered the repertoire of the washerwomen rather late.

The recorded washerwomens' songs tended to have a constant refrain, sung by the choir, and a variety of melodies sung by the lead singer. There seem to be no long, established songs, but, instead, many small verses which may be sung one by one or combined in different ways. As in so many other aspects of Scottish culture, sheep and other animals figure occasionally, as a reminder of the main occupation and of what was closest to people's hearts. The lead singers performed in very different ways, improvizing over a few notes in various

Figure 2.16. Women singing as they size cloth. The women to the left in the picture are grinding grain with a hand mill, under the supervision of the foreman. (Engraving from Thomas Pennant's *A Tour in Scotland*, 1722 [1776].)

combinations, while the choir refrains were constant, and often related to familiar melodies or types of melodies. In this type of music, too, lines of text and melodic phrases were repeated and gave rise to formal structures (Figure 2.17).

Work Songs and Tunes: Interplay between Simple Signals and Complex Beauty

Thus working music may contain sound structures forming simple signals with an unambiguous meaning relating to a given task, but it may also be complex and beautiful music for voice and instruments. These are the two ends of a long spectrum of music that has been an important aspect of the everyday life for many people, and it is sometimes such an integral part of general communication that an outsider finds it virtually impossible to describe the system theoretically. It is probable that working calls were originally conceived of as having a magical function. We recognize the structure of the falling shout from the "Kyrie eleison" and other invocations that were probably once used in a corresponding way for herding and at harvest time. The gradual shift from a magical to a work function and then to entertainment and finally sentimental value mirrors shifts in society at large. People have been able to transplant sound structures from one function to another. This is only possible when the melody, sound, and rhythm of the music have been composed with so much care and skill that it is considered worth the trouble of

transplanting from function to function. Of course the music always takes something of its previous function with it, and thus it becomes charged with both a sense of history and of present.

Literature

Anna Johnson's unpublished 1986 Ph.D. dissertation, "Sången i skogen: Studier kring den venska fäbodmusiken" (Songs in the Woods: Studies of the Music of the Swedish Pasture Culture), is accompanied by a parallel analysis of the music itself. It contains a survey of herding songs, made in accordance with the disciplines of the history of ideas and science, as well as a description of the world of the mountain pastures and the functions of this culture, and a survey of various investigations into the physiology of the voice and acoustics. It also has an excellent bibliography. Max Peter Baumann's study *Musikfolkore und Musikfolklorismus* (1976) was written at the time when West German scholars and others were preoccupied with "exposing" the myth of folklore. It has both a historical perspective and detailed musical analyses alongside a critique of ideology. Christian Kaden's studies, "Hirtensignale–Musikalische Syntax und Praxis" in *Beiträge zur musikwissenschatlichen Forschung in der DDRI* (1977) and "Utilit äres und Ästhetisches in der Struktur instrumentaler Arbeitssignale der Hirten" in *Studia instrumentorum musicae popularis* 2, (1977) (partcularly pp. 51–60) are semiotic studies with well-annotated bibliographical references. There are passages on the

Figure 2.17. A cloth-sizing song with a lead singer and a choir, in which the work at hand sets the beat. (Recording transcription from Mats Eden, *Scottish Tradition 3.*

music of the mountain pasture in various more general national studies, such as H. Tampere, *Estonskaja narodnaja pesna* (Estonian Folk Song) (1983). There is also a wealth of information in Zemtsovsky's different studies of Russian mountain pasture music. (For example, his 1975 study of calendar songs.) J. Vitolin's collections of Latvian folk songs also contain mountain pasture music, which he also discusses in his article "Die lettischen Hirtenlieder,"in *Deutsches Jahrbuch für Volkskunde* 13 (1967): pp. 213–222. Carl-Allan Moberg's study about Swedish herding calls, *Studien zur schwedischen Volksmusik* (Uppsala, 1971), is a classic.

As regards songs of harvesting, in addition to those quoted in the chapter, there is also an interesting paper by Z. W. Ewald, "Die soziale Umdeutung von Ernteliedern im belorussichen Poles," in *Sowjetische Volkslied-und Volksmusikforschung* (Berlin, 1967, pp. 259–291). This paper is a translation of a 1934 article from *Sovjetskaja etnografija.* There are very few musicological studies of work songs and the most detailed one, and still most-often quoted, is Karl Büchers 1896 study.

Three

Melodies Marking the Pendulum of Life and the Changing Seasons

CONCEPTS OF TIME IN THE PAST AND TODAY

Since time immemorial, people's lives have been guided by the changing seasons and the cycle of life. Today new measures of time, such as the end of the school semester and retirement age, have been added to the basic pattern. However, the traditional cyclical sense of time, for both the span of life and the calendar year, has remained and has not been superseded by a linear sense of time. Nature always manages to vanquish technocracy and artificial divisions of time. Such human inventions, whether religious or political, are always forced to adapt to the traditional cycles if they are to survive.

MUSIC THROUGHOUT THE CYCLE OF LIFE

Many things, including new behaviors and fashions, tend to mark the shift from childhood to puberty, from youth to adulthood, from adulthood to old age. Special cultural manifestations in song and instrumental music have also been associated with different ages. Virtually everywhere there are, or have been, lullabies and songs for children's games, for weddings, and for leaving loved ones behind.

Different musical expressions used in particular contexts take on special symbolism that leads to particular associations. Today, for example, the Simon and Garfunkel song "Bridge over Troubled Waters" stands out for many as the musical symbol of a wedding or a funeral, and thus it has moved from being a popular melody to being a "ceremonial" melody. Similarly, music played at a certain time of year serves the contemporary function of the ancient calendar songs. Because it is used towards the conclusion of the New Year's Day concert in Vienna with the Vienna Philharmonic, the *Blue Danube Waltz* has become a New Year's song. These relatively recent, generally recognized songs of seasonal and life cycles, however, are actually only a fragmentary aspect of the rich traditional fabric of psalms and folk songs that make up the musical pattern of our lives.

One might ask whether function and tradition have any bearing on the musical formulation of a rite or ceremony. Let us begin by examining the music of a life cycle, starting with singing by, and songs for, children.

Songs by and for Children

The even rhythm of a lullaby has always had a settling effect on children. It may be that lullabies are reminiscent of the way a fetus experiences its mother's steady heartbeat before the flood of sound and light begin to place demands on the ability of a baby to feel at ease. However, researchers have found that unborn babies are not entirely unprepared for what will meet them after birth, and that even the fetus is affected by sounds, rhythms, and tonal variations from the outside world. Thus it seems probable that every epoch and every milieu provides its newborn citizens with a gift: a unique set of musical patterns.

Theories about the Origins of Children's Song

Some melodic and rhythmic patterns occur all over Europe. One such example is the *sol-la-sol-mi* pattern of the "Ring-a Ring-a Rosy" theme. According to German folk music scholar F. M. Böhme, the only actual melody of all children's rhymes was a constantly repeated, two-beat motif circling round a single tone (Böhme, 1924, pp. iv–vi).

Böhme and other scholars assert that these children's songs and rhymes are remnants of ancient heathen folk songs, and this may be so. But the melody is probably more like an archetype associated with a formalized way of calling that seems to come naturally to humankind. It is then changed and developed, depending on the musical environment of the child. Later it is replaced by other patterns, and as children grow they become increasingly dependent on rote melodies. Moreover, every child has other individual forms of self-expression in melody. These, too, vanish with time and in relation to what music the child is exposed to. The more musical schooling a child has, in the home or elsewhere, the larger the store of familiar melodic and rhythmic motifs the child will be able to access. Children who lack musical schooling tend to present more "fragmented material" (Sundin 1978, Reimers 1983, Bjørkvold 1985).

Norwegian musicologist Jon Roar Bjørkvold (1985) refers to spontaneous singing by children as "our musical mother tongue." He bases this opinion on a study of singing by children over many years. He studied children between the years of four and seven in three different nursery schools. According to Bjørkvold, the sound symbols in the children's singing bear meaning, and the language of the songs is specific to each age group. He also found gender differences, indicative of "musical sociolects." Bjørkvold distinguishes among three main types of spontaneous children's singing: flowing amorphous song, fixed formulaic song, and complete melodies.

The first is a free, non-tonal song, the second has a basic repertoire of some fifteen formulae, and the third displays a wide scope, including a large element of older songs, despite the enormous pressure from the mass media to which children are exposed.

Bjørkvold 's view of children's songs is different from the traditional, historical explanatory model, which may be exemplified by a study carried out (1964) by Austrian musicologist Wolfgang Suppan, examining what he calls "everyday" songs.

In accordance with German scholarly tradition, Suppan sets out to prove how the melodies may have changed over the course of time, from a short, descending call of a third, *re-ti*, which he calls the "ontogenetic" primitive form of melody, and from another falling formula with an additional note, *la-sol-re*, to more "refined" forms (Figure 3.1).

Suppan presumes that these melodies are rooted in pre-Christian times. From the short, descending third call *roptersen* ("the calling third,") he follows a development from the pentatonic to the diatonic scale, claiming that his theory applies to all everyday songs from herding calls to children's rhymes, lullabies, working rhymes, and even songs of mourning (see also the corresponding theories with regard to calendar songs and songs of work, p. 71).

Although evolutionary views are increasingly questioned today, there is hardly any doubt that a falling formula, of a minor third or perfect fourth, for a call is fundamental to songs with texts referring to the life cycle and the calendar (see also p. 72). However, the origin of the variations is another question. There may have been variations from the outset, as ornaments added by an individual singer, or they may have come into being as the impact of other archetypes rooted in narrative song or instrumental music.

Swedish musicologist and music educator Lennar Reimers (1983) describes a falling melody line, sometimes beginning with a small leap and with repetition of relatively short melodic and rhythmic patterns, as unique to the melodies of small children in European environments. Falling little thirds or fourths are also characteristic, with the *sol-la-sol-mi* pattern and broken triads particularly common in German, Scandinavian, and Hungarian children's songs. (Figure 3.2).

Children's own supply of "spontaneous" elements in combination with the archetypes of their musical environment have led to a style for children's music which is then used by adults in composing lullabies and other compositions meant to reflect the musical world of the child. However, children have also listened to large numbers of songs belonging to the folk song repertoire of the adult. Chatarinus Elling (1858–1942), a Norwegian folk song collector, asked his informants about specifically Norwegian lullabies, known as *barnsuller*. He was frequently told that mothers sang whatever songs came into their heads, "so little crying babies probably heard the strangest things!" (*Norsk Folkemusikk* 1922, p. 58).

Figure 3.1. The stages of the development of the shout, according to Suppan's description. (Suppan 1964, pp. 260, 265.)

Figure 3.2. The melodies of nursery rhymes in the everyday life of the child. (a) A melody about debarking the wood for making simple flutes. (Germany: Brockpäler 1970, p. 89). (b) Spanish and Slovakian nursery rhymes. (*Songs from Liptov*, record jacket comments Opus stereo 9117 1211–14.). (c) A singing game based on a nursery rhyme, structured in short shouting phrases (Hungary: *Hungarian Folk music*, record jacket, LPX 18050-53 p. 16 IV A 8 b.)

In an article from 1960, "Bånsuller i Setesdal: Om Bruken av tradisjonelle Melodiformler" (Lullabies from Setesdal: On the Use of Traditional Melodic Formulas) (*Norveg* 7 pp. 13–27), Liv Greni studied one process of melodic composition which appears basic to both children's songs and other kinds of spontaneously improvised songs, such as nursery rhymes. The melodies appear to be variations on selected formulas from traditional melodic material. Greni distinguishes between three different basic formulae for melodies, which usually correspond to a short line of text such as the nonsense words *Bissa, bissa båni*. The melodic formulae are varied and ornamented with different cadential solutions. Many of them then comprise a sort of "core group," to which many different but related forms of variations may be added (Figure 3.3).

Children have their own private world, with traditions of their own to which adults seldom have access. Children teach one another and thus pass down customs from one generation to another without rote learning or written instructions, with some assistance from parents and teachers. Some of the children's games which have been retained appear to be from a time long past, when singing games were used in teaching and for pleasure, for children and adults alike. "London Bridge Is Falling Down" and "Ring-a Ring-a Rosy" are examples of these extremely old children's games. "Bro bro breja" (Figure 3.4) is a typical singing game in which a striking motif is repeated one or more times before it is replaced by a different melodic motif when the game goes into a new phase.

The rhymes are often short and simple, and collectors have only seldom rendered the improvised ornamentation of the motifs that they heard. One exception is Norwegian folk music collector Ludvig Matthias Lindeman.

A very typical wandering melody is "La folia,"

with its unique rhythmic and melodic profile (*New Grove*, vol. 6, p. 691). All kinds of texts have been set to it, from children's and calendar songs to political songs.

Some melodies recur virtually all over Europe. For example, one with a shout of a rising fourth or descending fifth of different variations is known as the "Fiskeskär" ("Fishing Rocks") melody in Sweden (Moberg 1950); not unlike "Row, Row, Row Your Boat." It is probably both a march/wandering melody and one of the "building blocks" that was invented and developed in different places and contexts.

Like the "Fiskeskär" melody, many other children's songs and lullabies use the range of the first five notes of the minor scale. A song from the Isle of Man, (Figure 3.5) is based on a constantly

Figure 3.3. a) Greni's three "basic formulas," and (b) the most common formulas. (c) Examples of Greni's analysis of the melodies of two lullabies. The arrows indicate shifts in pitch in relation to equal temperament. Parentheses indicate individual variations. (Greni [1960], pp. 15,16, and 18.)

repeated phrase similar to the ones we have described above in other kinds of narrative song.

The children's song from Palermo (Figure 3.6) appears to be improvised and "functional." The varied melodic arch shifts into a monotonous parlando with very few notes.

The Portuguese song in (Figure 3.7) uses the upper third of the minor triad as material for the rhyme itself, while the minor third below is a kind of shout that appears to emphasize the rocking motion of the song.

Many melodies using the first five notes of the major scale use *do* only as an introductory note and for occasional support, while the real structure of the melody is based on the second through fifth notes of the scale (as in Karelian laments).

The melodies from Romania and Greece (Figure 3.8a and b) are, in fact, two versions of the same melodic formula. At least as they were conceived by the collectors, the Greek version is much freer in its melismatic ornamentation.

Children's Songs Discovered and Transformed Into Cultural Heritage

Children's songs and culture were "discovered" in the eighteenth century in much the same way as

Figure 3.4. Four variations on the nursery rhyme "Bro bro breja" from Sweden and Norway: (a) Stöylen (1899) p. 31, no. 74. (b) Hellgren (1905) p.83, no. 61. (c) Nilsson (1980), p. 108; (d) Sung by Greta Naterberg in the early nineteenth century. (*Folkmusikboken* 1980, p. 42.)

the music of indigenous peoples, peasants, and shepherds was discovered. Although children's music was not collected as systematically, it was frequently the object of artistic interpretations or used as the source of inspiration for original compositions (see, for example, Schumann's 1838 *Kinderscenen*, op. 15). This, in turn, appears to have influenced the tradition of children's songs, which came to include many reminiscent of the Viennese Classical and early Romantic traditions.

Today there is a new dimension to the musical tradition of children and young people, transcending language barriers and national boundaries, and consisting of African-American music, pop, and rock. At the same time, many of the old singing games are passed down, more or less intact. In recent decades they have been collected and docu-

Figure 3.5. Lullaby from the Isle of Man. (*Folksongs of Europe* [1956] p. 60, no. 125.)

Figure 3.6. Lullaby from Palermo, Italy. (*Folksongs of Europe* [1956] p. 80, no. 125.)

mented in many European countries. They have also been recorded and sold, and these recordings have served to reinforce their survival and dissemination.

In the past, these melodies spread because they were associated with everyday life, related to herding, harvest, love songs, and laments. Today they are passed down through the mass media, which has become the mechanism for passing along knowledge and traditions, even competing with music education, in some respects, for this role.

INSTRUMENTAL MUSIC AND SONGS ABOUT LOVE AND WEDDINGS

Moral Songs

The children of Europe, even when very small, learned about the rules and regulations of matrimony through singing games, such as "London Bridge" (see also p. 47). There were also songs in which young girls learned the hazards associated with tasting the sweet pleasures of love prior to marriage. Such songs were sung by young women at all levels of society. The young women of the salons, for example, could use them to flaunt their own virtue and revel in the misfortune of others. One of the most important duties in the life of a young woman was "saving herself" for her future husband. This also applied to young girls without means, who could not rely on financial or family

Figure 3.7. Lullaby from Cercosa, Portugal. (*Cancionerio* 1981, p. 14, no. 1.)

aid in the marriage market. A "fallen woman" usually had only one way out: prostitution. The troubadours of the market place had plenty of songs about girls who let men trick them. These songs were usually set to popular melodies and written by city dwellers. There were, however, also romantic songs about "free marriage," young couples in the pastures who held their own marriage ceremonies without the involvement of either church or state. What began as melodies and texts used as herding calls were sometimes developed into little sketches which might later provide inspiration for stage plays and operas (Figure 3.9).

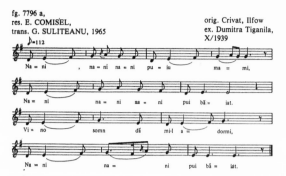

$a\blacktriangleleft$ $b\blacktriangle$

Figure 3.8. Suliteanu has shown how Greek and Romanian lullabies rest on the same structure, within the range of a tetrachord but beginning one note below it. Cf. p. 66. (a) Romanian lullaby. (b) Greek lullaby. (Suliteanu [1985] p. 190f., nos. 4 and 5.)

Dybeck gives one such example in *Vallvisor och hornlåtar* (Herding Songs and Horn Tunes):

A shepherd and shepherdess had a child, and kept it in the forest in a cradle of braided reeds, hanging from a birch. As they also had their master to serve, they took turns looking after the infant, and kept one another apprised of his condition like this: (example of a song). One evening they were in the woods together, and the shepherd gathered green branches for a mat to cover the ground. The couple fell to their knees, said their prayers, and considered themselves wed. At some later date they were discovered and exposed by a gentleman passing through the forest. Eventually all was forgiven, and the couple were married by a priest. (Dybeck 1846/ R 1974, p. 11)

Folk tales of forbidden love and its fruits have thus ignited the imaginations of authors and composers. This particular story exists in many versions, not only in Scandinavia but, for example, in Serbia as well—not always, however, with a happy ending. In a harvest song, a sort of ballad, from the village of Lokva on Mount Golija, the text recalls an event in the past which also took place during a harvest:

Jana's father asked for a *moba*.
He brought Jana down from the sheep
So she would sing for him to the line of
    harvesters.
For a long time they did not hear her voice.
When it was nearly sunset
Rade appeared, leading his sheep.
Jana began to sing loudly in a high voice:
"Did you water the basil, Rade,

"And shade it from the sun?"
Rade replayed through his pipe:
"Yes Jana, I watered the basil
and shaded it from the sun."
Jana has nine dear sisters-in-law.
The youngest one betrayed her.
Jana has a baby in the mountain.
                    (Serbian folk music *RTB* 2510057,
                            text in disk booklet)

Weeping Weddings And Singing Weddings

In Finland there were two widely divergent traditions with regard to wedding music. In eastern Finland (until this century) the wedding tradition was related to that of Estonia and Russia, as reflected in the *Kalevala* epic. The rituals of marriage, known as "the wedding play," included both weeping and singing. Traditional marriage ceremonies could also be found in western Finland until the 1920s, but they were not as old and were mostly imported from Sweden. Their special ceremonial melodies and dances were the march, the minuet and the *polska*. But before going on to discuss this instrumental ceremonial music and dancing, let us examine the eastern wedding-play ceremony, with its elements of weeping and singing.

Wedding plays were found in many countries, and were a series of sketches. Among the social classes that set store by preserving traditions, weddings have always been important. For this reason, weddings have been ensconced in ceremonies, particularly in eastern European peasant society, where pagan ritual and ideas were retained long after marriage became a Christian sacrament—or

Vallvisa

Figure 3.9. A pastoral dialogue from Sweden. (Dybeck 1846/
R 1974, pp. 11ff.)

an affair of state. Wedding ceremonies were associated with songs and with instrumental music as well, beginning in the eighteenth century. A study of wedding songs would probably reveal melodies and singing styles from many ages, with instrumental music a more recent element.

"Wedding plays" are another phenomenon to be found in some countries: They are a sort of tableaux that begin with the appearance of the matchmaker and follows the events until the bride leaves the home of her father. They include a whole repertoire of lyrical songs, including the laments that characterize one half of the play, known as the weeping wedding, and the jesting songs that make up the other half, known as the singing wedding.

Weeping weddings are known mostly from eastern Europe. The laments were usually performed as a dialogue between the bride and her mother or other women. The laments for weddings were longer and more highly ornamented than the laments for funerals. In Russia, just as there were professional mourning weepers, so there were also wedding weepers (Mahler 1960).

In the wedding play, the laments symbolized the emotions of the young woman soon to be torn from the home of her father and transported into a new environment, subject to the rule of her husband and his family, sometimes under conditions more like those for a slave than for a free woman. The tradition of laments may reflect an earlier time when brides were often abducted or purchased, so that a young girl had even less of a say in her future than when her parents and brothers decided to whom she should be betrothed.

Obviously, the weeping wedding play was women's territory. Imaginative poems included images of nature mythology, in which the bride was sometimes depicted as a white swan and the groom an eagle or a falcon, and reflected a boundless range of emotions. Deepest tragedy was occasionally broken by a ray of pure joy. The professional wedding weepers have been referred to as "the sisters and mothers of ecstatic shamans" (Kuusi/Honko 1983). Their laments could be heard for the betrothal, for the marriage ceremony, for the daughter leaving home, for the ceremony of acceptance into the new family. They expressed the grief of being uprooted and moving from one's own family to a new one. These songs also had an important ritual significance: the bride was expected to cry, even if she was looking forward to the upcoming wedding.

In the joyous part of the wedding play, the singing wedding, choral song was central. There were two choirs, one representing the family of the bride, the other that of the groom, and their songs compared the wealth and excellence of the one family with the poverty and misery of the other. These songs of jest toyed with the groom as well, and were sometimes so biting that the groom would have to be reminded that this was a tradition and all in fun. The choirs were like two teams, with the bride's side and the groom's side competing – a remnant of an ancient custom.

The melodies reflect the musical style of the region, with the emphasis on the very oldest songs. A few examples are given below, although it is impossible to do justice to the scope and diversity of wedding music, which would merit a book of its own.

The four Latvian wedding songs presented in Figure 3.10 illustrate different types of melodies: (a) formulaic melodies, in groups of related text phrases and repeated in varied forms from the first to the second lines in the text, (b) recitative-like melodies, sometimes tonally reinforced by a second part a fifth or a third below, (c) calling melodies in minor mode descending a fifth; (d) a number of what appear to be more modern melodies where one can imagine an accompaniment played on an accordion shifting between the tonic and the dominant.

Slovakian and Hungarian wedding melodies are often performed with free rhythm, with an ancient structure of tonalities, here ascending over the first five notes of the Lydian mode (Figure 3.11a), and featuring melodies with a more highly structured form (here A-B-A) (b). (Bartók classifies such melodies as reflecting the "old" and "new" styles.)

Although very similar wedding plays and music are to be found all over eastern Europe, there are interesting differences in detail, not least with regard to the melodies and their performance. Russian folk music scholar T. V. Popova claims that in northern Russia, the weeping wedding was more important, while the singing wedding was held in higher regard by the south (Popova 1955).

According to Popova, there were different songs for the different functions in the Russian wedding; for example, the "proposal of marriage" section was always concluded by a unison choir performing a wedding dinner celebration song (Figure 3.12).

Popova considers the seven syllables of each line of the verse, which consist of two groups, one of three syllables and one of four, as decisive to the structure of the melody's regular shifts between sections of four beats and sections of five. (See also the Latvian melody in Figure 3.10a, and the calendar songs.) In addition to laments, the weeping wedding had its lyrical melodies as well, sentimental and sorrowful. Some of these praised the beauty of the bride in poetic terms, others glorified her life under her father's roof that was now coming to an end. This lyrical folk melody, like so many other older Russian melodies, consists of two very different motifs. The first one, in this case, ranges over the first five notes of the minor scale, like the Swedish "Fiskeskär" melody described earlier. The second has a motif in thirds, replaced in the cadence by a motif with descending fourths. These weepers' melodies have similarities with many lyrical melodies.

Probably some songs have been retained more fully intact precisely because they were part of a closely guarded ritual, such as the time on the morning of the wedding when the women gathered to dress and adorn the bride, to braid her hair and place on her head the bridal crown or wreath.

Russian wedding songs have inspired composers, including Glinka, Dargomyzhsky, Tchaikovsky, Balakirev and Stravinsky, all of whom have interpreted the Russian wedding (see also p. 208).

Bulgarian wedding songs bridge the gap between Russian and, for example, Macedonian or Greek wedding songs. They may be built around fifths or fourths, but some are built on thirds, divided into minor and augmented seconds.

Greek wedding songs are richly ornamented and embellished in addition to their extremely interesting use of chromatics.

Earlier, wedding plays were common in large parts of western Europe as well. Tiersot (1889/ 1979, pp. 203–209) provides many examples from nineteenth-century France. For example, wedding songs from Gascony, known as the singing nation. There, singers accompany the betrothed couple

Figure 3.10. Latvian wedding songs with texts pertaining to various symbols associated with weddings and brides. (*Latviesu laulas musica* 1968, nos. 14, 25, 118, and 490.)

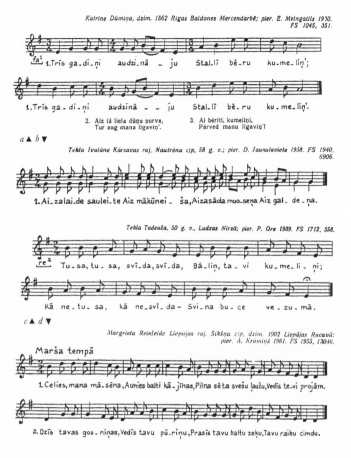

to the notary, back and forth to the church, at meals, for dancing, in the bridal chamber, etc. In Brittany, song was regarded as "the natural and necessary language of nature," and a singer was the proxy for the groom. Tiersot also indicates that the weeping wedding song had its equivalent

"On the wedding day the young girls sang local variants of songs of farewell to the bride, sometimes satirical, sometimes melancholy" (Tiersot 1889/1978, p. 203). Tiersot claims that French wedding-play songs, with the exception of the profane songs referring to meals and to the eve of the wedding day, were solemn and almost religious in nature, and were performed as if they had been psalms. Thus, with regard to the melodies of the wedding play, the church appears to have been more influential in France than in eastern Europe.

Today, wedding songs tend neither to be part of an overall wedding ritual nor very different from the more recent popular religious song repertoire. Examples of this include the polyphonic Italian

wedding song in Figure 3.13 and the wedding song from the Swedish-speaking part of Finland (Figure 3.14.) The latter is taken from a Swedish royal anthem, and carries associations with pomp and glory. Thus it also marks a transition to wedding marches and dances, which served to give weddings more modern flavor.

Instrumental Wedding Celebrations

Two other important distinctions, beyond that between traditional songs from wedding plays and newer ceremonial music, must be made between special ceremonial music only performed at weddings to symbolize aspects of the ritual, and dances and songs performed at weddings for entertainment.

Weddings for people of lesser means were naturally on a more humble scale. This accounts for the fact that wedding music described in the source literature (and cited here) reflects the strictly formalized wedding ceremony for the wealthy.

Figure 3.12. Song in praise of aquavit, sung at the home of the groom when he proposes. (Popova 1955, no. 59, p. 207.)

Figure 3.11. (a) This song, sung on the way to the wedding ceremony, is about birds losing their feathers, which are picked up by girls. Slovakian songs collected and systematized by Bela Bartók. (*Slovenské l'udove piesne* et al. 1959 vol. I no. 13 b, p. 144.); (b) the song of the bride to her girlfriends is about having a lovely wreath of wax and green myrtle around one's head. (*Slovenské l'udove piesne* et. al. 1982 no. 73, p. 130.)

The union of two families was considered an important event, and probably afforded an opportunity to perform the finest and very latest in wedding music. Therefore, many wedding marches were very modern in style, and were often written for elegent woodwind instruments. However, fiddlers also filled an important function at weddings and had a high status of their own. Although it was considered meritorious to employ a member of a regimental band, with bright brass buttons on his uniform to make the wedding procession posh. The fiddlers not only provided the wedding party with accompaniment as they paraded to and from the church, they also provided entertainment at the festive repast, and played for dancing in the evenings.

Music was performed on all the most popular, newest instruments. Traditional instruments such as the bagpipes, the dulcimer, the lyre, or the *nyckelharpa* (keyed fiddle) were gradually adapted to the needs of the new styles (see also Chapter 6).

In her novel *La Mare au Diable*, George Sand gives a detailed description of a wedding in the countryside: "The day before the wedding, around two o'clock in the afternoon the music arrives, that is the bagpipe-player (*cornemuseux*) and the hurdy

gurdy-player (*le vielleux*) with their instruments decorated by long waving ribbons, playing a ceremonious march." The fact that music was an important part of the wedding soundscape is clear from both artistic and literary descriptions. Figure 3.15 depicts a wedding in the town of Värend in the province of Småland, about which Johan August Berg, (1818–1902) a minister from Göteborg, rendered the following description:

When the procession left the home of the bride to make its way to the church, the minister, the bridegroom and the bridesmaids rode three times around the maypole that had been raised in the middle of the yard, and richly decorated with painted eggs and all kinds of ornaments. During this performance, according to the ritual, the bride was to weep and to look at her groom through her engagement ring at a moment when he could not see her.

(After the wedding)
When the minister and the groom had arrived at the farm, and as soon as they dismounted from their horses, the minister was to raise up the song: "Holy Trinity Stand by Us." The congregation was to join in loudly, accompanied by fiddlers, as they entered the home. A speech of welcome was held inside. It ended with "Come Holy Spirit, the Lord our God!" The procession to the church was led by the honoured elders, followed by the fiddlers, bagpipers, and oboe players. Then came the bride accompanied by the wife of the minister, and a select group of Amazons. The procession was forced to proceed rather slowly so that the heavy bridal crown, weighing one full pound, did not fall. Yet the music was to resound unceasingly! (*Helg och söcken* (Ceremony and Parish) 1973, p. 67)

Figure 3.13. Italian wedding song: dialogue between the bride and groom, and the guests. (Leydi 1973, p. 119.)

Figure 3.14. Finnish wedding song. (FSF VI 1964, p. 57 no. 9.)

On the Style of Wedding Songs

Instrumental ceremonial music covers a wide spectrum, with the common elements being loud, rhythmic music, and the variations characterized by the stylistic ideals of different epochs and countries. It is also always difficult to be sure of what causes these various traditions to be consistent or flexible. Let us investigate, for example, wedding melodies from islands close to one another off the coast of the Baltic states.

During two brief visits to Swedish-speaking inhabitants of the islands off the coast of Estonia, Otto Andersson (1879–1969) and Carl-Allan Moberg (1896–1978) independently collected wedding music. Andersson visited these islands on his way home from having studied folk music on the islands of Ormsö and Nuckö in January 1904. He noted down a number of wedding melodies, all of which were performed by a single bagpiper, Adam Söderström. Moberg journeyed to Runö in 1938 as part of a commission for Swedish Broadcasting, and collected a unique set of materials including choir songs and wedding music. Moberg transcribed his collection of wedding songs from Elias Schönberg (b. 1861), a shoemaker, fiddler, and mechanic.

The ceremony had been retained relatively intact during the decades that passed between the two collections, but musically great changes had occurred. The wedding melodies for the bagpipe transcribed by Andersson (Figure 3.16a) were characterized by a small range and a formulaic structure. The songs recorded by Moberg (Figure 3.16b) were considerably newer, and stylistically they fall into the category of marches, very common in sources from the late-eighteenth through the nineteenth centuries. It would be possible to conclude from this that the arrival of a new instrument not

Instruments such as trumpets, clarinets, oboes, and shawms were highly esteemed, and were clearly necessary for the music to be heard above all the other racket. The instrumental combinations were nothing but a hotch-potch of whatever was available.

In southeastern Europe the gypsies provided the music, and favored maximum festivity. Composer Franz Liszt and a gentleman by the name of Brassai discussed gypsy music (see Sárosi 1967, p. 116), saying:

> all the instrumental music of the gypsies runs parallel with the excessive ornamentation which permeates virtuoso European vocal and instrumental music . . . and all these fiorituras are actually nothing but rote fragments of European virtuosity. The highly praised irregularities of their music is not attributable to any form of idealized, isolated gypsy nature, but to the maimed and incomplete ways they were learned. (Quotes from Sárosi 1977, pp. 156f.)

In many of the Balkan states different types of instrumental wedding music of this kind have been developed since the eighteenth century. In Hungary, Romania, and the former Yugoslavia, a fusion occurred between the older gypsy traditions and the art music of the classical era, which could hardly be regarded as "maimed" today.

Connections with Arab culture as well may be seen not only in the *zurna* and large drum but also in the manner of playing and in the structure of the melodies.

Figure 3.15. Swedish wedding procession from Värend. The oboe and drum, the clothing and jewelery, the rifle shots and canon firing give a sense of peasant luxury. Watercolor by Bengt Nordenberg, Göteborg Art Museum. Photograph: Ebbe Carlsson.

only meant the rejection of an older one, but also the vanishing of older repertoire. However, in a study of wedding melodies from Rågöarna, Bo Nyberg shows that this is not a rule, and he questions the idea that the advent of the accordion meant the disappearance of the old traditions associated with bagpipes. He found, instead, that there was widespread conservatism with regard to wedding melodies, despite the establishment on the island of a new kind of popular music in the early twentieth century. He found, rather, that the accordion was influenced by the bagpipe, particularly with regard to accompaniment "where the drone of the bagpipe is often imitated" (Nyberg 1986, p. 137). Nyberg goes on to show that performances were, in fact "modernized," and that there was a transition from unaccompanied melody lines to more harmonized playing "in accordance with general practice in Swedish popular accordion music." For example, the phrases were shaped into recurring motifs and periods.

Wedding marches often reflect the entire spectrum of novelty, from tradition to innovation. In France, for instance, there are examples of marches with both vocal and instrumental performance, which appear to be extremely old (Figure 3.17). Sometimes nineteenth-century wedding marches can be found to have similarities to military marches, and are played on the same kinds of instruments as those used in wartime (Figure 3.18).

Many creators of wedding marches tried to be modern, thus taking up the stylistic traits of eighteenth- and nineteenth-century popular music. The peasant fiddler was often aware of the new developments in art music, and assimilated and adapted them to his own musical environment.

There were strict regulations in Sweden stipulating that the fiddlers were required to stop playing when they reached the portal of the church, where the music of the organist was to take over. This was a bone of contention throughout the eighteenth century, when the common people applied for permission for the fiddlers to play for the procession until the bride and groom reached the altar. It is possible that this was allowed by tradition even farther in the past, and that the peasants were skeptical of the new-fangled organ music. In fact, in some places in Sweden fiddlers have always been permitted to play in church, although only from the balcony.

Ceremonial Wedding Dances

Weddings had their ritual dances, for example, an abduction of the bride and groom from the unmarried to a dance for "old men and women." The melodies were often traditional, bearing as they did a relationship to the ancient ceremonies. Another example is the group of melodies for "lifting the crown," when the dancers removed the wedding crown from the head of the bride. (Figure 3.19).

The following is a description from the eastern part of the Swedish province of Småland in the 1770s:

The tables were then cleared and carried away while the guests were taken to another room until, after some time, the fiddlers took their places and began to invite the guests to dance to their songs. The minister would then take the bride by the hand and, after dancing a *polska* with her, turn to the groom and say: 'I dance for you.' After this the minister would take one more turn with the bride, and when

MARCHE NUPTIALE

Notée par J. CANTELOUBE en
1912 à Vic-sur-Cère (Cantal) ; jouée
par M. Lascroux, cabrettaire.

Animé

Lo deme-non Lo nostro nobio, Lo deme-non Coumo l'o-

-bon! Lo deme-non _ Lo nostro nobio, Lo deme-non _ Coumo pou

-don! Lo meno-ren piucè-lo, be-leu! Lo meno-ren piucè-

-lo! Lo meno-ren coumo pou-ren_, lo meno-ren coumo l'au-

FIN Ritoarnelle Violon, Vielle ou Cabrette

-ren! _

D.C

Figure 3.16. (a) Wedding melodies on bagpipes played by Adam Söderström, noted down by Otto Andersson on the Rågö Islands in 1904. (Andersson 1961 p. 22 no. 1.); (b) Wedding melody on violin played by Elias Schönberg on Runö island in 1938 for Carl-Allan Moberg. (Moberg 1960 p. 104 no. 1a "Vegaleikin".)

Figure 3.17. French wedding march for voice and, alternatively, for bagpipe, hurdy-gurdy or violin. (*Recueil de chants et de danses populaire*, p. 15, 1912.)

he was finished he would turn her over to the groom who, like the minister, would have two dances with her. After the first, the groom would turn to the most prominent man present, the father of the bride or his own father, saying: 'I dance for you.' In this way all the menfolk would dance with the bride, one after another and, if there was room, the bridegroom would first dance two dances with the bridesmaid and then with one woman after another, until he had danced with all the womenfolk.

Once the bride and groom had danced their obligatory dances, the guests danced however they pleased, and sometimes there were so many couples on the floor at once that they were like herring in a barrel, and always had to watch out for the couples around them.

After midnight when the last meal was served, all the young men gathered around the groom on the dance floor and began to dance a circle dance, with one man after another dancing in the middle of the ring with the groom. When every one of them had danced this way, they raised the groom on their shoulders and gave him drink. He thanked them for having been of his party, and by toasting with them he took leave of his life as an unmarried man. . . . This is called 'dancing out the bridegroom.' Then just as the young men and married men danced out the groom, the girls and married women danced out the bride, after which the bride was taken away and dressed in the garb of a married woman,

returning with her wreath in her hand. Then all the young women formed a ring around her, while her bridesmaid or one of the married women blindfolded her. Unable to see who she was approaching, she placed her wreath on the head of one of the maidens dancing around her. The belief is that the one who receives it will shortly be a bride herself. This is referred to as 'dancing out the wreath.' (Norlind 1919, p. 113f.)

Thus European wedding songs and music are intimately intertwined with the wedding ceremonies of each country. Some songs and melodies are undoubtedly of ancient origin, while many others were gradually incorporated from what was newest and best in each era. Wedding music is clearly an outstanding example of the wealth of rural European music.

Keening, Crying, Laments, and Funerals

Songs of weeping and laments have been heard in times of mourning and at funerals for thousands of years. Often the relatives of the person being mourned did the singing, but there are also traditions of professional weepers from almost all over

Per Nilsson Dahlberg

187. BRÖLLOPSMARSCH

Dahlberg hade ofta blåst denna marsch på klarinett under bröllopsfär-
derna till kyrkan.

Figure 3.18. Wedding march after Per Nilsson Dahlberg (1838–1920) in the form of a "mini sonata with coda" played on the clarinet (*Svenska låtar.* Skåne I 1937/R1978, p. 114 no. 187.)

a. MARSCH

Tredje reprisen har nio takter.

b. VALS

c. POLSKA

Figure 3.19. This dance is described as follows in *SvL Dalarna* IV p. 4 no. 10085 after Höök Olof Andersson, a fiddler from Rättvik, Sweden (1860–1936): This wedding song was performed to "'dance the bride and groom to the ceiling.' First the march was played (a) as the couple took the dance floor. Then a chair was placed in the middle of the floor, and the bride sat on it. One man lifted the groom to his shoulders, while the women, who were the only ones allowed to touch the bride, raised her chair up to the ceiling and lowered it again. During this ceremony a waltz was played (b), followed by a *polska* (c) with dancing round in a circle. Finally, the waltz was played again."

Europe. Some families even specialized in songs of mourning and developed them into an artistic form passed down from one generation to the next, setting the style for funerals over a large geographical area.

Even farewells other than that at death have been accompanied by singing, and thus, as we have seen, there were songs of weeping at weddings as well as when a young conscript went off to war.

In an 1802 article containing an overview of music in Russia, particularly in Moscow, there is a section covering songs of weeping when conscripts were taken away:

> At the [Moscow] town gate, there stood a crowd and from the centre of it I heard songs of sorrow. I walked over to the crowd, and found a lovely young peasant lass, whose bridegroom had been torn away from her to do his military service. She declaimed her misfortune with floods of tears, and also by recurrently banging her head against the wall. . . . She looked at him and fainted. (*Allgemeine musikalische Zeitung* 374 (23 March 1802).)

The songs of weeping women have always shattered the silence like a sword when young men were to leave them for the meaningless slaughter of war. Even today, there are television programs displaying women in the war-torn parts of the Middle East or the former Yugoslavia whose heartrending songs of weeping are the same cries of desperation that have echoed throughout the centuries.

Departures of close friends were also underlined by pitiful cries and laments. Such more or less ceremonial farewells were also common among the eighteenth- and nineteenth-century bourgeoisie.

Types of Lament

There is no question that the lament is one of the fundamental forms of musical expression. It releases emotions and ritualizes grief, making it easier to work through. There were songs of weeping, monotonous repetitions of formulae interrupted by cries and moans that triggered emotional reactions, and also more lyrical, melodic laments associated with the epic tradition. These were more distanced from grief. While spontaneous songs of weeping were generally at the very center of events—for instance, at wakes and in funeral processions to the graveyard—the epic lament was more retrospective and contemplative. However, there was no fine line of demarcation between the two, and the phrase *songs of weeping* will be used below as a general term, described as either spontaneous or contemplative.

Every area of the world has its songs of weeping, a state of being common to all humanity. At one time they were widespread in Europe. Their ancient heathen origins were, however, a burden to the churches of the Reformation, orientated as they were toward reason. However, the Greek Orthodox church, its Russian couterpart, and the Catholic church in Southern Europe were less hostile to popular mysticism, and songs of weeping lived on in eastern Finland, Russia, the Ukraine, Bulgaria, Hungary, the Balkans (including Greece), parts of Italy, Spain, Portugal, and Ireland. Songs of grief vanished faster from central Europe, especially from Calvinist and Lutheran areas (see Suppan, 1963, pp. 18–24). Songs of weeping are a fascinating form of art. They touch the deepest wellsprings of our emotions, even when we listen to them simply as outsiders. In our industrialized western society, fundamental human feelings associated with the cycle of life and death are often repressed. Our lifestyle tends to discourage discussions of old age and death. In more traditional communities it was normal to use singing as a means of preparing for dealing with the pain of final separation.

Below follows a presentation of the songs of grief of various nations and a discussion of regional similarities and differences.

Karelian Laments

In 1835 the Swedish collector Elias Lönnrot was travelling in Rukajärvi in Finland. While noting down a song, he suddenly found that he could not go on because for some reason one of the younger women was seized with an impulse to begin wailing at the top of her lungs, which was just terrible to hear. Everyone began to tell her:

'Cut it out, cut it out, Stop it now, already,' but once she got going she could not be stopped. So I finally got what I had been hoping for, the experience of hearing a real weeper in the spirit and the flesh, but I would gladly have paid her twice as much if she had been willing to listen to the others and cut it out sooner. She plagued my ears with her terrible wailing for a full half an hour, throwing herself into the arms of one person after another, as no one sings like that by herself, without her arms around someone else's neck. (Kuusi/Honko 1983, p. 80.)

To an outsider, the first encounter with the total release of emotions in was often a shock. There are many descriptions of the terror this heartrending screaming struck in the heart of a traveler or collector, many of whom felt unable to pass on the message of these songs to others.

Songs of mourning still exist in spontaneous forms in Karelia, alongside songs of a more narrative nature closely related to the runic song.

A. S. Stepanova and T. A. Kockim, scholars from Petrosavodsk, have described a treasure trove of ritual songs associated with ancient beliefs (1976). Today, this may be regarded as a national culture. Material which took decades to collect serves today as momentary impressions of the history of songs of mourning, stretching back over the centuries, like a "photograph" of something undergoing constant change. Some stylistic elements are so ritualized and canonized that they have been retained intact over time, while others vary. One group of melodies has become "synthesized with the poetic text" with regard to form, rhythm, metric accent, phrasing, etc., while another group is relatively independent of the text. The melodies have some internal regularities of organization with regard to what the scholars refer to as "intonations," basic pregnant melodic, rhythmic, or harmonic expressions that may be distinguished as musical units (see also p. 71 on intonation).

In Figure 3.20a, each melodic motif concludes on either A or G, and these notes serve as half and whole cadences, respectively. The text is not periodic, nor does it follow a given meter of verse, but is arbitrarily divided up by formula. The irregular beat can be explained by the necessity to accent the words correctly as they are pronounced.

Karelian local dialects are stylistically reflected in the melodies, there being three dialect areas from north to south, with the larger ones to the south.

There are, however, also small stylistic islands within each area.

One group of melodies has the range of a fourth with a predominantly major feeling, while another has the range of a fifth but predominantly minor. The singers can achieve great aesthetic variation even within the range of a fourth by limiting the individual notes of the scale to small independent units, varying their timbers, and using them in different rhythmic and melodic combinations. Songs of weeping from central Karelia display some of the elements of the songs from further north, but it appears that they have a larger range owing to the occurrence of more traditional melodic patterns (with influences from runic songs). There is also a stronger modality or tonality since the final note receives a prominent role in the actual melody as a recurring "tonic."

The five-note minor scale can be divided into two units, a second apart from one another, each having a range of a fourth: the fifth and the second steps comprise the limits of the upper unit, the fourth and the first steps for the lower (Figure 3.20b).

There is a resulting harmonic relationship between these two groups of fourths, with most of the tension at the shifts between the first and second steps of the scale, both striving to dominate within the melody and at cadences. This shifting is clearly noticeable in A. I. Vasilevaja's song, (Figure 3.20c.). Hoikka's song of grief (Figure 3.20d), however, is an example of how the combination of intervals has stiffened into the melodic formula of the "runic melody" (see p. 79) in which the first step fills its function in the final cadence as a tonic and the second as a dominant.

Estonian Laments

The small Vepsian minority in southeastern Estonia provides us with an interesting and unique type of mourning song, which has been analyzed by Estonian musicologists Ingrid Rütel and M. Remmel using a relatively simple melody-writing device that uses the melodies to produce a curve of frequency modulations. Rütel and Remmel conceive the melody of the lament as an alternation between glissandos and tonal plateaus, with the former being more prominent in traditional laments than in ones commissioned for a given occasion. They describe each individual phrase in a

lament as a kind of three-step model in which the first step is a descending melody line from the highest point, the third or fourth step of the tonality, to a kind of tonal center that is sustained, and thus emphasized. The melody then descends further, becoming a recitative with no fixed pitch within a relatively narrow range, followed by crying or sobbing, which has a rising curve. Each time a new syllable occurs the pitches are noted on a graph. This can now be transcribed as a simplified kind of music (Figure 3.21).

There are also laments of greater structural complexity that follow the same basic principle but that are linked together in sequences of several periods. In addition to this typical Vepsian type of melody, there is another, which appears to have been borrowed from Russian laments but whose melodic contour is entirely different. The highest and lowest notes are pitched elsewhere, the vocal ambitus is much higher, the strophic meter is fixed, and the intervals are more stable.

Russian and Ukrainian Laments

Lönnrot was not the only traveller to be terrified by women's songs of mourning. A similar description from nineteenth-century northern Russia may be found in F. Gladov's autobiography, *Tales from the Country*:

> They loved to scream in the village, for any reason or none at all, whatever their mood. The peasant women certainly had enough to weep and moan sorrowfully about, they screamed when someone had died, when a soldier was called to war, when a young woman married, when they met a traveller from another people who lived nearby, when they thought of the past. Earlier, not only the peasants but the Boyars, too, did this. And men performed the laments as well then. (Popova 1955, p. 93.)

Life in the village almost seems to have been governed by the women's songs of grief: their heartrending cries must have been an effective system of signals, with a great deal of emotional meaning and power. The primitiveness of the performance was a source of both fright and fascination.

> The two of them sat with their knees to their chests rocking to their songs of grief. . . . Their singing was slow and their songs were pleasing and captivating. I could distinguish none of the words as they were

Figure 3.20. (a) Karelian song of grief (Stepanova/Koski 1976, p. 444). (b) The two fourths contained within the first and fifth notes of the monir scale and their structural association (after Stepanova/Koski 1976, p. 447). (c) Song of grief by A.I. Vasilevaya (Stepanova/Koski 1976, no. 7 p. 461 f.). (d) Song of grief by U.P. Hoikka (Stepanova/Koski 1976, ex. 449.).

both singing different texts. They improvised their lament and very little of it was repeated. The mother sang her words, the grandmother her own. Alternately, they would start a new song. Their words did not come at the same time. Although one was

the leader and the other followed her melody, they were singing as if they were each alone and not listening to one another. Much of what they sang about was taken from everyday events of the world of Russian peasants. (Popova 1955, p. 94f.)

Many of the laments from northern Russia had the same melodic structure as *bilinïs*. This gave them more epic breadth and made them longer than the songs from central Russia and Belarus, which tended to be more lyrical.

Hungarian Laments

Siratók is the Hungarian word for lament, from *sirat*, meaning to grieve or mourn. It is possible to trace Hungarian laments from the eleventh through the mid-eighteenth centuries, when they began to vanish, not least owing to opposition by the Protestants. As early as the seventeenth century the church prohibited this type of mourning, stating that more restrained exhibitions of grief were preferable to emotional scenes: "No reasonable woman should display her narrow-mindedness by shouting like a madwoman, tearing her hair, and belting out inarticulate songs" (Corpus V, *Siratok*, 1966, p. 81). Changes in society resulting in traditions being abandoned in favor of new ways of thinking were just as fateful for the laments as were the admonitions of the church. As the bourgeoisie flourished in the nineteenth century, the intellectuals loved to ridicule the laments of the peasants:

> No matter whether the deceased was dearly loved or deeply hated in this life, he was cried over, particularly by the women. They would throw themselves at the coffin, airing their grief, expressing emotional words. Some people would follow grieving relatives showing the keenest interest in hearing the words, just to be able to recall them and make them the butt of their humor in company. One would have to admit that these grieving women ornament their lamentations with truly ridiculous statements. (Corpus V, *Siratók*, 1966, p. 91.)

In Hungary, since time immemorial, even the greatest villain had to be mourned with laments if he was to find peace in the kingdom of death. Otherwise there was a risk that he would not leave the living alone. At the same time, many people ridiculed this hypocritical display of morning from hired, professional weepers for the deceased.

Пример 1

Figure 3.21. Example of music for the same type of song of grief. (Rütel/Remmel 1980, music example 1, p. 187.)

If there is a rumour that someone has died in a village, his female relations rush to see the body of the dead man, and the mourners grieve with all their might. Every virtue the deceased had or might have had is declaimed loud and long with mighty shouts. And the funeral itself is even worse. The women outdo one another with their symphonic wails and their tales of the qualities of the deceased, even if death has come to a child of merely two years of age. If they finally run out of things to praise, they simply begin over at the beginning, calling even the most insignificant details to mind. (Corpus V, Siratók, 1966, p. 91.)

The lyrics sung by the weeping women were filled with clichés and empty phrases that sounded more like sentimentality than deep compassion. For example: "Oh dearest love of my heart, my dove, my faithful husband! Oh, if only you would speak briefly with me once again! If only you would give me a smile! Oh, oh, how could I ever forget you?" (Corpus V, Siratók 1966, p. 92). When Hungarian singers of laments were interviewed, one of them said that she prepared carefully while others claimed to sing completely spontaneously. Some of the older women said that the verses of the songs just came to them as if they were reading a book as they sat beside the deceased. The accumulated grief of many years of mourning for relatives and close friends helped them to sing even for the dead whom they hardly knew.

The laments of professional weepers were regarded as different from songs sung by mourning relatives. The former were more epic and narrative, with qualities characteristic of laments, while the latter appeared to be more spontaneous and emotional, like laments.

On the Style and Performance of Hungarian Laments

Corpus V, Siratók (1966), contains a detailed description of Hungarian songs of grief, raising many general issues. There were many regional differences in Hungarian songs of grief, with regard to both function and style. Some of the songs were influenced by Christianity, while others were older and heathen. The material in Corpus V was collected after the ceremonies rather than during them. This means that the songs (as annotated) were sung out of context and, not real expressions of mourning. This means of collection is, of course, more ethical than disturbing people in grief. It also made it easier for the singers to concentrate on their performance, thus presenting a picture that, although more holistic, was also more fragmentary and imprecise.

According to the description, an identical set of basic material was varied over a period of roughly half an hour. Sometimes it was possible to listen to more than one singer perform the same material, providing the opportunity to study individual stylistic traits. According to Kodály (1937), laments are the only kind of prose recitative in Hungary, and nearly the only kind of improvised song. Kodály also noted its variability. There was no indication of a time signature, and the melodic phrases were irregular in length and could be expanded and contracted according to the needs of the singer. Recitative songs of mourning are defined in the Corpus as a kind of speech-singing, performed according to the Hungarian rules of poetic diction, in which language elements are represented, first, in the meter of the text and, second, in divisions into irregular periods, arranged and determined by the content. Sometimes the recitative turns into a melody, and the free-verse structure into measured verse, and vice versa. Thus there is a sliding scale for laments, ranging from a fixed melody to a more or less spoken recitative.

Scholars have been unable to reveal any general regularities. Instead, it seems that a number of elements of style are subjected to continuous variation and that similarities in melodies that do occur cannot be explained by finding a traditional or cultural context. According to Kodály, the two main characteristic forms of songs of grief that cover the entire geographical area of the Hungarian language are the "wide" form (Figure 3.22a), in which the range may be a seventh, an eleventh, or a twelfth, and the "narrow" form (Figure 3.22b), with only half as large a range, referred to as "the equivalent" half of the wider form. The latter type dominates the northern part of the area. It usually has two motifs, ending on either the first or second steps of the scale.

These melodies have a descending melodic line, often divided into different bow-like phrases with interjected elements of recitative. There is no clear symmetry in the general formulaic structure, but the various parts do balance one another: a descending motif is followed by short bow-like motifs. The authors distinguished among five main groups of laments, including one recitative using the first three notes of the major scale with a specific Moldavian structure, with a limited range and different phrase endings depending on the length of the melodic formula (Figure 3.22b).

The note which is used for the recitation, in combination with the cadence, highlights a certain modality, of which there is a great variety: pentatonic, diatonic with groups of three to seven notes, major or minor, and those reminiscent of the church modes.

When laments were performed, there were gradual variations of pitch, great variations in the dynamics, and a great deal of shouting, moaning, and sighing. Traditions were mostly local, and, although they were heard and remembered, it was uncommon to adopt laments from elsewhere unless someone from a distant place married into the village. In such cases, the person brought his or her laments into the new cultural community. The Hungarian women also performed their songs of grief to a rocking motion, like lullabies. The comforting function is equally important at the end of life as at the beginning.

Mediterranean Laments: Sardinia and Corsica

In Sardinia the word for singing a lament, *attituidi*, derives from the word to nurse a baby, *attittai*. In Corsica, too, the melodies of laments are often the same as the melodies of lullabies, and both are sung to a rocking motion.

The lamenting tradition is still alive in Corsica and Sardinia (see and listen to *Musique Corse de tradition Orale* APN 82-1/3, *Archives sonores de la Phonotheque Nationale*, with excellent textual comments). Songs of weeping are an inherent part of the funeral ritual, with a very detailed ceremonial pattern. The songs may be sung by female relations or professional weepers. There are also two kinds of laments: the narrative *lamentu* composed for the funeral rite, and the more spontaneous *voceru* or *baddata*.

Wolfgang Laade has studied the structure of Corsican laments (1962), which he sees as fundamental to all traditional Corsican folk songs. He characterizes the melodic style as "female," because they are predominantly performed by women. The same melodic style occurs in lullabies and in men's attempts to imitate women with parodies on laments for dead animals. These melodies also spread to love songs and songs of political propaganda. There are a relatively small number of melodies–Laade designates twenty-two types–with a large number of variations. New texts are, however, constantly being written. The texts and melodies are independent of one another, so the same melody may be sung to various texts, and vice versa. They are performed in the same way as described above for the Karelian and Hungarian songs of weeping, in a recitative-type mode with flourishes and cadenzas on elongated notes. The final tone is held until the singer is out of breath. There are various structures, but the most common is, as in the Hungarian songs, a two-phrase structure. The tempo is between 40 and 152 MM. Although about 70 percent of the performances are in free rhythm, there are both three and two-beat bars. Here, too, the performance and structure of the text are interrelated, in this case as a regular meter. More of the melodies are in minor than in major keys, and a few are modal. Like the Karelian and Hungarian songs, the range of five notes is a common one. The final notes in the melodic phrases vary among the different parts of the song of grief far more than seems to be the case in the Hungarian equivalents. There is a sort of concluding formula that may be bow-shaped, like a descending curve, similar to what we have seen elsewhere. A syllabic style dominates.

The Sardinian and Corsican laments are not only for people (they may be for trees, for example), and there is a 1928 *lamentu* from Corsica mourning a hunting dog which is still performed today.

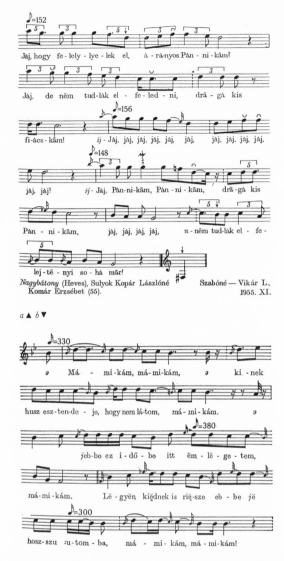

Figure 3.22. Hungarian songs of grief. (a) Song of grief by Sulyok Kopár Lászloné Komár Erzsébet, age 55. Recorded in 1955. (A magyar V, *Siratók*, no.45 p. 274.); (b) Song of grief by Szabó Ferencné Páncér Róza, age 45. Recorded in 1938. (A magyar V, *Siratók*, no.189 p. 697.)

Laade says that these are sometimes parodies. A lament may sometimes turn into a challenge for blood vengeance if the deceased was killed in one of the many family feuds that once caused so much bloodshed in that part of the world (Figure 3.35).

Contemporary Laments in Greece and Romania

Songs of grief have been heard on the Greek islands since antiquity. In her book *The Ritual Lament in Greek Tradition*, Margaret Alexiou describes

Sophia Lala, a woman she met who was then sixty-six years old and had done nothing but sing laments since the death of her husband and son. She never said no to a request to sing at a funeral, so that she could go on mourning her own deceased relations: "I only sing for mine, not for theirs," she said. Margaret Alexiou describes the route from a home to the cemetery as a soundscape of grief:

On the morning of the second day the slow tolling of the church bell summons the priest and the whole village to the house of the dead to accompany him on his last journey to the tomb. As soon as the bell is sounded, all over the village any water that has been standing in vessels is thrown away, and fresh water is fetched. Sometimes, the vessel too is broken. This is apparently an extension of ancient custom, from the immediate family to the whole village.

The body is taken up by four men, who in Thrace must be neither close kin nor newly married, and laid in the coffin. Mourning women throw on offerings of fruit and nuts—apples, quinces, walnuts and almonds—as a greeting to their own dead below. This ritual detail throws light on the opening phrase of so many dirges, giving it a meaning beyond its mere lyricism:

What shall I send you, my dear one, there in the Underworld?
If I send an apple, it will rot, if a quince it will shrivel:
if I send grapes, they will fall away, if a rose, it will droop.
So let me send my tears, bound in my handker chief.

As the priest enters with his censer, the lamentation reaches a climax, inspired less by the strange mourners than by the bereaved mother, wife or sister, who calls out a final reproach, just as they did for Hector. . . . (Alexiou 1974, pp. 42f.)

These songs are often performed as an intimate dialogue with the deceased, known as a *miroloj*, meaning "words of destiny." The melody of the following *miroloj* is highly formulaic:

"Dearest aunt, I wish you and yours a very good morning. How are you? Are things going well? Is there anything you need? The one thing we wish for you aunt, is that you will recover. We are fine, aunt, do not be concerned about us." (*La musique des Paysans de Grècee* Société francbais de productions phonographiques 6.2909.)

We might ask whether the tradition from antiquity is an unbroken one, or whether, irrespective of the singing of previous generations, each new generation has recreated its own laments spontaneously to help work through its own feelings.

According to Suliteanu (1985), a Romanian scholar, the traditions from Antiquity may be found in contemporary Romanian songs of grief. He bases this statement on characteristic elements of style in Romanian laments, including the use of a repeated final formula with notes held out after a rest and flute accompaniments (Figure 3.23).

In Greek sources from the fifth and sixth centuries, we can find similar laments with flute accompaniment. Suliteanu finds structural similarities between contemporary Romanian laments and ancient Greek ones, providing a geographical link. However, it is very difficult to distinguish between spontaneous elements of style that always characterize laments simply because they posses such emotional force and elements of style passed through oral traditions over long periods of time, not least because the only remaining older sources are literary.

However, it appears that the general spontaneous development of style elements was regional. If the regional style was archaic, the laments took on that style, and if the regional style was more modern, the laments were affected correspondingly. There is no question that spontaneous elements of style were very strong and gave rise to great similarities in laments all over Europe.

MUSIC AROUND THE CALENDAR

Annual cycles today and in the past

The division of the year into working periods and holiday periods is a relatively new phenomenon. In the agricultural society of the past, the year had natural divisions associated with planting in the spring and harvesting in the autumn. There were also the ancient heathen midwinter and midsummer cult periods.

The church used the existence of these traditional pagan festive periods to incorporate the celebration of saints' days or other important religious events into the cycle of the ecclesiastical year. All this was reflected in texts and melodies all over Europe until the nineteenth and twentieth centuries, when popular and art music, which utilized the new time divisions into work and free time to

a greater extent, and won out over the old ways (see also p. 101).

The role of song and music as bearers and mediators of historical traditions thus decreased as urban cultures took over. Song and music became more transient phenomena focusing on consumption and lost their traditional meaning.

The year has been divided in different ways at different periods in time and in different parts of Europe. For example, there appears to have been a mythologically-rooted division into the light and dark halves of the year. The division into calendar seasons is far newer, and most common throughout much of Europe. With regard to eastern Europe, however, scholars have found a different division: the calendar of the farmers and work in the fields. The winter season thus lasts from October to February, and the spring-summer season from March until July, followed by a short harvest period in August and September. There were folk songs associated with each respective season, and it would have been out of the question to sing a Christmas song at Easter time or a harvest song at Christmas. Singing was associated with a sense of community, encompassing both singers and audience.

In northern Europe the winter festival was eagerly anticipated, sorely needed to alleviate the hunger and privation that prevailed during the cold months of the year. Even the poorest could look forward to these special, festive days, with plenty to eat. In many countries people wore animal masks at midwinter, possibly a remnant of an ancient cult ritual. The Nordic Christian procession on Saint Lucia's Day, for example, included young boys dressed as "Christmas rams." In many parts of Sweden, there was also a bear dance at midwinter.

In other parts of Europe, especially to the east, there were midwinter processions from pagan times and earlier. These processions were made up not only of young men, but also of children, young women, and older adults. There were often separate processions for men and women, serving a sort of wish-fulfillment function as well as providing the opportunity to beg for alms. The processions would go to the neighboring farms or villages, and the songs would describe the kindness of the master of the house, the mistress, and the lovely children, as well as the virtues of the place itself. For this the singers were rewarded with a meal, and later with money. This tradition could be found all over Europe, and was initially not

Figure 3.23. Romanian song of grief with flute accompaniment. (Suliteanu 1985, ex. 13 p. 194.)

associated with Christmas. Singing processions were then made in the spring as well, the remnants of ancient spring pilgrimages from one farm to the next for the sowing ritual.

Before moving on to spring, however, let us examine Christmas and New Year's songs in some detail. These songs were rooted in a time far before the Christian era. They had many names. Those deriving from the word for calendar (Romanian *kolinder*, Russian *koladki*, Polish *koledy*) may be new names replacing ancient ones, although the old names may still be in local use (see also Propp 1963, p. 38). Practicing these songs, which were sometimes performed as part of dramatizations, has been regarded as a "school for rhythmically coordinated group song" (Kvitka 1973:1, p. 105). There were all kinds of performances. For instance, sometimes a soloist sang the verses and the choir the refrain (like the Swedish *Staffansvisa*, which is still performed that way today). There were many ways of dividing up the verses and refrains among soloists and choirs, including antiphonal performances with the two of the choir halves performing a sort of drama. (According to Zemtsovsky [1975], this form was used in Lithuania, Russia, Romania, Moldavia, the Balkans, and the Carpathians). These songs are always described as being performed with intensity, sometimes like something between singing and shouting. It is possible that this was once "a traditional way of trying to affect the forces of nature" (Kvitka 1975:1, p. 105–7), but it might just as well have been a natural way for the singers, who were outdoors, to try to arouse the master and mistress of the farm. It might simply have been the way people sang when partying, whether or not they were intoxicated. Medieval Christmas songs are related to, or may even have been taken from, the *djäkne* songs like the ones in the *Piae cantiones*.

Travelling scholars also wandered from farm to farm begging for their livelihood, and their songs were probably not unlike the songs of praise and alms-begging described above. As attempts were made to Christianize pagan customs, spiritual texts were also sung to secular melodies. This tradition is still alive today, for example, in Latin America.

Staffan Songs

Nordic *Staffan* songs provide us with good examples of the double function of the calendar song, combining older traditions with contemporary entertainment. Some of the preserved texts of these songs are structured like medieval ballads, using the imagery of the traditional legend of the story of Saint Stephen, Herod's groom, while others are nothing but alms-begging songs, in which Saint Stephen is more like a drunken farmhand. There is an example from southern Sweden of two *Staffan* songs transcribed on the same occasion, one of which is a two-line legendary song, the other a more recent alms-begging song. The stylistic levels of the two songs are very different. Figure 3.24a is almost modal in character, and is in the Dorian mode. Figure 3.24b, on the other hand, is a cheerful tune, with simple harmonies not unlike a popular nineteenth-century melody.

Staffan songs may be found in the other Nordic countries as well, and also in the British Isles. There is a two-line dance-tune variant from the Faeroe Islands, set to a typical Faeroese dance melody (Figure 3.24c). There is also a two-line variant from Finland, in which the melody of the refrain has been transposed an octave down, giving it a very strange appearance (Figure 3.24d).

Greta Dahlström, who collected this melody, explains it as follows:

> Some of the singers had trouble reaching the high notes of the melody, which was sung in unison, so they lowered the troublesome phrase by an octave. Gradually others, and then everyone began to sing

it that way, and now that is the only way it is sung on the island of Nötö (in the archipelago of Turku, Finland). It is not unusual for folk singers in this area to transpose for their own purposes parts of a melody that are too high for them. I have met old women who have done so with great dexterity and familiarity. (Dahlström, 1935, p. 72.)

There is an interesting example of a Danish, four-line *Staffan* song that is distinctly related to the older legendary melodies (Figure 3.24e). It has the same two-part structure as the two-line song from southern Sweden. The legendary Danish song was recorded by a woman from the village of Nørre Örslev in 1909 who had learned it from her mother. This indicates that *Staffan* songs were not only performed by young alms-begging men.

The most familiar version of the *Staffan* song today, "Stalledrängsvisan," is said to have come into being between 1550 and 1700, and to have been a distortion by the Lutherans of the old legendary song. (Celander 1927, p. 52). Saint Stephen suffered the common post-Reformation fate of the saints: dethronment. The four-line text has been sung to many melodies, with clear formal structures, some parts contrasting and others repetitive and using various dissonances creating a tension used for artistic effects (Figure 3.24f). The song has also been performed to traditional children's tunes and dance tunes, more contemporary dance music, and all kinds of sing-song melodies. When new versions of the text take root, the melody also tends to change.

Olof Broman, a Swedish minister (1676–1750) who kept a journal of his travels in the province of Hälsingland, was not particularly partial to the *Staffan* song. In his travelog, *Glysivallur*, he wrote:

I shall do no more than mention the ubiquitous *Staffan* song, sung by the young farmhands on the second day of Christmas, as they betook themselves throughout the parishoboes to gather food, beer, and spirits with which to make merry. This custom went on through 1690, when the authorities banned the custom of Staffaning. Their song began:

'Staffan watner fålar femb; hålt wäl Fålan min!' etc.

I find it difficult to believe that he wrote them himself, but rather think that it was patched together by someone else, in memory of his name. . . . (Jonsson 1967, p. 75.)

At Broman's time the *Staffan* song had already separated from the legend. It was being incorpo-rated into seasonal celebration, only loosely associated with Christian custom and ceremony, but closely allied with dancing and general merrymaking, as both the words and the melodies indicate.

Melody Types in Polish Christmas Songs

Poland has an exceptional wealth of Christmas songs of diverse origin. They are known as *koledy* and *pastoralki* (i.e., Christmas and shepherds' songs) and the melodies reflect the musical styles of different epochs. The eighteenth and nineteenth centuries saw the composition of large numbers of Christmas songs by both famous and anonymous composers. Many of these songs have become part of the orally transmitted folk song tradition. However, this was found all over Europe, not only in Poland. Some of the Polish folk songs also appear to be international and can be found in many countries. The 1985 Polish anthology *Polskie koledy i Pastoralki*, contains a mixture of sources of texts and melodies, and the esthetic result is highly successful. This is otherwise characteristic of the oral tradition. Various combinations of secular and sacred songs and melodies symbolize the combination of heathen and Christian traditions that comprise Christmas. (Figure 3.25a–i).

Most of the melodies of the Christmas songs in the anthology are related to the mazurka or other Polish dances (a and b). Some are minuet-like in style (c). Some were sung to recitative formulas (e), stylistically related either to narrative songs such as ballads (see also Chapter 4) or, as in this example, to Gregorian melodic formulas of two slurs separated in the middle by a long note. Many of the melodies can be traced to familiar religious hymns. For example, (f) uses the melody of *Dies est laetitiae*, a popular hymn. It is also similar to other sixteenth century hymns such as *Ecce novum gaudium* (see *Piae cantiones*, p. 31). Many of the melodies are structured in accordance with the traditional folk music principle of additions and variations. Oskar Kolberg transcribed (g) (see p. 14). In (h), the tonal pattern and use of triads in the melody, reminiscent of the baroque and classical periods, is one of many examples of songs which make use of a large proportion of what were newer stylistic traits. "Wandering melodies" such as the *La Folia* archetype in (i) are presented as themes and variations.

This collection of Polish Christmas songs shows

Figure 3.24. (a) A legendary folk song about "Staffan," and (b) "Staffan stalledrängvisa" from Vidtskövde in Skåne, Southern Sweden. (Otto John 1916, pp. 15 and 7.)

the elements shared by different musical environments—liturgical, secular, classical, folk.

The Romanian *Colinde*

In Romania there is a set of winter ceremonies beginning on Christmas Eve and concluding on Twelfth Night. The *colinde* ceremony, in which singers went from farm to farm to wish the owners well, began as a ritual associated with a longing for the return of the sunshine. The ritual was still in use and considered of magical import as late as the nineteenth century.

Bartók's collection of village folk music from Máramaroser in Romania includes examples of *colinde* songs performed by men as well as boys. Bartók reproduced nineteen such *colinde* songs. They generally consist of short verses of two to four lines and the same number of melodic motifs. The texts are often biblical but are not only about the Christmas season. Other themes include popular mythology, and some of the texts are sheer nonsense. The melodies appear to come from different strata (Figure 3.26), including cries unlike the music of the shepherds (a), pentatonic melodies (b), variants of the Swedish *fiskeskär* melody (c), and cheerful, probably more recent, melodies in the major (d). There are many different types of *colinde*. The most common is a three-line melody with an ABA structure, in which the embedded B line constitutes the refrain. Their performance is something between a recitative and a song, sometimes with very free rhythms.

Figure 3.24. cont'd (c) A legendary folk song about "Staffan" from the Faeroe islands. (Hjalmar Thuren, *Folkesangen paa Faröerne* 1908 p.139 melody example 86); (d) a legendary folk song about "Staffan" from the island of Nötö in the archipelago of Tuurku, Finland. (*Finlands svenska folkdiktning* V no. 23. See also Greta Dahlström's attempted reconstruction in "Staffan och Herodesvisans melody." *Budkavlen* 1935 no.2 p.67.)
(e) A "Staffan" song from Denmark. (*Danmarks gamle Folkeviser XI*, Volume two of the melodies 1938 p.128 f.); (f) "Staffan stalledrängvisa." Manuscript, Stockholm Royal Library, Afzelii manuscript Stockholm Royal Library, song archives, 126:4, p.74.)

English Christmas Carols

The fusion of the oral traditions with Christian popular hymns, transmitted orally and in writing, crystallized into a more or less stable collection of songs during the nineteenth century. Still, all kinds of improvisation and renewal were possible. In his *Folksong in England* (1967), A. L. Lloyd reproduces a song about the joys of the Virgin Mary. In the fifteenth-century version, Mary's joys were seven in number, but over the years, they were increased, and in the nineteenth century, around Christmas, some tattered poet of Seven Dials was encouraged to push his beer mug aside and scrawl some new joys for the Mother of God, increasing them to twelve.

Lloyd devotes an entire chapter to ceremonial song, describing door-to-door singing as an ancient tradition in which certain elements of style have persisted, including recurring refrains and alternation between march and dance rhythms. The songs may have originated out of a fear of starvation or a desire to tame the forces of nature. Some of the Christmas carols in Lloyd's volume share melodic similarities with folk songs from other cultures, for example, the Greek calendar song. What distinguishes the special "English" profile of these songs, however, is their descending pentatonic-sounding endings and their dance-like character. The Greek songs are of a more narrative, parlando type, closer to the hymns of Greek orthodoxy (see also Frye 1973, nos. 40, 66, 92, 108). Lloyd demonstrates that, in this context, the influence of function and ceremony on melodic structure may be more decisive than intercultural influences (Figure 3.27).

Fortune Telling Songs

According to Russian tradition, the new year was a time for looking to the future. At midnight on New Year's Eve (or at dawn the next morning), the young girls would gather and each would drop some object, such as a ring, into a bucket of water. The bucket was then covered and special songs were sung. Then an outsider would begin to remove the objects one by one at random. The girls whose objects came up first would hear songs of good fortune sung for them, but to those whose objects remained below there were only bad tidings.

Zemtsovsky (1975) describes the melodies of fortune telling songs as the common denominator of calendar songs throughout the year, and attributes this to their age and function. He says that most of the melodies have a range of three or four notes and are highly formulaic. There are some melodies with a larger range, but their songs exhibit the same pendulum motion.

The eastern European celebration preceding Lent, "butter week" had its own fortune-telling songs or incantations. Their theme was the end of winter. Butter week, seven weeks before Easter, was a time of fasting, singing, and ceremonies all over eastern Europe. It marked the transition from winter to spring. Butter week melodies, including songs for ceremonies ranging from ritual weddings to funerals at which straw effigies were burned, were stylistically varied, with elements from dance rhythms of Christmas songs to heavy melodies of laments.

Songs of Spring and Summer

The arrival of spring, and return of life once winter relaxed its iron grip, has been celebrated throughout history. Spring was celebrated with festivities and ceremonies, cries, songs, and instrumental music. However, it would be wrong to imagine that these celebrations were nothing but entertainment; the songs and the instruments were used to subdue forces both visible and invisible (see also p. 28). Many of the songs of spring were more like calls than songs. Cries were used to in the spring all over Europe, along with customs such as tossing wreaths into the water, baking special bread, and making special drinks. In eastern Europe the girls would gather on the hilltops and intone solemn laments not unlike songs of grief.

Zemtsovsky (1975) has made a systematic examination of these songs, finding the following melodic structure: *la-do-re* cadencing on *do*, *sol-do-re-mi* cadencing on *re* and *la-do-re-mi* cadencing on *do*. The interval structure of many of the melodies is in accord with that of the Swedish pastoral shouts, as is the construction consisting of small repeated motifs and variations (see Moberg 1959, p. 27). Similar recitative formulas can also be found in other parts of Europe. Other common constructions are question and answer, and descending thirds. Less frequently used ones include loud ascending shouts ranging from a major third to a sixth, seventh, or octave. There are also distinct regional melodic types which become apparent when the more complex structures are investigated. For example, there is one type of folk song characteristic of Belarus (Elatov 1974), the Ukraine (Kvitka 1973), and Russia (Zemtsovsky 1987), consisting of two lines of verse with a characteristic recurring rhythmic formula. (Figure 3.28, p. 72.)

Spring was welcomed in song all over Europe. In Denmark and southern Sweden, (which was part of Denmark at one time) May Day songs were

Figure 3.25. *Polskie koledy i Pastoralki*, 1985. (a) p.21 and 183, (b) p.57 and 184, (c) p.116 and 180, (d) p.134 and 186, (e) p.36 and 182, (f) p.95 and 173, (g) p.108 and 174. (h) p.113 and 175, and (i) p.142 and 177.

(and remain) an ancient tradition. Peder Jensen Roskilde, a Danish minister, wrote a spring song in the early seventeenth century in an attempt to suppress the obscene songs that were in circulation. He cleverly used the same meter and stanza pattern as the obscene song (based on a traditional melody), and the printed version states that it is to be sung to the same tune as its indecent prototype.

There was a special custom in Czechoslovakia and elsewhere on Palm Sunday and the day before, known as (Lazarus' Day). Young girls would sing and dance in pairs. Later, it was the girls rather than the boys who did the customary singing of well-wishing songs from farm to farm, known as *lazarski*. The *lazarski* were often formulaic in melodic structure. Local and regional variants have been transmitted, especially in southeastern Europe.

In Romania dances were (and still are) performed at Whitsuntide, both to encourage fertility and to protect against illness. These dances were very strictly structured and performed, and the dancers had to promise to respect the traditions. The leader carried a sword and the other dancers were equipped with sticks. They danced around a pole, draped in herbs and greenery. This dancing

Figure 3.26. Romanian *colinde* songs as noted down by Béla Bartók. (a) no.1, (b) no.5, (c) no.13d., (d) no.13c.

Figure 3.27. Christmas songs from (a) France, (b) Hungary, and (c) England, with related melodies. (Lloyd 1967, p.104.)

goes on throughout the Whitsun week, with dancers travelling from village to village to perform. The English Morris dance carries similar spring associations. Various spring games, often parodies of proposals and weddings, were in fact widespread throughout Europe, and associated with dancing, singing, and jesting.

Summer Songs and Autumn Songs

The Swedish midsummer celebration coincides with Saint John the Baptist's Day and provides another illustration of an ancient link between a heathen festival and a Christian observance. Midsummer songs are thus often about John the Baptist. In Latvia, midsummer celebrations focus on a mysterious individual known as Jāni, whose roots have been traced not to Saint John but to the Roman Janus cult. More than 1,000 Jāni songs have been preserved, all of which contain the word *ligo* in the refrain. Most of the melodies come from an

older stylistic stratum where the recitative melody is performed by the leader, accompanied by a choir singing in two parts, one singing a drone, the other varying the melodic motifs of the leader (Figure 3.29) (see also Apkalns 1977, p. 67ff; on other similar types of folk song sung in parts, see below, p. 118).

The European Community of Calendar Songs

Russian musicologist Zemtsovsky (1975, 1987) has studied calendar songs with a view to surveying the material and examining a possible connection between Russian calendar songs and those of neighboring peoples, from and including western Europe. The analytical method he applies was introduced in the 1920s by Russian musicologist Assafyev. It assumes that the music of any given time and place contains a certain number of sets of "intonations," or rhythmic, melodic, and tonal components.

Zemtsovsky attempts to define these "intonations" in songs of well-wishing and alms-begging on the basis of the hypothesis that there are basic rhythmic, melodic and sonorous structures that form groups of components, or "fields of intonation." According to Zemtsovsky, the rhythmic components of these songs are very similar, which indicates that they were probably danced not only in Russia but all over eastern Europe and in large parts of western Europe, such as France, Germany, Estonia, and Latvia (see Zemtsovsky 1975, p. 38). The concept of dance as he uses it probably consists of all kinds of organized movement, include

Figure 3.28. (a) Example of the spring song based on used as a basis for variations by (b) Tchaikovsky in his piano concerto no.1. (Zemtsovsky 1978, p.10 f.)

what we might call marches and dramatic dialogues.

He goes on to describe how a given rhythmic component, or "cell," multiplies, coming to dominate an entire performance. Take, for example, the simple formula in figure 3.30a, which is shaped and reshaped, sometimes with different patterns of intonation (b). Then certain turns in the melody (that is, intonations) strengthen the rhythmic cell, for example, what Zemtsovsky refers to as different formulas for choral calls (c). The actual intervals used are often descending, within the range of a third or a fourth (d). Zemtsovsky finds that there are melodies from all over eastern Europe that all have the same combination of these rhythmic cells and melodic turns. These similar intonations comprise a "field of intonation," which we might otherwise call a melodic style. The field is characterized by certain flexible regulations for the rhythmic and melodic cells, as well as by clear boundaries for what is acceptable within the field of intonation. Thus Zemtsovsky concludes that our way of thinking about music is not in terms of individual notes but in "complexes of intonation," phrases and melodic turns we remember, transmit, and apply in the folk tradition, and by strictly oral means of transmission. The individual notes are mobile within any given complex of intonation, and may vary in pitch, but the identity of the complex remains constant.

In this way, Zemtsovsky reveals regularities in our way of thinking about music; in the oral tradition we make individual melodic statements on the basis of a shared set of melodic, rhythmic, dynamic, and gestural expressions that combine into a common field of intonation (cf. spoken language). Our melodic statements are spontaneous, a product of the moment, created to express an idea in music. We then conceive of the different variants within the field of intonation, giving the whole an identity.

A field of intonation includes two forces, dynamic continuity and fundamental mobility. Together they comprise the horizontal and vertical tonal fields of intonation by removing what Zemtsovsky regards as occasionaly arbitrary.

Thus orally transmitted folk music is distinguished from written art music in that it consists of "folk-like mobile formulas of intonation." Some segments of the melodies are more stable than others, notably the refrains. In Ukraine, Belarus, Bulgaria, Romania, Hungary, and Greece, the melody of calendar songs tends to be built on intonations of a fifth. Such melodies are rare in Russian calendar songs. For this reason Zemtsovsky regards them as European imports; the "black sheep" of Russian folklore, and thus links between Russian and other European calendar songs.

Zemtsovsky postulates that long ago there was a sort of dictionary of intonations for European calendar songs in which the specific functions and semantics of the various melodic calls were described.

Did Calendar Songs, too, Derive from Calls?

The songs and tunes marking festive times of the year or the life cycle thus display great variation. They include everything from more traditional melodies, related to calls and simple speech-singing, often in combination with dance, to the melodies of the most recent popular music. Festive times have always been marked by a desire to both reestablish a historical context and provide the most current experience. Music was an important part of these occasions, providing signals of both past and present.

Hungarian Regös Melodies

Janka Szendrei, a Hungarian musicologist, wonders how it has been possible for the Hungarian calendar song, the *regös*, to retain its "primitive form" despite all the external pressure on it to change. Szendrei begins her search for an answer

Figure 3.29. Latvian midsummer song about the Janis Day which is about to begin. (Apkalns 1977, no. 29 p. 397.)

by presenting a *regös* melody which she sees as a simple call. The call consists of a simple, two bar melodic fragment. It has the characteristic ending, with the melody moving from the tonal center up a fifth. She claims that the melody was used in fertility rites owing to its ability to attract the attention of listeners, irrespective of whether it was performed vocally or instrumentally. Szendrei goes on to seek parallels in melodies from elsewhere. She not only finds similarities in songs from Athens (with its Byzantine liturgical hymn tradition), Romania, Spain, Poland, Bulgaria, and the southern Appalachians, but she finds that these similar melodies are also associated with some kind of fertility rite. She observed that when the melodic core came into contact with art music, it changed. However, she determined that what the melodies have in common, from their Byzantine to their folk music variants, is "a common ancestor, a primitive ritual melody resembling a call, based on some antique, shamanistic cult of nature" (Szendrei 1967, p. 50). Can we conclude that we may seek our musical roots in primitive ritual calls? The least we can say with certainty is that it does appear that some melodic formulas have a special capacity for being transmitted over long periods of time, or for being rediscovered and reappearing in similar contexts and functions.

Long ago, rural peoples could depend on tradition. Festivals were celebrated in exactly the same way they always had been, and people knew that many of the songs they sang had also been sung by their grandparents and great-grandparents in turn. Has this sense of tradition been broken today? Hardly. While the amount of entertainment available for instant gratification and immediate consumption has grown into a multinational industry, there are also counter-reactions in the form of an awareness of the need to preserve and create traditions in music and other areas.

Zemtsovksy, quoted at length above, has tried to answer the question of origins and to define stylistic strata. This is the same question posed earlier by Bartók and others. Yet even Zemtsovksy himself seems to question his methods. He notes that if we are to understand musical expression, we may need to stress function even more than has been done in the past, and that the historical dimension is helpful in explaining changes in function, external influences, etc. Many of the methods applied to analysis of melodies in folklore have been very useful, mainly in terms of creating some sort of order out of chaos. This has been vital to the development of scholarly collections and archives. But in general, in works on folk music, I believe that the dialectical relationship between function and melodic expression must be stressed. When it is, it is not surprising that links are found between the folk music of different countries. For centuries, the way of life in many places was very similar. The traditions that developed were natural, considering the conditions of production, whether they were hunting, fishing, herding, or farming. If we examine Europe as a cross-section of livelihoods, it is clear that there were (and are) great similarities between the lifestyles of different peoples.

We began this chapter by examining whether certain types of melodies and ways of singing might be associated with given occasions in a way that reinforced the experience of that occasion. The answer is certainly in the affirmative with regard to ways of singing. We have seen that the nature of laments also spread to other solemn occasions, such as weddings and celebrations of the arrival of spring. We also asked whether function and tradition affected choice and performance of melodies. We have seen a clinging to tradition and a desire for what is new. They reflect different sides of European folk melodies as they are sung both as the wheel of life turns and as the seasons change.

Figure 3.30. (a) A separate rhythmic cell and (b) its reformulation. (Zemtovsky 1975, Figures 1 and 24.)

Figure 3.30 cont'd. (c) Choral calling formulas. (d) Examples of common melody motifs. (Zemtsovsky 1975, Figures 5 and 9.)

Literature

A great deal has been written about children's songs. After them, laments are the type of life-cycle songs that have received the most scholarly attention, and perhaps they are also the most interesting. Research done in Hungary and in Petrosavodsk is of great interest. The Hungarian book *Siratók*, part of the fantastic series on Hungarian folk music (referred to here as Corpus) is available in English. Most of the research on Karelian melodies is in Finnish or Russian.

Aili Nenola-Kallio's *Studies in Ingrian Laments* (1982) is recommended for more detailed descriptions of laments.

A great deal has been written from the point of view of folklore about calendar songs, but not many collections of melodies are available, except for the Slavic area, where there are Kvitka, Elatov, and others. Zemtsovsky's books from 1975 and 1987 have extensive bibliographies. Lloyd (1967) is a very interesting work on calendar songs, as is Tiersot's classic work (1889/R1978). To my knowledge, it remains the only such work in French.

Four

"Bursting into Song" (Part I): The *Jojk*, Narrative Song, and Ballad

Bursting into song is a human need, although in our industrialized society we tend to confine it to the shower and to parties, with a few exceptions such as English pubs, Georgian restaurants, Swedish evangelical families and football (soccer) stadiums. Moreover, children sing as much as (if not more) than ever (see Chapter 3). This means that there is hope for singing to once again occupy the key position it held in many cultures before social inhibitions and, later, comparisons with the professional singers of the mass media silenced it.

This chapter is devoted to a few unique ways of singing and functions of song. At one time, these were central to certain ethnic groups and in some cases still have a special cultural identity, although they have gained new functions and the way in which they are performed has changed.

THE SAAMI *JOJK*

The *jojk* is a very special kind of song, still extant among the roughly 35,000 Saami (or Lapp) people who mainly live in northern Sweden, Norway, and Finland as well as on the Russian Kola peninsula. The *jojk* (meaning, roughly, "singing in the Saami way") has many variants. What is described below is a sort of common denominator of the original *jojk* and its later transformations.

Jojk Performance

The *jojk* is neither song nor speech, but a mode for the expression of feelings or telling a story in small, rhythmically varied motifs with dramatic shifts in dynamics and accent. There is a Saami word for this very special type of performance: *juoi'gat*. In the Saami language there are also special words for a *jojk* performed with words as opposed to a *jojk* that is only made up of vowels or isolated syllables. The singer often begins tentatively, feeling his or her way to the pitches and rhythmic motifs that will serve as a basis for their performance. Once the performer has this foundation, he begins to shape one or two motifs that develop into simple or complex structures. Edström (1988) has made a study of the stylistics of the *jojk*. In the southern Saami areas the older forms dominate, characterized by a "tense vocal technique. . . ." dummy syllables, a small number of notes . . . and various kinds of "sliding" notes (see p. 77 and Figure 4.1a). In the northern areas there are often pentatonic melodies lacking semitones or a mixture of melodies in which major tonalities predominate (Figure 4.1b).

Nils Hotti (b. 1905) from the Saami village of Könk m in Karesuando is a prominent *jojk* singer, and his performances are available on disc (*Jojk, Sveriges Radios jojkinspelningar*, sides 13 and 14). His *jojks* consist of long narratives interspersed with lyrical songs that appear to be passed down from generation to generation (see Arnberg et al. 1969, p. 34ff.). Hotti sings in Saami as well as in Swedish and Finnish. The melodic form is constant, but the pitch shifts upwards by approximately a major third during the performance. The bearing interval is the sixth. He uses stylistic means such as "sliding" notes and variations in pitch and recurring final descents and tonal shifts, and performs his *jojk* in a parlando style (Figure 4.1c).

Figure 4.1. (a) Edström 1988, p. 15 1:3:c. (b) Edström 1988 p. 75 12:5:a; (c) a *jojk* performed by Nils Hotti (b. 1905) from Könkärn Saami village in Karesuando, Sweden. The occasion on which this *jojk* was performed is described in the commentary on Nils Hotti's *jojks* (see Arnberg et al. 1969, p. 250f.). (Edström 1988, p. 80.)

Generally, the Saami song tradition is divided into northern and southern variants. In a travelog from a journey through Lapland in 1673, Johannes Schefferus described a Saami named Olof Sirma performing *jojks*. This description corresponds well to the *jojk* as performed today, confirming the endurance of the tradition. "The performer begins in his own fashion, choosing to sing louder or softer depending on his sense of the composition. Sometimes he repeats the entire song over and over. He sings on no special note, but performs according to his habit, and however it sounds best to him" (Arnberg et al. 1969, p. 6).

Petrus Laestadius, a missionary, described the *jojk*, 160 years later, as follows:

As the party sits having refreshments, and as people begin to feel the force of this nectar of life, the conversation grows more lively, more friendly. People cease speaking in prose, and begin to converse in song. The songs are simple and monostrophic, because the songs flow more easily that way. There are endless numbers of these melodies, referred to as *woulle*, or *wouleh* in plural. Some are melancholy, others happy, others proud, etc. (Arnberg et al. 1969, p. 8.)

Twentieth century musicologists have tried to describe the *jojk* more scientifically. Carl-Allan Moberg made the following notes in the log of an expedition from 1943:

A breath may be taken at any time. [My informant] sang with his lips nearly closed, as do nearly all the Lapps, singing with a rather tense voice . . . seemed out of breath, breathing heavily, which interrupted the song arbitrarily . . . an old-fashioned style that seemed highly authentic: his jaws were pressed tightly together, his mouth hardly open, his voice growing tenser and tenser, straining in crescendo-like coarse heaves, pressing the air between his palate and the

back of his tongue, down into his throat. (Quoted from Edström 1977, p. 121.)

Moberg attempts to specify the differences between the *jojk* and ordinary singing. His efforts to be objective and scientific in his descriptions is typical of twentieth-century *jojk* scholars. Mats Arnberg and Israel Ruong, however, have emphasized the aesthetic aspects. "Every *jojk* has a motif of its own. The *jojk* texts, melodies, and rhythms give us a picture of the Saami, their lives and work, an image transposed to and chiselled out from a uniquely Saami aesthetic force-field, theirs since time immemorial" (Arnberg et al. 1969, p. 14).

Ruong and Arnberg stress the personal, individual aspects of the *jojk*.

There are numerous other preserved, ancient singing techniques alongside the *jojk*, and it is interesting to examine how the *jojk* has been inspired by neighboring music cultures such as folk singing, the psalms of the missionaries, and the dance and popular music of the times.

In an 1818 article from the arts journal *Svea: Tidskrift för vetenskap och konst* (Svea, A Journal for Science and Art) entitled "Anmärkningar öfver gamla nordiska sången" (Notes on Ancient Nordic Song), German-born composer, organist, and voice teacher Johann Christian Friedrich Haeffner (1759–1833) describes one intermediate form of the *jojk*:

In the 1780s, some Lapps and their reindeer came to Stockholm. They told fortunes, and played music on drums, flutes and a kind of fiddle, as well as an instrument resembling a trumpet-marin [probably a *langeleik*]. . . . There were two men and three women. To me, all their singing appeared to be improvised. It was accompanied with gestures. It was more declamation than melody, sometimes slow, sometimes quick, sometimes solo and sometimes in unison. At times this mimed declamation verged on the sub-

render the intermediate form between the *jojk* and other kinds of music, as he implied in his remarks about their instruments.

Haeffner clearly found it difficult to describe this peculiar kind of singing, and his difficulties were exacerbated by the fact that he was describing not the "pure" *jojk* but a form probably "contaminated" by Swedish and Norwegian folk music. Part of his description is typical of the *jojk*, such as the declamation, the mimicry, and the improvisation. But, the unusual instrumentation was foreign to the nomadic culture of the Saami, and the drum he describes was probably not a troll drum. We may better understand the intermediate form Haeffner described in the early nineteenth century if we compare it with the 1980 Eurovision Song Contest. The Norwegian contribution was called *Samiid Aednan* and was based on a *jojk* by Saami musician Mattis Haetta. This is a contemporary example of a *jojk* presented as popular music, but the contest jury had nowhere near the same insight into the qualities of the *jojk* as Haeffner. There were also objections from traditionalists against merging the *jojk* with "commercial" music, which was regarded with skepticism. Other Saami, however, were of the opinion that this was a good way of spreading the *jojk*, as long as it was also retained in its original form (see also Johnsson 1986, p. 116).

Drums, Ritual, and Magic

When the Saami migrated west from their Asiatic camps, they brought the rituals of the cult of shamanism with them, including the shaman drum. Both are closely associated with the *jojk*. In pagan times the drum was used by the Saami priest, the *nåjden*, to make contact with the gods. The drum skins were painted in red with scenes portraying the higher forces of nature who were both the help and the bane of the drummer. There were also depictions of various other protectors or destroyers of life and property. They were omnipresent, but if he wished to commune with them he had to undertake a hazardous journey into the world of the spirits. Using the drum and a mallet, he would put himself into a trance. His soul would rise from his body, and, now a spirit himself, he would learn things about the future. Upon returning to consciousness, he was then able to interpret and share

Figure 4.2. Example of Johann Christian Friedrich Haeffner's interpretation of the song of the Lapps. (Quoted here from Geijer-Afzelius, *Svenska folkvisor* 2nd ed. from 1880, part III p. 90)

lime. The person declaiming appeared to be in a fury, his speech was like a brush fire. It was particularly so when he was predicting the future. . . . There was slow solo song with accompaniment on their instruments, and occasionally other voices chimed in. After a great deal of bother and concentrated listening, I concluded that their modulations could be roughly described as follows: [see Figure 4.2]. (Geijer/Afzelius 2nd ed. 1880: 3p. pp. I–XIV.)

When Haeffner's notations of the *jojk* are difficult to interpret, it is important to recall that this collector was trying to illustrate a very alien world of music in a way that must have appeared extremely sophisticated to his contemporaries. The cadencing and the "modulation" in the third staff may have been concessions to the musical taste of his times, but Haeffner might also have been trying to

his experiences and insights, pointing to the different symbols on the drum.

A Saami named Arvid Larson from Åsele described the drum as a fortune-telling instrument in 1740. "[O]ne Saturday he was in Nills Jonsson's hut when a man named Jox came in. Nills Jonsson had given him his drum the evening before, and Jox, using a hammer of horn and sitting for a while on the ground, he had beat the drum and, upon conclusion, declared that Nills Jonsson should not travel westwards" (quotes from Manker 1938, p. 406).

The Saami drums were often used both as musical instruments and instruments of fortune telling, often on occasions when *jojk* were performed. Thus Saami drums are a symbol of a highly developed culture with a unique world of the imagination, a combination of wisdom and mysticism.

But the missionaries and the government officials were equally cruel and wily in their efforts to make the Saami abandon both *jojk* and drum. Linnaeus's travelog from Lapland bears testimony to what can only be described as rough methods of capturing the ancient fellow traveler of the nåide (shaman) and taking him to the underworld. In it Linnaeus describes how he costumed himself as a Saami, and equipped himself with hammer and drum. His factual observations of the spiritual life of the Saami show understanding and tolerance of a kind that was completely foreign to his ecclesiastical contemporaries.

Since the Middle Ages the Saami have felt the impact of the lifestyles and cultures of the south, but they have somehow managed to incorporate these foreign elements in a way that has enriched rather than extinguished their own culture. Thus, for example, today the *jojk* is not only a relic from the past but has been integrated into hard rock and other forms of contemporary music. For the Saami, the forces of change have always gone hand in hand with an awareness of the importance and strength of their own cultural heritage. Both the musicians who make the *jojk* part of contemporary electronic music, seeking a lifestyle adapted to the present, and the vocalists who perform ancient monovocal jojks with increasing piety, looking to the past, are equally committed to seeing the *jojk* preserved.

The *jojk* has also inspired different composers to interpret the world of the Saami, from the eighteenth-century German-Swedish composer Abbé

Vogler to young avant garde composers today, such as Rolf Enström, who won the Prix Italia in 1987.

NARRATIVE SONGS FROM THE EAST

Finnish *Runic* Songs

Like the *jojk* of the Saami, Finnish runic song can hardly be considered "singing" in the traditional sense of the word. It is more like a mixture of recitative and calling, with some melodic features as well. The runic song might well be described as a kind of drama including both the imitation of sounds from nature, and mime.

A number of runic melodies were noted down in the late eighteenth and early nineteenth centuries. These appear to have been reliably transcribed, although it must be borne in mind that the aesthetics of the time often meant that they were tidied up and modified. Figure 4.3 is a runic melody published by the explorer Acerbi (1795). The melody has the usual piano accompaniment, and Acerbi wrote in a note:

"Having heard the melody performed in various ways, I render variations as I have heard them. *Nota bene* that I am indebted to Herr Schwenke, music master in Hamburg, for the bass part to all the melodies given below, some of which are brilliant pieces of scholarship."

It is possible that the folk song variations arranged for piano or other instruments contain other versions of the same melody noted down by other collectors, so they are not necessarily products solely of the imaginations of the arrangers. The first version of the melody is made up of two short phrases, grouped as a question-and-answer in accordance with the structure of the verse. The basic interval of this common kind of runic melody is *sol-la-do-re* (G-A-C-D). B-flat is not used as the final note in a cadence, and appears to have less weight in the melody than the other notes. Thus the foundation appears to have been a semitoneless scale with a supplementary minor third.

Textual Meter and Melody

The actual narrative is the basis of the runic song, interspersed with lyrical elements. It is probable that there was a sort of grammar of folk poetry

Figure 4.3. A runic melody. (Acerbi II 1802, appendix p. 325.)

handed down from generation to generation (see also Laitinen 1985, p. 39). The poetry was based on the *Kalevala* meter, with free grouping of the lines of verse. This grammar contained alliteration, repetition, and recurrent patterns. Probably the oral tradition did not mean learning runic songs from the past by heart but rather rendering earlier versions of them as closely as possible. If a person was familiar with the grammar of folk poetry, he could shape his song during the performance, and he knew how to make the transitions between narrative prose and lyrical poetry, where to interject incantations and joking verses, and how to set his pitch and rhythm. More recent runic songs only contain the remnants of this kind of improvized speech-song. The melodies that have been preserved appear to be crystallized structures, possibly a selection from a wealth of material no longer available to us. The stories themselves have been gathered into an epic poem, *The Kalevala* (see p.14). This process of transformation was not unique to narrative song in Finland, Estonia, and the area of Russia from which the runic song probably once migrated to the north. We can see the same historical development expressed in relations to the *bilinï*, the *duma,* and heroic songs from the Balkans.

Performance

In ancient times, the leading singer had an assistant, who repeated the final verses or, if the singer required a break, repeated an entire verse. Sometimes both singers were accompanied by a *kantele* player.

Figure 4.4a and b show pairs of runic singers, but more than a century apart in time. Figure 4.4a comes from Acerbi's journey in 1795. In it, the singer is accompanied by a *kantele* player. Figure 4.4b is a photograph of two runic singers from 1894 (FMQ 1-2 1985 p. 8). This unusual Baltic and Finnish form, in which a lead singer alternates with another who follows, appears to have a common origin. The prologue to the *Kalevala* describes this type of performance:

> Let's strike hand to hand
> fingers into finger-gaps
> that we may sing some good things
> set some of the best things forth
> for those daring ones to hear
> for those with a mind to know
> among the youngsters rising
> among the people growing—
> those words we have got
> tales we have kindled
> from old Väinämöinin's belt
> up from the Ilmarinen's forge
> from the tip of Farmind's brand
> from the path of Joukahainen's bow
> from the North's furthest fields, from
> the heaths of Kalevala.

(This and all subsequent quotations from the *Kalevala* are from the Keith Bosley translation, *The Kalevala: An Epic Poem after Oral Tradition*, by Elias Lönnrot, *The World's Classics*, Oxford: Oxford University Press, 1989.)

This ancient way of singing runic melodies, with two men holding hands and alternating in song, had virtually disappeared in the nineteenth century when the *Kalevala* songs began to be collected. By that time, they were simply recited.

We can get one step closer to the performance of runic songs in their musical environment if we examine the musical events described in the *Kalevala*. Väinämöinen, the hero, is seeking someone with whom to perform the songs alternately, with the second singer repeating the ends of the verses. It was a great honor to be the second to a prominent singer. The song about the wedding describes Väinämöinen's search for a singing partner. If he cannot find a willing or suitable singer, he is prepared to sing alone. These songs were

Figure 4.4a. A runic singer performing. Acerbi I 1802, alongside p. 226. Sketch from a farm in Järvänkyla, Northeast of Tuurku.

performed on very different occasions, one of which was weddings. Their purpose was both to embellish the beauty of one's own home and to highlight the poverty of the home of the other party. Special singers were hired for weddings (songs 20, 21 and 29).

The *Kalevala* describes in detail both instruments and instrument-making. One example is in "The broken knife" (song 33). The fighting spirit of Kullervos the shepherd is depicted in a painting by Finnish artist Akseli Gallen-Kallela (1865–1931) in a fresco at the Helsinki Vocal Academy. He portrays Väinämöinen in many situations (Figure 4.5).

He made a pipe from cow-bones
from an ox-horn a hooter
a trump from Birdcherry's leg
a whistle from Brightie's hock
and he peeped upon his pipe
he tooted upon his trump
three times upon the home hill
six times at the lane's entrance.

That mistress of Ilmari
the smith's hag, the fine woman
    long lolls without milk
sprawls without summer butter.
She heard playing from the swamp
    ringing from the heath;
    she says with this word
    she spoke with this speech:
    'Be praised, God: a trump
    sounds, the herd comes! But
where did the serf get a horn
and the toiler find a trump
    that he comes playing
    he trumpets tooting
    blowing through my ears
    going through my head?'
Kullervo, Kalervo's son
uttered a word and spoke thus:
'From the swamp the serf has got a horn
brought a trump out of the slime.
Now your herd is in the lane
the cows at the byre-field's end:
    come and light the smudge
    go and milk the cows!'

Figure 4.4b. The Jamanen brothers performing verses from the *Kalevala*. The brothers are sitting in the same position as the men in the Acerbi sketch, and as described in the *Kalevala*. Sometimes the bearers of tradition were photographed like this to give a genuine, ancient impression. (Photograph: I. Inha. Photography museum of Finland FMQ 1–2 1985, p 8.)

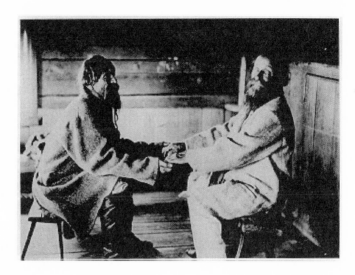

There is also a detailed description of the making of the *kantele*, or *kannel*, the magical instrument that accompanied the runic song and provided it with such a mystical shimmer (song 40, "The Pike"):

> I wonder what these—
> these pike-teeth, this wide
> jawbone—could become
> were they in a smith's workshop
> with a skilful craftsman, in
> a mighty man's hands?
> The smith Ilmarinen said:
> 'What's nothing becomes nothing
>   a fishbone no tool
> even in a smith's workshop
> with a skillful craftsman, in
>   a mighty man's hands'
>
> Steady old Väinämöinen
>   put this into words:
> 'But surely these could become
> a kantele of fishbones
> were there women who knew how
> who could make an instrument of bones.'
>
> When no one else came forward
> and there was none who knew how
> who could make an instrument of bones
> steady old Väinämöinen
> made of himself a maker
> took the shape of a shaper: he made an
> instrument of pike bone
> produced a joy for ever.
> What was the kantele's belly from?—
> 'twas from the big pike's jawbone
> What the kantele's pegs from?—

> they were made from the pike's teeth.
> What the kantele's strings from?—
> from the hairs of the Demon's gelding.
>
> Now the instrument was made
> and ready the kantele
> the great pikebone instrument
> the kantele of fish fins:

When Väinämöinen made his new *kantele*, his main material was no longer the jaw of a pike, but ordinary birch wood. In fact, every part of his instrument appears to be of less mystical origin (song 44):

> Steady old Väinämöinen
>   ponders in his brain:
> 'Now some music would be good
> and some merrymaking right
> for this new state of affairs
>   upon these fair farms;
> but the kantele is lost
> my joy has gone for ever
> to the farm of the fishes
> to the crags of the salmon
> to the sea-trough's keepers, to
> the Wave-wife's eternal folk
> nor will it be brought again
> nor will Ahto give it back.'
> . . .
> Then old Väinämöinen formed
> from the birch an instrument
> carved it through a summer day
> hammered at a kantele
> on the misty headland's tip
> at the foggy island's end
> carved a belly for the kantele

Figure 4.5. *Concert Finnois.* Poster advertising a series of concerts of Finnish music at the Paris World Fair in 1900. The illustration is a motif from the Kalevala, depicting a young maiden cutting off her hair so that Väinämöinen can use it to string his kantele (see end of song 44, below).

a soundboard for the new joy
a belly out of tough birth
a soundboard out of curly birch.
The old Väinämöinen said
  he declared, spoke thus:
'Here's a belly for the kantele
a soundboard for the eternal joy;
but where shall the pegs be got
  the screw be fetched from?'

An oak grew in a barnyard
a tall tree at a year's end;
on the oak were shapely boughs
on each bough was an acorn
on the acorn was a golden whorl
on the golden whorl was a cuckoo.
hen the cuckoo calls
and utters five words
gold wells from its mouth
and silver pours forth
on a golden knoll
on a silver hill:
from there the kantele's pegs
the screws for the curly birch!
The old Väinämöinen said
  he uttered, spoke thus:
'I've got the kantele's pegs
the screws for the curly birch
but still something is missing:
Where should I get the strings from
for it, put on the voices?'

He went in search of a string.
  He steps through a glade:
a lassie sat in the glade
a young maiden on the marsh.
The lass was not weeping, not
indeed was she rejoicing
but just singing to herself:
she sang to pass her evening
hoping a bridegroom would come
thinking about her lover.

Steady old Väinämöinen
yonder crept with no shoes on
without toe-rags he tiptoed;
  then when he got there
he began to beg tresses
and he put this into words:
'Lass, give some of your tresses
  damsel, of your hair
  for kantele strings
voices of eternal joy!'

The lass gave of her tresses
some of her fine hair;
gave tresses five, six
even seven hairs:
from there the kantele strings
sounders of eternal joy.

Of course, no ordinary mortal can handle a magic *kantele.* The celebratory *kantele* must be played by a hero (see song 41:1–36). Väinämöinen also plays the part of a Finnish Orpheus who enchants people and animals with his music.

The Meaning of the *Kalevala*

To the Karelian farmers, the poems in the *Kalevala* provided an alternative reality in which anything was possible for heroes and mortal men. Reading the *Kalevala* today can give no more than a faint hint of what this was like. We must use our imaginations to recreate the toughness and privation of the long evenings, the momentary excesses of wedding festivals, and the dancing shadows caused by burning sticks of peat.

In the form which we meet it today, the *Kalevala* is a complete epic, as mentioned above, collected and integrated from different runic songs by Elias Lönnrot (see p. 14). There was probably no such epic prior to this. The unique narrative tradition behind the *Kalevala* is said to have begun some

4,000 years ago. The art of creating runic songs is said to have followed the Finns as they wandered north, leaving cultural traces in both Russia and Estonia. In the late Middle Ages, the runic song took inspiration from the French ballads as they reached Finland via Sweden, and thus these ballads also affected the *Kalevala* tradition. This may be the point at which the process of melodic crystallization began, resulting in what we now conceive of as *the* runic melody.

Lönnrot's collected epic begins with a creation myth and ends with a poem describing the hero, Väinämöinen, a child of the goddess of the air, as he leaves the Suomi people when the virgin Mariatta (the virgin Mary) becomes pregnant with the help of a lingonberry. We leave the *Kalevala* with this Orpheus of Finland after he has attempted in vain to kill Mariatta's son, the king of Karelia. Väinämöinen wanders to the shore of the great sea where, for the final time, he sits down and sings, after which he prepares to leave the Suomi shores forever:

> Then the old Väinämöinen
> goes full speed ahead
> in the copper boat
> in the coppery punt
> to where mother earth rises
> and heaven descends
> and there he stopped with his craft
> with his boat he paused; but he
> left the kantele behind
> the fine music for Finland
> for the folk eternal joy
> the great songs for his children.

The *Kalevala* gave the Finnish culture its identity. Poets, painters, and composers have constantly returned to this epic, finding in it new inspiration to portray the destiny of their people. Today, hard rock bands and television producers give us their versions of an apparently inexhaustible and indestructible heritage of ideas, stories, visions, and love poetry. Today, as in the past, the *Kalevala* is performed using pitch and rhythm, although the music of the *kantele* is usually replaced with that of a symphony orchestra or rock group (see also *Finnish Music Quarterly* 1–2 [1985]).

The Russian *bïlinï*

The *bïlinï*, or Russian narrative heroic songs, are related to runic songs in terms of content and, most important, in terms of function. Like the runic songs, *bïlinï* represented the history and memory of the peasants. Many *bïlinï* have been annotated and recorded. Before we examine their general performance and melodies let us become acquainted with one of the singers and one of his songs.

Our singer's name was Nikita Fedorovitch Ermoli, born in 1885. He lived in the village of Truskovksy on the Slime River, in the comidad of Archangel. As a child, Nikita Fedorovitch had learned *bïlinï* from troubadours and others. As an adult, he was one of the best known local *bïlinï* singers. He would sit on the river bank singing and drowning out the whistles of the passing steamboats.

The melody to which he sang the *bïlinï* about Ilya Muromez in Figure 4.6 is structured like the runic song: a range of a fifth with the second and fourth steps found at bearing points in the melody (accented phrases and descending endings), and the third note, the minor third, less outstanding. As shown in the illustration, the melody is very stable with small rhythmic and melodic variations. Now and then the singer dips a whole note below the base note. The rhythmic structure of the melody appears to completely dominate the meter of the text.

The two illustrations in Figure 4.7a and b are taken from a series of amateur sketches from 1852. The first depicts the meeting between the hero and Solovey the robber; the second shows Ilya's meeting with Vladimir in Kiev. The story of Ilya Muromez, and the demise of the Russian heroes, may be summarized as follows:

> Ilya had been immobilised for thirty years, when one day, two gods in disguise came to him and told him he was going to become a great hero. Ilya hastened to Kiev, 'his horse galloping as fast as the hawk flies across lakes and rivers. The tail of his horse swept away entire cities.' On his way to Kiev, Ilya overcame the many cunning tricks of Solovey the robber, and freed three maidens in distress. Ilya dragged Solovey the robber to the palace of Prince Vladimir, arriving in the midst of great festivities. To prove his superiority he challenged the robber to wrestle with everyone present. Only Ilya and the Prince can keep the robber from throwing them to the ground. Ilya murders the robber, and is given the seat of honour at the Prince's table as a token of gratitude for having freed the country. The other heroes receive him like a brother. He and his new-

found hero friends set off on new adventures. After a tremendous duel, Ilya pokes out the eyes of his heathen enemy, and carries his head back to the enemy camp on a lance. After this deed, however, his luck turns. He is challenged again by some of the surviving heathens, and as he fights them some magic makes them double in number. The former heroes are forced to flee to the mountains, and many of them are transformed to pillars of stone. This was the end of the Russian heroes.

The Structure and Performance of the *Bilinï*

The poetic language and performance technique of the *bilinï* are very special. A *bilinï* is linked together by a recurring melodic formula. Various poetic techniques, such as assonance (vowel rhymes, internal rhymes or half-rhymes), are used to weave the language into the tonal entity. *Bilinï* are not adapted to any particular meter. Their textual structure is very free. Some of the singers have a special introduction called the *zapev* which sets the stage with huge, imaginative descriptions of nature, out of which the *bilinï* narratives arise almost imperceptibly. Sometimes *bilinï* begin with a question, such as, "Who knows the *bilinï* about Ilya Murometz; who knows the stories of the past?"

The melodies are often performed differently by different singers, and are not connected to specific texts. The stories progress through highly patterned melodies, punctuated with recurring phrases that serve as cadences. Many of the melodies only use a few notes. When they are expressing strong emotion, they often rise to a higher pitch, but otherwise they are extremely stable, especially the final phrases. This distinguishes them from the Ukrainian *duma*, which tend to have freer variations (see opposite). The wandering singers, poets, and *bilinï* tellers accompanied themselves on a *gusle*, a cithern-like instrument. There are many variants of the *gusle*, some of which are similar in appearance to the *kantele* (see Chapter 7, p. 136).

The History of the *Bilinï*

Bilinï were sung all over Russia. In addition to the northern monophonic type used in the example, there were polyphonic *bilinï*, and *bilinï* with instrumental accompaniment from central and southern Russia. The only place where the *bilinï* lived on until modern times was in northern Russia near

Archangel. These were the *bilinï* that were annotated and recorded. This area is also where the name *bilinï* arose in the 1840s. It is thought to have come from the Russian word for "what has been." According to the singers from Archangel it means "the old things." This is now the accepted interpretation.

In earlier times, *bilinï* were familiar all over northern Russia, and were sung at work. When the fishermen were free, they would gather their boats into a circle and the best singer would begin to sing his story.

Until quite recently, peasants and fishermen thought the *bilinï* recounted true history. All they knew of ancient Russia were warrior heroes, bold and courageous, terrible to meet in combat, but kind and protective of the weak.

The origins of the *bilinï* are shrouded in the mist of history. Some scholars believe that the early *bilinï* were medieval heroic songs performed at the royal courts, and that when they began to be outmoded as real history among the boyars, they were taken over by the peasantry and mythologized. Although historians have identified real people and places in these old songs, no one considers them a reliable historical source.

Later, the *bilinï* were "discovered" by the intellectual middle classes (see Chapter 1). Early collections were made by devoted amateurs. In eighteenth- and nineteenth-century manuscripts, *bilinï* are mixed with prose narratives describing ancient Russian heroes. During that early period of collecting, many scholars were driven by the idea that the simple peasants had a set of morals, a language, and a lifestyle that could serve as an ideal for the depraved aristocracy.

In nineteenth-century northern Russia there were still families that specialized in singing the *bilinï*. The songs were passed down from father to son and mother to daughter. *Bilinï* singers had to be over the age of 40 before they were allowed to perform. Not until then were they considered to have sufficient wisdom and knowledge.

The *bilinï* have become part of the Russian national culture, not unlike the *Kalevala* in Finland. At the beginning of Glinka's opera *Rusland and Ludmilla*, a Russian storyteller appears with his *gusle*, telling tales of Russian heroes and their traditional feats, a kind of Russian Homer. Reinhold Glière's symphony No. 3, op. 42 (1909–11) also portrays Ilya Muromez, the *bilinï* hero.

УСТЬ-ЦИЛЕМСКИЙ РАЙОН
СТАРИНА ПРО СТАРА КАЗАКА ИЛЬЮ МУРОМЦА
(К тексту 35)

Figure 4.6. *bïlinï* from 1961, p. 501 no. 1.

The Ukrainian *Duma*

The Ukrainian narrative song is referred to as the *duma* (or sometimes *dumka*, plural *dumy* or *dumky*). Although it bears a relation to *bïlinï*, it also has many independent stylistic features.

Singing the *Duma*

Many *dumy* begin with a special melodic motif, a *zaplatjka*, which both sets the atmosphere for the coming narrative and delimits the musical material (i.e., the notes to be used). This introductory *zaplatjka* is sung without instrumental accompaniment after a few initial chords on the *bandura* or short melodic phrases on the hurdy-gurdy. These are the traditional instruments for accompanying *dumy* (see also Chapter 7 on instruments). The real story, the *ustupi*, begins after the *zaplatjka*, and is interspersed with instrumental passages. A *duma* concludes with a virtuoso instrumental solo.

Duma melodies, (Figure 4.8a–d), like *bïlinï*, are highly structured, often with the range of a fifth or a fourth. In particularly dramatic passages, however, the range is expanded to an octave or more,

and the pitch also rises so that the voice of the singer tenses up The recitative song is extremely melismatic, with the augmented second serving an important function. Instrumental accompaniment is central to the performance.

A *duma* has four parts: (a) the introductory *zaplatjka*, (b) the "sigh," a recitative on a single note, (c) a more melodic recitative, and (d) an embellished final formula. The lines of verse may vary in length from a few syllables to nearly twenty. The *duma* is often in a kind of Dorian mode with a raised fourth, which gives the melody an exotic flavor that "helps to stress the text, describing the suffering of the Cossacks under the Turks" (*New Grove* 19, p. 411). The melody in Figure 4.9 illustrates the way in which *duma* melodies have affected the structure of other Ukrainian folk music, in this case a lyrical song. In some respects, the *duma* is related to the lament, and Ukrainian laments are known as *dumak*, a diminutive form of *dumka*. Nineteenth-century composers, particularly Polish and Bohemian ones, were inspired to write instrumental music reflecting the special sound of the Ukraininan lament. Dvorák's *Dumky* Trio, op. 90 (1890–1891), is an example.

Figure 4.7. Ilya Murmometz on his way to Kiev. Along the road he meets Solovey the robber. (a) He outwiles him and arrives as the palace of Prince Vladimir (b). Amateur drawings from 1952. (*bilinï*, 1960)

The History of the Duma

While the *bilinï* is thought to have originated in the early Middle Ages, scholars date the origin of the *duma* to the fifteenth and sixteenth centuries. Initially, these were political songs, written by the *kobzars*, professional folk singers who played the *bandura* or *lira* who were part of military expeditions and revolts, and whose function was to encourage the participants to resistance and action.

A *duma* may describe a war. For example, the invasion of the Tatar lands by the Turks or the later seventeenth-century invasion of Poland. A *duma* may also describe social injustice, portraying right and wrong with a strong sense of morality. There are even *dumy* about the October Revolution. Perhaps they were once improvised with the aid of the kind of "poetics" that scholars believe to have been used when runic songs and *bilinï* came into being. However, the preserved versions appear to be more like narrative epics, passed down through the oral tradition, than improvizations. Where has this wealth of tradition gone? In his memoirs, Shostakovich wrote:

> Since time immemorial folk singers have wandered along the roads of Ukraine. They're called *lirniki* and *banduristi* there. They were always blind men—why that is so is another question I won't go into, but briefly, it's traditional. The point is, they were always blind and defenseless people, but no one ever touched or hurt them. Hurting a blind man—what could be lower?
>
> And then in the mid-thirties the First All-Ukrainian Congress of Lirniki and Banduristy was announced, and all the folk singers had to gather and discuss what to do in the future. 'Life is better, life is merrier,' Stalin had said. The blind men believed it. They came to the Congress from all over the Ukraine, from tiny, forgotten villages. There were several hundred of them at the Congress, they say, It was a living museum, the country's living history; all its songs, all its music and poetry. And they were almost all shot, almost all those pathetic blind men killed.(Volkov 1979, p. 165.)

According to Shostakovich, the players of the *bandura* and *lira* were not the only wandering minstrels to meet with this fate: the 1920s and 30s were the period when "our great national art heritage was destroyed."

Istoria ukrainskoj musiki (1981) indicates that the economic and social changes in the later nineteenth century had a negative impact on folk music, but that the impact of the October Revolution was positive.

Before we embark on a general survey of the origins, age, and tradition of the types of narrative song presented here, let us examine one type of heroic song that lived on (in relative isolation) well into the twentieth century.

NARRATIVE SONG IN THE BALKANS

The Perfomance of Heroic Songs

Although the runic song, the *bilinï*, and the *duma* were more or less obsolete by the time collection and recording began, Balkan narrative song was

Figure 4.8. Ukrainian *duma* (Gordintjuk 1979, p. 18 f.) (a) *Zaplatija*, (b) simple recitative, (c) melodic recitative, and (d) embellished final formula.

Figure 4.9. Uraininan folk melody influenced by the structure of the *duma*. (Gordintjuk 1979, p. 31.)

still being written and changed far enough into the twentieth century for it to be studied, both in terms of compositional creativity and the melodic and textual limits in performance.

Heroic songs from the Balkans were closely intertwined with the *gusle* (see p. 138). The Balkan singer accompanied himself on this instrument, (apart from the rare occasions when heroic songs were performed unaccompanied) in situations of work or travel. It was also very rare for the singer to be accompanied by another person. No other instrument ever competed successfully with the classic *gusle* for accompaniment of heroic songs.

Instrumental Accompaniment on the *Gusle*

Heroic songs open with an instrumental introduction. The *gusle* player holds the instrument angled vertically between his knees, with the fingers of his left hand on the string. Without pressing the string to the neck of the instrument, he plays a kind of harmonic, producing the unique sound of the *gusle*. Once the player (the *guslar*) has the "feel" of the instrument, he finds a suitable opening pitch for the song. The accompaniment then follows the various melodic and rhythmic variations of the

song which, in turn, is restricted by the pitch, determined as described above by the position of the fingers on the neck of the *gusle*. Only five notes are used.

Transcribing the actual performance of a heroic song is a highly complex process, since neither the song nor the accompaniment observe the rules governing traditional notation. Moreover, the performance is a matter of intricate interplay between text and music, and between instrument and song, which no attempt to put on paper could do justice (Figure 4.10). Still, transcription may be the only way to attempt to describe the internal mechanisms of this type of song. As the notation indicates, the voice is far more mobile than the *gusle*, which occasionally bursts into quick complex phrases in the vocal rest at the end of a verse (Figure 4.11). When *guslars* came into contact with music adapted to the tempered scale, they "corrected" their intervals by changing to ordinary whole tones and semitones. Musicologists have mourned this adaptation, regarding the change as a kind of "levelling."

This transition from traditional local audiences to urban European or Europeanized ones is in full swing among *gursle* propagandists known as *nova intonacija*, and what *gursle* player would not like to have such an honorable and profitable status? (Wünsch 1934, pp. 53f.)

These are the chromatic *guslars* we have heard on recordings ever since the 1930s, referred to scornfully by Wünsch as "village tenors."

Singing and Performance

The melodic core of these songs consists of three notes with the range of a minor third, d^1–f^1. Normally, the singer begins on the second note, e^1. This is the basic narrative note, and as the song increases in intensity, it is replaced by a higher narrative note. The pitch is varied constantly, depending on the dramatic content of the song, shifting upwards in exciting parts and downwards in calmer ones. This is clearest in the alternation between the two narrative notes. The higher one, the auxiliary note, is reached either step by step or in a leap. It is sung loudly, and its length varies with the dramatic intensity of the song. When special emphasis is needed, the singer may jump to a higher pitch.

Except for the two narrative notes, the other notes are ornamental. Every syllable is accorded one note, and there is a characteristic descent at the end of each verse. The performance of these songs is so dramatic that sometimes syllables may be dropped at the end of a verse or a new line suddenly inserted, abruptly interrupting what might have been an instrumental interlude. But the listener does not get lost, because the established pattern is always in place. The singer also uses a great deal of body language to emphasize the dramatic passages. There are many detailed, animate descriptions of this kind of performance, with the singer accelerating or slowing down, raising and lowering the pitch, stressing important individual words, relating to the audience as an actor, and miming the story. Heroic actions and successful revenge are described with head held high, chest inflated, and grave facial expressions. On very dramatic occasions, the singer's voice can rise by as much as an octave. The performance varies from simple recitative to ordinary singing. Textually, groups of verses are characterized by parallelisms, repetitions, assonance, end rhymes, and concluding refrains. The rhythm is entirely contingent on the metric structure of the text which is

Figure 4.10. This transcription was made by Béla Bartók after a recording made by Milman Parry and Albert B. Lord during a collection journey in Yugoslavia in 1934–35. Their collection contains some 350 epic poems, performed by 90 singers in 23 villages. Bartók made the following comment on this transcription of the performance of Ibrahim Massinovic: "The player usually uses the index, second and fourth finger on his left hand, but seldom the third finger. The singer of no. 34 only used the first finger, and thus only played one note (an A) in addition to the tone of the open string (a G). The G clearly functioned as a final tone, which appears to have been an established rule of *gusle* playing, confirmed by hundreds of examples. . ." (p. 240 f).

This song is about Himziberg the hero, who goes into battle accompanied by two fellow Albanians. He survives two battles, but is injured in the third, and sends his horse back to his mother and his sword and watch to his brother.

decasyllabic with a central cesura. This is intuitively imprinted on the mind of the singer, and can be compared with the way in which a speaker knows grammatical rules. Different rhythmic groups may crystallize, usually containing three to four units.

After a certain number of verses, the alternation between dramatic and lyrical passages comes to a climax. The dramatic gradations of melody and text are not necessarily parallel. Sometimes there is the impression of a dialogue between them, in which one party can surprise the other with an

HALILI QET NGA BURGU NË KRAJLI BYTEMET ALINË

AIKP. bob. 244/1
Mbledhur: Q. Haxhihasani
Transkrip: B. Kruta

Këndoi: M. Ndou
Palaj — Shkodër, 1963

Figure 4.11. Benjamin Krutas' transcription of the opening phrase of an Albanian heroic song. This song had both an instrumental *gusle* introduction and an embellished interval. Compared with the previous example, the *gusle* thus played a more prominent role. Krutas' transcription is more schematic than Bartók's, and more intended for use by musicians than for detailed musicological analysis. (Kruta 1984, p. 113.)

unexpected message. This further enhances the artistic intensity of the song.

It may be the very fact that there are so few functional notes that makes it possible to perform long epic poems to music. The singer can shape the dramatic performance using a limited number of recurring modes, each of which has its own characteristic pitch. The audience knows what is coming and can easily follow and empathize with the action. By making them both stable and flexible the structure of the texts also made it possible for these heroic songs to go on for hours before captive audiences.

The Contents and Evironment of Heroic Songs

These Balkan folk epics center around the family, the extended family, and the clan. Events focus on heroic exploits, just as in the *Kalevala* or the *bilini* and *duma* songs. Until the nineteenth century, life was very much like it had always been, with tightly knit families and clans and a strong patriarchy. And as long as these heroic songs remained a living art form, new ones were written about the heroes of every generation. For example, there were songs glorifying the partisans during World War II, with tanks and machine guns replacing horses, bows, and arrows. The traditions surrounding the he-

roic song can be traced back to medieval literary sources, and their themes reflect the collective memory of the people. The world-view of these songs is that of the solitary warrior, upstanding and candid, in the best cases just and fair, but often implacably vengeful.

In a country constantly plagued by invaders and bandits, it is logical for the myth of the solitary hero to survive, changing shape as times and ways of life change. The people fled from their oppressors to the inaccessible mountains. This was where the *haiduks* launched their attacks for centuries against the Ottomans, as did the partisans against the Germans in World War II. They all had the heroic songs ringing in their ears.

Heroic songs are still being written today, but the tradition has been substantially transformed and no longer cultivates the individual aspects of improvisation. Rather, it has become a fixed melody with poems reflecting the identity and history of the region or nation. Three different heroic cultures are distinguished: the patriarchal culture rooted in the Dinarian Alps, the *haiduk* groups, and the Muslim knights in Bosnia and Herzegovina, who were allowed to retain their feudal rights under the control of the Turks and lived with this medieval form of government until World War I. Each group had its own forms of heroic songs (Braun 1961).

The intent of the heroic poems is realism, but they glorify reality for the enlightenment of the listener and to incorporate the ideals of heroism. The elevated nature and uniqueness of the songs are also evident in the language used by the singer in the structured improvisations on old words and expressions, a long tradition sometimes even incomprehensible to the singer himself. The language of the songs was a sort of written language for illiterates, an artistic, linguistic expression of war, love, and everyday life.

> O mountain, my ancestral home,
> How many times have I crossed you,
> And led a band of heroes,
> And carried the heroes' standard!
> Many a mother have I made to mourn,
> But especially Mujo's mother.
> I slew her son Mujo,
> and forced his father
> To roast his own son,
> And I forced his mother

To eat her own son's flesh,
And I forced his sisters
To dance for him,
And to sing songs for Mujo!
                    (Bartók/Lord 1951, p. 263, no. 5)

Blow, blow cold wind!
Come to me beloved,
Into my white dwelling!
Bring your white horse with you,
and tie him a branch of the rose tree.
Let the rose envelope him in its fragrance,
And let his spirit be filled with longing.
                    (Bartók/Lord 1951, p. 263, no. 4)

These poems were never gathered into a coherent epic, which tends to happen when the singers become literate and begin to write down songs for themselves or their pupils. Later, literary versions appear. In cultures where this has happened, we know that both the improvised aspects of the song and the memories of the singers have undergone a process of change.

An oral song tradition almost never has long, firmly structured cycles. It is, by nature, improvised, but bound to a set of models, themes, etc., and its framework is free-verse meter and flexible melodic structures, as found in the Balkan heroic poems.

In Bulgaria, Romania, Greece, Georgia, Turkey, and Albania, there are variations on this kind of improvised, heroic poetry, exemplified here in versions from Serbo-Croatia and other parts of the former Yugoslavia. In parts of Albania, a home without a *gusle* (or *laouta*) is known as an "abandoned home" (Miso 1985, p. 194, see also Chapter 7). The transcriptions published in Albanian scholarly journals are far simpler than the ones given here, which has both advantages and disadvantages. Although they indicate less about the complex internal structures, for instance, they are easier to overview. This is an advantage not least if, as in Albania, there is an aspiration for the heroic song to survive, to glorify even present-day heroes (see Figure 4.11, p. 89).

NARRATIVE SONG IN THE WEST

During the feudal era, heroic poetry was an important art form in the west as well. We find it,

for example, in the medieval *chanson de geste*. There are extant texts of heroic ballads from the Irish and Scottish medieval courts, but very little is known about the melodies. It is assumed that they were sometimes sung to familiar popular melodies, often of sacred origin. There were texts and melodies at many levels of society. There is a strain of Scottish heroic poetry from the late seventeenth century, for example, in which the heroes were the clan chieftains.

The Irish *Sean-nós*

The ancient style of narrative song from Ireland, the *sean-nós*, still exists today. These songs were performed by a soloist, in Irish Gaelic. Poets in this narrative song tradition can be traced back to the early eighteenth century. As was the case with the corresponding Balkan songs, the audience reacted to the singing at performances with stereotyped shouts or joking comments. The historic narratives were sometimes local, sometime religious, and sometimes more like songs of work. They have been regarded as "the shared experiences and hopes of the audience"(O'Canainn 1975, p. 80). *Sean-nós* melodies were embellished either melismatically, with added intervals, or rhythmically. Some singers gave more emphasis to the words than the melody, while others developed an expressive interplay between the two.

Sean-nós Performance

At an official folk music festival in Ennis (on the west coast of Ireland) in the summer of 1988, a ten-year-old girl took the stage as soon as the formal opening ceremony had been completed. She was all alone on the stage, in a frilly pink dress, with black patent leather shoes and curly hair. Suddenly, without so much as a gesture, she began to sing. Out poured a song, a traditional Irish *sean-nós*, sung in Gaelic (as it must to be truly authentic). Because of this language restriction, the tradition has lived on only in the linguistic communities that have refused to accept English as their first language.

Not only is the *sean-nós* alive and well, it appears to be growing and changing. *Sean-nós* are sung by both young and old as part of the nationalist sentiment that also includes spreading and encouraging the use of Gaelic in everyday life. The *sean-*

nós is performed in a different way from the ordinary ballad, in that single notes are made unique and embellished in a way reminiscent of old folk chorales. O' Canainn (1978) interviewed a prominent *sean-nós* singer, Diarmuid O'Súillebháin, who defined the *sean-nós* as follows:

> Well, it's the kind of thing that's very hard to define. Can I put it this way—when I hear it I think I recognize it, but I don't think it's easy to put into words. For any kind of singing a good voice is desirable but it's not necessarily the most important thing in traditional singing. The overall style is what matters—the approach to the song and, of course, the song itself. I don't know—take for example a simple thing like breathing. If you take a breath at the end of every line, like a child reciting poetry, it becomes boring after a very short while. That's one thing, for example, running the lines into each other. Then there are various ways of making emphasis that are not used in classical singing or that kind of thing. A person doesn't have to raise his voice to emphasise something—he can pause before it or after it or say it in a certain way. Then, of course, there are the various ornamentations, double ornaments and so on. You can slide from one note to another and perhaps flatten a note somewhat or even shorten (sharpen?) it according to the meaning of the song. All these sort of things together are style: they don't all have to be in one song but some of them should be evident together to make a unit that I would recognise as something worthwhile. (O'Canainn 1978, p. 113.)

O' Canainn's transcription of O'Súillebháin's song (Figure 4.12), is an illustrative example of exactly what the singer describes. The breaths, marked by a V, are not at the end of the verses. The stressed syllables in the text are sung on long, unembellished notes. The letters A, B, C, and D mark five different phrases in the song. These are varied in different ways.

The Icelandic rímur

The Icelandic *rímur* has been selected for detailed investigation as an example of western narrative song. It has been studied in depth by the Danish folk music scholar, Svend Nielsen (1978).

Nielsen regards the *rímur* as a branch of the tree which also includes the southern Slavic epic, the Russian *bilini*, the runic song, and Irish and Scottish narrative song.

Nielsen uses the concept of "intonation," as applied by his Danish colleague Thorkild Knudsen, to characterize the unique melodic structural features of folk singing. (Compare the concept as it is similarly used by Zemtsovsky and other Russian scholars.)

This concept implies that the metric structure of the text determines the choice of melodic structure. Parts of performances may sound very much like ordinary singing, while others are much more in the style of Icelandic *kvede* poetry. (The verb *kvedha* denotes a manner of singing associated with the performance of *rímur* (see below).) Nielsen's informant was Thordur Gudbjartsson (b. 1891). Thordur's performance technique remained unchanged throughout the eight year period when Nielsen was collecting and analyzing his *rímur*—the melodic structures remained identical from year to year. This is attributable to the fact that his *kvede* style used only a limited number of melodic phrases or intonations, each one belonging to a certain line in the verse. There are intonations for the beginning and end of each verse, and there are special combinations of patterns. Thordur learned this *kvede* technique in his childhood from older singers. He said that some of the melodic phrases he used were ones he had learned, while others were his own invention. His familiarity with all these intonations and with the grammar of the *kvede* style made it possible for him to perform any text at any time in that style. He would vary his musical patterns just like any improvising musician, whether jazz, rock, or classical. Some intonations occurred much more often than others. According to Nielsen, Gudbjartsson simply gave priority to the intonations he had in mind at the moment, leaving others more dormant. When Thordur took up a particular intonation at the beginning of a song, it would then recur in verse after verse. This is the technique that gives the *kvede* form its stability. It also explains why some stylistic traits are prominent at one performance, only to be absent altogether from another. Nielsen also noted that Thordur tended to begin his *kvede* on the third note in the scale, to give himself more freedom to choose intonations.

Rímur Performance

Thordur kept a distance from the narrative. The *rímur* performed in *kvede* style, like the Russian *bilini* but unlike the Balkan heroic songs, was "ob-

Figure 4.12. "Cuil Duibh-Re," a song in the *sean-nós* style performed by Diarmuid O'Súilleabháin from the west of Cork, transcribed by Tomás O'Canainn (1978, p.114). The song begins with a lament over the sad and gloomy River Lee, a tragic sight in comparison with Ireland's finest river, the Gaortha, and its paradisical surroundings. It ends with a song in praise of Toon.

jective," giving the listener freedom to choose his own interpretation and attitude towards the narrative. Because Thordur did not base his intonations on those of ordinary language, we have no reason to think that spoken language was used as a basis for this technique.

Nielsen registered performances using different types of melody-writer, in an attempt to distinguish between recitation, *kvede*, and song. In the examples given here, (Figure 4.13) prepared at the Department of Musicology at Uppsala University in 1971, the upper line indicates pitch, the lower one volume. Nielsen's description of how the *rímur* was performed is based on analyses of such registrations, as well as interviews and his own efforts to render music in the *kvede* style. He characterized *rímur* melodies as follows:

Verses performed in the *kvede* style have the following fixed patterns of meter and structure:

1. The "*kvedha*" notes are longer than the spoken sequences, but shorter than the sung syllables.
2. The length of vowels varies, while conso-

nants are more stable. It is the length of the vowels that determines the tonal character, since vowels carry the tone.
3. The shift from one syllable to the next is often unclear.
4. The *kvede* notes are tremulous, and fluctuate by up to a semitone.
5. There is a kind of vibrato on the final note, which is held.
6. Although the pitch of each individual tone is often in the shape of one or more "arches," it is possible to discern various tonal steps. In other words, there are fixed limits to pitch positions. However, our perception of the *kvede* song is deeply affected by our tendency to interpret what we hear as being in or out of tune.

The *Rímur* Texts

The *rímur* texts are long narratives in verse, based on the Icelandic sagas and other stories. The bard shaped the story into the molds supplied by the various complex meters or invented a new meter of his own, which became the basis of a new *rímur*. The art of the *rímur* was invented in the fourteenth century, probably inspired by the French narrative verse tradition as well as the Icelandic sagas. In the art form of the *rímur*, historic events from different eras are reflected. The *rímur* are also unique in that they have been preserved in written form since the very beginning. They reached the height of their popularity in the early nineteenth century, at which time they also began to be transformed into a more antiquated, historical genre. There is evidence that the *rímur* were once danced to (cf. the Faroese ballads). Later, they were entertainment for long winters' evenings. One person sang the *kvede* while the others listened.

Reception of the *Rímur*

It was often the case that the listeners of a *rímur* would pick up the last syllable of the verse and hold it while the singer prepared for the next one. Even today, the singer always holds the final note.

Travelers from intellectual circles were unable to appreciate this peculiar technique. For example, after a visit to Iceland in the mid-eighteenth century, Danish mathematician Niels Horeboe wrote,

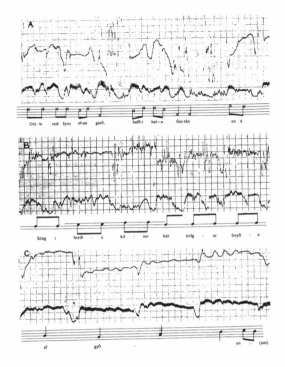

Figure 4.13. An example of Svend Nielsen's registration of the *rímur*, carried out at the Department of Musicology, Uppsala University, using the MONA melody writer. (Re: MONA, see also Bengtsson et al. 1972, p. 107.)

Their only entertainment, on the occasions when they are served a meal, is to whine the old Icelandic heroic ballads, of which they know quite a number. These are performed to a rather crude melody, as they know nothing about music and have no instruments. . . . (Bergendal, 1986)

The eighteenth-century Icelandic authorities considered the text and name of the *rímur* shameful, and during the nineteenth century it was considered unworthy of the efforts of singers. Not until the late nineteenth century, when the *rímur* tradition had begun to disintegrate, did it begin to be written down and thus revived. Bjarni Thorsteinsson's notations were published in *Islendsk thójdhlög* in 1906–1909. This collection contains no less than 250 *rímur* transcriptions. This collection, along with recordings, provided the basis for the current revival of the *rímur* in Iceland, where it is cultivated at special *rímur* clubs.

SIMILARITIES, RELATIONSHIPS, AND ORIGINS IN THE HEROIC SONG TRADITION

If we compare the different kinds of narrative song described above, we can see certain similarities of theme as well as of tone and rhythm of performance. However, there are also great disparities between the traditions.

Most of the genres of narrative songs can be regarded as art forms, developed in order to pass along insights and knowledge to others, via the oral tradition, about history, nature, and contemporary society. The pitches and rhythms gave the stories added dimensions of drama, excitement, and beauty.

The epic songs appear to have followed the regulations established by tradition with regard to verse meter, standard expressions, and the other repeated regularities that endowed the improvized narratives with a structure. The choice of motifs for these traditional songs was also restricted, which further contributed to their uniformity.

Seen as a whole, the narratives shaped an oral vision of the world that was successively destroyed as written world visions made their entry. They focused on glorification of power, but not on that of the traditional heroes. Thus it was only in illiterate peasant communities that these heroic narratives survived. Gradually, owing to the work of the collectors and their ideological reinterpretations, the songs were transformed from living renditions of history in song to a part of the poetic "folk" heritage. The Russian *bilinï* appears to have undergone this change as early as the eighteenth century. Although the Balkan heroic songs were strongly influenced by other musical cultures, they retained their ability to depict even the heroes of modern society in the form of heroic song.

Ghizela Suliteanu (1985), a Romanian folk musicologist, claimed that contemporary Greek and Romanian music folklore contains elements from the ancient, classical Mediterranean cultures. She saw this as confirmed in the Romanian folk ballad, where she found not only typological and ethnic relationships with Homeric epic poetry but also historical connections.

In this chapter, beginning with the Scandinavian *jojk*, we have followed the principles of melodic regularities. They follow the lines of the verses, varying according to the intentions of the singer, often with a descending fifth serving as the core tonal material. The question, then, is whether the similarities are necessarily explained by a shared tradition and its subsequent dissemination. Could it, instead, be the presentation technique, related to performance of oral narrative for an audience when the interplay between words and music are not yet defined by written conventions? Over time, epic song became a fixed art form, with memorized texts and firmly structured melodies, the purpose of which was to serve as a collective memory rather than a dramatic instrument. It was then turned to the service first of the bourgeoisie and later of the socialist state as historical symbol of the right to freedom and grandeur of the past.

Once the structures were in place, the epics were successively standardized instead of improvised, and became folk songs in which were expected expressive melodies far from the simple regular ones that made the narrative song unique. Thus fixed melodic structure was one of the signs of the changes a narrative song went through once it began imitating the pattern of music based on written notes. Let us now follow this change in another case of standardization from narrative song to ballad.

BALLADS IN EAST AND WEST

Western Europe also had its medieval epic song tradition. However, the tradition appears to have withered in the thirteenth and fourteenth centuries, giving way to shorter songs of a different, more dramatic nature. These were presented as little scenes, in which family troubles, historic events, and traditional motifs passed by, sometimes as brief, sententious descriptions, sometimes as dramatic dialogues. The songs consisted of verses which, in the English and Scottish tradition, were concluded (and sometimes divided up) by refrains. Some— but far from all—of these ballads were danced to, as their names indicate. In other words, it is actually inappropriate to classify the entire genre as *ballads*, but the term is so accepted today that it would be difficult to replace it, not unlike the term *folk music*, also too widely applied. The genre has different names in different countries. It is known

as the *romance* in France, Portugal and Spain, and in earlier Swedish literature it was simply referred to as the *folk song*. The term *ballad* has thus long been used as a neutral term covering the entire genre all over Europe.

Some of the ballads that have been preserved are similar to the free renditions of a story from the Balkans described above. As time passed, however, the texts were frequently written in advance, and composed melodies correspondingly replaced the more improvised type of performance we saw in the Balkan heroic songs. There is no clear line of demarcation between this older kind of epic song and the ballad. For example, there are numerous *bilinis* which are to be regarded more as dramatic ballads than as epic songs.

New ballads were constantly being written and added to the original tradition, beginning in the sixteenth century and were often published. In the eighteenth century a form of literature known as the *ballad* arose as well. Today, people associate the term *ballad* with all kinds of music. Depending on their own musical taste, twentieth-century ballads can be performed as jazz, folk music, or rock. Below, the definition of the term *ballad* is restricted to mean only songs directly or indirectly rooted in the medieval narrative song tradition. A ballad is also an integral part of the tradition of composed, lyrical folk songs. The line of demarcation chosen here has been set only for practical reasons, and is not to be regarded as rooted in the aesthetic philosophy of performers.

Carriers of the Ballad Tradition

In contrast to the epic song tradition, where the performers were men, the art of the ballad belongs mainly to women, who were also the composers of most of its traditional songs.

For this reason, let us begin with two women singers from different eras and classes. The first is Anna Gordon Brown, a minister's wife. She was born in 1747 in Aberdeen, Scotland, where she also died, in 1810. The other is Svea Jansson, a Finnish-Swedish housekeeper, born in 1904 on the island of Nötö in the Tuurku archipelago of Finland and died 1980 in Västergötland, Sweden. Each of them contributed a melody to the collection of tunes to which *Herr Olof and the Elves* could be performed (see Figure 4.14).

Anna Gordon Brown was the daughter of a

professor at King's College, Aberdeen. She learned the ballads in her childhood, both from one of her maternal aunts and from her old nurse. Anna Brown wrote down her texts herself, and received help in writing down the melodies. She was also a poet in her own right. Sir Walter Scott contacted her when he was studying the Middle Ages, and Brown noted down given melody on more than one occasion. Bertrand H. Bronson (1969) compared two of the versions and concluded that she was not operating on the basis of a single, fixed version, but rather "a fluid entity that was integrated into her intellect, and could be called to mind as words and music when she wished" (Bronson 1969, p. 71). According to Bronson, Brown represents the type of singer who gives birth to a new work of art at every performance, combining given models of lyrics and music differently each time. This explains why there is no "original." The original is created by the individual who notes down the song as performed. This version is then "frozen" for posterity. Brown constantly re-created her songs, altering the material at each performance, in accordance with her inclinations of the moment.

Swedish musicologist Märta Ramsten (1981) has depicted three great women singers, one of whom is Svea Jansson. Svea had a repertoire of some thousand songs, and she continued to learn new ones throughout her life. Like Anna Brown, she wrote her texts down. Her repertoire included singing and dancing games, love songs in the folk tradition, shanties, comic songs, lyrical love songs, ballads, psalms, and, later in life, popular hits. Twenty-two ballads are included in the more than six hundred songs recorded by Matts Arnberg on behalf of the Swedish Broadcasting Corporation in 1964. Svea Jannson is also available on disc (Caprice CAP 1156). She sings perfectly in tune, with a very straightforward style and with great emphasis on the words. She alters neither the melodies nor the texts, but renders them identically from performance to performance. This distinguishes her as a singer from Anna Brown. Svea's strength was in exact preservation and rendering of a tradition, rather than in recreation.

The History of the Ballad

There are conflicting theories in research on the origins of the ballad. One school of research asserts that a ballad began as a new creation and later became a sort of model; ultimately a final version was accepted and passed down. The other school opposes this theory, claiming that a ballad was a single "work," created once and for all and then varied—and often mutilated—by rough treatment over time. There has been a great deal of speculation as to the origins of the ballad, particularly whether they began as formal, written works of art or as improvized folk songs and poetry. It is possible that a detailed study of the melodies can shed light on this issue. Bertrand Bronson has made several such detailed studies.

Although it appears difficult to be more precise than providing general descriptions of ballad melodies, the situation changes radically if we concentrate on the ballads of a given region (see p. 99, summarizing Vargyas's study of Hungarian ballad melodies). It therefore seems questionable whether studies of melodies can elucidate the eternal question of whether ballads are formal works of art or improvised folk music. In fact, the question itself is somewhat dubious, because here as elsewhere we have the constant and paradoxical interplay between the written and the oral cultural traditions.

Indeed, much of the conflict between improvising or memorizing a ballad may not be as great as certain researchers claim. The question seems related more to ideology than to historical research. Some historical scholars insist that there must be one originator from whose work the tradition emanates, whereas others claim that each time a musical or textual idea is performed, a work is born. It seems very difficult for us to depart from the latter view in which the ballad, in its performance, is a complete occurrence. The interplay between performer and audience, the spirit of the times, and social components are central to an understanding of the textual and musical structure of the individual ballad.

Comparative Studies of Melodies

The transcribed version of a melody only provides us with a very rough picture of the real performance. Still, a traditional comparison of transcribed ballad melodies might help us to answer the specific question of the development of melodies. Another approach, exemplified in the study by Ramsten (1981), is to study the repertoire of individual singers (see Rosenblad 1986).

Figure 4.14. (1) *Norske Folkeviser* 1853XL, p. 355; (2) Thuren/Grüner-Nielsen 1923; (3–13) *Dgf* XI: 1976, 47 1–11; (14) *SMB* 29 E; (15) *SMB* 29 Ga; (16) *SMB* 29 K; (17) *SMB* 29 L; (18) Child ballad no. 42:1, 2; (19) Thuren 1908, p. 99 no. 20a.

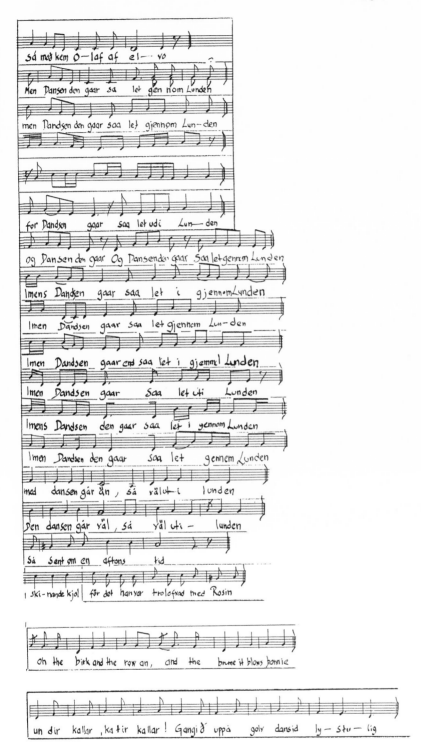

Figure 4.14 cont'd. Melodies for *Herr Olof and the Elves*.

Let us begin by concentrating on one single ballad performed in various countries (mainly Scandinavian) to many melodies. This ballad is *Herr Olof and the Elves*, about which a great deal has been written and discussed.

One traditional way of examining ballad melodies is to investigate them in relation to a single text. This method makes it possible to discuss whether or not the text and the melody can be separated, whether older kinds of texts are associated with older ways of performing, etc. However, the methods also have disadvantages, including the loss of contact with the individual performer, who becomes an anonymous supplier of an aesthetic and social unit. We attempt to put forth this kind of synopsis of the melody of a given text in Figure 4.14. (See previous page.)

The melodies surveyed here come from the Faeroe Islands, Denmark, Norway, and Sweden. There is also one English ballad, "Clerk Colven," the story of which is very similar to *Herr Olof and the Elves*. Five of the melodies can be distinguished in form from the rest. Four of them have internal refrains and one, the English ballad, has four-line verses and a final refrain. The melodies of the four songs with internal refrains are based on brief melodic motifs, a kind of melodic cell. The danced version from the Faeroe Islands is also regular in structure, based on motifs with three and five notes (no. 19). The characteristic motif of the Norwegian version (no. 1) is a melodic cell consisting of a major third plus a minor second and vice versa, as in the first phrase of the refrain, which has the order Bb'-a'-f#'-g', with a change of register after the refrain. The last line of each verse and the final refrain all have the same melodic motif, ending "open" and "closed," respectively. No. 16 is also based on regular motifs, but its melody has been shaped more holistically, either by the individual who noted it down or by tradition. No. 17 is also more of a whole, despite the fact that it was noted down by a less experienced annotator. Nos. 16 and 17 are both in minor keys and are typical in many ways of older Swedish songs, both ballads and lyrical love songs, such as in the motif: e'-g#'-a'-b'-c²-d², which centers around b'. These two melodies also contain a very common phrase in Nordic folk music, namely c²-b'-g'. Most of the Danish melodies appear to be of one and the same type, leaning towards the major (nos. 3–6, 9, 10), while others have more clearly structured melodic cells (nos.

7, 8). The motifs of the refrain are more closely related to one another than those of the verses.

The English melody, as transcribed by Anna Brown, contains only one single motif, repeated alternately as open and closed lines of verse. The refrain consists of two repeated motifs. This is the only melody that has been preserved in the English tradition. The melodies of *Herr Olof and the Elves* include both those that appear to be fixed structures that have developed, and those in major or minor keys or closely related tonalities. It is difficult to decide whether there is a relationship to the *rímur* melodies (see p. 92) or whether this is a case of a fixed, structured melody. As in most instances we only have access to one version of the melody. Probably it is the latter (i.e., a strophic song in which the same recognizable, holistic shape is retained), although the melody varies from one verse to another.

Performance

Thorkild Knudsen has considered whether the form of the ballad might not be contingent on its means of performance. It is his opinion that both the Faeroese and Danish ballads were originally sung while danced in line dances (see also p. 184), and that they were not only used for dancing on special occasions but were also sung in the evenings when members of a household sat together carving, carding, spinning, etc. The Danish word for these evening activities was *kvöldseta*, and the songs were referred to as *kvöldsædeviser* (evening-sitting songs). According to Knudsen, in the *kvöldsædeviser*, the narrative is more concentrated, the tempo shifts more frequent, and the rhythm less monotonous than in the danced ballads (see Knudsen 1961). However, the ballads from places other than the Faeroe Islands may never have been used for dancing but originated strictly as sung ballads.

The Faeroese *kvaethi* dance is probably more directly related to the medieval, danced lyrical song, although it is not unchanged today. Rather, it is a living phenomenon in which medieval and ancient Nordic heroes stand alongside current events, just as in the Balkan heroic songs and the Irish *sean-nós*.

A *kvaethi* dance may contain up to one hundred strophes or verse groups with both an internal and final refrain, or four-line verses with final refrains.

The Nordic and English ballads have the same kinds of strophes, which may be regarded as characteristic of the northwestern European ballad tradition. The verses move the narrative along, while the refrains provide recurrent lyrical images or comments. The melodies are often diatonic, highly structured in nature, and begin with a narrow range interval. Today, the Faeroese *kvaethi* have become a national cultural manifestation, and are performed on Independence Day (29 July) as well as between Christmas and Lent (see also p. 184).

Dissemination

As mentioned above, it is a commonly-held notion that, in one way or another, these songs from all over Europe formed a coherent network binding together otherwise disparate cultures:

> It is not motifs that travel, but ballads as units, often accompanied by their tunes; and so long as the movement is limited and recent, the evidence of identity is incontestable. *The Lament of the Robber's Bride* is the same thing in the Balkans, the Ukraine, and Czechoslovakia; The Rumanian *Marcu and the Turk* is a translation of a Serbian or Bulgarian original; *Roman and Olesa* is found in Poland . . . and the Ukraine; the *Murderous Wife* is sung in Czechoslovakia and Poland. The gypsies of southern Hungary sing ballads of German and Greek origin among others inspired by the conditions of their own life. *Anrus and Death* is the variant of the Greek *Digenis and Charon*. There is movement of ballad literature all over Europe, just like the movement of books. The transition is from mouth to mouth and not hand to hand. (Entwistle 1939. p. 77.)

Many songs were carried from place to place by wandering troubadours, even across the boundaries of languages and nation-states. One well-documented example is the migration of the English ballad along with the immigrants to North America (see the work of Cecil Sharp).

Lajos Vargyas (1983) has proven that there was a great deal of borrowing of French material in Italy and the Iberian peninsula. In Spain the tradition of older epic songs is stronger than in Portugal. Greece, too, borrowed from French ballads. Vargyas refers to the French empire in Cyprus from the thirteenth to fifteenth centuries as one possible transport route. There are also connections between France and England, as well as France and

Germany, but German scholars have often claimed that the transmission was mostly in the other direction. Although eastern Europe has always been marked by emigration from German-speaking western Europe, it appears that some of the connections between the German and Slavic ballad were via Hungary, where the ballad tradition is extremely rich. Traces of the French ballad tradition can also be found in Poland. The Hungarian tradition appears to have spread south towards Greece.

According to Vargyas, there was a Roman Catholic cultural zone in eastern Europe, stretching from Bohemia to Poland, Hungary, Croatia, and Slovenia, which was in direct contact with Germany, Italy, and France. Serbia, however, was more influenced by Turkish dominion and remained quite apart from the west. Thus Vargyas finds a clear line of demarcation for southern Slavic folklore between songs of the same type with anti-Turkish attitudes in regions belonging to the Habsburg empire and pro-Turkish attitudes in regions belonging to the Turks. Towards the east was the Byzantine sphere. This explains the relative isolation of Russia, which only had a few channels open north towards Scandinavia, west toward Poland, and via the Carpathians toward Hungary. This helps Vargyas to explain "the exclusively western ballad types, distinguished from the epic song of the Czechs, Poles, Hungarians, Slovaks, Croats, and Slovenians, and the mixed forms of the Serbs, Bulgarians, and Russians." Vargyas also notes that the fact that the peasants all over Europe had a relatively homogeneous life style, which facilitated a continuous cultural interchange, could also explain the similarities in ballad types. He is more doubtful about the possible courtly origin of the ballad and prefers not to see it as a watered-down cultural form. He believes that the constant flow of migration led to contact between peasants across linguistic and political barriers. The Jewish population may have been important cultural intermediaries. This would be an interesting area for further study.

Shared Stylistic Elements

Does a study of the ballad melodies provide evidence of all this migration? Are there shared stylistic elements in the ballad melodies all over Europe? In the past, the search for "wandering melodies" in order to chart connections occupied many scholars (Danckert 1939, Wiora 1957). The difficulty, however, was in knowing how to determine melodic similarities and interrelationships on the basis of material which is generally limited to one version of the first verse of the melody of each song. Important components such as performance and tonal quality were impossible to access. In his 1983 study, Vargyas used a new approach. He restricted his material to Hungarian ballads, and tried to determine where the various melodies came from, primarily in relation to Hungarian folklore.

Vargyas found that most Hungarian ballad melodies go hand-in-hand with certain song types, the same melody being performed to all the verses. The melodies are often structured like traditional Hungarian folk songs (i.e., with four motifs and a regular rhythm). The melodies are developed so as to fit the number of syllables in each verse: six, eight, or twelve.

Vargyas distinguished the following melodies, all of which are also typical of Hungarian folk music:

1. Ancient pentatonic melodies with the shift of a fifth.
2. Related pentatonic melodies with a descending melodic line.
3. Ancient recitative melodies.
4. Melodies directly traceable to laments. According to Vargyas, these are often recitative songs in major or minor keys with a range of up to a sixth, divided into two alternating motifs that may shift from free to strictly regular metric rhythms.
5. Bagpipe melodies with a narrow ambitus, related to lament melodies.
6. Less common melodies of the type referred to by Bartók (1925) as "the new style."

The ballad melodies were also used for lyrical love songs, just as the ballad texts were sometimes performed to wandering or liturgical melodies.

Vargyas was particularly interested in the wandering melodies with regard to the connection between French and Hungarian ballad melodies. He was convinced that France was the original source of the European ballad. For example, he regards two similar melodies, one Danish and one Hungarian, as reflecting, "The strong French connections of Hungarian ballads allow to some degree a possible agreement" (Vargyas 1983, pp. 258ff.).

The next agreement, however, should be that the Danes and the Hungarians have preserved some common medieval tune in two fringe areas of European culture. True, the Hungarian melody is rarely linked to a ballad text, but is extensively sung to the words of a dawn love song (something like the *aubade* or *Tagelied* type). The consistency of tune-text combination in this case makes a historical connection likely and explains the tune's association with the ballads. The Hungarian melody has assumed pentatone features, probably as secondary.

The Hungarian ballad melodies consist of a layer of traditional Hungarian melodies rooted in laments and other recitative melodies as well as in bagpipe melodies from areas with a rich ballad tradition. In addition there are liturgical songs, both as connections between individual texts and melodies, and as whole melodic families based on them. Liturgical songs, like ballads, originated in the Middle Ages. Wandering melodies are western in origin. Vargyas and Bartók consider the ballad and the dance to be mutually exclusive phenomena of the peasant cultures of Hungary, Romania, and Slovakia.

Vargyas's classification and analysis make it possible for us to begin a more thorough study of ballad melodies in Europe. If we had access to the same information from every region in Europe, we might be able to begin to confirm or reject the various research efforts to establish the ballad as a uniform genre in Europe. Vargyas had no doubt whatsoever:

Along the paths of dissemination discussed above common themes and within them, common types and motifs may have developed which every nation could make use of at will: signs of ill-omen, evasive replies in delicate human situations, deceptive answers instead of plain speech, sending on false tracks of the returning hero, commonplaces of formulas and formal characteristics of the common elements of presentation, common types of refrain and strophic construction, distribution of text portions within the strophe, variations of a given strophic form, free application of the repetitive devices, etc. All these constitute a network of poetic inventions which essentially differs from any other kind of poetry, and which is uniform in nature to such a degree as if it has been brought about by one nation. Therefore the European ballad claims a special treatment in distinction with all comparable poetic achievements—if any—that should have appeared at some by and large identical stage of social development and in a fairly similar psychological surrounding in other areas where the epic poetry of earlier times offered ground for a kindred genre to come into existence. Outlines of a similar genre can be detected for a more or less identical stage of social development in the Caucasus; yet the results there are far from approaching the refinement of the European ballad, and are devoid of all the characteristic features common in the entire European ballad area. Therefore we think it is not to the prejudice of scientific thinking if we regard the European ballad as a uniform poetic achievement paralleled nowhere in the world. (Vargas 1983 I, p.109.)

When the ballads in the west were first collected and printed, a dialectic began between the oral and the written traditions. Not until the early nineteenth century, moreover, did the written text tend to be accompanied by the melody. In other words, text collection often led to the separation of words from music. An individual wanting to perform a song of which he or she knew only the words simply had to find "a pleasant melody," as the printed broadsides sometimes put it, unless the collector suggested a suitable, familiar melody, often that of a hymn (see also Jersild 1975, pp. 70ff.). The fixed structure of the strophes in many of the narrative songs led to the melodies being naturally shaped as a number of varied motifs, which often joined to form a kind of arch. However, this does not mean that scholars who claim narrative song in the west is an art form, created once and for all and then memorized, are correct. It only means that the "grammar of popular poetry" of the ballads is more fixed, and possible variations in structure more restricted than is the case, for example, for the Balkan heroic songs. Nor is there any evidence that a complex strophic pattern necessarily means that the melody was fixed and structured. On the contrary, the *rímur* has already provided evidence that this does not have to be the case. Another example is, Italian epic song, the *storia*, still performed today by wandering minstrels or *cantastatorie*. The fixed point of these songs is the structure of the verse, ottava rima, with eight lines to a stanza and eleven syllables to a line, in a complex rhythmic pattern. The performance is in the form of a recitative (i.e., there are no fixed melodies).

This is also true of the Spanish and Portuguese romances. Their melodies consist of both recitative, structured melodies and more lyrical ones, with different styles and characteristics. Some romances

were performed to familiar popular melodies, for example, the *fado*.

The Origins of the Ballad Melodies

It seems probable that as soon as they came into the picture, "composed" melodies for narrative songs began to affect both the creation of new melodies and the way in which they were passed down. At that point, performers began trying to re-render the performances of others as closely as possible, just as if they were memorizing printed music. Thus there was a change of attitude, from creativity to reproduction. On the other hand, this also meant that there was more concentration on performance and interpretation than before. This is similar to the situation of nineteenth-century keyboard performers, who made the transition from improvization to the rendering of printed works. The ballad was also probably transformed with the advent of published music and by the new idea of ballads as "works of art." Listening to a narrative song packaged as a disc or cassette is another phase in this development. However, things may in fact be coming full circle. When people learn things by heart from recordings, they can, in turn, reproduce ballad performances once they have integrated the grammar and stylistic language of the art. Their renditions will be a return to the oral tradition instead of performances from the printed page.

Literature

Studies of the *jojk* and the musical culture of the Saami have been made by Edström (1977), Arnberg et al. (1969), and Manker (1938). In *The People of Eight Seasons* (1963), Manker gives an introduction to the lifestyle of the Saami. A book on the *jojk* was published just as, this volume was going to the original edition of press: Rolf Kjellström, Gunnar Ternham, Håkan Rydving, *Om jojk* (1988).

The work of Kuusi and Honkos on the history of ancient Finnish poetry is an instructive introduction to the runic song. In *Finnish Music Quarterly* 1–2 (1985) there are various interesting articles on the *Kalevala*, and on Finnish and Estonian music. Russian *bïlini* have been published in several series, and there is extensive literature on them in Russian. Good introductions can be found in B. M. Dobrovolski's and V. V. Korgusanov's 1981 study. To my knowledge, the most recent independent study of the *duma* was made by F. M. Kolessas in 1920. Kvitka (1973) also covers the *kobza* and the *duma*. Becking's study from the 1930s on instrumental and vocal technique is still of interest. Bartók/Lord (1951) and Lord (1960) are classics, as is Braun's study of Serbo-Croatian heroic songs. Interesting studies of Albanian narrative song have been made by Kruta (1984), Daja (1983), and Haxhihasarie (1982).

Ballad melodies may be studied in the work of Bronson (1969). Entwistle's 1939 book has a chapter on tunes, pp. 40–53. Vargyas's 1983 book is already a classic. General information on ballads can be found in many studies on folklore and comparative literature.

University of Rochester Press

REVIEW COPIES

P O Box 9 Woodbridge
Suffolk IP12 3DF

Telephone 01394 411320; fax 01394 411477
Bank account: sort code 60-24-45; account 86033840
Giro account 237 6156
VAT registration no: GB 102 7864 81

Invoice number   119664
Date   07/01/1998

Account code   P70077

CHARGE TO:

Simon Frith Reviews Editor
Popular Music
John Logie Baird Centre
University of Strathclyde
GLASGOW G1 1HX   Scotland
Via

DELIVERY TO:

Your order reference   Quantity ISBN   Title

Titles to be supplied

Price Discount Total

Published price: £36.00 /$49.95   Publication date 03/07/1997

This title is sent for review. We would be grateful for two copies of any review that may appear

Please quote the full title as follows:

A History of European Folk Music

Terms: days   Currency: Sterling
Account type: 12   Representative:

Any queries relating to this invoice must be notified in writing within 7 days
The legal title to these goods shall remain with Boydell & Brewer Ltd until payment is received in full

Five

"Bursting into Song" (Part II): The Lyric Song and the Hymm

LYRIC SONGS, SPIRITUAL SONGS, AND HYMNS

What Is a Lyric Song?

As early as the sixteenth century, composed folk songs began to become the property of the bourgeoisie in Western Europe. Subsequently, composed songs also spread to the peasants and artisans.

I refer to these, for want of a better term, as "lyrical songs." The lyric song existed from antiquity, and can also be found both in literature, as lyric poetry, and in the form of song passed down in the oral tradition. Lyric songs are characterized by their fixed structure of lines and verses in a great variety of combinations, and often with some kind of final rhyme. Their melodies are not subordinate to the text, as we have seen was the case in most narrative song and in songs of work. Instead, the melodies are complex little works of art, standing in an independent relationship to the texts.

Paths of Dissemination for Lyric Song

Beginning in the sixteenth century, lyric song spread to larger audiences through inexpensive printings, known in England as broadsides, in Germany as *Flugblätter*, in Russia as *lubotjnaja* and in France as *feuilles volante*.

In a study from 1975, Margareta Jersild classified broadside songs into (1) historical and political songs (2) songs about local events, (3) spiritual songs and (4) profane songs with no special connection to events or society. This last, very large, category is dominated by love songs.

The songs were spread via hawkers, who often set the words to suitable melodies themselves. In Sweden, for example, they were often hawked by young women who would buy the printed lyrics from the publisher and then sing them to familiar, local tunes. In other cases, the broadside texts included a recommendation of a suitable, well-known folk song or hymn (Figure 5.1). Some very popular melodies were used for all kinds of texts. Jersild's study goes on to group the broadside melodies by type, revealing that some of them were surprisingly enduring and widespread (see Jersild 1975, p. 218ff.).

A folk singer using broadsides usually take tunes already well-known. The names *feuille volante* (French) and *flyveblad* (Danish), i.e., "flying leaves," indicate that the survival of the printed-text form is dependent on their being sung to already-familiar melodies. Why should a singer and seller in the market place take the risk of presenting a newly invented tune which might be disliked by the audience so that the "flying leaves" fell dead to the ground? Giraudon (1985, p. 68) gives some examples of the origin of melodies to *feuilles volante* from Basse Bretagne:

1. The oral tradition.
2. A well-known melody. The missionary Grigon de Monfort (1673–1716), for example, used drinking songs and dance tunes for his *feuilles volantes* with religious texts.
3. Many melodies, used for the same text.

It was recommended that the singer use a well-known tune, a melody he or she liked or that was

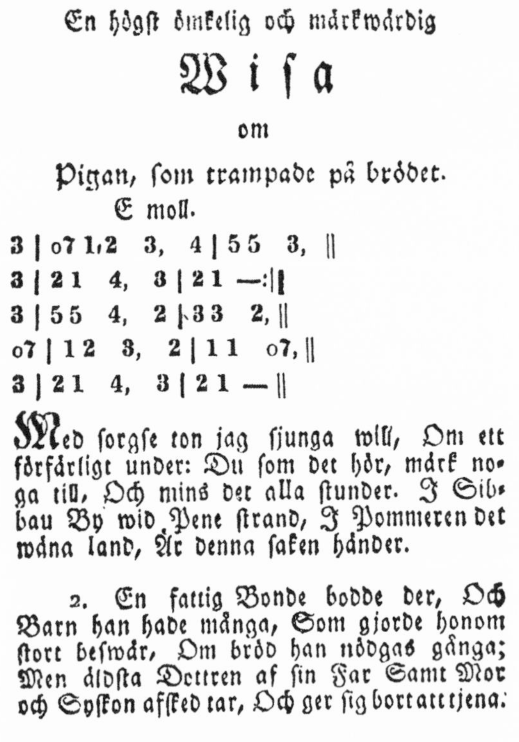

En högſt ömkelig och märkwärdig

Wiſa

om

Pigan, ſom trampade på brödet.

E moll.

3 | o7 1,2   3,   4 | 55   3, ||

3 | 21   4,   3 | 21 —:||

3 | 55   4,   2 |·33   2, ||

o7 | 12   3,   2 | 11   o7, ||

3 | 21   4,   3 | 21 — ||

Med ſorgſe ton jag ſjunga will, Om ett förfärligt under: Du ſom det hör, märk noga till, Och mins det alla ſtunder. J Sibbau By wid Pene ſtrand, J Pommeren det wåna land, Är denna ſaken hänber.

2.   En fattig Bonde bodde der, Och Barn han habe många, Som gjorde honom ſtort beſwär, Om bröd han nödgas gånga; Men äldſta Dottren af ſin Far Samt Mor och Syſkon affked tar, Och ger ſig bortatt tjena.

Figure 5.1. An example of the melody to a broadside song: "The Girl Who Stepped on the Bread" in figure notation. This melody is taken from a hymn, "Good Lord, Punish Me not" (chorale book from 1697, hymn 27). The rhythm is easily derived from the meter of the text, and the melodic motifs were adapted to the length of the phrases.

easy to sing. Another possibility was for the singer to make up a melody. Giraudon mentions an informant who sang all her broadsides to the same tune. Of course, there are also examples of singers who sang different tunes to the same text.

The interplay between function, text, and melody gives the broadside its special character. One function is to spread propaganda for religious or political ideas. Later broadsides describe natural disasters, royal weddings, etc.—the sort of news that readers today receive from the tabloids.

Giroudon emphasizes that there was a gradual transition from more or less intellectual writers of broadsides, such as semi-educated clergymen, to writers who were more representative of the man in the street and who, with the help of the publisher, wrote lyrics for local occasions such as weddings. Such broadsides were printed in small series and distributed in very limited areas.

Many pictures of singing *colpoteur* or *cavassers*

show them with a violin, or later an accordion, in their hands. The presentation of a broadside by a playing and singing seller rather than just a hawker was, of course, noisier and more spectacular. Thus the broadside provided the most commercial entertainment of folk culture in its time.

As described above, the tune was the vehicle by which the message was spread. Today, MTV videos are made by amateurs, semiprofessionals, and true professionals, not unlike the broadside in its time. The music video also has the same bad reputation among the official cultural establishment today as did the broadside.

The main dissemination of lyric songs took place among countries with otherwise close cultural contact, where people were accustomed to one another's languages, and translation was commonplace. One well-documented example of such dissemination is the spread of the lyric song from Germany to Denmark, and then to Norway, Sweden, and Finland (see also Schiørring 1950).

Lyric Song and Its Regional Profile

In central Europe, during the cultural revolutions of the Reformation and the Counter-Reformation, the folk song underwent a radical transformation. The melodies became streamlined, were either in major or minor, had regular rhythms ,and were structured as either ABBA, AABB, or ABCA, depending on the verse and meter of the lyrics. Melodies also began to change with the prevailing fashion. The melody line, for example, consisted largely of arpeggios, suggesting tonic-subdominant-dominant harmonies, since the music of the countryside had also begun to adopt functional harmony and a more vertical view of music. However, there were also factors that inhibited change; as long as there were still songs that remained closely tied to work and ceremonies, the traditional, regulating factors would remain and would affect the selection and structure of new songs as well.

Sometimes the lyric song would encounter the older oral song tradition, well-rooted in society, and there would be a merger of tradition and renewal; the templates of lyric song would be applied to traditional folk songs, and it would not take long for the peasant and artisan balladeers to begin composing in the new style themselves. This was the process that gave rise to regional profiles.

In many parts of Europe, folk musicians have always had a remarkable ability to improvise songs on the basis of given meter and rhyme schemes. This is an ancient art, and the confrontation with new song types led to stylistic change and sometimes to the occurrence of a whole new genre.

Nordic Song Competitions: The Norwegian *Stev*

The Norwegian *stev*, a single-stanza verse, was originally a competitive song form. Newly improvised *stev* were performed alternatively with existing ones. There are two kinds, referred to as old and new. The old *stev* is like a four-line ballad verse with no refrain and an ABAB rhyme, while the new *stev* is AABB. The old *stev* can be traced back to the Middle Ages, while the new *stev* has been found in versions only from the nineteenth century, although it may have originated far earlier (see Sandvik 1952, p. 22). In the mid-nineteenth century, in the Telemark region of Norway, *stev* singing was a very popular form of entertainment. When dinner had been eaten, the beer came out, and, after certain formalities, the "drinking *stev*" began. Everyone was expected to contribute. The women responded to the men, answering every *stev* with one of their own. The old *stev* were regarded as the finer ones, while the new ones were a sort of "teasing songs," describing prominent people and current events (see also 1981, pp. 80f.).

Sandvik has studied the new *stev*, describing them as similar to Scottish folksong, in verse and melodic structure. This should not be surprising, considering the similarities between Scandinavia and the British Isles. Gregorian chants may also have been among the prototypes for these *stev* (Figure 5.2a). Paradoxically, this endows the melodies of the new *stev* with the impression of being older than the old ones. According to Erik Eggen, the *springdans* (a dance in triple time, such as *springar*, *gangar*, *springleik*, or *pols*) can be regarded as having contributed to the melodies of the *stev*, as some of them have an upbeat of three eighth notes (Figure 5.2b). Sandvik, on the other hand, claims that there is not a single *stev* that can be used for a *springdans*, and that the explicit declamatory style of the *stev*, as well as its shifts from two- to three-beat rhythms, are contrary to the rhythmic requirements of a

Figure 5.2. Norwegian *stev* melodies. (Sandvik 1952, nos. 1 and 2 p. 39, no. 8 p. 41.)

dance. Still, he claims that the *springdans* is not to be entirely ignored, and that the new type of verse can be assumed to have many origins (Figure 5.2c). Discussing the *stev* in this way highlights many issues of principle. For example, does a new type of verse necessarily imply a shift to new kinds of melodies? It appears as if the tradition of the new *stev* came at the time of a new wave of creativity, in which many different types of melodies, new and old, were included. As the text was developed by the performer, melodies from hymns or lyric songs were not slavishly adopted. Thus it appears that freedom of choice in relation to melody and melodic structure was greater when the text was invented by the performer than when it was adopted from a printed source. When a printed source was involved, there was more of a tendency to seek an existing melody, to which the new text was suited in style and fashion.

Song Competitions in Southern Europe

There is a long-standing tradition of song competitions in Italy, the Basque region, and elsewhere. For example two men in a local pub might compete to see who could improvise verse faster (and better) to powerful, traditional melodic motifs. Occasionally they might use existing melodies in their entirety, but in general they improvised on the basis of traditional motifs.

"Black Sheep" in Finnish Runic Song

In areas with a strong, unique song tradition, such as Finland with its runic song, lyric songs developed as a separate popular genre, completely foreign to what came before it. Thus folk songs in rhymed verse were "black sheep," coming to Finland from the west, often from Germany via Sweden. In the nineteenth century, folk singers spread such songs all the way to Karelia where, previously, runic songs had reigned virtually uncontested. Melodies in major or minor keys replaced the previously wide variety of tunes in various modes. Gradually, too, printed broadsides came to dominate over oral dissemination.

English Folk Songs with Peculiar Melodies

Lloyd (1967) assumes that there are two different strains of lyrical songs in the English tradition.

An analysis of tune outline, harmonic structure and phrase formation alone–disregarding the subject-matter of the texts–would probably confirm that while English folk song is unitary, two stages are nonetheless perceptible. We may call these stages the "early tradition" and the "late tradition." Put roughly, the flourishing time of the early tradition falls roughly between, 1550 and the middle of the eighteenth century. During the later years of that century it began to give way to a new style of song that persisted vigorously for a hundred years until the second half of the nineteenth century (p. 171).

The origin of the first strain can be dated because the mid-sixteenth century was characterized by some class mobility and by a wealth of contact between rural and urban areas. This led to the development of a large corps of semi-professional musicians, supplementing their incomes by playing at weddings and other celebrations, (to the an-

noyance of the official musicians to whom they were nothing but unlawful competition).

The Romanian *Doina*

The Romanian *doina* is a type of lyric poetry that can be described as free variations on a number of more or less fixed melodic elements, assembled into more or less fixed patterns. The *doina* proper, according to *New Grove*, is "a term which Brăiloiu and succeeding Romanian folklorists used to describe a specific style of melody, a particularly lyrical melopoeia in free form, based on improviation with some more or less invariable melodic elements. This sort of song is popularly called *lung* (long) or *prelung* (prolonged), *de coasta* (of the slopes), *de codru* (of the forest), *de duca* (of departure), etc." (Vol. 16, p. 134) (Figure 5.3).

Nature and love are the commonest subjects, but *doina* may also be realistic descriptions of working life. The oldest songs are characterized by tense vocal timbre, reminiscent of the calls of the Swedish cowherds (see also p. 115–116). The form appears to have remained unchanged for a very long time. The melody, based on a modality centerd on d^1, circles around the fourth and fifth notes of the scale, which are introduced by a long note ending with a sudden leap up to the fourth or fifth note. Repeated descending figures interrupt the improvised sections. The style of the songs is closely associated with calls of both shepherds and harvesters, but the *doina* had no ceremonial function. The nineteenth century saw the breakthrough of modern melodies, but the traditional *doina* style remained in actual use until the mid-twentieth century, when it came under the protection of folk music groups who safeguarded the traditional form.

The Russian *Chastushka*

The Russian *chastushka* arose in the late nineteenth century as urban and rural areas became more separate. The *chastushka* is a kind of improvised folk music, the text of which can include anything: verses from traditional lyric song, proverbs, classical poetry, and old humoresques. The *chastushka* is a two-part song, in which the two halves may appear to have nothing to do with one another, consisting, perhaps, of a description of nature and an emotional song. Upon closer examination, however, psychological parallels tend to appear

Figure 5.3. Doina. (Alexandru 1980, no. 26 p. 168).

Figure 5.4. A *chastushka* on the pleasures of country living, the steamboats passing by, and the swift passage of youth. (Zemtsovsky 1967, no. 119 p. 107f.)

(Stephan 1969). There is another type of *chastushka* in which the theme is consistent throughout and in which the rhyme scheme, the form, and the meter interact to provide a structure for the narrative. This strain of the *chastushka* is still alive in Russia. It should be added that melody is not an obligatory element in the *chastushka*, which can also be recited rather than sung. The recitation is often accompanied on the accordion, the instrument which gained its popularity in conjunction with the development of the *chastushka* (Figure 5.4) (see also Chapter 11, p. 212).

Hungarian Lyrical Songs in the "Old" and "New" Styles

As early as the 1920s, Béla Bartók claimed that Hungarian lyric songs could be traced to the early nineteenth century, where they arose under increased influence from the west, usually via Bohemia and Moravia. Their formal structure is classical in style, but they were transformed during their migration from the middle to the peasant classes, where they took on original, artistic forms. Bartók and his successors have described the development of a European music style moving through cultural spheres, in shifting forms, and in disparate epochs. They see the development as having begun in Bohemia and Moravia, where both industrialization and urbanization revolutionized society. This led to the growth of a flourish-

ing petty-bourgeois musical culture in which even more popular forms of art music became widespread. They then spread rapidly to Hungary, according to these scholars as a consequence of the cultural and political process of liberation of the Hungarian peasant class in the nineteenth century. This, they say, explains the "optimistic tone" of nineteenth century Hungarian folk music, often referred to as the "new Hungarian" style (Szomjas-Shiffert 1979).

Bartók's Analysis of the "Old" and "New" Styles

Let us examine, in somewhat greater detail, the Hungarian songs and research of Bartók. His research has been, and remains, extremely influential with regard to what is considered old and new in the music of eastern Europe, and with regard to how it has been analyzed. Large collections of Slovakian, Romanian, and Serbo-Croatian music, for example, have been classified according to Bartók's system.

As mentioned above, Bartók early discovered the unique traits of Hungarian folk music (see p. 19). His basic thesis was that the music of the peasant class consisted of melodies that were spontaneous expressions of the musical feeling of that class. They instinctively altered musical forms of expression coming from a higher (urban) culture, to suit its own outlook and disposition (Bartók 1981, p. 1). Bartók claims that, "It should be admitted that practically every recent European peasant music known today arose under the influence of some kind of 'national' or 'popular' art music" Bartók 1981, p. 1).

This music also had its limitations in time and space. Bartók went on to describe what he called "popular art music," in which folk music styles were combined with stereotyped structures from art music (p. 2). It was this composite that became what Bartók called the "new style in Hungarian peasant music" (p. 3). Bartók did not believe that the individual peasant had the ability to create new melodies, but that his musical instincts were sufficient to reformulate the musical elements at his disposal. He claimed that this strong musical instinct expressed itself in the formulation of variations of different melodies, just as their performances were characterized by changes in rhythm and melody—a kind of improvisation. This could develop into a series of changes from one performer to the next, leading to a situation in which the relationship of the final link to the first was unrecognizable. Bartók strove to define the stylistic elements characterizing peasant music.

Taken in a narrower sense, the term peasant music connotes the totality of the peasant tunes exemplifying one or several more or less homogeneous styles. Thus, in this narrower sense, peasant music is the outcome of changes wrought by a natural force whose operation is unconscious; it is impulsively created by a community of individuals who have had no schooling and is a natural product as much as the various forms of animal and vegetable life. (Bartók 1981, p. 3).

This explains how some of these melodies are

excellent examples of aesthetic perfection, small masterpieces far superior to the popular art songs of the upper classes. Bartók also provided examples of cross-influence of different peasant cultures having various levels of musical understanding. He saw this mostly as a downward motion, from top to bottom. He went on to classify the peasant melodies according to a scholarly system, determining their various musical styles and origins by introducing a classification system which was (later) also applied to types of folk music other than Hungarian, and which is therefore deserving of special attention.

Philip V. Bolhman refers to Bartók's combination of lexicographic methods and classificational criteria of genetic and historical patterns as "one of the most masterful syntheses of diverse approaches" (Bohlman 1988, p. 40).

One example of how Bartók presented his ideas and the concepts underlying them can be found in the following quotation from the English translation of his book *The Hungarian Folk Song*. Bartók begins by complementing Finnish folklorist Ilmari Krohn, whose basic concept for lexical classification Bartók modified.

All the tunes are reduced to a common final (g^1).

1. We divide the tunes according to the number of their lines (a tone-line is that portion of a tune allotted to one line of the text) into two-line, three-line, and four-line tunes.

2. A further classification is based upon the pitch of the final tone of the various tune-lines. The final notes will be indicated by figures for simplification according to the following table:

accidentals being added when needful: e.g. ♭3 = [figure].

The final note of the chief caesura will be marked ☐, that of the previous melodic line ⌐⌐, that of the following ☐; which means that [♭3] [5] [4] indicates a four-line tune whose first line ends with [figure], the second ending with [figure], and the third with [figure].

3. Further sub-groups are determined by the number of syllables to a tune-line; the order of these sub-groups follows that of the numbers. These numbers are indicated by small-font Arabic numerals, separated by commas.

4. Finally, the tunes are grouped according to their compass. (Bartók 1981, p.6–7.)

Bartók goes on to present an analysis in which he tries to determine the relative age of the different types of melodies. According to this analysis, "primitivity or complexity refers to the melody structure," where he defines various stages of evolution, from short tunes of one-bar or two-bar motifs to four-line tunes with an architectural plan. According to Bartók, the rhythm can also be conceived as belonging to various stages of evolution. The first is *tempo giusto*, a strict rhythm associated with body movements such as those of work or dancing; the next is a parlando-rubato rhythm, gradually independent of the body's motion, adapting to the rhythm of the words, followed by *tempo giusto* rhythm again, but this time evolving out of the parlando-rubato performance. Bartók then describes three stage of evolution and divides Hungarian peasant music into (1) tunes in the old style, (2) tunes in the new style, and (3) tunes that belong to neither style, and thus represent a mixed style (Bartók 1981, p. 6–11).

Figures 5.5–7 consist of melodies each of which has four sections. The final notes of the sections in 5.5 are d², b¹, and g¹, described using the numbers 5, 3, and 1. There are brackets to mark the beginning, middle, and end of sections. The sections in 5.6 end with g¹, d², and a¹, described using figures 1, 5, and 2, with the necessary brackets. The sections in 5.7 end with g¹, d¹, and g¹, described using the numbers 1, 5, and g¹.

The sections are also classified by the number of syllables they contain, denoted with Arabic numerals and separated by commas. The number of syllables in the figures described above are twelve in 5.5, eleven in 5.6 and thirteen in 5.7.

Last, the melodies are classified by range, denoted by figures for pitch, in combination with hyphens. The range for 5.5 is g¹–d² = 1–5, for 5.6 f1–a2 = VII–9, and for 5.7 g¹–g² = 1–8.

Bartók based his work on the hypothesis that "primitive" melodies were older than the less primitive or more complex ones, and thus he posited the following stages of development:

1. short melodies with motifs of one or two measures, such as Romanian dance melodies or Arabic peasant music;
2. three or four segment melodies with a fixed, enclosed form and no definite architectonic structure;
3. four segment melodies with an enclosed form and a definite architectonic structure (AABA or ABBA).

With regard to rhythm, Bartók envisaged three stages of development:

1. from *tempo giusto*, described by Bartók as a well-disciplined rhythm with notes of equal value, typical of music for movement, such as dance or work, to
2. a parlando-rubato rhythm that came into being when the melodies had separated from the rhythm of movement, becoming freer, and enabling (in turn) an adaptation to
3. the *tempo giusto* rhythm that arose when the rubato performance again became more strict.

Bartók's world view, marked by evolutionist trends, and coupled with his conception of the peasant classes as unable to create but able to improvise, as well as his critical view of the influence from urban cultures, must all be borne in mind when we try to understand his classification system. Music in category A was not function-bound and was based on isometric text segments of between 9 and 12 syllables, in parlando-rubato rhythm and, somewhat later, in *tempo giusto*. These melodies were characterized by their pentatonic scales. Examples of the structure included ABCD, ABBC and A⁵B⁵AB (the figure 5 marks the transposition of a motif by a fifth). These melodies may be regarded as Hungarian creations, as no other people were known to have a musical style of the same character. Music in category B, the "new style," was music with an architectonic, closed structure, either AA⁵BA, AA⁵A, ABBA or AABA. The tonalities of these melodies are Dorian, Aeolian, or major, or they have some kind of liturgical characteristics. Their typical rhythm is *tempo giusto*.

Many of Bartók's hypotheses about the age and origin of the melodies have been canonized today, and his evaluation criteria have become unwritten, aesthetic law for appraising folk music. Although some aspects of his historical interpretation have been questioned by later scholars with differing opinions (see Kodály 1961, Nagy 1962, and Szomjas-Schiffert 1979), for example, as to the Hungarian provenance of the "new style," his studies generally still serve as the norm.

Figure 5.5. Bartók 1925/R 1965, no. 2 p. 253.

Figure 5.6. Bartók 1925/R 1965, no. 101 p. 280.

Figure 5.7. Bartók 1925/R 1965, no. 177 p. 301.

Cataloging and Analyzing Collections of Melodies

> The extreme form of the penetration of classification to the specific is the gradual replacement of observed and collected tradition with the system that has purported to define it. (Bohlman 1988, p. 50.)

> Whenever one talks about folk music in a systematic way, one engages in some form of classification. (Bohlman 1988, p. 51.)

Since the late nineteenth century, all efforts to make comprehensive analyses of folk music have been coupled to studies of collections. The analyst and collector have generally been one and the same individual, who has both attempted to illuminate the structure and origin of the melodies and to establish some general order to enable future scholars to approach the material from new angles.

The history of the study of folk music is dotted with such figures, many of whose work was an attempt to respond to a key question, asked by Dutch scholar D. F. Scheurleer in 1899: "What is the best method of arranging folk songs and popular songs in lexical order on the basis of their melodic (not textual) characteristics?" This was also the title of his article (Scheurleer 1899).

Many people felt the urge to respond to this question, not least Scandinavians, including Finnish musicologists Ilmari Krohn and Armas Launis, and Swedish musicologist Tobias Norlind. (Bartók developed Krohn's fundamental ideas more fully.) One of the things on which they based the system was the main notes of phrases grouped according to their final notes.

The early twentieth century saw many attempts at finding an acceptable method of cataloging songs on the basis of what was considered by scholars to be applicable to any given collection (for a Nordic overview, see Dal 1956, pp. 389–398).

In other parts of Europe, different systems were developed and adapted to the collections of various countries by scholars including Feilaret Kolessa in the Ukraine (1916), and Otakar Hostinky and Vladimir Helfert in Czechoslovakia (see also Markl 1969.)

Professor Bertrand Harris Bronson of Berkeley used punch cards for his studies of melodies in the 1960s, thereby sowing the seeds of what have now become hi-tech databases. Bronson also used statistical methods and graphic overviews (see, for example, his "About the Most Favorite British Ballads" and "Toward the Comparative Analysis of British- American Folktunes" in *The Ballad as Song*, 1969).

1969 also saw the publication of a collected volume in Bratislava entitled *Methoden der Klassifikation von Volksliedweisen*, edited by Oskár Elschek with the assistance of Doris Stockmann. This volume was the proceedings for the first working conference on cataloging, held by the then Folk Music Council. Since that time there has been an active study group working on systematization of folk music under the auspices of the Folk Music Council, which later became the International Council for Traditional Music (ICTM).

In *Methoden der Klassifikation von Volksliedweisen*, Wolfgang Suppan described the history of cataloging melodies at the Deutsche Volksliedarchiv in Freiburg. His experience, confirmed at many other archives and research centers, indicates that cataloging principles based on the observations of individual scholars seldom survive that scholar. When he or she stops working, other researchers try to assert their own ideas as useful for general cataloging systems. Suppan also discussed the possibility of applying methods of analysis from art music to folk music, for example, adopting music theorist Heinrich Schenker's methods of analysis.

Another article in the volume, by Alica Elscheková, described a system of classification used to categorize 12,000 Slovakian folk songs with the aid of data analysis. The objective was to find a deeper means of melodic, typological identification. This analysis was based on examination of the course of various melodic motifs, patterns of intonation, cadenced notes, and number of measures. Elscheková's principles can thus be recognized as building on those of Krohn and Bartók. However, the structure of Elscheková's analysis allows for data analysis of a large amount of material in order to show typological similarities and differences. She called for more such studies of classification, in order to acquire enough material to study morphology and musical stylistics in individual folk music cultures.

The present day is a dynamic period in terms of the classification of melodies at various archives all over Europe. In the future, this will probably enable exciting comparative research of a kind not yet possible today. A large number of problems, however, remain to be solved, particularly as interest is focusing more and more on recorded material, while the "herbarium of dried notes," or written music, appear to be increasingly relegated to the status of secondary reference material.

Composed Lyric Ballads Claim the Field

As mentioned above, many of the songs that became popular folk songs were not anonymous. One example is the vaudeville song *Plaisir d'amour*, text by Jean-Pierre C. de Florian (1755–1794) and melody by Jean-Paul É. Martini (1742–1816), a music teacher from Nancy. Often only one part of a composition, in this case the rondo, became a folk song because it was remembered and hummed by the audience on their way home from the music hall.

In comments on his own collection, Levin Christian Wiede touches on the difference between the composed songs which became generally familiar to the peasantry and songs that only existed in the oral tradition. One of his examples includes different versions of the melody to which *Den fromma fru Signild* (Pious Madame Signild) by Anna Maria Lenngren was performed. The original melody was composed by amateur musician Carl Erik Gleisman (1767–1804), and was published in part 4 of Olof Åhlström's, *Skaldestycken, satte i Musik* (Pieces by the Bard Set Down in Music) from 1795, no. 2, (Figure 5.8, p. 113).

Of the four melodic variants Weide noted down, two (nos. 2 and 3) were close to the original, while the others (nos. 4 and 5) showed clear signs of being personal renditions (see definition of the term below).

Wiede also gives examples of songs from the theater becoming folk songs in early-nineteenth-century Sweden:

Of all songs, the one rendered here, taken from a modern play from abroad, *The Little Drummer*, should be mentioned as having won a place as close to the hearts of many people as Swedish folk music, undeservedly. I mention it here simply as an example of the wondrous ability of the peasantry to comprehend and re-render, on occasion. This song was performed, to the letter and to the note as given here, by a crofter's farmhand, A. P. Österberg, who worked at a croft under the Skenås estate in the parish of Östra Husby. My lack of knowledge of the song performed in the theatre makes it impossible for me to tell how close or far his version was from the original, but I can safely say that his performance was surely as good as that of many people we see on stage. (Ling 1965, pp. 117f. no. 248.)

The renditions by folk singers of variations on familiar songs were long considered a negative phenomenon. Scholars criticized such variations as having been sung to death. However, in 1941 Walter Wiora introduced the term *personal renditions* (in Swedish *omsjungning*). Thus he introduced the concept of the transformation of a melody as an artistic re-creation of a familiar song.

Many melodies sung as part of the oral tradition were simultaneously part of the printed, arranged song repertoire.

Composers of Lyric Ballads

The closer to the present we move in time, the more names we know of composers and authors of songs. Many of the songs of Carl Michael Bellman (1740–1795), for example, became folk songs via broadside distribution. The eighteenth century also saw the coming of a change in attitude towards the general public on the part of composers. Seventeenth-century composers felt their work was being trivialized by the people (see Klusen 1978). During the course of the eighteenth century, however, composers and poets began to take pleasure in knowing that their works were performed at marketplaces and in pubs. Composers whose works traveled this path included Mozart and Schubert as well as a number of names less well known today, including Johann Adam Hiller (1728–1804), Johann Friedrich Reichardt (1752–1814), Johann Abraham Peter Schulz (1747–1800), and Christoph Ernst Friedrich Weyse (1774–1842). Schulz described his methodology as follows, "I made every effort to keep my melodies simple and comprehensible, thus making them appear familiar. . . . The entire secret of the tone of popular music lies in its apparent familiarity" (Hermann-Schneider 1980, p. 264).

Poets and composers now began to see 'the people' as their main audience, and wrote songs specifically for soldiers, apprentices, and country people. Many

composers succeeded in finding the 'popular tone 'folk song enthusiasts were seeking. Some of their compositions, including *Der Mond ist aufgegangen* with a text by Matthias Claudius and music by J. A. P. Schulz, or W. Müller's/Schubert's *Am Brunnen vor dem Tore* truly became folk songs. (Klusen 1978, pp. 60, 104.)

Some themes, such as the Tyrolean songs, were so incredibly popular from the outset that they never reached the zeniths of Parnassus. Beethoven's "Tyrolean Aria" from 1816 is virtually the only alpine romance attributable to a great composer. Alpine romance, instead, became the favorite theme of the popular composers, not only in music hall entertainment, but also in light concert repertoire and music for the royal courts. Hildegard Herrman-Schneider has made an interesting study of one such composer, a court musical director by the name of Ignaz Lachner from Munich, whose work centered around alpine scenes and peasant caricatures. It was natural for Lachner to write such music as part of a long-standing tradition. Entertainment at the courts of royalty and nobility had focused on the peasants since the sixteenth century, with actors dressed as peasants, and entertainment featuring peasant music and food. Tyrolean folk music spread rapidly across Europe and to the New World. The Alps were no longer seen as a gray, wild, terrifying area, but as a basically idyllic, friendly region offering pleasant adventure. As the tourist trade picked up speed, Tyrolean songs multiplied like wildfire, performed by native inhabitants, now in the obligatory folk costume.

Many popular composers latched onto this new public interest. Pianists such as Ignaz Moscheles performed paraphrases for the piano of *Les Charmes du Tirol* and prima donna Henriette Sontag performed Tyrolean songs at her concerts in the 1820s (see also Salmen 1980, p. 71).

Gradually, a combination of some of the stylistic traits of yodelling (see p.32) and clichés from the world of entertainment led to the development of a national Tyrolean style, deeply rooted in popular tradition and also associated with other forms of popular music. "This led to the continued debasing of the original qualities of Tyrolean song as one kind of genuine alpine music." (See, for example, *Tyrolean Song, Yankee Doodle for the Zither*, published in Chicago (Salmen 1980, p. 72).)

Salmen has compared this interest in things

Figure 5.8. *Den fromma fru Signild* (Pious Madame Signild). Original version composed by Carl Erik Gleisman and published in Olof Åhlström's, *Skaldestycken, satte i Musik* (Pieces by the Bard Set Down in Music), (2–5) Four versions heard sung by the peasantry of the province of Östergötland, and annotated by Levin Christian Wiede. (Ling 1965, p. 61.)

Tyrolean with the contemporary interest in the gypsy *csárdás*, the Venetian *barcarole* and the Andalusian *bolero*. It is very clear that this new wave of popular music not only washed in over little old bourgeois piano teaching spinsters and, moreover, boosted the tourist trade, but that it also found its way to the servants' rooms and the farmhands' cottages, where it may have played an even more important role than it did for the middle classes as an escape from dull routines (Figure 5.9).

Alpine romances reached Sweden as well, *Alprosen* (The Alpine Rose) being one example of a familiar song with Tyrolean elements in the melody. It is based on triads and sixths, embellished and ornamented after every leap, and with the emphasis on emotionally charged, prolonged high notes.

Lyric Ballads as Patriotic Folk Songs

Political nationalism was a primary motivation for the writing of lyric ballads and songs for the people, and there are many examples in the romantic spirit. Ever since the Middle Ages, the folk song was a documented propaganda tool, and now it became a flourishing support for the ideas of the nation-state.

In late seventeenth-century Scotland, a kind of patriotic song grew up with texts in Gaelic and melodies with a narrow ambitus (a fifth or a sixth, generally structured on the pentatonic scale) and with a very special rhythm of its own. Although we often know who wrote these songs, they have been passed down as part of the oral tradition exactly as if they had been anonymous. This new kind of lyric song competed increasingly successfully with the ballad, the objective narrative of which was now replaced with more emotional texts, often with a sentimental flavor that appealed to the middle classes. The first time these songs were anthologized, as Allan Ramsay's *Tea-table Miscellany* from 1724, the book went into eighteen editions. One of Ramsay's colleagues, James Johnson, was ambitious enough to want to become "a musical patriot for his country" (see Harker 1985, p. 19). He eventually published a monumental volume of Scottish folk songs, *The Scots Musical Museum* (1787–1803). Johnson collaborated with the poet Robert Burns who collected, arranged, and wrote new texts to folk melodies. The treasure trove of songs they assembled, in contrast to the efforts of other collectors in different European nations, truly served as the basis of a living folk song tradition. To transcribe the music, Burns used assistants, although he, too, was personally able to note down the melodies of the simple peasant (Figure 5.10).

The popularity and dissemination of these ancient Scottish songs is thus closely associated with the national movement which, in turn, gave rise to new folk songs and poetry. These new songs were widely spread throughout the population and passed down orally from one generation to the next. Thus they correspond to what we refer to as *folk songs*, despite the fact that their creator is known.

POPULAR HYMNS

The texts of popularized hymns were always taken from an official hymnal and the melody was often, though not always, borrowed from or inspired by an official, published version. Popularized hymns were to be found where religious services contained congregational singing. However, they actually originated at devotions held in the home and other meetings outside the church, where more personal kinds of singing and reformulations of melodies could take place without liturgical intervention.

Moberg describes the following from the island of Rågö:

> Hymns were sung not only in church but, to a large extent, during work and breaks from work, and in the home. Just one generation ago devotions at home were a part of everyday life, beginning in the month before Christmas and following the entire ecclesiastical calendar year according to the traditional prayer books. Grace, 'All Eyes Trust in Thee' was always said before meals, and a hymn sung to conclude the meal, usually 'Christ We Now Thee Praise' or 'We thank Thee Lord for Thy Loving kindness.' . . . Mrs. Maria Melin, one of Moberg's informants, said of that it was sung one verse per week every Sunday throughout Lent, to conclude the meal. In those days, 'At the Hour of Ten, Think then of God' was still sung after work. Many hymns were sung during a vigil, on the Saturday night before a funeral. Hymns would be sung through until four or five o'clock in the morning, and then people would sleep until it was time for the funeral. (Moberg 1939, p. 24.)

Popular variants of hymns mostly developed in places where there was neither an organ nor a per-

Figure 5.9. The melody and the first verse of "The Alpine Rose." (*Från skrapare till hackare* 1972, p. 44.)

son who could read music. In such places, members of the congregation would develop their own versions in the local style, or even set the words of a hymn to a local melody. Thus popular hymns had their regional flavors, for example, the kind of ornamentation referred to as *krus* (a "frill") in the province of Dalacarlia in Sweden. Similarly, the rhythmic structure of these popular hymns was often colored by the local song tradition which, in turn, was affected by the linguistic intonation of the region. The tempos were often slow and reflective, not least because so few people could read well.

Popularized Hymns in Different Countries

Moberg introduces his analysis of popularized hymns from the island of Runö with a general description of their sources and annotation. His introductory survey covers the Nordic area only, and he justifies this by saying that there were no "direct equivalents beyond the Nordic cultural region," and that his was probably the last collection that would ever be made (Moberg 1939, p. 9). On this point he was proven wrong, variations on popular hymns were later found to exist in nearby countries such as Scotland, and they, too, were well worth collecting.

However, we can uphold Moberg's thinking to the extent that these popularized hymns were mostly found where the religious services contained congregational singing, in Lutheran congregations far from urban centers. In Sweden, many popularized hymns have come from the provinces of Dalacarlia and Skania. There were two reasons for this. The tradition remained strong long after the advent of organs, as well as of zealous parsons and organists who created order in the congregational singing, and interested collectors existed in

Figure 5.10. "Green Grows the Rashes," text by Robert Burns, in James Johnson, *The Scots Musical Museum I* no. 77.

these areas during the final flourishing of these hymns. They realized how important it was to preserve them (see Moberg 1939, p. 6ff., on Johan Enninger (1844–1908) and Nils Andersson).

Collection of popularized hymns began early in Finland, where there was also an early scholarly edition, Ilmari Krohn's *Über die Art und Entstehung der geistlichen Volksmelodien in Finland* (1899). The collecting work for this volume was completed sixty years earlier (see Moberg 1939, p. 14).

In the Faeroe Islands, Danish hymns were introduced and took on regional color. Their style was very Nordic, with every note sung slow and ornamented or stressed. The melodies were often altered to suit the different verses.

In Norway religious songs became a vital feature of traditional song. As mentioned above, Ludvig M. Lindeman (1812–1887) applied for a travel grant with the intention of "bringing to light these hymns, from the mountain areas, regarded with such contempt and misunderstanding" (see Sandvik 1960, p. 16).

It was his experience of popularized hymns that inspired Evald Tang Kristensen (1843–1929), a Danish schoolmaster, to devote himself to collecting Danish folklore. Moberg cites a Swedish clergyman:

The congregation was not the least bit interested in my way of singing and had simply no desire to be corrected by me. They persisted in singing their way, and I realised that they were never going to change. For this reason, I was forced to change my way of singing to liken that of my congregation, and to learn

their music so that I could sing it. . . . Once I began to sing as the visitors to my church wished, they were satisfied.

The Scottish highlands also has its own metrical kind of popularized hymns, the psalms, in Gaelic. These hymns came to Scotland after the Reformation, and as so few people could read, the cantor would sing a phrase that the congregation would repeat. This developed into a tradition still used in some places.

Style and Performance of the Hymns

It should be noted that not everyone was as open-minded as Lindeman and Tang Kristensen, and that some people found congregational song with popularized hymns objectionable and disturbing. Asbjörn Hernes has written an essay entitled *Salmetone og menighetssong* (The Sound of the Hymn as Congregational Song), which contains some drastic descriptions of these popularized hymns by music-lovers. In 1851 Swedish scholar and composer Gunnar Wennerberg wrote:

I beg of the members of the congregations of our Lutheran churches to keep their screaming mouths shut during the hymns, and listen to a choir that *can* sing, instead. If they must sing at all, let them enjoy themselves to their hearts' content at their home devotionals (Jeanson 1929, p. 74).

Norwegian author Henrik Wergeland, who came of ecclesiastical stock, was no better. He wrote in *Folkebladet* no. 12 (1832) under the heading *Forslag till Kirkemusik paa Langfredag* (Suggestions for Church Music on Good Friday):

In most places we have no sacred music. The Lutheran freedom of individual singing has led to a storm of cacophony in our churches, making the singing of the choir sound like a far-distant echo of comb-playing, despicable, whining women's voices sufficient to send any sense of religious feeling, dissecting what might remain of religious feeling, replacing it with fury, ridicule, and thoughts of the madhouse. Possibly one or two hymns could be open for all, but the rest should be performed by people who can sing and read music. (Hernes 1940, pp. 180f.)

Hernes renders various similar statements from Norway about organists whose singing is terribly tremulous—"the louder they can shout the better"—and congregations who compete in trying to drown out the organist, even arranging competitions with a prize for the person who could sing loudest (testimony from Lars Roverud in 1815). It is important to note that all these writers make trained singers their standard for comparison.

The introduction of new hymns has always been a matter of controversy between parishioners and the ecclesiastical establishment, and still is today. In his church journal from 12 and 19 March 1843, Pastor Thams Buskmann from Aure in Norway, himself a prominent musician, describes his difficulties in getting new hymns accepted: when new versions of two hymns were performed by a well-trained choir, his congregation fled the sanctuary in a wild tumult. At a later service, the pastor had the doors closed and, after the sermon, explained that he was now going to perform these hymns for the congregation himself. The parishioners began running around the sanctuary as he sang. Some people sat still and listened, but once they were outside the congregation began to plan the continuation of the demonstration the next Sunday.

> The next week I repeated the routine from the previous Sunday, and sang one of the hymns again. After I had begun, some of my parishioners began to sing a different melody from the back of the room, with such dissonances that the best-versed vocalist would hardly have been able to continue. I could read disapproval of this premeditated chaos in the faces of those nearest me. It is my understanding that the ringleaders were shoemaker Ole Halvorsen Eide, tailor Anders Leerdal, and farmhands Anders Jonsen Gredset and Niels Andersen Sundbye. (Hernes 1940, p. 176f.)

Although today hymns and spirituals are usually performed to written texts and melodies, there are still many local variations in style and performance. Hans Bernskiöld made a study of congregational song in the Swedish Missionary Society in 1986. He discerned the wide spectrum of song, from traditional to revised, as well as the fact that congregations have always exhibited resistance to accepting new musical and religious phenomena. His study also points out the gap between the more popular, functional song and a kind of song that seeks to adapt to the changing aesthetic trends in music. Music is a highly integral part of the activities of various churches and today, as in the past, this means that special styles and methods of performance develop there.

SINGING FOLK MUSIC

Although singers themselves have not expressed much enthusiasm for the project, musicologists have had a great desire to classify various historical layers of music, much as geologists classify layers of the earth. There is evidence, however, that singers had already classified their songs, distinguishing between special songs reserved for ceremonies or specific tasks and songs that did not have this connection.

Now that musicologists have begun to be more interested in individual songs and styles, a new research area has arisen: studies of vocal performance of folk music. Female musicologists appear to have shown a greater interest in this area than their male colleagues, who have preferred to concentrate on instrumental folk music.

Ingrid Gjertsen, a Norwegian folk music scholar, has characterized singing techniques in folk music by comparing folk song with conventional classical vocal techniques.

> In European classical music, the ideal voice is a full one, with a great deal of scope and volume. In accordance with this idea, the human body gives rise to resonance in prescribed ways, so as to give the voice fullness. As opposed to folk music, in classical music the voice is located more in the head than in the body of the singer. The mouth is supposed to be wide open, and the voice has to be loud in order to resonate. Folk singing has very different conceptions of both scope and volume, as well as resonating differently. The voice is further forward, at the front of the singer's mouth, and is more nasal. It resonates in a more concentrated fashion. Folk music is distinguished from classical European music not only with regard to use of the voice, but also to general performance. The melodic lines develop more freely in folk music, with regard both to melody and rhythm. Folk singers tend to stress the consonants in the text, which also affects the tonality and rhythm of the music. The voice part seldom goes straight to a defined pitch. Instead, it takes a circuitous route, using either glissandos or small embellishments. (Gjertsen 1985, p. 214.)

Using Sound Analysis Equipment to Study Song

As early as 1972, Ola Kai Ledang studied song performance in the melodies of religious Norwegian texts using sound-analysis equipment. His findings correspond to Gjersten's verbal description in many respects. One of the problems often discussed in this context is how to relate the individual note, the separate "components" of the flow of the music we regard as melodies when we write them down. Seeger discusses this in his study of variations on the ballad of Barbara Allen (1977). It is also discussed in an article of methodological interest by Alf Gabrielsson and Anna Johnson (1985), in which they attempt to combine verbal "listening descriptions" by interpreting the results of analyses made with sound-analysis equipment. This study was based on the chorale "Bereden väg för Herran" (Make Way for the Lord), and is an analysis of three choral variations sung by Finn Jon Jonsson (1853–1936) and his children, Finn Jonas Jonsson (1888–1965) and Kersti Nygårds (1896–1970). Each one had their own variant of melody, although they basically followed the same version. The scholars then had two professional singers, Rolf Leandersson (b. 1933) and Stefan Parkman (b. 1952), record the chorale, first on the basis of written music and then after having listened to a sound analysis made by melody analysts at the Department of Musicology at the University of Uppsala.

The musicologists found that the performance of the folk singer was a melody line with constant glissandos between notes and long "approaches" to the first note of every phrase. According to the scholars, much more happened between and in the course of every note when the folk singers performed the song than when the professional vocalists performed it. They found that written music led to much more tightly bound approaches than the songs performed by folk singers who learned them by ear, and that the folk singers exhibited far more variation from one performance to the next. Writing the music down was also found to affect the way the melody was perceived, encouraging the reader to see the melody more as a series of individual notes than as a flowing continuum.

Is Vocal Expression Based on Speech?

In a study of a 1986 performance by folk singer Lisa Boudres, Susanne Rosenberg (1986) concluded that her "vocal expression is based on speech" (p. 76), and that she creates contrasts, for example, by exaggerating some sounds, binding syllables together using nasal sounds to develop new semantic constellations. Her singing was also found to be characterized by ornamentation, and the meaning-bearing qualities of the text were overshadowed by the "sound qualities of the text" (p. 77).

The Impact of Other Vocal Styles

Bartók described Hungarian folk song as it changed under the influence of urban vocal styles.

As the new style is still flourishing, it is far less difficult to collect examples of it than to collect examples of old-style tunes. The latter are obtainable from elderly people only, who at times—on account of their age—cannot easily be persuaded to sing, and whose memories are not infallible. It very seldom occurs that we find several people in the same place who sing old tunes: indeed, we may rejoice if in one village we encounter one person who remembers old tunes. But as regards the new tunes, the position is far different. These are fashionable; every boy and girl knows a good many of them. People sing them in unison while working in the fields or marching, so that indeed we hear 'the spontaneous expression of the peasant's musical instinct,' as the stock phrase would have it. And we are able accurately to observe the mode of performance. Of course, it is collective singing that provides the most useful opportunity.

The Hungarian peasant uses only chest voice. Whenever singers pitch notes in the head, we may presume that urban influences have been at work. The performance has strong rhythm. When marching, singers assign a quarter note to each step: hence $\quarternote = 100$, a pace which many consider as the normal tempo of new-style tunes. But if only one person is singing and especially singing to a listener, the pace is often slackened, and sometimes to excess. [. . .] Another remarkable practice—one might almost say, a malpractice—should be mentioned. [. . .] It is connected with the steadily growing compass of tunes: in the case of a tune whose compass is 1–10 or even 1–12 [. . .] it is not always easy for the singer to select a pitch which will enable him to intone with equal ease all the low and all the high notes. Hungarian peasants do not devote much care to select a suitable pitch, but they simplify difficulties in proportion as they occur: whenever a note is too high or too low for them, they transpose it by an octave, regardless of design and rhythmic conditions. This they will do *ad libitum*, perhaps several times in the course of one tune. (Bartók 1981, pp. 50f.)

Greta Dahlström made similar observations with regard to Finnish folk singers, i.e., that they did not hesitate to shift up or down by an octave if their vocal registers were insufficient for the song (see p. 66).

There are many stylistic traits specific to folk music that are in stark contrast with the principles of classical music. For example, Tomás O'Canainn (1978) mentions nasalization in the *sean-nós* (see also pp. 90–91). Will these vocal techniques live on, or will they vanish under the pressure of new techniques for popular music? It appears that "folksy" singing is on the rise. It is unfortunate that so little has been written about how the singers themselves see their performance–this is a huge unexplored research field.

On Polyphonic Folk Song

Folk song collections often give the impression that folk singing was a solo art and that folk songs were performed by a single vocalist. Although there was quite a lot of this kind of performance, there is also a great deal of evidence for sing-alongs. In her study of folk songs in Altmark, Magdeburg, Germany (1962), Doris Stockmann found various forms of group folk singing. In the past, it was common to sing together in German villages, with young and old joining in groups. Such groups have been described, and their songs were noted down in collections from the mid-nineteenth century through 1950, when they began to die out. Traditional occasions for singing were gradually made superfluous by the existence of organized choirs. The *Koppel*, i.e., choirs with eight to ten members that met and sang in the evenings in the village streets during the warm months of the year, were especially important. Their repertoire included all kinds of folk songs, dance music, romances, and, later, popular hits. By 1955 this kind of evening voluntary vocal entertainment had virtually vanished. There was also a winter equivalent, the indoor *Spinnkoppel*. This meant that there was singing year round. Stockmann's examples are mainly of monophonic songs. When there are several parts, they tend to run in thirds or parallel sixths.

In household and pub singing in Germany today, this latter kind of singing may still be heard, as well as in Austria and the nearby countries to the east. "Hector Berlioz described various kinds of polyphonic folk music he heard in Italy. He mentions two-part songs which were more or less in tune, the barbarian shepherd songs similar to their Turkish counterparts, and street choirs who appeared to have learnt what little they knew about music by frequenting the theatres." (*Memoirs*, 1803–1805, Berlioz 1980, p. 171f.)

There were other kinds of polyphonic singing in Europe (for example, from Georgia and Albania), some of which have been described by scholars as extremely complex. However, this complexity may simply be the perception of the unaccustomed listener. The singers who grew up with this music see the polyphony as a fundamental prerequisite to performing the music at all, as many collectors have discovered upon requesting individuals to sing their part so that it can be transcribed by the collector. The singers have reacted with incomprehension, as these vocal harmonies are, to them, an indivisible collective entity.

Perhaps the most varied and highly refined form of polyphonic singing in Europe is to be found in the Carpathians, the Balkans, and, not least, Georgia. The wealth of variation is so great that it is almost impossible to overview the remarkable harmonies, combinations of voices, and types of singing.

In Georgia, singing in harmony was recorded as early as the 1930s by an expedition from Leningrad, including Ernst Emsheimer (*MGG*, "Mehrstimmigkeit").

Georgian folk music is generally performed in three-part harmony, each part having a special name depending on its function in the particular piece. In eastern Georgia, two soloists often perform, alternately singing the higher part, and with a rhythmic drone permeating the text. Dissonance is avoided.

In western Georgia, on the other hand, folk music is characterized by a highly complex polyphony, in which the parts are allowed to develop following established patterns in accordance with a long tradition, and irrespective of whether consonances or dissonances arise (Figure 5.11). Not until the end of the song do the parts join together in a long-awaited unison. The melodies are performed by the middle voice, which is accompanied, above and below. It is common for parts to cross, meet up in seconds, move in parallels, and suddenly leap. One very special technique in this type of song is a sudden upswing into falsetto, where the melodic motifs take on distinct profiles, often within the range of a seventh. In Georgia there are also songs for two choirs, one of which sings as a group of soloists and the other in traditional four-part polyphony. Emsheimer also emphasizes the special melodic formula with which the lead singer initiates the song. The tradition exists in both eastern and western Georgia. The eastern variant is an independent phrase, the western an introduction to the play between the melodic lines. The rhythm is a free recitative or melismatic form in eastern Georgia, while in western Georgia the rhythm is rapid and pulsating, with a basic beat divided into sections with defined time signatures.

In the 1960s Doris Stockmann, Wilfried Fiedler and Erich Stockmann visited southern Albania, where they found that different people had their own very special kinds of polyphonic singing. Their ambition was to survey geographical districts, and determine the variants of style and performance of the vocal polyphony found there. In the whole area, the singers stood in a semi-circle, as close to one another as possible. If there was a drone, the soloists sat either opposite or beside one another, thus providing a focus around which the choir was centered. When the scholars tried to move the singers around in order to be able to record better, they found that the singers were unable to perform their song if they were not in their usual positions. The song groups were generally composed of either men and boys or women and girls, but seldom included members of both sexes. Every village also had one or two soloist couples who performed together. Generally the men were more willing to perform for strangers, while the women tended to be shy and not forthcoming. However, both the men's and women's groups had wide repertoires, including love songs, legends, historical songs, seasonal and holiday songs, and, not least, general songs for social occasions. However, only women sang lullabies and laments. Very few instruments were found in this area, and the only types were wind instruments that would be found in animal-herding cultures plus short-necked lyres and tambourines.

The drone-based songs in several parts were mainly performed by men. Stockmann (et al.) describe the performance as a drawn-out drone from the choir is overlaid by two solo voices, each with its own melodic line. One of the soloists remains the lead voice throughout the song. This part is called "take it." The other soloist comes in later, and is called "the attendant" or "cut voice." The çamëria drone-song begins with the drone of the choir intoned by one or more individuals first and then taken up by the others, after which the first soloist initiates a solo phrase. The choral part is known as iso, from the Greek. The singing is based on the vowel e, which is held out as if it were being played on an instrument. Three singers must perform the iso part. The choir continues even when the soloists pause.

In her melodic analyses, Doris Stockmann shows that there is clear regularity in the structure: the soloists shape a sort of melodic double phrasing that sometimes corresponds to one or more segments of text. One textual segment can also, however, be formed by one or more melodic motifs. The lead voice sings the complete text while the other soloist only repeats selected parts. Some segments of text are repeated, and there are also many elements of improvisation (Figure 5.12).

The çamëria drone-song is based on five- or six-note scales. The range varies from a sixth to an octave. One common stylistic feature is a descending movement with rich ornamentation. Thus the singer begins with a high note or quickly moves up to one. Toward the end, the melodic line descends (sometimes steeply, sometimes less so), concluding with the drone. Stockmann distinguishes among different types of harmonies in the drone.

There is a tendency to strive for consonant harmonies. The rhythmic structure is more or less free, sometimes of a stricter sort, sometimes quite parlando-like. The songs are narrated in different ways, depending on the nature of the text. The soloist often approaches ecstasy in the performance. The two singers fill different functions: the leader is to sing with a loud, full voice and be highly familiar with the texts, while the second adapts in order to create harmonies and dramatic dialogue.

Several studies have been made of polyphonic Albanian songs with more or less systematic examinations of regional differences, and examples of the adaptation of these songs to new functions, such as for political purposes have been provided (see Kruta 1981, 1984:1 and 2; Daja 1983).

Alica Elscheková (1981) has studied singing in several part harmony in the Carpathians. Her methods include analysis of melodies, using a statistical-mathematical model. She began by divid-

Figure 5.11. West Georgian polyphony (Nadel 1933, p. 21 no. 12).

ing the material in relation to the number of parts and how they were performed the function of each part, and the relationship between the scale and motives of each part. She also studied the succession of harmonies formed by the parts as well as the various forms of cadences and the counterpoint. She went on to list different types of polyphony, examining the composition technique used to structure the phrases, including the movement of parts, drones, ostinatos, canons, parallels, etc. Elscheková accounted in detail for regional differences, providing an impressive survey of variations in polyphonic structures.

It is interesting to ask whether it is possible to determine the age of polyphonic vocal music. Elscheková provides the following hypothetical description of what happened when monophonic music became polyphonic through the influence of urban culture.

The monophonic melody was first given another part either a third above or below the melody. When there were two soloists, the one singing the lower part was to incorporate the harmonies I, II, VII, I, in the cadences. In polyphonic song the thirds were gradually replaced by fifths, and the fifths were then filled out with thirds under the influence of string ensembles and urban music.

Elscheková established important distinguishing criteria between older and newer polyphonic music: the former included various kinds of intervals, and concluded in unison, while the latter used more thirds, which also dominated at the cadences (Figure 5.13a and b).

How Did Polyphony Arise?

We can only speculate as to the origins of vocal polyphony, its connections with western art music, etc., as there are no truly reliable sources. One well-worn hypothesis is that there was a kind of center in the Carpathians. From there, various threads were spun, leading to western medieval vocal polyphony and "popular" polyphony in Georgia. However, the idea that popular polyphony originated in art music models now appears to have been permanently shelved. New literature from Georgia (and elsewhere) indicates that songs in three-part harmony were performed there long before the School of Notre Dame came into being.

There has long been similar discussion with regard to the Icelandic *tvísöngur* (twin-songs). *Tvísöngur* is a remarkable type of song in which the upper and lower parts constantly cross, in a two-part counterpoint in which the fifth is the most common interval. This kind of song was performed in Iceland as early as the early Middle Ages (the first evidence is from 1324–1331). It was taught at schools throughout the seventeenth century and remained part of the folk song tradition into the twentieth. The *tvísöngur* was mainly performed by men on special occasions and at religious services. It is more probable than with Georgian polyphony that the source of the *tvísögur* was medieval organum, although it is impossible to say with certainty.

Traditional attempts to trace the sources of popular polyphony back to one or another medieval liturgical polyphonic phenomenon is (and will surely remain) a field of great speculation for music historians and folk musicologists. We must, however, bear in mind that it has been proven elsewhere that cultural phenomena bearing similarities to one another are not necessarily related.

Swiss polyphonic yodelling, the *Gradhäbe*, is one

Figure 5.12. Albanian polyphonic song performed by men, and an analysis of the structure and harmonic progression. (Quoted from Stockmann/Fiedler 1965, example no. 3 p. 101, and analysis p. 44 and 50.)

kind of polyphony the source of which seems possible to trace. The following story comes from Appenzel (published in 1890).

> If a group of yodellers have gathered on a 'day of rest' [there were two official dancing days per year] and they want to produce a new yodel, they stand close to one another in a circle, bow their heads and put their arms around each others' shoulders. Also, they often used the sound from cow bells. One of the best yodellers sings the melody [Loba, Boverla] while the others hold a monotonous base note [like that of a bagpipe]. (Baumann 1976, p. 172.)

Thus the *Gradhäbe* is a kind of polyphonic, improvised journey based on simple basic triads, providing the yodeller with harmonic support for his melodic twists and leaps. The name is regarded as being related to *gerade halten* (holding out evenly) and may be an attempt to imitate the bagpipe. There are many kinds of *gradhäbe*, from simple drones to homophonic support in combination with various kinds of cow bells. According to Baumann, the *gradhäbe* can be traced (in terms of textual or melodic evidence) back only to the second-half of the eighteenth century (p. 202). Perhaps this was when it originated. We may never know. (See also pp. 37 and 162.)

The Testimony of a Singer

Before we move on from folk song, let us meet an informant of Hungarian folk musicologist Bálint Sarósi as a counterpoint to all the scholarly theories mentioned here. He was a farmer by the name of Péter Sándor (1900–1976), and he may have held the answers to many of our questions about origins and layers, and how traditions were passed down. He claimed that he sang what he pleased and made up new songs when he forgot the old ones.

Bálint Sarósi has written:

> I knew him from childhood, he was a *székely* from the village where I was born. My first memory of him dates from spring plowing, the year I was six or eight, and drove the plow with my father. I was leading the horses, and enjoying listening to another plowman whistling beautifully from a nearby hill. Sometimes he burst into song, only to be whistling shortly thereafter again. Then there was a sudden pause, after which he returned his stubborn horses to the furrow, adding a series of curse words to his whistling. A moment or two later he was singing again, having picked up a lovely old hymn, as if to make up for his swearing. He went on, picking funny songs and laments alternately out of the storehouse of his memory. [. . .] [Later, during a recording session in 1958] As we were talking he suddenly remembered the melody of an old *székely* folk song, although he could only recall fragments of the words. Seeing my disappointment, he was immediately prepared to console me, by saying, 'Never mind, I'll have it by tomorrow.' And he recreated the old folk song from the fragments of text he recalled, so that it sounded authentic. His knowledge of the tradition and his ability to create verses made it possible

FSAV-979-1-350; Šarišské Jastrabie, Levoča, drei Mädchen; A. Elscheková 1963, Heuen-
telied

a ▲ *b* ▼

F. Kolessa 1938/83, S. 87

Figure 5.13. Polyphony in the Carpathians: (a) Slovakia, and (b) the Ukraine. (Elscheková 1981, p. 171 and 196.)

for him to replace the bits he had long forgotten without hesitation. (Sárosi 1986, p. 24f.)

Literature

A great deal of research on folk songs has been published (see, for example, the bibliographies appended to the articles on the music of various countries in *New Grove* and in journals such as *Ethnomusicology*, as well as special bibliographies such as *Europäische Volksmusik*, edited by Erich Stockmann). Various folk music archives have special publications, such as *SUMLEN*, the yearbook of the Swedish folk music archive.

With regard to Sweden, Märta Ramsten's presentation in *Folkmusikboken* (1980) is an excellent introduction. Margareta Jersild's description of the instructions regarding the melodies of broadsides (1975) is also a review of the cultural history of the use of the folk song. Doris Stockmann's study of folk songs in Altmark (1962) is unique in that it combines historical and sociological perspectives. Bartók's 1925 work is a classic work still worthy of the attention of anyone interested in analysis. A. L. Lloyd's *Folk Music in England* (1967) is a work of an entirely different kind, comprehensive and readily accessible. Every country has at least one such popular presentation, which often also includes a collection of folk songs.

Six

The Playing of Folk Music (Part I): Spontaneous Sound Makers, Acoustic Working Equipment

WHAT DO MUSICAL IN-STRUMENTS TELL US?

Some of the early acoustic tools and musical instruments that characterized the rural soundscape can still be heard today, either in their traditional environments or in museums. When music is performed today, however, it is generally on instruments that can be tuned to one another. The jarring sound of the ratchet, previously used at the hunt and elsewhere, has now been relegated to the stands at international football matches. Today we have ambulances and fire trucks that blow their sirens to keep traffic and pedestrians out of their way. In the past, other instruments were used to ward off wild animals (see Sevåg 1973, p. 18f.)

The sounds and the harmonies with which we live become integral parts of our identity. When we see older instruments, we can ask ourselves what the sounds of the past were and what melodies were played on them. In this way, instruments become memories of sound.

Instruments cannot be indelibly associated with a single context. They have been used for different purposes and in different ways at different points in time and in different environments, not to mention by different players. It is even risky to try to distinguish between "folk" and "art" instruments: the percussion section of a symphony orchestra, for example, contains many scraping and clapping instruments very similar to old tools. Beginning in the eighteenth century, folk music has also increasingly been played on art instruments. During the nineteenth century, when it became possible to mass-produce them, the har-monica and the accordion quickly became regarded as folk instruments because they came into use by a broader spectrum of the general public than the elite lovers of classical music.

WHAT IS A FOLK INSTRU-MENT?

We begin this chapter by examining some of the pieces of everyday sound-making equipment that are fundamental to all instrumental music. There are tree trunks we just cannot resist making noise on, blades of grass that just have to be whistled, and bottles and tins just waiting to see if we can make music with them. This sound equipment has been used by generation after generation without any sense of passing down a tradition. In Chapter 2 we looked at working tools used for music-making. We go on to see how these tools were used not only at work but also as musical instruments at dances and on ceremonial occasions. We shall also see how instruments originally used in a particular context do not stay bound to it, but spread to wider functions and environments. There is a constant circulation of instruments from one stratum of society to another, as financial and ideological barriers fall away. An instrument which at one point is regarded as refined and exclusive may suddenly be rejected as vulgar. This was the fate of the accordion in the nineteenth century. The violin moved in the opposite direction in the late sixteenth century. Having been a simple dance instrument, it achieved its zenith in art music, at the same time never losing its popularity amongst the people.

The same basic principles of construction apply to spontaneously created sound-makers and to specially constructed musical instruments. In the hands of a virtuoso player, spoons serve as a stupendous rhythm and sound instrument, comparable with professionally made castanets (Figure 6.1). Henceforth, the term musical instrument as used here applies to any sound-making object used in any type of musical context.

How can we define what we mean by folk music instruments? I have settled on using the societal aspect as my line of demarcation. A folk music instrument (FMI) is any instrument used for certain functions and in certain environments external to the feudal court and the church and beyond the public and private musical milieus of the bourgeoisie. Today, FMIs are a valuable supplement to art and popular music instruments.

This definition has many problematical aspects. Some FMIs were played at the courts, especially on the occasions when the royalty and nobility would dress up and pretend they were peasants. It was impossible to ban first the fiddle and later the violin entirely from the church, and fiddlers sometimes played in both the chancel and from the organ loft. Both the domestic salons and the public concerts of the bourgeoisie sometimes contained FMIS. Today, numerous folk instruments are used when rock, jazz and art music are performed (not least at what are referred to as medieval musical performances). It is possible that we should consider the synthesizer and the electric guitar as the FMIs of our times, as their popularity and the number of people who play them can be compared with the Jew's harp and bagpipes in the Middle Ages, the violin in the seventeenth century, and the accordion in the nineteenth. Perhaps the young people who have established the Stockholm Synthesizer Fiddlers are the most genuine folk musicians we have today. However, in order to be FMIs, instruments, at any given moment, must have been around for a century or so and be associated with a certain folk repertoire, style, and environment.

Categorization and Description of Musical Instruments

An instrument loses its status as "musical" if, as happened to the keyed fiddle in Sweden during the nineteenth-century revival movement, it is transformed into a feeding dish or a toy boat for children. We may well ask whether a guitar never taken down from the wall or a piano used only as a stand for photographs is a musical instrument or a decorative object. If a description of sound-makers and instruments is to be meaningful, *instrumentalists* must be included as well as the sounds they produce in the form of signals or music. The instrumentalists are, in turn, dependent on the social context as mentioned above, which is often decisive to the function of the instrument. The demand for a holistic approach has developed gradually in instrumental scholarship. However, it has proven difficult to develop a reasonable model for including *everything* in a description of all the ways an instrument can be used. Any number of efforts have been made to systematize instruments, and models have been developed, but they have often turned out to be difficult to apply in practice (see also *New Grove*, vol. 9, p. 238, Bielawski 1979, Kvifte 1986).

The scholarly work that comes closest to providing the holistic approach is *Handbuch der Europäischen Volkmusikinstrumente (1967)* by Ernst Emsheimer and Erich Stockmann. It focuses on the following aspects of instruments: material, construction, how they are played, repertoire, function, dissemination, and history. Instruments are regarded as an integral part of a musical chain that links *context-instrumentalist-instrument-music* into a whole.

The chain is subject to certain variation. For example, itinerant fiddlers had to be flexible in adapting their performance and style to the context. If the repertoire or sound of the instrument is changed too drastically, or if the context is extremely foreign, the chain may break down or be replaced by a new one.

Any given study of musical instruments puts its main emphasis on some link of the chain. In this chapter, the primary concentration is on general cultural issues, while the instrumentalist's technique in handling the instrument, the repertoire, and the function of the instrument or of the music are regarded as secondary. The material with regard to these latter factors is so extensive that each separate instrument would be worthy of a study of its own.

The issue of the historical and cultural role of an instrument has been dealt with as long as there has been instrumental research. The early studies, not unlike Bartók's efforts to study melodies, were carried out with a view to practical results. In the late nineteenth century organologists (such as Mahillon) began contemplating how to arrange the instruments of the world into a system that could be applied at museums, exhibitions, and archives. Soon there were serious theoretical studies aimed at providing a general systematization of instruments (Hornbostel/Sachs 1914; for a survey, see Kvifte 1986).

Ernst Emsheimer and Erich Stockmann's system, developed for categorization of folk music instruments in the 1950s, was central to the development of folk music research in Europe (1964). They based their system on the Hornbostel/Sach (1914) classification of instruments into *idiophones* (that produce their sound from the substance of the instrument itself), *membranophones* (for example drums), *cordophones* (stringed instruments), and *aerophones* (wind instruments). They went on to supplement this system with descriptions of the way the instrument was played and its history. Their system formed the basis for the monumental *Handbuch der europäischen Volksmusikinstrumente*, mentioned above, which is to contain a volume on every European nation. The volumes are organized by region, and the original ambition was that every country would have its volume. In some ways this is problematic, in that the instruments have not respected these geographical boundaries. Still, the volumes available to date (Hungary, Bohemia-Moravia, Slovakia, Switzerland, Slovenia) describe such a wealth of instruments and types that there will have to be a radical change in our picture of the European soundscape.

Ernst Emsheimer has drafted an overview of the types of instruments represented in the first five volumes, (Figure 6.1). It clarifies that Slovakia has by far the largest number of types of instruments, not owing only to the rich tradition in that country but also to the fact that so much collection work has been such done there. In the final analysis, when all the surveys of folk music instruments in Europe have been completed and supplemented with dissemination maps, we will be able to see the European soundscape in detail.

Origins and Dissemination

The origins and dynamic history of an instrument are difficult to trace, even if information is available as to the phases of its development. Efforts have been made to trace this process in relation to folk music instruments still in use today. *The galoubet-tambourin, instrument traditionnel de Provence*, by Maurice Guis, Thierry Lefrancois, and Rémi Venture, is an excellent example from 1993. The situation is even more complicated with regard to instruments from longer ago, for which the only sources may be archaeological finds, literary examples, or works of art.

Many folk music instruments were very widespread, probably because they originated at roughly the same time in various places with similar functional prerequisites, or because they spread from a single center of culture in many directions. Undoubtedly, many factors contributed to the spreading of these instruments.

Among those found at archaeological sites all over Europe are many types of flutes. New finds are constantly providing us with examples of extremely costly, richly ornamented flutes in addition to simple ones that were made from readily accessible animal bones until the end of the nineteenth century (see also Moeck 1969, Homo-Lecher 1987, Lund 1985).

"Universal" Instruments

In other words, it appears that certain instruments, such as the flute, were universal from an early stage, if we draw our conclusions on the basis of the many finds from across large areas and the varied designs and playing styles (see Leisiö 1983). To some extent, the same can be said for single reed instruments (of the clarinet type) and for double reed instruments (of the oboe type), which are found in a wide range of forms as separate instruments or, for example, as parts of a set of bagpipes. Many scholars have tried to find a typology for all these flutes. Moeck (1969), for instance, worked along the lines of the Hornbostel/Sachs hierarchical system and produced a study of different types of European fipple flutes, dividing them into groups with formulas for

1. the type of flute (fipple flute = recorder, tongue or lip flute = the air flow is determined by the tongue or lips, transverse, open-holed long flute),
2. overtone flutes,
3. the number of holes,

4. the presence or absence of a thumb hole,
5. the location of the sharp edge of the block in fipple flutes (i.e., whether the sharp edge was on the same or opposite side of the flute from the holes).

On the basis of these criteria, Moeck goes on to present an impressive survey of European fipple flutes, including both archaeological finds and flutes from popular musical milieus. Virtually all hierarchical studies lead to the conclusion that the instrument in question has developed from a primitive to a more complex form during its lifetime. However, this was not always the case in reality. In the same volume of *SIMP* (no. I) where Moeck's study was published, Elschek (1969) put forward a different kind of systematization he called "typological access in work with folk music instruments."

Using graphic symbols, he illustrates various kinds of

1. drilling,
2. means of making a sound,
3. constructions and how to blow,
4. location, shape, and means of production of the holes, and
5. material and means of production of the flute.

Elschek then combines these various elements, but not in a hierarchical way. Allowing differences and similarities between ways of playing, principles of construction, materials, etc., to determine the system opened up potential for new kinds of comparative studies.

Different typologies or systems of instruments have fascinated not only scholars but also the instrument-makers themselves, who have invented various symbols for instruments, etc. One example is the Swedish keyed fiddle, where the instrument-makers have developed a system of classification, including the "double bass fiddle," the "silver bass fiddle," and the "chromatic keyed fiddle," on the basis of their own and the fiddlers' typologies. Thus the counter-fiddle got its name from the placement of the strings on either side of (counter to) the drone string, the silver bass fiddle the "new kind" of overspinning gut strings, which probably transformed the sound more than other changes in the instrument, and the chromatic keyed fiddle from tangents that allowed it to be played in any key.

European Folk Instruments
Idiophones:
swords or sticks for dancing
spurs for dancing
spoons
cymbals
xylophones
triangles
threshing beaters
sounding-board (board with wooden mallets)
clapper-board (board with one hammer on the top   that strikes the board when it is swung).
wind clapper-board (hammers attached to an arm, equipped with a propeller).
cow bells
bells
rattle-stick (dancing staff with rattling rings)
sleighbells
scraping sticks
washing board
noise makers
box ratchet
Jew's harp ★
saw (bowed) ★
scraping board (wooden object scraped with a stick)

Figure 6.1. Musical Instruments in *Handbuch der Europäischen Volksmusikinstrumente* (1967) by Ernst Emsheimer and Erich Stockmann.

Who Makes Folk Music Instruments?

Folk music instruments have traditionally been made by the performers themselves or by instrument-makers close to them. Beginning in the eighteenth century, more and more instruments were also made by professional urban instrument makers. In the nineteenth century folk music performers began to purchase mass-produced instruments from factories, not least by mail order.

The building of one's own folk instrument is, however, still an important element in folk music cultures all over Europe. Today, instrument making often takes organized forms, and courses in instrument-making are frequently held in many places in Europe.

Spontaneous Instruments in Musical Games for Adults and Children

Surely every parent will remember a moment of desperation when their toddlers were banging on anything in sight, especially anything that made a loud noise. The child's curiosity about sound is a

Membranophones:
tubular drum
friction drum★
mirliton (singing membranes such
    as a paper-covered comb)

Cordophones
musical bow
box zither
dulcimer
necked lutes:
    long-necked lute (guitar type)
    hurdy-gurdy
fiddles of different shapes and sizes★★
violins, cellos and double basses
bass fiddles of different shapes
    and sizes
percussion double bass
    (such as the gardon)
harps ★★

Aerophones:
whips
air reeds
    (such as a blade of grass
    held between the
    thumbs and blown into)
lip reeds (such as a piece of birch
    bark placed to the
    lips so as to make a vibrating noise)
rotating aerophones (such as a twirled piece of wood
    on a string)

whirling aerophones (such as a button on a ribbon,
    which is twisted and becomes "elastic", which
    makes the button vibrate)

edge instruments (with or without finger-holes):
transverse flutes
carved flutes
end-blown flute
fipples flutes ((= duct flutes, recorders) with and
    without finger holes)
double duct flutes
vessel flute with duct (= ccarina)
straw, reed or bark oboes
clarinets made of bird feathers, plant stems, etc.
    (ideoglottal = with the reedcut out of the instru-
    ment itself)
wooden or metal clarinets (with a separate mouth-
    piece (heteroglottal = a separate reed)
tárogató (a special type of clarinet with a conical
    wooden tube and an oboe mechanism from late
    nineteenth century Budapest).
bagpipe with with blowpipe or bellows
    organs
harmonicas★
accordions
animal horns
wooden trumpets
metal trumpets

★

Figure 6.1 cont'd.

kind of pleasure associated with the discovery of music that often vanishes when the child is adapted to the norms and regulations of its social environment. Many pieces of sound-making equipment and "musical instruments" are made of readily available materials: a blade of grass held between one's thumbs is a wonderful "oboe," a split dandelion stalk with a "tongue" a fine clarinet, etc. Such instruments are spontaneously made, and are for temporary use.

    Materials that can be shaped to produce simple or more advanced instruments include everything from pieces of wood and bark to fruit peels and bones, plastic tubing, empty coffee tins, and disused pens. Igor Cvetko (1985), a Slovenian folk music scholar, documented the ability of children to make musical instruments both by using their own imaginations and by emulating the instrument repertoire from the adult world. He also described the various materials used in different times, reflecting the traditional principle of using what is at hand. Pan flutes were traditionally made from reeds, for instance, but can also be produced from

plastic tubing or from cardboard. Simple metal objects may be transformed into exciting percussion instruments, and disused household goods, such as a wooden clog or a cigar box, may be transformed into interesting stringed instruments (on Slovakian fiddles, see also p. 159 and Figure 8.7).

    The following story has been told about the first instruments belonging to Anders Frisell, who later became a prominent Swedish fiddler.

> When Frisell was about seven, he and his older brother made a fiddle from hand-cut roof thatch, and he began to learn simple melodies on it. However, his parents, who were in the grasp of one of the more pious revival movements, brought his playing to and end and burned his fiddle as if it had been a tool of the Devil. A year or two later his brother made him a better one, very much in the shape of a proper fiddle, with strings of ordinary, homespun sewing thread (*SvL Dalarna* III p. 174.)

Today there is also a special "DIY" methodology to encourage children to make their own simple instruments from everyday materials. This educational theory has been criticized in some circles as preventing children from coming into contact with "real" instruments either in the home or in their pre-school environments.

Children's Instruments with a Magical Past

Some musical instruments for children are similar to older, magical instruments, but have been adapted to fill new functions. One outstanding example is the clapping instruments used during Lent in the Freiburg area of southern Germany (Habenicht 1985). These remarkable "noise making boxes" (*Kastenratschen*) (Figure 6.2) are produced by adults for children. Each instrument consists of a sounding box with eight hammers, which can be lifted by two rows of eight pegs mounted on a cylinder with a crank. The pegs lift the extended arms of the hammers, one by one. The arms extend beyond the head of the hammer, and when the pegs let go, the hammer strikes the top of the box, making a terrible din. The instruments are only played during Holy Week, at the high mass held on the evening of Maundy Thursday after the church bells have tolled during the Gloria in excelsis. The priests then exchange their own bells for clapping instruments, which is the signal for the boys to get their own special clapping instruments ready. At the high point of the Mass, they start to "play" their instruments, one by one, and the noise increases. On the morning of Good Friday, the boys go around collecting money. No one knows exactly how old this custom is, but noisy instruments have been used on symbolic occasions associated with death or illness since the Middle Ages.

In early times the whining or cracking noise produced by swinging something rapidly through the air was used both in magical contexts and for working functions in the adult world. Norwegian musicologist Reidar Sevåg (1973, p. 22) provides examples of how people in Norway used a kind of bullroarer to abate the high winds or to call the crew of a fishing ship to work (Figure 6.3). There are still magic rhymes children know to make the bark loosen from a stick so they can turn it into a flute or a pipe (Brockpähler 1970, Emsheimer 1984).

In the early world of the imagination, sound was a powerful force. Many of us born prior to 1940 will recall that when we were children it was

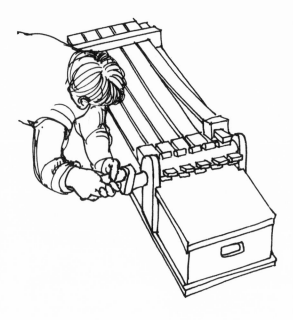

Figure 6.2. Box ratchet. (Sketch after Bachmann-Geiser 1981, p. 37.)

considered unsuitable, if not sinful, to whistle. According to Sevåg (1973), this may be associated with older ideas about the danger of sharp noises, like whistling on a blade of grass "The old people claimed these sounds would bring down the rain. They called it 'blowing rain.' It made the old women angry when the children would blow on their little reed pipes in the spring. They said it would make the weather cold and nasty. There was even a proverb for it: 'Whistling makes it wet'" (Sevåg 1973, p. 23). Children take in the sounds of the world around them in a process of learning to understand and integrate a cultural pattern. In noisy urban environments, children naturally seek out strong, aggressive noisemakers. In this way, the musical instruments used by children are a measure of the quality and structure of the soundscape in their society.

The Reed Pipe

The painting from 1889 by Christian Skredvig, aptly entitled *The Reed Pipe*, shows these instruments being made in the spring when the sap was rising. This made it easy to loosen the bark from the wood, which was first soaked then beaten and twisted.

Today this instrument, once a spontaneous creation, has been monopolized by the musical instruments industry, and is available in plastic for use as a folk music instrument or tourist souvenir. It has lost all connection with the season when the sap was rising. This has been portrayed by Norwegian musicologist Ola-Kai Ledang, using a model that illustrates various ideological, cultural and societal factors in the process:

1. the instrument originated in the herding tradition;
2. it was transported into a new environment by a folk musicologist, who endowed it with new functions;
3. a cultural entrepreneur reshaped the instrument to adapt it to serving as
4. a tourist souvenir and
5. an instrument for use by proponents of local culture and folk music;
6. the mass media strengthened the position of the instrument as a national folk instrument.

Ledang's model was based on the following underlying information: musicologist Eiving Groven made scholarly studies of the reed flute or pipe, as well as introducing it as a folk instrument at fiddlers' competitions (*kappleikar*) and on radio broadcasts. In 1960, a man by the name of Egil Storbekken began making metal pipes. Later, when plastic became more common, plastic pipes were gradually used in more and more contexts.

The *Launeddas*

Many of these apparently simple instruments are actually extremely sophisticated. One example is the *launeddas*, a Sardinian triple clarinet. The *launeddas* consists of a pipe played with the left hand and attached to a drone pipe, with yet another pipe for their right hand (Figure 6.4). This instrument is one of a wealth of reed instruments, traceable back to ancient Egypt and disseminated throughout the Mediterranean area. Weis Bentzon (1969) has studied this instrument in detail, and poses two hypotheses about it:

1. that the *launeddas* was a local form of the common double pipe, developed in the first century B.C., and
2. that it was part of a subgroup of simple clari-

Figure 6.3. Bullroarer. (Sketch after Sevåg, p.23.)

nets, most of which died out in the late Middle Ages, or were incorporated into the bagpipe family.

During the 150–200 years in which it is possible to follow the instrument closely, many of its details have changed.

The *launeddas* is easy to make but difficult to keep in working order for a long period of time. It is necessary to locate the exact type of bamboo needed to make a good instrument. In order to play it properly, it is necessary to know a great deal of theory and to master the performance technique. The instrument can be found in various tunings and with different scales. The instrument also had its own special notation, which it has now vanished, consisting of a system of symbols indicating which holes were to be open and which closed, using signs for which holes were to be covered by the right or left hand. The *launeddas* was played for line dancing at Cabras in northern Sardinia, as well as for song, marches, and religious ceremonies, (see also Bentzon 1969 which includes a special volume of transcriptions and illustrations.)

The Irish Tin Whistle

In twelfth-century Dublin, the bone flute was played in the same places as the tin whistle is played by buskers today. Simple wooden flutes are also depicted in romantic Irish paintings of the eighteenth century. As always, it is difficult to know

Figure 6.4. *Launeddas.* (Sketch after Weis Benzon 1969, part 2, p. 149, plate I.)

of labor. The hunter can entice the bird out of the bushes with the aid of special shouts and whistles in addition to using his pipe. The shepherd used both shouts and noise-makers. Norwegian herring fishermen and Swedish milkmaids used both calls and horn signals (see p. 23). Songs of labor and sounding instruments used at work were all associated with herding, fishing, farming, and hunting.

Horns

It is not certain that everyone who used instruments at work had ambitions of playing beautiful, enticing music. In one of his studies of herding music, Larsen (1986) pointed out the importance of being aware of who was using the instruments in question.

> When performance technique and instrument handling are discussed in conjunction with popular use of sounding equipment, it is important to consider what type of musicians or players were involved. There is a risk that the instrument is seen in isolation from the user. It must be stressed in this respect that horn blowers were non-professionals. They were seldom regarded as musicians in their own culture. [For example, 'horn blowers' were distinguished from 'musicians'.] Rather, the horn player was judged in terms of his ability to get the relevant work done. The horn blower was an animal herder and could, as such, use many different tools, of which the herding horn was one. This says nothing, however, about their playing skill. . . . When Zorn arranged competitions, thereby promoting an advanced technique, the instrument took on (at least) one new function. (Larsen 1986, p. 9f.)

Clearly, it is not necessary to interpret everything played on an instrument as "music." In his earlier research, Larsen (1977) described the production of instruments intended to be played as *prillarhorn*, or horns on which to play melodies, including ones with a single reed similar to those of the clarinet family (see also Sevåg 1973). Folk music competitions and tourism have contributed to the survival and development of the aesthetic function which, in many cases, may originally have been marginal.

Bark Horns or Wooden Trumpets

More traditional music can both influence and inspire change in folk music genres. For instance, the instruments used in military bands affected the

whether the history of these flutes is unbroken. One thing is certain, however: the flute has always been a much-loved instrument in Ireland, especially among children. Today's whistle, like the Norwegian reed pipe, is also a popular tourist souvenir today, sold with a teach-yourself manual and a tape of Irish melodies. There are two types of whistles, one with a conical bore (Clarke's whistle) and one with a cylindrical bore. Both have six holes, and can be played over a large range by overblowing. different blowing techniques also offer a large variety of timbres. Many Irish folk musicians who perform on instruments such as the violin or the concertina also play the whistle for variation. Today it is also a well-established ensemble instrument.

Tools of Work as Instruments of Music

A terrified milkmaid in the mountains who tries to frighten off a wolf or a bear by blowing into her horn has no musical ambitions, nor does the hunter trying to scare up the birds with his pipe. The fiddler on the ship's deck whose job is to keep the sailors working has to find his rhythm, as does the bagpiper meant to keep the harvesters working steadily. Although they use musical instruments, they use them as *noise-making working equipment*. Such instruments are closely related to calls and songs

production of herding horns in later years, not only in terms of attempts to improve their acoustical qualities, but also to bring some of the charm, power, and strength they represented in their properties as war-making instruments to the herding culture (Figure 6.5). The influence went the other way as well–herding horns were sufficiently loud to be used as signaling instruments by the military if necessary.

Sevåg (1973, p. 60) reproduces part of a military document from 1811 describing the dilemma facing the Norwegian army during the blockade by the English, when Norway was cut off from Denmark and had no access to instruments for military signaling. The commander general instructed his officers to "make use of what is known as the herding horn, a wooden wind instrument."

Wooden Trumpets

In Poland, the Ukraine, Czechoslovakia, Sweden, and most of the Balkan nations, herding instruments include a large number of wooden trumpets of different designs and lengths (see, for example articles by Emsheimer [1969], Dević [1977] and Baumann [1977]). There are straight and curved ones, with conical or cylindrical bores, some of which are one meter long and reasonably manageable, as well as some huge, awkward, five-meter trumpets. Some are used only for signaling, while others also have various musical functions (see also Chapter 2).

In some cultures, including Scandinavia and most of the Balkan countries, herding instruments and music making on various tools has become a serious art (Larsen 1977; 1979; Leisiö 1983; *Atlas of Folk Music Instruments* SSSR 1963; Sárosi 1967; Leng 1967; Elscheck 1983).

The *Kaval* and the *Fujara*

Dragoslav Dević (1985), a Slovakian instrument researcher, has used "long flutes" to show how the influences in the Balkan region come and go, from east to west and vice versa. His example is the eastern Serbian long flute, the *duduk*, which was crossed with an instrument called the *kaval* from nearby countries. The result was the *cevara* which, in turn, became another variant that spread in northwestern Bulgaria by the name of *goljam duduk*. The words *kaval* and *cevara* both mean "reed," and *duduk* means "pipe" (Figure 6.6).

Figure 6.5. Sketch of a Finnish horn blower playing. (*Rapapalit ja lakutimet* (Old Finnish Instruments) 1985 p. 12.2, figure 4.)

There were also hybridisations of instruments from different social classes, for example the *fujara*, the eastern European herding instrument, the name of which means "to blow" in Slovakian. The instrument (Figure 6.7)has a small pipe through which the air enters. The air is then led to the fipple through a channel. The instrument may be up to two meters long, and has three holes quite far down the body of the instrument, which makes it difficult for short people to play. The holes are generally evenly placed, according to the principle of equidistance. The player adjusts the intonation. The first four overtones are relatively easy to produce. For natural reasons, the instrument must be played in a standing position. The tongue serves as a sort of value. The basic tone is difficult to produce, and most of the playing is done on a limited number of overtones (Elschek 1983, p. 160). The *fujara* is mostly played in the mountain areas of central Slovakia. It is played outdoors from spring through autumn. Young shepherds learn it from their older colleagues, whose styles and ideals of performance may differ from one another. The performer plays and sings alternately, and the melodies are herding songs and "bandit songs," a kind of guerrilla song from the times when their country has been occupied by foreign powers.

Figure 6.6. Two *kaval* players. (Sketch after musicians in the "Dobroudja" group, disc *Balkanton* BH A 10336.)

Figure 6.7. Sketch after a photograph of a *fujara* player named Juraj Kubinec from Utekac in Slovakia. (Elschek 1983, Abb. 47.)

The *fujara* is known as the queen of Slovakian folk music, and is played mainly by the chief herders, while the others make do with simpler types of flutes. It is considered to have evolved from an earlier type of long flute with three holes. This construction is reminiscent of the bass recorder and the bassoon. The earliest evidence of the instrument is from the mid-eighteenth century, and is closely associated with seventeenth-century bandit songs. Thus it appears that the *fujara* came into being at approximately the same time as many art music instruments, and at a time when many art instruments became folk instruments and began to be popular in European folk music (see also chapters 7 and 8).

Descriptive Music Played on Herding Instruments

Shepherds developed instrumental pieces or motifs associated with different elements of their labor: "taking the sheep to their morning pasture," "taking the sheep up the mountain," "sheep bells in the pasture," "driving the sheep to the spring," "the sheep drinking water," "milking the sheep,"

"cheese-making," "butter churning," etc. (Stockmann 1960, 1965, 1974, Macievsky 1972). Descriptive pieces of music of this type–which may be said to have a primarily aesthetic function–may also have a practical function. If two shepherds are driving their sheep to water at the same time, a collision can be avoided if they can hear one another's music for "driving the sheep to the spring." The same holds true for knowing that one's neighbor is milking, making cheese, or churning butter.

Bells and Cow Bells

Instruments found at archaeological digs, such as horns, bone flutes, bells, often have contemporary counterparts, many of which are still in use. In older times, these had magical connotations (Sevåg 1973, Lund 1985, Emsheimer 1985). For example, with the advent of Christianity in peasant society, it was thought that the power of Holy Communion could be transferred to the domestic animals with the aid of cow "charmed" instruments. These "cow communions" bear witness to how all kinds of spiritual beliefs, both heathen and Christian, were used. A combination was, of course, more effective than just one. Ernst Emsheimer has studied the magic function of the animal bell from stories of these "cow communions" and elsewhere.

In Sweden on midsummer's eve the tradition was that the people on a farm would go out together and pick all kinds of flowers, binding them into wreaths that were hung in the farm house. When the wreaths had dried, they were hidden away until the autumn, when the animals were brought in for the winter. When the bells were removed for the winter, they were filled with the dried wreaths and hung away in the farmhouse until Easter morning. The dried, powdered flowers were mixed with flour to a paste, with which the bells were filled. One of the women would then go into the barn and stand by the opening for the manure . Another woman, would then hand her the bells. Each animal would then be fed a spoonful of the paste from a silver spoon, each animal being fed from its own type of bell. When the bells were empty, they were hung onto the animals to which they belonged, and they remained there until autumn came around again. This ceremony was thought to make the animals obedient to their herders all summer long. It was known as the cow communion, and was considered so important that the two women who implemented it dressed in black, as if they were going to communion themselves. They probably also had special words to say when feeding the animals their paste, but these words were secret. The cow communion was also thought to protect the animals from all evil while they were grazing, as well as to make them give a great deal of milk during the summer months. (Emsheimer 1979, p. 15.)

In Switzerland and Austria, and parts of southern Germany, cow bells still play an important role both as working equipment and musical instruments. In her book on Swiss folk instruments, Brigitte Bachmann-Geiser (1981) provides a survey of both riveted and cast bells. Bells are named after their appearance and sound: *Bumele* (which can also mean a fat woman), *Rumple* (to make noise with a hollow object), *Chlepfe* (a snapping sound), *Chlopfer* (to knock). The bell openings are oval or rectangular, and are wider or narrower depending on the desired pitch. Bells are played only by men, and bell-playing is still done today in the Swiss cantons of Appenzell and Saint Gallen when alpine dances are held, and for tourist exhibitions.

There are descriptions of bell playing as an accompaniment to yodelling (see pp. 27–28) from the 1790s, as well as detailed descriptions from the mid-nineteenth century, when tourism had taken firm root in the Alps. "After an outing [to Altenapler Sattel], a shepherd boy entertained us from a haystack with shepherd music similar to a journey in the Alps by setting three alpine bells in rhythmic movement, and making his harmonious yodelling heard between the ringings" (Bachmann-Geiser 1981, p. 24). The sound combination of bells and cow bells gives an acoustic experience that can make celebrations very special and, moreover, unique from place to place, creating a regional identity. This kind of music has been played since the Middle Ages, and many bells have been preserved, from the 1620s and onwards. These audible symbols of the past appear to be resistant to the pressure to change from both the mass media and changing lifestyles. Thus they stand out as an example of a kind of music that has been encouraged and reinforced by the tourist trade, although in a somewhat revised form.

Elsewhere in Europe, bells also have a very special meaning. In many parts of southern Europe, the new year is a time for blessing tools and animals. In the Walachia region of Romania, poems were recited to the beat of the friction drum and the cow bell, both of which were considered to have magical powers. There is often a magical function bridging the working and aesthetic function of these instruments. All three of these functions for whips, bells, and cow bells as well as rattles, are used at different seasonal celebrations in many countries in eastern Europe.

Seven

The Playing of Folk Music (Part II): The Transformation of Musical Instruments

MEDIEVAL INSTRUMENTS IN POPULAR MUSIC CULTURES

Many of the instruments represented in medieval iconographic and textual sources exist in contemporary folk music cultures all over Europe. These include various kinds of box zithers, bagpipes, hurdy-gurdys (*lira*), keyed fiddles, fiddles, Jews' harps, flutes, horns, and many more. To abandon an instrument when it is still functioning is foreign to any society outside the laws of the modern market economic system. Important ideological cornerstones of these cultures include tonal identity and continuity with the past. Thus instruments were not replaced. What did happen was that individual, local, and regional variants developed, since creativity and imagination were not under pressure of the demand for constant renewal and new ideas but were secure in the embrace of tradition and function.

This chapter provides a description of certain types of instruments and their dissemination in Europe, and attempts to trace the causes of their variation. It focuses on those instruments that were widely spread, paying less attention to locally restricted instruments.

Zithers and Lutes

Chapter 4 described the singers of runic songs, *bïlïnï*, *dumy*, and Balkan heroic epics, all of whom sang to instrumental accompaniment. The accompanist, whether or not it was the singer himself, made the important discovery of the melody as

something intrinsically special, separate from the text. Once this discovery was made, an interplay began, dramatizing the performance by alternating between verbal and musical expression.

The *Kantele*

The reader will recall that the hero of the *Kalevala*, Väinömöinen, played the *kantele*. In 1828, when Elias Lönnrot was collecting runic songs, he noted that "a *kantele* can be found on the wall of every home" (Asplund 1983, p. 79). However, during the course of the nineteenth century the violin cornered the market and the *kantele* tradition died out everywhere but in Karelia, Pohjanmaa, and central Finland. Renewed interest in the *kantele* began at the end of the nineteenth century, and there followed scholarly expeditions aimed at finding both instruments and songs. *Kantele* festivals also began to be held at this time.

The *kantele* (Figures 7.1 and 7.2) is generally regarded as having been brought by migrant peoples from what is central Russia today toward the north. Along the way, variants developed including the *kankles* in Latvia, the *kannel* in Estonia, and the *kokle* in Lithuania (Figure 7.3). The *kantele* is also related to the oldest form of Russian *gusle* (see below). Early *kantele* were made from hollowed out birch to which the top was secured with the help of birch bands. The oldest known instruments had horsehair or gut strings. The instrument sounded completely different later, when it was made with steel strings. The *Kalevala* depicts a more magical *kantele* made of fish bones, as well as a more realistic variation on Väinömöinen's birch *kantele* (see the quotations

Figure 7.1. A ten-stringed *kantele.* Sketch after a photograph of *kantele* player Petri Patronen. (After Asplund 1983, p. 45.)

Figure 7..2. Women gathered around a modern-type *kantele.* It has more than 20 strings, like a modern zither. This kind of *kantele* is played from a table top. (Sketch after Asplund 1983, also, cover of the record "Kansansoittoa *kanteleilla,*" Kansanmusiiki-instituuti Kaustinen.)

from the *Kalevala* describing the *kantele* in Chapter 4). Most of the instruments that have been preserved, however, are made of fir, pine, or other soft woods. The oldest preserved instruments are from the seventeenth and eighteenth centuries, and are relatively small (see also Asplund 1973, p. 81). In the nineteenth century, the technique of hollowing out the instruments was abandoned in favour of making them from planed boards, which changed the sound of the instrument. As the *kantele* developed, the number of strings increased. The earliest *kantele* had five, and the chromatic models from the 1920s had thirty-six. In between was the late-nineteenth-century "Karelian *kantele,*" with ten strings, the body of which was still made from a single piece of wood. The contemporary concert *kantele* can be quickly retuned and its strings mechanically damped.

The oldest *kantele* was played while held on the player's lap or on a table. When it became larger and had more sophisticated technical structure, special *kantele* stands were also developed. The *kantele* was more than just an instrument to accompany a singer. It was used to play instrumental dances of many different kinds (Asplund 1983). Both the older and the new *kantele* tradition are strongest in central and eastern Finland. The *kantele* is also con-

Figure 7.3. Sketch of a young woman playing the *kanklès,* the Lithuanian equivalent to the Finnish *kantele.* Sketch from a performance at one of the traditional singing festivals common to Lithuania, Latvia, and Estonia, at which there may be hundreds of people playing the *kanklès,* the *kokle,* and the *kannel,* and dressed in folk costume. (V. Jakelaitis, *Song festivals,* 1984. Sketch after p. 48.)

sidered an important instrument at the Sibelius Academy in Helsinki for students learning to teach Finnish folk music.

The *Gusle*

The Russian *gusle* is closely related to the *kantele*, and their histories run parallel. The oldest *gusle* was played by the itinerant *bïlïnï* story tellers. Their helmet-shaped instrument could still be found in the early twentieth century (Figure 7.4a). The *gusle* was also played by northern Russian peasants and fishermen, and was taken over by amateur musicians in the eighteenth- and nineteenth-century circles of the bourgeoisie and nobility. Originally a hollowed-out, gut-stringed instrument with five diatonically tuned strings and one resonating bass string, it became a many-stringed instrument assembled from many parts. The eighteenth century *gusle* was also built into a frame (compare the *kantele*), after which it took on the same status as the harpsichord and clavichord in the salons of the bourgeoisie and the nobility (Figure 7.4b). The earliest collections of Russian and Ukrainian folk melodies are associated with the *gusle*, as the collector, V. F. Trutovsky, was both a court singer and a chamber guslest (see also Figure 11.5, p. 205).

In the early twentieth century, a simplified *gusle* was developed with four different registers: piccolo, primo, alto, and bass. It was incorporated in the 1930s into Soviet folk music orchestras, along with the dombra and *balalaika* (see below).

Figure 7.4a. Helmet-shaped Tartar *gusle* (known by the Tartars as a *guslja*). (*Atlas* 1963 sketch after p. 56 no. 27.)

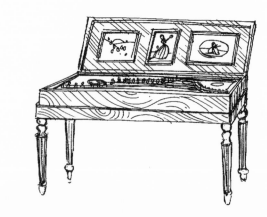

Figure 7.4b A *gusle* built to compete with the harpsichord and clavichord, probably from the later eighteenth or early nineteenth century. (*Atlas* 1963, sketch after p. 149 no. 34. See also Vertkov 1969, illustration to p. 141.)

The French *Epinette*, the Norwegian *Langeleik*, the Swedish *Hommel*, the European *Dulcimer*, and the Hungarian *Cimbalom*

Medieval music making was dominated by various instruments of the zither family. The zither was established as a popular instrument for home use in different social classes in several waves of popularity beginning in the sixteenth century. In Norway the instrument developed from a medieval instrument, the *långspel*, documented in several Nordic iconographic sources, to become the *langeleik* (Figure 7.5) (Sevåg 1974, Ledang 1974). The corresponding instrument as it developed in France was the *epinette* (Figure 7.6) played mainly by women. In Sweden, the *hommel* was a popular instrument of the zither family in the eighteenth and nineteenth centuries, mostly in bourgeois environments (Figure 7.7). There is also an Icelandic version of the *långspel*, that is related to its Norwegian counterpart. Many zithers appear to have developed in bourgeois milieus and to have been borrowed by folk musicians relatively late, such as the *hommel* during the course of the eighteenth century.

Figure 7.7. A Swedish *hommel*. (Sketch after a photograph of hommel player Otto Malmberg. Stig Walin 1952, fig. 84 p. 154.)

Figure 7.5. A Norwegian *langeleik* and its performer. There were both melody strings and accompaniment strings, used to vary the sound. (Sketch after Ledang 1979, p. 20 and *New Grove*, vol. 2 p. 504.)

Today, the *dulcimer* can be found in many parts of the world, and it appears to have been popular in Europe as early as the seventeenth century. Like the bagpipe and the hurdy-gurdy, it went through a number of social reassessments, particularly during the eighteenth century. Itinerant soloists gave the instrument a high reputation and contributed to its popularity, even among professional rural musicians. Gypsies in Romania, Hungary, and Slovakia used it in their ensembles. The concert *cimbalom* came into being in the late nineteenth century and inspired Franz Liszt, Zoltán Kodály, and others to compose national folk music. It remained popular as an instrument of entertainment and is still a vital part of folk music ensembles today in many eastern European countries (Figure 7.9).

The *Dombra* and the *Balalaika*

Both the *dombra* and the *balalaika* have predecessors in the east: in Uzbekistan, for example, there is a stringed instrument known as the *dumbrak*, the *dumbara*, and the *dombra* (see *Atlas* 1963, p. 575). The *dombra* (Figure 7.10) is older than the *balalaika*, and is regarded as having come into being with itinerant sixteenth- or seventeenth-century Russian singers. The younger *balalaika* can be traced back only to 1715 (see *Atlas* 1963, p. 29). In the late nineteenth and early twentieth centuries, new kinds of *domras* and *balalaikas* were made by Russian folk music enthusiasts and instrument builders such as V. V. Andrejev and G. P. Ljubimov, and a new performance technique took shape. At this time the idea of grouping instruments into families was also born and implemented in many folk music orchestras with large numbers of instruments.

Figure 7.6. A French *epinette* player. (Sketch after Marcel Dubois 1972, p. 179 illustration 3.)

This makes them one of many bridges between older traditional peasant music and more recent bourgeois music for entertainment, as well as between city and country music.

A zither in which the strings are struck with hammers, known as the *dulcimer* (or *hackbrett*) (Figure 7.8), is an instrument with a long history that probably originated in Persia (see Kettlewell 1973).

Figure 7.8. A Polish *dulcimer.* (Sketch after a photograph of Polish dulcimer player Jósef Sowa. Cover for disc *Rzeszowskie wies Piatrkowa,* SX 2349.)

Figure 7.10. A *dombra* player. (Sketch after inter alia, *Atlas* 1963, p. 149 nos. 38–41.)

Figure 7.9. A Hungarian *cimbalom.* (Sketch after a photograph of Hungarian *cimbalom* player Kálmán Balogh performing with a Swedish folk music group, Orientexpressen. From disc "Havanna Club." Origo 1007.)

The *Cobza,* the *Bandura,* and the *Tambura*

The *cobza,* a Romanian pear-shaped lute, is said to have come from the Turks. It is used to accompany ballads and is also an ensemble instrument in the *lautari* (see also ensemble) (Figure 7.11).

The *cobza* is, in turn, said to have been the model for the *bandura,* an unusual hybrid instrument which is a cross between a zither and a lute. The number of strings on the *bandura* is said to have

grown from seven or eight diatonically tuned strings to thirty or more chromatic ones. The instrument is held in the player's lap. The left hand fingers the bass string, which runs to the peg box, while the treble strings are fingered or plucked with a plectrum as on a zither (Figure 7.12). There are different styles and methods of playing in different parts of the Ukraine. The *bandura* appears to be a Ukrainian construction from the eighteenth or early nineteenth century. In the twentieth century, particularly after the October Revolution, *banduras* have been made in all sizes, from soprano to double bass, and the instrument is now part of large folk music ensembles (see also Chapter 4, p. 86).

The *tambura,* with its long neck (Figure 7.13), is played all over Albania, the former Yugoslavia, and Bulgaria. It is part of a large family in Turkey and parts of the Middle East and central Asia. The number of strings varies between two and twelve, four being most common. One or two are melody strings, the others are drones. There are regional variants of the *tambura,* adapted to different functions. Both epic songs and love songs are performed to *tambura* accompaniment. The combination of *tambura* and drum is another indication of the association of the *tambura* with musical cultures in the East.

The *Bouzouki*

The Greek *bouzouki* is a substantially younger relation of the Arabian long-necked lute known as the *buzuk* . The *bouzouki* has been regarded with skepticism by purist folk musicologists, who have regarded it as spoiling the older lyre tradition. This sense of indignation has increased since the *bouzouki* began to be played with electric amplification. In the 1970s, the *bouzouki* was introduced as a Swedish folk instrument via the wave of English folk music. According to Jan Winter, the *bouzouki* made its breakthrough in Swedish folk music when Ale Möller played it in many different styles in the 1980s (Figure 7.14). Thus the *bouzouki* is an instrument that has succeeded in transcending most of the rigid boundaries in folk music.

We can thus discern a pattern regarding the kinds of zithers and lutes mentioned here:

1. they were based on ancient prototypical instruments, probably with histories of many hundreds of years;

2. performers and builders adapted their construction to suit the constant stream of new functions and new musical trends;

3. when an instrument ceased to change, it became a museum piece unless

4. it had matured to a form which, if changed, resulted in a worsening of the instrument. At this point the variations were limited to increasing the number of strings.

The Bowed *Gusle* and Other Bowed Lyres

Gusle

The *gusle*, a remarkable instrument, also has numerous older Arabian relatives (see also chapter 4). It may first have been found in western and central Asia. Wünsch (1934) assumes that it came to Europe under the influence of Islamic culture in the tenth century. It was used exclusively to accompany the performance of heroic songs, and has become a symbol of all the freedom fighters in the Dinaric Alps. The playing string is made of horsehair, and the bowl-shaped body of the instrument is covered with a sounding board made from an animal hide. Until World War I, every player made his own instrument, according to the stipulations of a very strict tradition. In the 1930s, *gusle* production began to be considered a handicraft, and local variations were replaced by a more uniform style. Today, the Albanian *gusle* appears to be the one made most closely in accordance with the ancient tradition (see Miso 1986) (Figure 7.15).

Figure 7.11. A Romanian *cobza*. (Sketch after a photograph in Alexandru 1956, fig. 84 p. 154.)

Lyres

Other instruments related to oriental stringed instruments include the different kinds of lyres (Greek *lira*, Croatian *lirica*, Bulgarian *gadulka* or *kemene*, Turkish *kemençe*, Italian (Calabra) *lira*). There are two main types: the pear-shaped and the straight *lyra*, related to the Turkish *kemençe*. The pear-shaped variant is hollowed out from one piece of hardwood. It has three strings of sheep or cat gut, and is usually tuned in perfect fifths, sometimes in a combination of fourths and fifths. The uppermost string is for melody, the middle string may be used for either melody or creating drone, and the bottom string is always for drone. Some of these types of instruments have a soundpost running from the bridge via one of the holes to the soundboard. Leydi/Guizzi (1985) have described the spread of this instrument from Greece and Bulgaria to Italy.

Not until the early twentieth century did the lyre receive serious competition from the violin and the guitar. Older lyres share many stylistic features, including the pear-shaped pegboard with the peg for the middle string at the top, the semicircular holes, the shape of the bridge, the location of the soundpost, and the fact that the instrument is held in a vertical position when played (see also Leydi Guizzi 1985, p. 164f.). Like the *dombra* and the *balalaika*, then, the lyre originated in the east and took on regional profiles with new

Figure 7.12. The *bandura*. (Sketch of a singer, a member of a Ukrainian choir and bandora ensemble, accompanying himself on the bandora. Cover for disc Melodi C30 196559000.)

Figure 7.13. The *tambura*. (Sketch after Anoyankis 1979.)

functions such as being used for accompaniment and in ensembles (see, for example, the Bulgarian ensemble *dubrujan trojka*, consisting of a *gadulka*, an accordion, and a set of bagpipes or *kaval*). The triumph of the violin also inspired certain changes in the shape of these lyres. The lyre, like the *gusle*, was used to accompany heroic songs (see Atanssov 1981, p. 120ff.). Atanssov also writes of blind *gadulka* players and singers.

The Bagpipe in Europe

This section is devoted to the bagpipe, because, with its pungent sound, its societal origins, and its life amongst the rural peasants and itinerant beggars, the bagpipe may be regarded as a kind of symbol of European folk music (see also Chapter 1). The bagpipe is also an example of an instrument with a remarkable ability to survive or be reborn. In many countries the bagpipe-playing tradition dwindled to almost nothing and then blossomed again, growing beyond all its previous bounds.

From the British Isles in the west to Russia in the east, from the Italian peninsula in the south to Scandinavia in the north, there are both illustrated sources and references in old documents giving evidence that the bagpipes were present from the Middle Ages onwards.

Many surveys have been written on the subject

of the bagpipe. Those most useful in preparing this section are Anthony Baines (1960, new edition 1973) and Francis Collinson (1975). There are also a large number of detailed studies of various bagpipe traditions, including Sárosi (1967, the Hungarian bagpipe) and Elschek (1983, the Slovakian bagpipe). The "Scottish Tradition" series, published by the *School of Scottish Studies*, contains a different kind of valuable information on bagpipes. These are studies of *individual* bagpipers, with their melodies on cassette tape (nos. 4 and 6, 1981, 1982). The series *Strumenti musicali populari italiani* (1983), provides yet another variation on the theme; presentations of different instruments, with musical examples on cassette. A book about the Nordic bagpipe, *Säckpipan i Norden, Från änglars musik till Djävulens blåsbälg*, (The Bagpipe in Scandinavia: From Angel Song To Devil's Bellows) edited by Per-Ulf Allmo, was published in 1990.

In 1981, Leif Eriksson and Per Gudmundson published a leaflet (no. 25) in a series published by the Dalacarlia Museum in Sweden. The leaflet is written with anyone interested in the bagpipe in mind, but particularly "anyone who wants to learn to play the instrument." This leaflet was part of a regional education campaign on the subject of the bagpipe as a folk instrument; it resulted in a bagpipe renaissance in Sweden. Figure 7.16 contains the presentation of the instrument and the description of how to hold it. This leaflet is a model of educational, informative literature.

There is evidence of the bagpipe in Sweden as far back as the fifteenth century (Rehnberg 1943, Allmo/Winter 1988). However, the bagpipe originated far earlier. The exact date of origin depends on how one interprets source documents, works of art, and various uncertain archaeological finds. It is also a question of whether we believe that all bagpipes stem from the same tradition or that there are various independent traditions based on different inventions. The bagpipe is generally regarded as having been invented by the Sumerians and having been assimilated by the Greeks and Romans. The connection between this early evidence and the later European bagpipes, which first appeared in the late twelfth century, is uncertain, as there are no source documents from the intervening centuries.

In chronicles and illustrations, the instruments can be followed back to the sixteenth and seventeenth centuries: a seventeenth-century Romanian chronicle mentions the bagpipes being played at court, indicating that it was at home in the ruling classes there as in England, Scotland, and France at that time. Nineteenth century historians, including T. Burda (1877), writing about the Romanian bagpipes, talk about them as having been in existence "since time immemorial" (Habenicht 1974, p. 123). This was probably true. In many places there is an uninterrupted tradition of bagpipes from the Middle Ages through the nineteenth century, when they became a regional phenomenon, remaining in places where the tradition was particularly strong, such as Czechoslovakia (see Kunz 1974, p. 128). Rather than examining theories of diffusion, we now follow attempts to characterize different regional types of bagpipes. (The article entitled "Bagpipe" in *New Grove* follows the same development and contains literature references.)

The Name of the Instrument

The two main parts of the instrument, the "bag" and the "pipe," generally give the instrument its name, although in some languages there is a component of *ram* or *goat*. (Ronström 1986, p. 3). In any given region, there may be various names (Sárosi 1967, p. 86). For instance, the Italian *zamponga* also has numerous regional names.

Figure 7.14. *Bouzouki* player Ale Möller and Hardanger fiddler Gunnar Stubseid from the cover for the disc *Rameslåtten*, Sirimusic SMLP 008. (Photograph: Jan Harald Rismyr.)

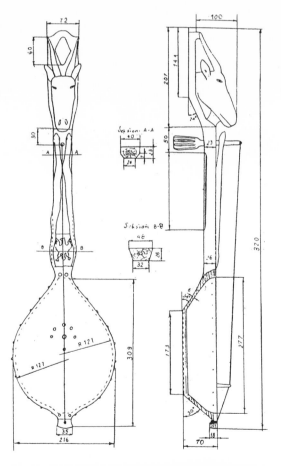

Figure 7.15. Design for an Albanian *gusla*. The article entitled, *La rôle et la function de la lahouta* (1985) by Pirro Miso also contains a series of informative production drawings.

Figure 7.16. Description of the bagpipe and how to play it. (Eriksson/Gudmundson 1984, p. 10–11 and 18).

The parts of the bagpipe
Materials and tuning for bagpipes made by Leif Eriksson:

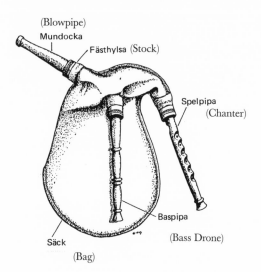

(Blowpipe)
Mundocka
Fästhylsa (Stock)
Spelpipa (Chanter)
Baspipa
(Bass Drone)
Säck
(Bag)

The **chanter** is also known as the *tappelstock* (i.e. tap-stick). It has six finger holes on the top and one thumb hole underneath. It is made, like all the other wooden parts of the instrument, of lathed birch. The range of the chanter is one octave, from about e^1 to e^{11}. The scale, rather like that of *spilopipor* (folk recorders) of today, is detailed here:

You will find that it initially requires a great deal of effort to attain this tuning. Because the reed is a rather primitive sound-producer, the bagpipe is sometimes difficult to control. The tuning of the bagpipe may vary, but the central note (with the three lower finger holes uncovered) tends to be between a and b flat. Bagpipes that are tuned higher than this sometimes tend to have a major scale instead (the third, the third tone from the central note, is raised one half-step).

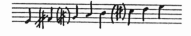

The **bass drone** maintains a tuning around e, and is the lowest tone of the pipe. The lower part of the bass pipe is moveable, and has holes to facilitate tuning.

The **blowpipe** has a non-return value, a leather patch that prevents the air from flowing out of the bag in that direction. The **bag** is made of bark-tanned calfskin, with three stocks where the pipes are attached.

The reed has been cut from a natural reed, and sealed at one end. A little tongue is cut out of the reed, and is lifted slightly by a thin string we call the tuning string. Such reeds produce the sound in both the bass pipe and the chanter.

How to play:
Look at the picture and try to imitate the posture of the player. Of course, you must find the position your body feels best in, but the picture gives you somewhere to start. Hold the bagpipe under your left arm, so that you can easily reach the chanter, and so that your arm presses the widest part of the bag. The most common way of fingering the chanter is to use the bottom of your fingertips, sometimes as far in as under the first knuckle. In other words, your fingers should be quite straight on the chanter.

The most difficult aspect of playing the bagpipe, for a beginner, is probably the fact that it is necessary to do two rhythmic movements at once and separately. You fill the bag with air from your lungs, pressing the air out with your left arm. The breathing tempo will depend on the qualities of your bagpipe and on how demanding the melody you are playing is.

The technique for playing is as follows:
Fill the bag with air through the blowpipe. When it is almost full, there is enough pressure for the pipes to begin to sound. Begin pressing your arm against the bag, but only hard enough to keep a steady tone. Stop blowing. When you stop, the leather valve is activated again, and the only way the air can escape is through the pipes. Only press so much air out with your arm that you will be able to refill the bag in one breath. Take a deep breath and fill the bag with a gentle, steady stream of air. At the same time, allow your left arm to follow the bag up as it is filled. Keep listening to the note, and try to keep it steady. As soon as the bag is full, stop blowing and start applying pressure with your arm again.

Thus, the first thing you will learn is to keep the pressure even and the tone steady. To begin with, you can make this a little easier by blocking the hole in the bass pipe, and just practice making a steady tone in the chanter. Later, add the bass pipe and practice keeping the two pipes in tune with one another.

When you begin to feel confident at this, it's time to start fingering a simple melody. You can prepare for this step by putting the chanter into your mouth directly and practicing the fingerings. Make sure the bag is always sealed–it will make your practicing much easier!

Crafting and Performance Technique

Just as many of the names in different languages have similar connotations, the craftsmanship and performance techniques of the bagpipe appear to have been pan-European, with a cross-cultural connection to India and many other countries where the English and Scottish military bands were musical models. At the same time, it is clear that there were strong regional elements. The bags themselves were made of many different types of hide, most frequently goat or sheepskin, but there are examples of dogskin and horsehide as well. In later days, the bags have been made of rubber, and today there are synthetic materials as well. Using a sort of bellows to produce the sound also appears to have been a later invention, as do the ingenious systems of keys and the "regulators," groups of three covered pipes with double reeds in different registers: tenor, baritone, and bass. The player can use the regulator to obtain certain chords simultaneous with the playing of the melody. These latter inventions appear to have been made beginning in the seventeenth and through the mid-nineteenth century, a period during which the bagpipes made the rounds of virtually all the social classes.

In addition to these extremely tangible interventions in the history of the traditional bagpipe, there were also more timeless differences, including the number of pipes (the melody pipe with a varying number of contrapipes, drone pipes, and their bore) and the kinds of reeds used. In different parts of Europe there were bagpipes consisting of various combinations of the basic parts, but it is difficult to draw conclusions from these instruments as to their age and origin. Often it is necessary to go on rather vague assumptions.

The bagpipe is a noisy instrument. With the aid of one or more of the pipes, the constant drone or drones are achieved. These two musical properties—loudness and drone—reflected a medieval musical stylistic ideal that lasted for a long time in many popular cultures. It was not until the late eighteenth century that they began to die out in favor of a *subtly nuanced* music based more on functional harmony. This was also the time at which the above-mentioned regulators came into being.

Social Functions

Although the bagpipe can be said to have been a universal instrument in medieval Europe, it is necessary to distinguish between the bagpipe as a stationary instrument, rooted in the ceremonies and traditions of a given culture, and the bagpipe as an instrument in the hands of itinerant musicians. There was sure to have been reciprocal influence between these two groups, but popular belief has it that it was the itinerant bagpipers who gave rise to the tradition of stationary instruments. In his book on the Swedish region of Västerdalarna, Maximilian Axelson wrote in the mid-nineteenth century: "a Spaniard captured in Venjan is said to have been the first person to play the bagpipe in these parts" (Rehnberg 1943, p. 48; see also Allmo/Winter 1988).

Generally, it must be borne in mind that written documentation of European cultural history is unevenly distributed from country to country. This means that no single source can be the basis from which overall conclusions with regard to the existence or spread of an instrument are drawn. Every piece of evidence speaks only for itself and in its own context. With regard to England, we know from many literary sources and chronicles that during the sixteenth century bagpipes were played at virtually all spring festivities, weddings, court entertainments, and military actions (see Collinson 1976, pp. 106f). As late as 1663–1664 William Tollett was appointed official bagpiper in Charles II's royal chapel, and a set of medieval bagpipes figures in Hogarth's painting *The Election Entertainment 1755*. After that time, there was very little mention of the bagpipe.

The Bagpipe in the British Isles

How, then, do we explain the fact that the bagpipe tradition was retained and developed in Ireland and Scotland? There are many hypotheses about this. In ancient times, Scottish bards appear to have played the harp. It was not, however, a particularly loud instrument in battle. One theory is that the use of bagpipes in battles between the English and the Scots was decisive to the outcome of the battles, and thus the bagpipe became a symbol for the Scottish people of their struggle against English imperialism, notwithstanding the fact that their opponents used the same instrument for both signaling and inspiring their soldiers.

The official Scottish war bagpipe was the "Highland pipe." The pipe has a conical bored blowpipe. It produces the notes of a G-major scale (but with C-sharp instead of C), and includes an extra note at the top–a². Certain intervals are tuned in a way that differs from both equal and just temperaments.

How old, then, is this Scottish bagpipe tradition? There are suspiciously few convincing pieces of evidence for the presence of bagpipes in Scotland in ancient times (see Collinson 1975, p. 125f.) The first certain proof is from 1549, when a Frenchman described the wild Scots using their bagpipes in battle. This was the time at which the MacCrimmons clan began a long period of service as bagpipers under the MacLeod clan. It is said that they transformed the bagpipe from a peasant instrument to an art instrument, developing complex melodies, *ceol mor*, out of simple piping tunes, *ceol beag*. Where did the MacCrimmons clan come from? Some would have it that they were Irish, others that they were native Scots. A third theory, that they were Italians from Cremona, is the bane of any true Scots nationalist (see Collinson 1975, p. 146).

The complex melodies for the bagpipes, *ceol mor,* are very similar to sixteenth-century variations for the virginals. Today, every melody runs through a strict pattern of variations, with different kinds of variations for different types of melodies, There is an interview from 1982 between Peter Cooke and a famous bagpiper, George Moss (b. 1903), describing the structure of a *pibroch* variation. The following is the beginning of the long description of the build-up of variations, their characteristic features, and names:

George Moss: The word *pìobaireachd* itself, pìo-air-eachd–three syllables, is Gaelic for piping, any piping, not just the *ceol mor.* . . . .

What was called in Gaelic "*ceòl mor*" is just derived from the ancient form of music and–pipers sort of–cultivated it and put–variations . . . .

The variations of a *pibroch* are–melodic variations that are just another version of the ground, and–rhythmic variations that use the skeleton of the ground and build up from bare notes up to the *crùnluth mach.*

Get a tune like Glengarry's Lament, composed by a piper to Glen–the last MacDonald of Glengarry–

. . . the first phrase. The main notes are A-C-E-C and that occurs in every variation all the way

through. The first variation to that is the *siubhal*–goes this way–

That's just the main notes of the ground with a low A between each beat. Now the next one is the same melody notes, but not the low A between but another of the melody note–like this–

Now–the next one–a variation could be played called the *leumluth*. It would go this way, but it just didn't happen to be played with this tune–but it follows that type of variation–

Peter Cooke: Is that a rhythmic variation?

George Moss: Yes, they're all that in this tune, because the–they're not just the elaborately graced *urlar*, they go on to the rhythmic variations right away. [booklet pp. 18–19].

In order to retain the highland pipe as a national symbol it was necessary to train pipers, as well as to resist all temptation to play Scottish national melodies on *other* instruments. The collection of *pibroch* by Donald MacDonald, "pipe-maker" from the later 1810s, probably published in 1818, is an effort both to make the Scottish melodies generally accessible for music-making and to provide instruction about the traditional highland pipe (see also p. 17). The title page contains the following statement:

A Collection of the Ancient Martial Music of Caledonia, called *Piobaireachd*, as performed on The Great Highland Bag-Pipe, now also adapted to the Piano-Forte, Violin, and Violoncello; with a few old Highland Lilts, purposely set for the above modern instruments. To which is prefixed, A Complete Tutor, for attaining a thorough knowledge of the pipe-music. Respectfully dedicated to The Highland Society of Scotland, by Donald MacDonald, Pipe-Maker, Edinburgh.

According to the preface, there were people who did not regard the music in the volume as worth preserving, as well as people who played it on other instruments simply for the fun of music-making. The author goes on to remind the reader that these melodies once nurtured their warrior forefathers, and that they are surrounded by a sense of adventure and romance. He also justifies his publication in the spirit of patriotism, a desire "to redeem from the waste of time what was dear to our Fathers. He describes his intention as rendering the pipe music for performance on the highland pipe, as well as making it adaptable for the organ, pianoforte, violin, and German flute. The preface continues:

Strangers may sneer at the pains taken to preserve this wild instrument, because their ears have only been accustomed to the gay measures of the violin, and 'lascivious playing of the lute;' but it has claims and recommendations that may silence even *their* prejudices. The Bag-Pipe is, perhaps, the only national instrument in Europe. Every other is peculiar to many countries, but the Bag-Pipe to Scotland alone. In halls of joy, and in scenes of mourning, it has prevailed. It has animated her warriors in battle, and welcomed them back, after their toils, to the homes of their love, and the hills of their nativity. Its strains were the first sounded on the ears of infancy, and they are the last to be forgotten in the wanderings of age. Even Highlanders will allow that it is not the gentlest of instruments; but, when far from their mountain homes, what sounds, however melodious, could thrill round their heart like one burst of their own wild native Pipe? The feelings which other instruments awaken, are general and undefined, because they alike to Frenchmen, Spaniards, Germans, and Highlanders, for they are common to all. But the Bag-Pipe is sacred to Scotland, and speaks a language which they only feel. It talks to them of home, and of all the past; and brings before them, on the burning shores of India, the wild hills, and oft frequented streams of Caledonia, the friends that are thinking of them, and the sweethearts and wives that are weeping for them there!

The Lowland bagpipe never gained the same national status as its Highland counterpart. It appears to have been a more everyday instrument, one of the bellowed bagpipes regarded as being of more recent origin. Its three drone pipes are gathered together into one section. There is a variation on the Lowland pipe related to the Irish *uillean* pipes. These pipes did not survive the competition from what was probably their older brother, the Highland pipe.

Prototypes for new variations on bagpipe design may very well have been tested out as folk instruments before becoming part of the repertoire of professional makers. However, in Paris the international center of woodwind instrument-making in the seventeenth century, bagpipes were an object of professional design. These seventeenth-century pipes had two important new design features:

1. the blowing is done by a bellows rather than through the mouth;
2. the drone pipes are equipped with valves permitting pitch changes of the drone bass notes.

The incentive to change the bagpipe was the increasing interest in all things rural and simple—of the peasantry—which was exactly the same incentive that gave rise to the first collections and arrangements of folk songs (see also chapter 1). The French bagpipe, known as the *musette*, was designed as a "chivalric" shepherds' instrument. It was a bellowed bagpipe and featured technical advantages. The Marquis de Gueidan, a prominent politician, had a *musette* included in his portrait, an instrument with ivory ornamentation, gold fringe, lace, and ribbons. The new instrument probably spread from the Paris workshops to the British Isles and to the rest of continental Europe. It was praised by Mersenne in his famous *Harmonie universelle* (1636). The French invention had also been mentioned positively a decade earlier by Michael Praetorius, the German composer and encyclopedist, in the third volume of his *Syntagma musicum*. We may never know exactly how more recent instruments developed out of a combination of medieval traditions and new inventions, but it is probably safe to assume that technical progress was an important factor in the survival and competitiveness of bagpipes.

Let us also consider the history of the Irish bagpipe which, according to Breandán Breathnach (1976), can be traced back to the eleventh century, when it was already in use as a martial instrument.

The special martial Irish bagpipe, the *píob mhór,* appears in illustrations from the sixteenth century and was also a well known instrument in the rest of Europe. Vincenzo Galilei describes it in his *Dialogues* from 1584. It appears to have been a large, awkward instrument until the eighteenth century, when it was equipped with a bellows, patterned after the *musette.* At that time the register was also extended from nine notes to two octaves, and in addition to the three drone pipes in different registers, various regulators were also successively added. In the mid-nineteenth century, three of these were joined together (see above). The nineteenth century instrument, which became a national status symbol, was also made in mahogany, brass, and ivory. (For a detailed description of the *uilleann* pipe and the playing technique, see Buckley 1979.)

However, doubt has been cast by Paul Roberts and others on the theory that the French design affected the domestic construction of the *uilleann* pipe. In a article in *Common Stock,* the journal of the bagpipe society of the Lowlands and the border country between Scotland and England, (vol. 1, no. 2, November 1984), Roberts attacks the traditional view of the history of the Irish bagpipe. By way of introduction, Roberts emphasizes the leading position of Great Britain as a bagpiping nation, claiming that the most sophisticated types, i.e., the "small pipes" and the *uilleann* pipes were to be found in Northumberland. According to Roberts, the *uilleann* pipes were widespread in northern England and southern Scotland in the eighteenth and nineteenth centuries. For this reason, he claims that the Irish bagpipes were of Anglo-Saxon origin, parallel to or deriving from the intermediate-length Lowland bagpipes. The instrument was known as the "union pipes" from the mid-eighteenth until the early twentieth century. According to Roberts, the word *uilleann* is the invention of musicologists. He bases this statement on a theory propounded by Grattan Flood (1911) that *union* was a distortion of *uilleann,* meaning elbow.

Roberts found a description of a bellowed bagpipe from as early as 1746. Roberts says that this book was written for the English upper-class reader, and may be regarded as one of many bits of the pastoral craze that eventually gave rise to collections of folk music (see Chapter 1). Roberts thus determines that the instrument developed gradually within the bagpipe district in northern England and southern Scotland, claiming that this evolu-

tion may be seen as the consequence of new kinds of music requiring a larger register.

Throughout the nineteenth century, the instrument became more and more regarded as Irish, possibly because it became more popular in Ireland and less so in England and Scotland. It is also possible that there was a parallel development in Ireland, with the same shifts in musical style as in England and Scotland.

Roberts also found a candidate for the post of inventor of the regulator: David Hatton (1769–1847) from Yorkshire. Roberts's conclusion, then, is that the union pipes were an English-Scottish invention for the upper classes, later exported to Ireland. In *Traditional Music in Ireland* (1979) Tomás O'Canainn also states that the bellows-played bagpipes could hardly have been an Irish invention, as the same type of instrument was to be found in both England and France.

It is often difficult to determine where an instrument or type of instrument originated. Scholars are often blinded by a sense of national chauvinism. It requires both courage and determination to contradict habitual assumptions, in musicology as elsewhere. Whatever we may think about the origins of the *ullieann* pipes, it is clear that they survived the dwindling interest in the bagpipe in the late nineteenth and early twentieth centuries, at which time a new love of things local was triggered, not least among the expatriate Irish, who assured its position as a national symbol. Important elements in this process included regular lessons for children on the pipes and publication of large collections of melodies (see pp. 17–18).

Continental Bagpipes

Using maps, Baines has shown the dissemination of different kinds of bagpipes in Europe on the basis of Curt Sachs's discovery that typological differences can be determined by examining various elements of the design such as the conical or cylindrical bore, the use of single or double reeds, and the use of one or two pipes with a varying number of holes. Different design properties appear to have been of varying importance in different regions, which require their own technical solutions (see Sárosi 1967, Habenicht 1974, Elschek 1983, and Strumenti 1983).

Bellowed instruments were found all over Europe, sometimes in glorious solitude, sometimes alongside those blown through the mouth. In the

Sorbia region of eastern Germany, there was a fine tradition of making beautiful instruments, sometimes in the shape of a "goat" (Figure 7.17a). This *kozot* (goat) may have horns and skin, but the resemblance to the ram stops there. It was made of fine hardwood, with pipes decorated with precious metals. These instruments were constructed from the late eighteenth century until they began to die out in the mid-nineteenth century.

In France (See Figure 7.17b) the peasants retained the medieval type of bagpipes in many places (for example, the *biniou*, also referred to as the *cornemuse bretonne*). In many other places, the bagpipe also survived without radical alterations. In southwestern Europe the *gaita* bagpipes are still played today in ensembles on ceremonious occasions and in processions such as the Easter processions in Portugal and Spain (Asturria, Gaicia, and Moniho), and in Italy.

Italy has various kinds of bagpipes. The northern Italian version, the *piva*, has a conical bore, a double reed, and seven holes, and is quite rare today, while the southern Italian version, the *zampogna*, has two cylindrical pipes, one for each hand, and a single reed. Both these instruments fought a losing battle with the accordion. However, the *zampogna*, at least, appears to be surviving, and has many regional variants (see Strumenti 1983).

Let us devote some attention to the *zampogna*, which is played in the company of the shawm, the tambourine, and the triangle. Just before Christmas the *pifferari* appear. A great deal has been written about this phenomenon, including the following by Berlioz in his memoirs:

Figure 7.17a. Large bagpipes from Sorbia in eastern Germany, a *kozot* (goat). (Sketch after Raupp 1976, Abb. 1.)

Figure 7.17b. The French *Biniou* or *cornemuse bretonne*. (Sketch after *New Grove* vol. 2, p.106.)

In Rome I only encountered one folk instrument I would be inclined to describe as a remnant from antiquity, the *pifferari*. This name referred to itinerant musicians who came down from the mountains, just before Christmas, in groups of five or six. With bagpipes and *pifferari* [a kind of reed instrument], they would play concerts of sacred music, standing in front of a depiction of the Madonna. They usually wore brown robes, pointed caps, like bandits, and were rather wild, and mystical in appearance, with a special originality. . . . The bagpipes, with the support of a large *piffero* playing the bass part, sounded out in harmonies of two or three notes, with a smaller *piffero* playing the melody above all this; the other instruments were two short *pifferi*, played by children twelve to fifteen years old. The air trembled with trills and cadences, embellishing the country tunes with a flood of peculiar ornaments. . . . Close up,

this music is so loud as to barely be tolerable, but at some distance these remarkable orchestras make an impression few can resist. (Berlioz 1980, p. 152.)

Louis Spohr, too, could bear the sound of the *pifferari* from a great distance, although it rather bored him. Farther back in time, composers, including Corelli, Bach, Handel, and others, alluded to the *pifferari* directly in their music.. This Christmas melody can be found in many arrangements and variations, including contemporary ones.

This popularity cannot be attributed to the beauty of the melody alone. A contributing factor is that the use of this melody and the combination of sound qualities signaled the Christmas spirit. Such symbols die hard, and even if they were considered crude at some point, as was clearly the case in the nineteenth century, they tend to be softened by composers, who attempt to give them an artistic context. In this way, paradoxically, interest in the crude version of the *pifferari* music was also maintained. (See also the *Brussels Museum of Musical Instruments*, Bulletin Vl–1/2 [1976].)

Further to the east, in the Balkans, we find many kinds of bagpipes. There were also many in Hungary (Sárosi 1967), Poland (Trojanowicz 1979), Belarus, Russia, Ukraine, Georgia, Estonia, and Lithuania (see *Atlas of Musical Instruments in the USSR* (1963), with its wealth of illustrations).

Performance Technique

Owe Ronström, a bagpiper himself, has formulated the following four principles for the bagpipes:

1. the continuous sound;
2. the drone or pedal-point accompaniment;
3. the "special" tonal quality (nasal, buzzing, high-pitched, etc.)
4. the quick, hard attacks. (Ronström 1986, pp. 4f.)

The relatively simple melodies undergo constant variation. One of the distinguishing features of the bagpiper is his ability to ornament and embellish. For bagpipes with two pipes, one pipe is used to achieve quick movement between notes accompanying the melody, sometimes giving rise to a kind of dominant-tonic pattern. When dance music is played, these accompanying notes are important in that they mark the rhythm. The special staccato effect of the bagpipes is obtained by the piper lifting his finger immediately after playing the melody note, allowing the bass tone of the pipe to sound freely.

Although it is difficult for anyone but a bagpiper to write or read about the details of performance technique, if we devote a few moments to a good transcription/annotation, we can learn a great deal about bagpipe playing.

The Christmas melody presented in Figure 7.18 as sung, recited, and played by Jozef Antalik (b. 1914) from Nitra in Slovakia was performed on a four-channel pipe and a drone, where the melody pipe produces five notes, and the counterpipes provide occasional reinforcement of the G-drone with any of the following notes: d^1-g^1-d^2-g^1.

The Hurdy-Gurdy

In many ways, the hurdy-gurdy is a very interesting instrument to compare with the bagpipe. It, too, was widely disseminated in Europe, beginning in the Middle Ages and continuing today. It was played everywhere, from the church and concert hall to the marketplace and dance floor. The earliest evidence of its existence comes from France and Spain, and since the Middle Ages, France has been the home of the hurdy-gurdy. It was a very popular instrument with French peasants, and was also adopted by the aristocracy, including composers, in the seventeenth and eighteenth centuries. Itinerant bagpipe and hurdy-gurdy players from Savoy delighted people all over Europe, in cities and in the countryside, beginning in the seventeenth and lasting through the nineteenth century. The name of the instrument often contained a descriptive epithet (see Bröcker 1973, p. 7, 232f.; Allmo/Winter 1985, p. 8–11). The epithets usually referred either to the wheel or winder on the instrument, or to its place of origin. For example, *lira tedesca* was a way of marking, in Italian, that the instrument was regarded as German in origin. By way of a cultural-historical comparison with the bagpipe, let us now consider the hurdy-gurdy as both an itinerant and a stationary instrument.

The Design of the Hurdy-Gurdy

The body of the hurdy-gurdy contains a mechanism composed of a keyboard with a number of tangents that, when depressed, bear down on the melody string or strings, passing through the box housing the tangents. There is also a wooden wheel coated with resin. The wheel is made to rotate by a crank, and thus acts as a bow, playing the drone strings. It is thus able to produce two or more notes simultaneously with the drone (see *New Grove* vol. 2, p. 261).

The *Grodda-liran* (Figure 7.19) is a particular type of hurdy-gurdy coming from a traditional eighteenth-century family of folk musicians from the Swedish island of Gotland.

The Spread of the Hurdy-Gurdy

To some extent, we know about the spread of the hurdy-gurdy during the Middle Ages from preserved documents. However, written sources described instruments by ambiguous names. It is also impossible to know whether the hurdy-gurdy-playing angels painted on church ceilings really indicate that the hurdy-gurdy was known and used in that community or whether the artist just copied them from some other work of art. It does appear

7.18. A Christmas song sung and played by Jozef Antalik, from Nitra, Slovakia on a four-piped bagpipe. Note the rich variations around the given notes in the melody. (Elschek 1983, p. 228, illustrations 64 (a) and (b).)

that western Europe was the main home of the hurdy-gurdy in older times, although even in Hungary it has been traced back to the sixteenth century although, as a folk instrument it appears first in the late eighteenth century (Sárosi 1967, p. 55). The hurdy-gurdy was also known in Bohemia as early as the fourteenth and fifteenth centuries (Kunz 1974, p. 74). Moreover, it probably also spread in different "waves." This makes it difficult to decide whether any given instrument came with one of these later waves or belongs to a longer historical tradition. In some places, the hurdy-gurdy seems to have died out, its last use being associated with certain ceremonial uses; in eighteenth-century England it was used to accompany songs. It is said that in Oxfordshire and north Wales people would wander from place to place, singing to the accompaniment of the hurdy-gurdy (Bröcker 1973, p. 299f.). In Bohemia as late as the 1870s, schoolboys would march the streets to the sound of hurdy-gurdy and drums on February 3, Saint Blasius's Day (Kunz 1974, p. 74). The first mention of the hurdy-gurdy in Poland, the *lira korbowa*, is from the seventeenth century, when it is said to have been played by a village musician at the court of Count Lew Spieha (Kopec 1979, p. 142). After this, it was mentioned in various literary sources, often as an instrument played by beggars and old men. There are also stories of how young men were blinded to force them to join the hurdy-gurdy players, and that these blind musicians were well received at marketplaces and other public gatherings (see also Kopec 1979). The hurdy-gurdy was found in Russia, Belarus, and the

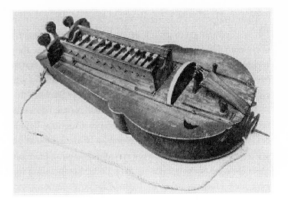

Figure 7.19. The original *Groddan lira*.

Ukraine in the nineteenth century, but there do not seem to be any sources mentioning it in older times. The instrument became popular in new designs in the 1930s (see Atlas 1963, instrument nos. 93–95 and the description on page 37). Although the hurdy-gurdy was far more popular and in greater use in the Nordic countries than one might guess, there does not seem to have been a firmly anchored tradition. Instead, it seems to have appeared sporadically here and there, probably where there was inspiration from itinerant players and where there were instrument-makers.

Wandering through the Social Classes

According to Bröcker (1973, p. 399), the downward social mobility of the hurdy-gurdy in the late

Middle Ages was related neither to the nasal tonal quality of the instrument, nor to its drone, nor to the limited register it was thought of as having, but rather to the social status of the musicians who played it. The hurdy-gurdy had become the musical identity of many beggars. Thanks to its loud, penetrating sound it was a perfect instrument on which to accompany group singing, not least spirituals and hymns, which were the songs that triggered the charitable feelings of all good Christians. See, for example, Allmo/Winter (1985, p. 62) on an early eighteenth-century hurdy-gurdy playing, hymn-singing beggar from Norrköping known as Jöns the *lira* player.

There were may women among the beggars and itinerant groups, and so it is not surprising that the hurdy-gurdy also became thought of as an instrument for women. Early romantic drama and opera often contained a beautiful young woman who played the hurdy-gurdy, and the art of the times also depicts many pretty young women with the instrument.

However, the status of the hurdy-gurdy-player was probably comparable with that of a prostitute. Bröcker (1973, p. 388) quotes the story presented in 1670 by H. J. Ch. von Grimmelhausen, of *Der seltzame Spinginsfeld*, an outstanding violinist who married the hurdy-gurdy-playing daughter of a beggar. She was known to play in all kinds of places, and on all kinds of occasions from doorways to dances to church occasions. Spinginsfeld tried to make her change her ways and to improve her social status, for example, by getting her to dress in fine clothes like him. The storyteller claims that, despite her social background, this couple won a certain amount of renown for their music. In paintings of musical ensembles, women hurdy-gurdy-players can also be found. This is proof that their repertoire was not at all limited to song accompaniment.

In France, the hurdy-gurdy was far more successful as an instrument of the aristocracy in the seventeenth century than the *musette* ever became. Bröcker (1973) lists a large number of handbooks in hurdy-gurdy-playing. The instrument changed radically after about 1715, when bodies of both guitars and, more important flutes, (beginning in 1720), from the workbenches of professional musicians, began to be used in the production of hurdy-gurdies. The playing mechanisms and strings also began to be made professionally at about this time,

and many extremely elegant and expensive hurdy-gurdies were made in fine hardwoods and with mother of pearl insets. As the social status of the instrument began to rise, new repertoire developed (see Bröcker 1973, p. 311ff.). Music for the hurdy-gurdy, in addition to anonymous pieces, has been written by composers like Vivaldi, Haydn, and Mozart. Neither the new music nor the new performance styles appear to have rubbed off on the instruments played by beggars and peasants (see Bröcker 1973, p. 337). Despite its new status among the urban aristocracy, the hurdy-gurdy lived on as an instrument of city beggars and country peasants in the French provinces, particularly Bourgogne, Limousin, Auvergne, Nivernais, and Bourbonnais in Poitou, as well as Brittany and Normandy. The key area was then, and remained, in the Berry district.

The upward social progress of the hurdy-gurdy did not take place without protest from connoisseurs of music, and their criticism grew throughout the course of the eighteenth century. It must be seen as part of the struggle between the representatives of the "enthusiasts of nature" on the one hand and the "friends of the fine arts" on the other. Economic factors were certainly one of the determining elements when various parties took sides in the debate. Why else would Michel Corette (1709–1795) deliver such bitter criticism of the hurdy-gurdy in his guitar manual from 1762, and yet, twenty-one years later, when the popularity of the instrument among the aristocracy was dwindling rapidly, go on to write a book on hurdy-gurdy playing entitled *La belle vielleuse* (The Lovely Hurdy-Gurdy Player). (For more details on Corette, see *New Grove*, vol. 4, p. 801f.) Most of the champions of the aristocratic status of the hurdy-gurdy alluded to its origins in antiquity. Being referred to as the lyre of antiquity gave the instrument sufficient historical clout to shroud its simple social background. However, the hurdy-gurdy also had its opponents. In his attempts to show the superiority of the guitar over the hurdy-gurdy in his guitar manual, Corette describes the demise of the hurdy-gurdy at the hands of the furious gods of art!

After being accepted for some time in the world of art music, the hurdy-gurdy changed in appearance, and we recognize traits of the finer hurdy-gurdy in the instruments of later itinerant Savoyard players as well as in those of the peasants, from

France in the west to Russia in the east. At the same time, the art prototypes, in turn, were always shaped with a view to the musical and social functions of the instrument in the rural environment. Today, the hurdy-gurdy is a central instrument both in performance of medieval music and in various revival movements. Its renaissance began in France, where parts of the rural population have always appreciated the sound of the hurdy-gurdy. Hurdy-gurdy playing is now a popular movement, not least in Germany, where there are constant courses in both making and playing the hurdy-gurdy. Its revival in Sweden is described in Allmo/Winter (1985), whose research can be seen as a reflection of this newly triggered re-interest in the survival of old instruments and traditional music, albeit new in forms:

1965: Swiss folk singer and musician Renée Zosso performed at the Museum of the History of Music in Stockholm.

1967: Swedish musician and instrument-maker Styrbjörn Bergelt constructed a hurdy-gurdy.

1976: Felix Wolf, the conservator of the Museum of the History of Music in Stockholm, made a drawing of a hurdy-gurdy from Enånger.

1976: Eugen Joss constructed an instrument from Wolf's drawing. In 1978 he made a drawing of his own, which won great renown, as did his later designs and descriptions.

1980: The first kits and instrument-making courses were held in the southern Swedish town of Lönsboda.

1984: The hurdy-gurdy was used in the production of a play based on a novel by Victor Hugo.

1985: Allmo/Winters's book, *Lirans hemligheter* (The Secrets of the Hurdy-gurdy), was published.

The Keyed Fiddle (*Nyckelharpa*)

The *nyckelharpa* (keyed fiddle) has been in existence since the Middle Ages (Figure 7.20). Most of the evidence for the instrument in early times comes from Sweden, and only a few examples are found in Denmark and Germany. Although instrument researchers have gone through medieval written records and various pictorial representa-

tions with a fine-toothed-comb, new evidence of the instrument still surfaces from time to time. It is clear that the instrument was relatively well known in Germany. This is evident from the two best-known sixteenth- and seventeenth-century books on musical instruments in Germany: S. Virdung's *Musica getutscht und ausgezogen* of 1511 (reprinted in 1931) and M. Praetorius's *Syntagmatis musici tomus secundus* from 1619 with the *Theatrum instrumentorum* of 1620, where the instrument is represented with considerable exactitude (reprinted in 1958). The many stone-carvings and paintings in churches including the *nyckelharpa* found in the northern part of the Swedish province of Uppland and in occasional church frescoes in other parts of the country indicate that the instrument had an especially strong hold on the Swedish cultural scene. Sweden also has the only proven instance of a surviving medieval instrument of this kind. Strong cultural impulses have played a part in the existence of the *nyckelharpa* with a gamba- or violin-like body; these replaced the medieval, guitar-like body. The *nyckelharpa* has change in body form, rows and numbers of keys and tangents, basic principles of key mechanism, and particulars of strings in connection with later instrument builders. Apart from traditional home music-making and accompanying dancing, the instrument is now used in theater music and as a Swedish symbol. The new generation has researched and taught and experimented its way forward, and thereby created a vast bank of knowledge. All this seems to have taken place in Sweden, as there is no evidence that the instrument existed elsewhere after 1650. However, we shall see when we examine different kinds of fiddles that there were similar local variants in other countries.

Bowed Harp (or Bowed Lyre)

In 1903, Otto Andersson, a young Swedish student on a literary grant in Finland, made the remarkable discovery of fiddlers who played a hitherto unknown *lira*-like instrument, the bowed harp, on two islands off the coast of Estonia, Ornsö and Nuckö (Figure 7.21). The instrument had a rectangular body, with four strings running to a yoke. Some of the instruments Andersson found had been equipped with violin bodies. Another type of bowed harp, with a small sounding hole, had previously been discovered in Karelia. This instru-

Figure 7.21. Players of the small (left) and wide (right) holed bowed harp. (Sketch after a photograph of fiddlers Semoi Tuptsin and Juho Villanen in *Kansan Musiikki* 1981, plate after page 144.)

Figure 7.20. A *nyckelharpa* (keyed fiddle) performer with a chromatic keyed fiddle (Sketch after a photograph of Hans Gille, keyed fiddle player.)

ment, the *jouhikantele*, appeared to be more primitive and of an older type.

Andersson became fascinated with the problem of the origin of these stringed instruments. He therefore made extensive excursions in search of related instruments. He found similarities in a Welsh instrument known as the *crwth*. Later, in a medieval sculpture in the cathedral in Trondheim, Norway, he found something that might be regarded as a link to the tradition of the few Swedish examples of bowed harps. Swedish musician scholar Styrbjörn Bergelt made great use of Andersson's sources when he initiated the revival of the bowed harp with the aid of two elderly fiddlers, who recalled the instrument from their childhood on the island of Ormsö.

The Traditional Harp

The harp, a chordophone in which the direction of the strings runs perpendicular to the soundboard, was found virtually all over medieval Europe, although it may have been most widespread in Great Britain. *Harpa* was the old Norse word for any stringed instrument, and was even at one point simply a synonym for "musical instrument." On the continent, the harp became a popular instrument for bourgeois salon music in the eighteenth and nineteenth centuries. It particularly inspired Italian itinerant musicians (see Leydi/Guizzi 1985). In Ireland, however, the harp remained an instrument of the bards through the eighteenth century. The bards were musical entertainers, combining old traditional melodies and newer stylistic influences. Some of their melodies are still popular Irish folk songs today. In Norway there is both iconographic evidence and preserved instruments that indicate that harp playing was a tradition in the wealthier agrarian families. Today in Norway the harp is enjoying a renaissance both as a folk instrument and as an instrument in early music ensembles, thanks to musicians such as Tone Hulbaekmo and Sverre Jensen.

How Did They Survive?

The popular instruments with medieval predecessors have survived because they have such a special tonal quality as well as other distinguishing musical characteristics. They and the music played on them have come to symbolize anything from peddling to traditional ceremonies. Some of these instruments have been charged with national ideologies, often with an element of historical nostalgia. In order to be able to survive, they have had to assimilate new trends coming from the outside from, for example, professional instrument makers, without losing their identities. The revivals, in the form of renewed interest in the truly old folk instruments such as the traditional bagpipes, hurdy gurdies, and keyed fiddles, may be regarded as a parallel to the "authenticity movement" that has led to the development of using "original instruments" in the playing of music from the Middle Ages, the Renaissance, and the Baroque period. Folk fiddles stand somewhat separate from this development, as they have had a more direct relationship with the violin since the seventeenth century. The Jew's harp is also in a category of its own, for although it has changed in shape over the course of the centuries, it has lived in rather splendid isolation as a hand-crafted pocket instrument.

Literature

Two of the best of the many surveys on the bagpipe, to my knowledge, are by Anthony Baines (1960/new edition 1973) and Francis Collinson (1975). There are also several detailed studies of individual bagpipe traditions, such as Sárosi (1967, on Hungarian bagpipes), Roland Hollinger (1982), and Elschek (1983, on Šlovakian bagpipes). The series *Scottish Tradition*, published by the School of Scottish Studies, contains a great deal of valuable information on the bagpipes, with studies of individual bagpipers accompanied by recordings on audiocassette. Another series, *Strumenti musicali populari italiani* (1983) provides a variation in which different types of instruments are presented with musical examples on cassette. A study of the Nordic bagpipe was published in 1990 by Per-Ulf Allmo et al.

Marianne Bröcker has written an extensive monograph on the hurdy-gurdy (1973), Stig Walin has written on the *hommel* (1952), Nils Andersson on the bowed harp (1930) and Ling on the *nyckelharpa* (1967).

Eight

The Playing of Folk Music (Part III): Musical Instruments for the People

FIDDLES, VIOLINS, AND BOOKS OF FIDDLERS' TUNES

From Fiddle to Violin and Back Again

The fiddle was one of the most popular instruments of the Middle Ages. It was both a high-status instrument and a very popular dance instrument. Different types of medieval fiddles survived in music of the countryside long after they had been replaced by gambas and violins in feudal and bourgeois urban musical contexts. The replacement process is not easy to follow because it is difficult to sort out the instruments by name, and there is very little direct evidence. There also appear to be a number of hybrid forms when the violin began to conquer the scene in the sixteenth century. In some places the medieval fiddle tradition was so strong that the violin never fully took over, but only affected certain details of the instrument. In other places, the popularity of the violin resulted in some primitive prototypes, especially for children. These may have been similar to the older fiddles or not at all related to them. We have already seen how the lyres, the hurdy-gurdies, and the bowed harps were inspired by the violin. In this chapter we examine the even more violin-like popular instruments and follow the violin as it conquered the rural areas of Europe. This often went hand in hand with the spread of musical literacy and the mastering of instrumental technique.

In many places, for example in Poland, instrument-makers and fiddlers tried to adapt the sound of the violin to previously created instruments such as the bagpipe or older fiddles. Some hybrids of the violin, string instruments like the double bass or the cello, but with a drone, appear to be attempts to use modern instruments but retain the older sound structure. One example of this tradition is found in Resia, a valley in the Italian Alps.

Instrumental Technique

When the violins arrived on the scene, although attempts were made to simply transfer the playing technique from older instruments, new playing techniques also appeared to arise spontaneously. These had very little to do with either older string-playing or with the art music tradition. A Swedish fiddler known as *Menlösen* ("the fool") is a very good example of self-taught playing, with the violin held tight under his arm. Mostly, however, violin technique was developed by master fiddlers, who were very familiar with the accepted way of playing the violin. This gave rise to a conglomerate of individual styles, which would gradually come to be regarded as regional style, folk music, dialects. The fiddlers gradually learned to read music and cultivated an interest in the latest discoveries in violin technique and violin making. In the first half of the eighteenth century, for example, the violin methods of Francesco Geminiani and Leopold Mozart were familiar to some fiddlers in southern Sweden. Wherever the violin appeared, so did books of fiddlers' tunes. This confirms the idea that reading music often went hand in hand with learning to play the violin (see also Chapter 1).

Music on Paper

Fiddling books often came into being when dance musicians began to note down their own songs in order to recall them and to teach them to their students. A wide variety of books of fiddlers' tunes have been preserved but probably many more are still waiting to be recovered. In Finland, books of fiddlers' tunes based on songs have been published since the late nineteenth century, and in the early twentieth century, songs by Finnish-Swedish fiddlers were also published (see Ala-Könni 1956, pp. 109f.).

The following are examples chosen from among a wide array of books of fiddlers' tunes.

Joan Rimmer (1978) has published two volumes of dances from Friesland, one containing dances by a fiddler named Wieger Michiels Visser (1801–1886). These are arranged as suites, and were written for the wealthy Friesian merchant families who traded with the British Isles and the Netherlands (Figure 8.1). These connections are clear in the music, as the same dances can be found in English, Scottish, and Dutch collections. Rimmer's second volume, on music written by Andries Kiers (b. 1851), contains what Rimmer's analysis indicates to be more Continental elements. The music in both volumes is for the violin. They contain minuets, Anglaises, waltzes, schottisches, mazurkas, *hoppsas*, quadrilles, and other types of popular dances of the times.

In Denmark in 1987, Jens Henrik Koudal published an annotated facsimile edition of the *Large Notebook* of Rasmus Storm from 1760, known as *En fynsk tjenstekarls dansemelodier o. 1760* (The Dance Melodies of a Servant from Fyn) (Figure 8.2). This is unique material, containing minuets, *polskas*, a few Anglaises, folk songs, marches, and hymns. Koudal also provides a survey of eighteenth-century Danish dance music manuscripts, including some four thousand melodies; the material of musicians, composers, and dancing masters between 1600 and 1800 (pp. 22ff; see also Koudal's bibliography, which contains references to a large number of European books of fiddlers' tunes from Finland, Germany, Poland, and elsewhere).

The same year, 1983, saw the publication of an extraordinarily beautiful facsimile edition of *Das Kralsche Geigen spielbuch. Eine Buddisiner Liederhandschrift vom Ende des 18. Jahrhunderts*. This book was written by a Saxon musician, Miklaws Kral, between 1780 and 1790. Kral was registered as a military trumpeter and was killed in Russia in 1812. The book contains a wide repertoire of wedding dances as well as a large number of folk songs and instrumental melodies, providing an overview of musical events in Lausitz during that decade (see also the preface to the facsimile edition by Jan Raupp) (Figure 8.3).

Swedish oboe player Gustaf Blidström transcribed a collection of minuets and *polska* dances while he was imprisoned in Tobolsk in 1715–16. The volume contains some three hundred pieces (Figure 8.4). Kjellberg (1983, p. 126) points out, when describing the *polskas*, that "a division also becomes tangible between art and folk music songs of *polonnaise* and *polska* types" (see also Landtmanson 1912 and Ala-Könni 1956, pp. 25f.).

The actual transition from the traditional folk music repertoire of the fiddlers to an increasingly popular common dance repertoire is described by David Johnson in his *Scottish Fiddle Music in the Eighteenth Century* (1984), where he follows stylistic developments in different Scottish books of fiddlers' tunes. Johnson deals the death blow to the myth of the anonymity of instrumental music and its independence from art music. Scottish fiddlers' music, played on the violin, was a melting pot containing everything from traditional bagpipe music from the Highlands to extracts from Corelli's Christmas concerti. Johnson assumes that before 1860 it was possible for a fiddler to master the entire repertoire by ear. However, when the violin came on the scene, it brought with it a new style and new dances that were increasingly learned from printed music. The effect of the appearance of such books of fiddlers' tunes, both handwritten and printed, on music played in Scotland was enormous (pp. 6f.).

According to Johnson, when the violin arrived in Scotland, it met up with two related medieval instruments.

> The native musical traditions which the violin found on its arrival in Scotland included fiddling. This was carried out on two bowed-string instruments played, like the violin, on the arm: the medieval fiddle and the rebec. The violin, however, was so superior to either of these—being more resonant, expressive, and grateful to play—that within a generation every fiddler who could afford to buy one, or knew how to make one, had transferred to it. The violin thus acquired the ready-made status of a 'traditional' Scottish instrument.

Figure 8.1. Waltzes after a Swedish fiddler named Wieger Michiels Visser (1801–1886). (Rimmer 1978, p. 96 no. B 46.)

Figure 8.2. Minuet from *Rasmus Storms nodebok* from 1760. (Koudal 1987, no. 12.)

In the opinion of Johnson, the violin skewed the balance of power among instruments.

> What is clear, however, is that the arrival of the Italian violin altered the balance of power between 'fiddles' and other Scottish instruments. The violin brought new types of dance, new ways of making variations, with it from England and the Continent, and added them to the existing fiddle repertory; it also began to purloin the idioms of other instruments. By 1740, Scots fiddling had become a kind of cultural melting-pot. (Johnson 1984 p. 3.)

By around 1760, the violin had become "the instrument of Scottish traditional music" (p. 4). Some fiddlers there had always been able to read music, and more and more learned during the course of the century. Many fiddlers intended to publish their songs. Johnson has divided melodies from before 1720 into those based on either five notes, two chords, or Italian harmonics (*passmezzo, antico,* or *moderno*). This is followed by a section with Scottish salon pieces, long cycles of variations, and

pieces based on bagpipe music, minuets, sonatas, dance music, etc. Johnson's collection shows how important it is to see a musical culture as a whole and not from an overly narrow perspective (Figure 8.5).

Today, there are a large number of books of fiddlers' tunes forthcoming as publications from various archives. For example, the *Österreichsches Volksliedwerk* with different local archives (such as the one at Steiermark) publishes them in small, convenient folders. Sometimes these books of fiddlers' tunes also contain dance descriptions. Hartmut Braun's collection, *Tänze und Gebrauchsmusik in Musizierhandschriften des 18. und frühen 19. Jahrhunderts aus dem Artland,* is one example. Helga Thiel, Franz Eibner, and Hermann Derschmidt have authored scholarly papers on the violin in European folk music (1975), which illustrate the significance of the violin in Austria. Derschmidt emphasizes the importance of books of fiddlers' tunes as a bridge between folk and art music, indicating that fiddlers were often recruited from social classes other than the peasantry. "Most folk musicians were probably craftsmen: carpenters, shoemakers, tailors, etc. They often played under the direction of a schoolmaster who also saw to it that the melodies were transcribed and learned . . ." (pp. 164f.).

What Do the Books of Fiddlers' Tunes Contain?

In her study and publication of the folk music collection of Einar Övergaard, Märta Ramsten (1982) examines the question of the extent to which books of fiddlers' tunes rest on ancient traditions and to which extent they represent the introduction of new repertoire. Övergaard (1871–1936) was one of the

Figure 8.3. Wendian dances from Miklaws Kral's collection from 1780–90.

Figure 8.4. Minuet from Swedish hautboy player Gustaf Blidström's collection from 1715–16. He annotated them in the French violin clef (soprano clef). See also Landtmanson's transcriptions from 1912.

greatest connoisseurs of Swedish folk music of his day, and he possessed detailed knowledge of style and performance. He was extremely skeptical about the value of the books of fiddlers' tunes he had seen. In a letter to folk music collector Olof Andersson dated 20 February, 1929, Övergaard wrote, "In those days, I deeply despised written music. In my opinion, only the 'oral' tradition was worth anything. Of course I would look through the books of music that came my way, but since I never found them to contain the tunes played in the region, I left them to their fate (Ramsten 1982, p. 21). Övergaard referred to the fiddler from the province of Hälsingland, known as Snickar-Erik (Erik the carpenter), whose melodies he transcribed and from whose own fiddling book Andersson had borrowed melodies for the huge volume of Swedish folk tunes, *Svenska låtar* (Swedish Melodies) (1922–1940/R1972–1978): "My main source from the area was, in fact, Snickar-Erik. What is strange

is that the excerpts from his fiddling book used in *Svenska låtar* do not contain a single one of the melodies he played for me (Ramsten 1982, p. 18). Ramsten concludes that Övergaard distinguished between "genuine" fiddlers and schooled performers of folk music, and she provides a number of convincing examples.

As early as 1951, Carl-Allan Moberg had criticized *Swedish Melodies*. In his opinion, the fiddling melodies it contained had been indiscriminately selected from books of fiddlers' tunes.

"There is no way of being certain where they come from, what traditions they render, or what they actually reflect of Swedish folk music" (Moberg 1951, pp. 47f.). This attitude toward printed music, a denigration of the "written" tradition, emanated from a romantic view of the tradition of genuinely playing by ear. This attitude inhibited some fiddlers from using printed music as a source for "genuine" music-making. Today, however, this attitude appears to be a thing of the past, and the number of books of fiddlers' tunes is on the rise.

Having investigated the books of fiddlers' tunes, let us now return to the different violin-like instruments and their immediate kin in an attempt to see whether the interplay we have found between the folk and art music traditions is corroborated by the construction and performance of the instruments. We begin in the northwestern corner of Europe, in Norway.

The Norwegian Hardanger Fiddle

The Hardanger fiddle was mainly played in western Norway, in the Telemark area and in some of

Figure 8.5. Scottish "folk music" for the violin from the eighteenth century: "The East Nook of Fife" from Bremners *Scots Tunes* from 1759. (Johnson 1984, p. 40.)

the valleys where people held most firmly to traditions. It appears to be a perfect example of a violin-like instrument adapted to a very special musical tradition: the shape of the fingerboard and the bridge make it possible to play a drone and accompanying notes, and the resonance strings made it possible to create a tonal color that was very popular in the seventeenth century, such as in the viola d'amore. Sevåg gives the following description (*New Grove*, vol. 13, p. 327).

> The harmonic aspect of Hardanger fiddle music is more intriguing but should preferably be examined in terms of drone style. One purpose of the many different tuning patterns in Hardanger fiddle playing is to enable drone effect based on the first and fifth (and occasionally even the third) degrees of the scale to be used with melodies of differing character. However, all four open strings are frequently used as variable drones below and above the melody, producing deviations from the common tonic to dominant drone effect. The extent to which this occurs depends on both the character of the melody and the tuning pattern adopted. Players also change tunings to give the instrument different tone colours, a means of variation used during wedding festivities. Another important way of enriching the harmonic effect is to stop both melody and drone string simultaneously with the first finger; this device further increases the number of drones available and, used imaginatively, achieves surprising harmonic effects.

The Hardanger fiddle has a separate repertoire from the more generally known Norwegian fiddle, the *flatfelan*, the Hardanger fiddle having a far more capricious relationship to the phrasing and melodic styles of art music.

The question of the origins and age of the Hardanger fiddle is a highly controversial one. A monograph by Bjørndal/Alver written in 1966 puts forth various theories, one of which is that its first occurrence dates back to the *Jåstadfela*, (Jåstad fiddle) inscribed "Ole Jonsen Jaastad 1651." It is, however, possible that the year was inscribed at some later time, as the next known fiddle is dated 1710. According to Bjørndal/Alver, these two instruments are very different, the latter having been influenced by the violin. Sevåg (1971) expressed some doubt that the Hardanger fiddle originated so early, but Blom (1985) supports the theory of Bjørndal/Alver. The main cause for skepticism about the age of the Hardanger fiddle has to do with its resonance strings. In any case, it appears probable that the Hardanger fiddle came into being sometime in the seventeenth century and was possibly modelled on an older fiddle. There is no doubt that the violin was also a source of inspiration and possibly even a prototype, and that the very strong local music tradition endowed the Hardanger fiddle with its unique construction and contributed to its repertoire (Figure 8.6).

Hardanger fiddlers have developed their own set of terminology that provides us with an excellent example of what happens to music theory in the popular tradition. The terms include *tonekrullar* (which corresponds to embellishments), *skutlenote* (which corresponds to second position playing), *kvævetoner* (which correspond to perfect fifths), and *tvigrep* (which corresponds to double stops). Many of these terms indicate how close the terms of popular and professional music theory were to one another.

The Violin in Eastern Europe

In Finland, too, the violin became a peasant instrument in the eighteenth century, particularly in western Finland where there was contact with Sweden. Violins became very popular for wedding music, as they were regarded as the finest there was to offer (see p. 65).

In Estonia, Latvia, and Lithuania, the violin became an accepted folk music instrument during the eighteenth and nineteenth centuries, often in combination with various *kantele* instruments (see p 165).

In Poland there was a very strong tradition focused on older types of fiddles (see Steszewsky 1975, Dahlig 1985), and thus the Polish violin was rebuilt and adapted to this fiddle tradition, and so that its tone would be suited for the dominant type of bagpipe in Poland. The following description

from a wedding in Wolsztyn, Poznan, in 1861 indicates how the peasants used the sounds of different types violins to their advantage:

> From the time when the guests are invited to partake of the first evening meal, the fiddler uses an unpretentious, highly screechy violin known as the *mazanki* or, if he does not have one, he binds about half the neck of an ordinary violin to make it emit a screeching sound like that of the *mazanki*. Throughout the time the *mazanki* is being played, the groom is obliged to serve his own vodka and beer to the guests. . . . As soon as the violin begins to play, the guests bear their own responsibility for supplying the beer and vodka. [Steszewskij 1975, p. 23].

In the nineteenth century the Polish *gęśliki,* an older type of fiddle related to the Russian *gudok,* was complemented by both a new instrument, the *suka,* which was clearly influenced by the violin, and the above-mentioned *mazanki*. Local variations on the cello and double bass also occurred. The latter were known as *basetla* or *basy* and were made in the old fashion, by hollowing out a log for the body.

In Slovakia we meet other violin-like instruments, including the *oktávka* (octave-violin), the *shlopcoky* (box-shaped violin) and a double bass with a frets, the *korovo basa* (or bark-bass, as the frets were made of bark) (Elschek 1983) (see figure 8.7).

The violin probably made its way to Romania and Hungary with the music of the gypsies who also expanded the instrument's repertoire and incorporated it into their traditional ensembles. In Hungary, a cello-like instrument known as the *gardon* was also used almost as a percussion instrument to provide a sort of rhythmic accompaniment (Sárosi 1971).

In northern Italy concomitantly with the entrance into the world of art music, variants of the violin for performance of folk music developed the instrument's repertoire. Bousquier/Padovan (see Leydi/Guizzi 1985) describe one example of this tradition from Valle Variate, south of Monviso in the Italian Alps. The dances for which it was used included country dances as well as the gigue, the bourre, the courant, and other dances associated with the art music of the Baroque. The melodies were performed with different kinds of improvised ornaments and rhythmic variations. Double stops were also used, but seldom vibrato.

The instrument retained its popularity as a dance instrument far into the twentieth century,

Figure 8.6. A Hardanger fiddle. (Drawing after a photograph of fiddler Sören Nomeland from Setesdal. *New Grove Musical Instruments* 2, p. 126.)

despite increasing competition from the accordion. (For the influence of the violin on lyre instruments see p. 154).

The migratory routes of the violin all over Europe can be traced, but the examples above suffice to indicate the main principles, which can be summarized as follows. The violin was constructed in the late sixteenth century and spread quickly north in the hands of itinerant Italian ensembles and virtuosos. Its rapid spread may also be attributed to the many visits of European nobility to Italy, "the land of music," and their tendency to hire Italian musicians at their courts. Secondary centers of dissemination sprang up relatively quickly in France, England, Poland, Bohemia, Sweden, and elsewhere.

The violin entered Sweden in the 1640s, and was well established in England by 1660. Although the earliest social classes to accept it were the aristocracy and the upper bourgeoisie, the violin probably soon became popular in other social classes. In fact, there was some initial resistance to the violin among the upper classes. There is evidence that the English regarded it as a simple fiddling instrument because it lacked the tonal quality of the gamba. As an instrument to accompany dancing, however, the violin was a success. With its beautiful piercing sound and its infinite technical potential, it stood out as a brilliant competitor to traditional instruments. There were more factors involved in the success of the violin in various popular music environments than simply the introduction of the instrument itself. The violin brought in its wake a new attitude toward art music, more

and more fiddlers learned to read music, and new types of dancing were soon introduced. This new repertoire of dances in rural environments developed into various artistic styles, while in urban environments it was soon abandoned in favour of new trends, cities being fickle places even in the eighteenth century. The gigue, the bourrée, or the country dances of northern Italy, the *polskas*, mazurkas, and minuets of Scandinavia, and the English dances of Scotland, are examples of folk dances that kept their hold in the rural environment longer than in the cities.

The violin was a musical instrument meant to be listened to by large audiences, first at court celebrations, later at concerts and public opera performances. In consequence, it was a high-status instrument, highly charged and male-dominated. Just as the violin has become a predominantly male instrument, the cittern, initially intended for home use, became the province primarily of women. The violin soon also became the instrument of the gypsy musicians in Hungary, who were the intermediaries between the popular music of the bourgeoisie and the music of the peasants (see Sárosi 1967, 1975, 1977).

We will return to the violin when we discuss ensemble music, where it often had to keep company with a ragtag collection of instruments spanning the spectrum from old bagpipes to accordions.

Instruments Constructed for "the People"

The nineteenth century saw the first professional production of instruments intended for the general public. Until that time, instruments were exclusively produced for the performance of art music, either in public or at sophisticated private salons. Until the 1960s, mass production was regarded as a sort of levelling of music in society, and authority after authority thundered about the imminent total collapse of music (see Kjellström 1976, pp. 79ff.). Undoubtedly, however, this mass production was an important stage in the democratization of music that, in turn, was a prerequisite for the wider acceptance of art music.

Mass production of violins was sanctioned by the champions of folk music, not least in Scandinavia, whereas mass production of the harmonica and accordion was condemned. The accordion truly meant a change, since traditional melodies could not normally be played on the re-

Figure 8.7. Slovakian folk violins and double bass. (Drawing after a photograph of a string trio from Liptovske Sliace. Elschek 1983, Figure 15a.)

stricted single keyboard. Moreover, it had a very special sound, with an intonation determined by the maker and not, as with the earlier instruments, by the individual fiddler, who had a tradition to follow. However, what the denigrators of the accordion and harmonica were never prepared to admit was that suddenly there was an increase in the number of amateur performers. Thus music gained a far greater quantitative spread than ever before. In any art form, such popularity must always precede qualitative differentiation. The history of the accordion is still in progress, as is its integration into traditional folk music cultures. It began as a supporting instrument to the violin, and later became part of the popular tradition in its own right. How did this transition occur? It took a number of decades, from 1822 when Friedrich Ludwig Buschmann constructed the first prototype until many years later when hundreds of thousands of accordions were being sold. If we are to understand the full course of events, we must begin with another instrument of mass production, the Jew's harp.

The Jew's Harp

Judging on the basis of archaeological finds, as early as the Middle Ages the Jew's harp was already a very common instrument. In contrast to the flute, of which there were undoubtedly many more, the Jew's harp was made not of a readily accessible material but of iron, available only to the blacksmith. In addition, the skills of a blacksmith were needed to produce and assemble the metal frame and the strip of which the instrument consists (Fig-

ure 8.8). The Jew's harp was an extremely popular instrument, found in the possession of young men of all walks of life.

Alberto Lovatto (1983) has shown the Jew's harp to have been at the height of its popularity in the seventeenth to nineteenth centuries centered in Austria, Germany, Italy, and Great Britain. Its commercial center was Boccorio, Italy. The history of the Jew's harp can be traced back to 1524, and there are receipts of sale from many epochs. A Jew's harp often had a rather elegant box, a necessity for protection of the instrument's sensitive vibrating strip. Nineteenth-century production was extremely impressive–1,536,000 Jew's harps were produced in Boccorio alone. According to Lovatto, 114 million Jew's harps were made between 1600 and 1850. In Molln, Austria, eight to nine thousand Jew's harps were produced per day, resulting in about 2.5 million per year (Sevåg 1973, p. 126).

In the eighteenth century the Jew's harp made a brief foray into the salons of art music, with itinerant virtuosos playing their lighter repertoire on it. The early nineteenth century also saw a Jew's harp "epidemic," when the virtuosos used an "arc" of Jew's harps to enable them to play in different keys and to give them an expanded range over which to play their melodies.

The true home of the Jew's harp, however, was the dance; the participants would dance in their stocking feet in order to hear its sound. Literature provides us with the example of a beggar named Aron, who played his Jew's harp cheerfully in the evening, like a cicada, and who also accompanied dancing. This is a Swedish hexametric poem by Ludvig Runeberg, *Älgskyttarne* (The Elk Hunters):

Figure 8.8. A Jew's harp. (Drawing after a photograph by Per-Ulf Allmo.)

The beggar Aron warmed himself alongside old Rebecka.
Aron got his Jew's harp all ready. Rebecka rocked slowly, stroking the dabbled cat on her lap.

(Song 8, verses 14–17)

The Harmonica and the Accordion

Das Akkordeon, published in Leipzig in 1964, claims that Buschmann experimented with the Jew's harp in conjunction with his discovery of the "free strip" or "tongue." Birgit Kjellström (1976), a Swedish instrumental scholar, questions its importance, claiming that Buschmann's father had already discovered a tongued instrument, the *Aelodikon* (Figure 8.9).

However, from another point of view the Jew's harp was important: it was pocket-sized. Buschmann's first instrument was a harmonica that he wanted to name the "aura." Unfortunately, this name was already in use, designating the instrument that consisted of an "arc" of Jew's harps. According to Kjellström, Buschmann then decided to call his instrument the *mundaeoline*. Thus the harmonica came into being, although it was long popularly confused with the term Jew's harp. Kjellström also tells us that the first *mundaeoline* was not actually intended as a musical instrument but rather as a tool for organ tuners. Buschmann also added a bellows onto his mundaeoline so as

not to have to blow himself. This idea was so appealing that an order for a *handaelon* was placed in 1822, and thus the accordion was born. The instrument was not at all originally intended for plebeian use, but for the young ladies of the city, who were attracted by its ease of performance. By the 1860s the accordion was already a best-seller, although it soon lost its attraction to the middle classes, who had plenty of time to devote to more advanced musical pleasures. The growing scores of young sons of the working classes, on the other hand, found the accordion to be just what they needed. On it, they could quickly learn the popular new melodies. The accordion sounded bright lovely and loud, and it was a relatively robust instrument. Unfortunately, there is not much more to say about it. "We can thus merely speculate as to the role of the accordion in gilding an otherwise difficult life in the impersonal foundry settings and factory communities, in forest workers' shanties and in railwaymen's' barracks" (Kjellström 1976, p. 31). The accordion was soon incorporated into various ensembles all over Europe, and regional variants developed, such as the English *concertina*, the French *accordion musette,* and the Russian *bajan* (Figure 8.10).

Today, the accordion is regarded as a classic folk music instrument. We, in turn, have the mass-produced instruments of our own times to be annoyed with, the electric guitar and the synthesizer.

Who knows whether, fifty years from now, the story of the synthesizer as an instrument of wide dissemination will have reached its conclusion and will have joined the ranks of historic traditional instruments? The one thing we do know is that, although the period in which an instrument is "in style" grows shorter and shorter, the length of the period does not affect the absolute lifetimes of instruments: bagpipes and hurdy-gurdies are played just as frequently today as they were during the Middle Ages, along with seventeenth-century violins and nineteenth century accordions.

Clay Pigeons and *Ocarinas*: Instruments with Ancient Predecessors

A large number of flutes have an egg-shaped or elongated air space rather than the usual tube. Such flutes can be traced to the cradles of human civilization, and at some points they have been highly valued. These instruments function rather like

Figure 8.9. Swiss accordion production. A free strip or through tongue means that the sound is created with the aid of a flexible tongue moving freely through an air stream created by the player's breath. In the illustration we can see one of the gentlemen making the mechanism itself, and the woman of the house working on what will be the bellows. (Bachmann-Geiser 1981, Tafel 42.)

whistles, or like blowing into conch shells. Clay pigeons, or *ocarinas*, are popular children's instruments and tourist souvenirs today. The shape for an earthenware or clay *ocarina* (Italian for "gosling") that is generally accepted today is attributed to an Italian, Guiseppe Donati from Budrio. (*New Grove Dictionary of Musical Instruments*, "Ocarina".) The ocarina is found in different sizes, and Italian ocarina ensembles play a wide range of popular and light music (Figure 8.11).

The *Tárogató*: The Popular Stepbrother of the Clarinet

Other important instruments to European folk music, alternatives to the violin, are the clarinet and the oboe, both vital to the many wind ensembles that formed throughout the nineteenth century.

The *tárogató* is a remarkable hybrid of the old Eastern oboe and various attempts to make new constructions and adapt old ones. The clarinet inspired the present form, which came into being in the late nineteenth century, made by the V. Jozsef Schunda firm of instrument-makers in Budapest. The *tárogató* has a noteworthy history with certain parallels to the transformation of the bagpipe. The so-called *Magyar tárogató* reflects very clearly the Hungarian relationship to the Turks. It was an instrument used for military purposes against the Turks and was therefore also known as the *hadisip* (war pipe). But its construction was at the same time stimulated by Turkish instruments. It was also known as the Rákóczy pipe, because it was used during the revolt of the patriots against the Austrians in the early 1790s under Count Ference Rákóczy. After the Rákóczy Movement was defeated, the instrument was prohibited. However, the *tárogató* was still very popular and used at weddings as well as by tower guards. Its popularity faded during the course of the nineteenth century, and it was then, in the spirit of nationalism, that the new construction consisting of a long clarinet-like instrument with a conical wooden body and the mechanism of the oboe appeared (see Sárosi 1967, pp. 82–88).

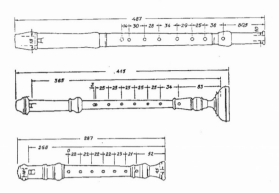

Figure 8.12. Norwegian recorders: (top) an "ordinary" recorder, known as the *bystadsflöjt* (the city flute), *sjöflöjt* (the sea flute), etc. to distinguish it from domestic ones (middle and bottom), are illustrated here from Sevåg 1973.

Figure 8.10. An English *concertina* player. (Sketched from an illustration in *Musikinstrument från hela världen* 1979, p. 80.)

Figure 8.11. An *ocarina* player. The *ocarina* has a long history, beginning in stone age societies, where fruit shells and seashells made natural vessel flutes. Whistling into one's hands gives the same effect, but somewhat muffled. (Drawing after *Hungarian Instrumental Folk Music*, disc text 1980, photograph no. 8, p. 22.)

The German Recorder Becomes the Norwegian *Sjöflöjt*

Just as the violin and the clarinet had their more popular counterparts, the recorder also inspired new prototypes of common wooden pipe-flutes (Kjellström 1964, 1977, Sevåg 1973) (Figure 8.12). In Norway this German import is known as the *sjöflöjt* (sea flute), *tyskflöjt* (German flute), or *bystadsflöjt* (city flute). The name was later transformed from *tysk-* (German) to *tyss-* and *tusseflöjt,* an indication of how an import can only gain acceptance once it feels familiar. Sevåg gives examples of inexpensive imported recorders from Germany in the eighteenth century that competed with the skillfully produced domestic flutes. This inspired the makers and players to develop impressive individual traditions, outstanding examples of which can be found in the areas of Telemark and Gudbrandsdal. Satisfying the demand for a traditional instrument and supplying the new tonal quality and intonation was undoubtedly a difficult tightrope for a local flute manufacturer to walk. Thus the musical instruments described in this chapter make it possible for us to interpret both the musical and musical-sociological changes in European society. The constant musical circulation of the social classes is certainly one of the keys to a rich variety of music in society. In the next chapter, we go on to survey examples of combinations of instruments in all kinds of ensembles.

Literature

Handbuch der europäischen Volksmusikinstrumente(1967) and *Studia instrumentorum musicae popularis* (1967–) are, as described above, monumental works including scholarly documentation of the folk music instruments of many countries. The Soviet *Atlas of Folk Music Instruments* (1963) indicates the connections between Asiatic and European types of instruments. Monographs are also constantly being produced on the instruments of individual countries. Leydi and Guizzi (1985), for example, have put Italy on the map with regard to its folk music, though previously the country was relatively little-known.

Figure 9.1b. "Spontaneous" ensemble of hurdy gurdies, reinforced by a dulcimer, bagpipe and accordion, playing for outdoor dancing. (Photograph: Per-Ulf Allmo.)

Nine

Folk Music Ensembles

FORMS OF ENSEMBLE PLAYING

Fiddlers' and folk music festivals all over Europe offer opportunities for two kinds of music-making to take place (Figures 9.1a. and b.):

1. formal music-making, where established ensembles perform on the stage;
2. informal music-making, where two or three fiddlers get together and play.

There are similar opportunities for vocal music-making at the major choir festivals, such as the ones held in Tallinn, Riga or Vilnius; dancing and singing takes place all night long after the official program for the day has been completed.

Moreover, there is a kind of organized, spontaneous music-making known as "unison playing." The following is a description by Gustav Wetter (1901–1977), a Swedish folk music collector and festival organizer:

> I tried to get all the fiddlers together on the local playing field to play a unison waltz from Uppland, which I had dutifully mailed to all the festival participants in advance so they could learn it. Oh, Lord, what a sound! No more than fifteen of the hundred fiddlers knew the melody. However, five of the fifteen played the second repeat, five played the third repeat, and the rest tried playing both the first and fourth repeats. The remainder of the crowd just played along with tonic and dominant chords in F major, looking left and right. When I tried in the best conductor's style to indicate that we might all stop playing at once, it took at least sixty seconds for

> the message to get across to the last of the players. (Hembygden 1954, no. 4, p. 69.)

Otto Andersson has described (1958) a similar effort to get all the fiddlers at a convention to tune to the same pitch and play a melody at the same tempo. His effort succeeded, after persistent practice.

Many fiddlers' societies did begin with spontaneous unison playing, as did many more professional folk music ensembles. Norwegian Hardanger fiddler Gunnar Stubseid tells of his first encounter with Ale Möller (see p. 159 and Figure 8.6):

> I met Swedish bouzouki player and folk musician Ale Möller for the first time in 1986 at a folk music festival in Sweden. We found ourselves playing together late one night in a hotel room. I noticed at once what a good combination the bouzouki and the Hardanger fiddle made, and how nicely the use of the plectrum emphasised the bright, dynamic rhythm of the music from Säterdal. This was a new experience for me, a fiddler who had long been looking for a fellow player who could highlight the unique features of this music and its hay-making ambience. Playing with Ale gave my own music-making a new dimension [Rameslåtten,disc on SIRMUSIC label].

Similarly, Sárosi (1972) has described how a young Hungarian zither player can commonly be accompanied by rhythms played on spoons, the seat of a chair, or a tabletop.

There are many examples of our spontaneous desire to make music together and the pleasure we derive from it. Such pleasure may also be disturbing, for example, when a child at a concert cannot contain the desire to participate in the music-making, or an amateur violinist cannot refrain from fingering in the air from his seat in the audience. The spontaneous joy of music-making is what unites amateur and professional musician, cutting across all genre boundaries.

Folk ensembles are often, of course, modelled on art or popular music ensembles. Playing may begin spontaneously and then change and develop through the performers' contacts with other types of music. An ensemble of two is often the core of large ensembles. In an interview from 1987, Ulf Gruvberg discusses European folk-rock music. He was a member of such an ensemble himself (Folk och rackare), and was of the opinion that many of them began like his own did; with a couple of guitarists playing together and later expanding and changing in line with new trends, stylistic demands and the influence of new contacts. In the 1970s, Alan Stivel started an ensemble with instruments including the Celtic harp, the bagpipe and the bombard. The ensemble later expanded to include electric and acoustic guitars, violin, banjo, Irish flutes, dulcimer, organ, electric bass and drums . . . . These ensembles sprang from duos, and are characterized by great flexibility with regard to musical style and instrumental composition. Duet-playing appears to be an ancient tradition in folk music playing, alongside the tradition of individual performers.

A Historical Perspective on Duo Ensembles

The Pipe and Tabor

The jester, playing the one-handed flute and drum known as the pipe and tabor, was probably the most common one-man duo of the Middle Ages (Figure 9.2a). These instruments were to be found all over western Europe, and were known in Provence as the *galoubet*, in Germany as the *Schwegel*, and in the Basque country as the *txistu*. There is written documentation of their existence as early as 1260, from which point they are mentioned occasionally in medieval ballads and chansons as instruments which accompanied dancing. In Germany, Switzerland, and Austria they gave way to the flute and accompanying drum and after 1700 they began to be regarded as folk music instruments. In England they were used to accompany Morris dancers at Whitsun into the nineteenth century, after which they were gradually replaced

by the violin and concertina. They are still in use in southern France, from Provence to the Pyrenees, in the Basque country, Spain, Portugal, and Italy (Figure 9.2b).

The Basque *txistu* was played in ensembles and can also be found in a bass variant, the *txistu aundi*, which cannot be played with one hand. Such ensembles therefore have an extra drum. They may also have a soprano variant, the *txirula*.

The wealth of folk culture in the Basque region is rooted in the Middle Ages, as is clear not least from the dances performed at various religious and national celebrations. The *txistu* has gradually changed, and been extended to satisfy more recent demands placed on instruments used to accompany dancing. What explains the survival and adaptation of this instrument? Could it have anything to do with its function as a sound symbol of the region, which endows it with a cultural identity, as discussed above? In this particular case, the one-man duo also gradually dissolved to be replaced by two instruments played by two different musicians, and the flute-family instrument also expanded into a family of instruments.

There were similar one-man duo instruments, but they did not survive as long. This applies to the French combination of flute and drummed epinette (see Marcel-Dubois 1972, p. 183).

What factors beyond the desire for spontaneous music-making have contributed to the creation of duos? Usually, curiosity about a new sound combination and what it can do is involved, but it can also be the result of a desire to retain old ideals of sound. An example of the latter is to be found in the Resia Valley in the Italian Alps. This valley is the home of a Slovenian minority group that has developed a special ensemble known as the *cytirati*, consisting of violin (*cytira*) and cello, with the violin playing the melody and determining the rhythm and tempo while the cellist chooses a suitable drone. Strajnar (1972) has tried to determine how the inhabitants of the Resia Valley continue to play only the violin and cello in this unique kind of duo, despite the fact that their migrant-worker background brings them into contact with many types of instruments from elsewhere in Europe. His conclusion is that they have quite simply developed this ensemble to replace the bagpipes after their disappearance. This is true not only in the Resia Valley, it appears that the need to replace the bagpipes with other instruments was

Figure 9.2. (a) Medieval one-man pipe and tabor duo and drum from Härkeberga church. (Photograph: N. Lagergren, ATA.) (b) Spanish one-man duo on the pipe and tabor from twentieth century Tenerife. (*Magna antologia* 1979, p. 46.)

an important point of departure for the creation of ensembles in many parts of Europe.

Instrumental Duos in Various Types of Interplay

The two instruments in a duo may interact, as in a dialogue, in which one instrument provides for the chord accompaniment or takes on a polyphonic function (see, for example, Todorv 1972). Alternately, they may complement one another, the instruments playing either in unison or in octaves, or playing a drone and a melody. The complementary function tends to be a sign of an older tradition or a conscious revival, while chord accompaniment and polyphonic playing reveal the influence of the dialogue between art music ensembles and folk music.

The Dialogue Function of Instrumental Duos

There appear to be many relatively new combinations of instrumental duos. For example, in a study of Bulgarian ensembles from 1972, Todorv mentions the *gadulka-tambura* as one new combination,

as well as describing a "modern" dialogue between the *gadulka* and the *kaval* in polyphonic playing and harmonization.

Another example of the growing numbers of duos in dialogue with one another is that of the *bouzouki* and the Hardanger fiddlers given above. The earliest documented duos, in eighteenth-century books of dance music, were violin duos playing dance music (see p. 155).

The Complementary Function of Instrumental Duos

Despite the fact that they are both drone instruments, the French hurdy-gurdy and the bagpipe are a very fine combination. In this case, what makes them complementary is their sound. As early as the eighteenth century, bagpipes and violins were a regular combination with a truly complementary function. The ancient bagpipe, blown in antiquity and having a primitive animal appearance, and sound was combined with the violin, the queen of art music instruments. In this case, what makes them complementary is that the fiddle doubles the bagpipe's melody at the octave, while also adding extensive ornamentation (see Elschek 1983, no. 34, p. 211).

Playing in Unison and Playing in Octaves

Playing in both unison and octaves appears to have been frequent in folk music as early as the eighteenth century. The keyed fiddle and the hurdy-gurdy had strings for both unison and octave playing, just as the bagpipe had pipes for both.

In Norway and some parts of Sweden, a special expression was used to describe playing on two violins or Hardanger fiddles in octaves. This was referred to as playing "roughly and resoundingly" (*grovt och grant*). In his 1973 book, *Pols i Rörostraktom*, (Polish Melodies in the Röros Area), Sven Nyhus writes that it was already common in 1850 for two fiddlers to provide dance music together, playing "roughly and resoundingly" (Figure 9.3).

Today, such playing is a stylistic feature of many Swedish fiddlers, used consciously to give performances an archaic touch. Such performances otherwise have the precision of a professional string quartet, with deliberate and exact replication from one occasion to the next.

In principle, any number of fiddlers can play in unison and in octaves, and it does not require any special type of organization. Dragoslav Devic (1981), a Yugoslavian instrumental researcher, has described a recorder ensemble from the village of Vitovnica near Petrovac in Serbia. The ensemble was composed of six players, performing on recorders of different sizes in unison and in octaves. The musicians were farmers and shepherds who had been playing since they were children and who played, in the traditional manner, to accompany dancing. Neither organization nor ideology can be traced to this ensemble structure. It arose simply out of a spontaneous love of music. There are similar kinds of ensembles virtually all over the world. There are also descriptions of gypsy musicians playing in parallel octaves in seventeenth-century Hungary (Sárosi 1967, p. 109).

This doubling of octaves by the violins was a stylistic trait regarded by eighteenth century music-lovers in Berlin as invented by Haydn and characteristic of Viennese taste in music. Berliners considered it comical, naive, and a breach of the rules governing classical music (see also Finscher 1974, p. 86). Today, we might wonder whether Haydn was inspired by folk music ensembles or vice versa, or whether these two types of octave-playing developed independently of one another. According to Finscher (1974) it is possible to "follow the way in which, step by step, Haydn added more and more of the features of folk music to his string quartets" (p. 15). Haydn may also have been inspired by the rough and resounding playing of the folk music groups in which he played in his youth.

Unison/octave-playing, as well as use of the drone remained part of folk music and are distinct characteristics of folk music ensemble-playing even today. We shall now examine developments in central Europe, where Viennese popular music developed into two separate trends, the string quartet and the gypsy ensemble.

The Gypsy Orchestra: A Sister of the String Quartet?

In seventeenth- and eighteenth-century Italy, Germany, France and, most importantly, Bohemia, a plethora of ensembles grew as the instruments in the violin family gained popularity. We find them in the salons of the nobility, the homes of the bourgeoisie, the cloisters, and the churches. The musicians in these ensembles made their livings by combining domestic service and musicianship Some of them were itinerant musicians. Many writers have borne witness to their musical skill. Charles Burney gives us one description, from Rome in the 1770s:

> As soon as I arrived at the inn, a group of musicians appeared below my window. There were two good violinists, a cellist and a woman vocalist, and their performance would have made people's eyes pop out in England. Here, however, they receive as little attention as we pay to coal carriers and oyster mongers. (Burney 1980, p. 73.)

Other travelers from eighteenth-century England sang the praises of ensembles in Germany. These musicians, like wandering minstrels, entertained people for a few florins. Despite their poverty, their musical level could compete with that of first-class English artists (see also Knight 1973, p. 10).

Seventeenth- and eighteenth-century composers wrote pieces with more pastoral features, using drones to imitate the sound of bagpipes. Thus it is not difficult to imagine how country fiddlers, many of whom were well schooled in music (see

Figure 9.3. Anders Sjövold and Ola Skott playing "roughly and resoundingly" in *Leken hass Knut Elven.* (Nyhus 1973, p. 55.)

Böhmen), further reinforced their "rural" sound by introducing more of the stylistic traits of folk music. Popular instruments such as the dulcimer were also included.

According to Macàk (1972), there were string duos of two violins in Slovakia, one playing the melody and one the accompaniment, as early as the sixteenth century. Later, a cello or a small bass fiddle were added, after which the melody and the accompanying instrument were doubled. Thus the string trio, quartet, or quintet came into being, consisting of one or two first violins, one or two seconds, and a bass fiddle.

As mentioned above, during the seventeenth century there were ensembles with bagpipes and stringed instruments, with one violin playing the bagpipe melody embellished an octave higher while the other instrument accompanied. In the mid-eighteenth century the dulcimer came onto the scene, followed by the clarinet. These instruments added a new tonal dimension to music. However, the tradition of the bagpipe was not broken; its drone or the shift between the notes of the two drone pipes, was now taken over by the cello or the double bass, which provided a rhythmic bass part and a harmonic foundation without adhering to chordal progressions. Thus neither the harmonic shifts between dominant and tonic functions that charac-

terized popular music nor the sophisticated harmonic progressions of art music gained much of a foothold in the folk music of central Europe. Listeners expecting certain familiar harmonic patterns protest when they hear a Hungarian, Slovakian, or Romanian folk music orchestra, where the harmonies are unpredictable.

The second fiddle basically had the same function as the viola in earlier string quartets as a supportive tonal filler, but the harmonic shifts always remained of secondary importance in comparison with the function of providing the basic rhythms. Gypsy musicians were of the utmost importance in training these folk ensembles (Figure 9.4).

Sárosi states that the first gypsy orchestras to achieve fame performed in northwestern Hungary, near Vienna and Bratislava. Its members could read music and were very familiar with the Viennese tradition. The famed gypsy musicians from Galánta are described in *Pressburger Zeitung* as excellent musicians who also played art music. They played in "gentlemen's orchestras" from printed music, performing symphonic works as well as music for dancing. According to the author of the article, they were closer to being schooled musicians than "natural" ones (see also Sárosi 1977, p. 72).

The gypsies were receptive to new fashions in

Figure 9.4. A gypsy ensemble consisting of a violin, clarinet, dulcimer and *gardon* (an instrument of the cello family) from a Hungarian village in the 1840s. (Print by Domokos Perlszka after a drawing by Miklós Barabás. See also Sárosi 1977, plate 21.)

music. They were hired musicians and played what was put before them. This brought them into contact with many different instruments and styles, which they then combined in new ways. When they were in rural areas playing peasant dances and ceremonial songs, these new elements from popular and art music were incorporated, adding new tonal dimensions and stylistic traits. When they played in the cities, they rendered melodies and stylistic traits from rural music, which added a feeling of the wild and exotic. This inspired many amateur composers among the bourgeoisie to write folk songs or rhapsodies, and writers to compose their literary equivalents. Franz Liszt's Hungarian rhapsodies, for example, are based on popular urban gypsy music.

The significance of the gypsies as musicians can also be seen statistically. As early as the eighteenth century, gypsies were employed by the Hungarian nobility. In 1782 there were 1,582 gypsy musicians in Hungary, and in 1963 there were 9,929, 3,159 of whom had full-time employment (Sárosi 1967, p. 110f.). Peasant ensembles were more conservative and not as easily influenced from the outside as the gypsy orchestras, which rapidly absorbed new trends and rendered them with great virtuosity (Elschek 1983). Today, in Slovakia, Hungary, and Romania, as well as other nearby regions and countries, ensembles consisting of strings and occasionally of other instruments, such as the dulcimer, *fujara*, or the clarinet, still exist in much the same way as in the nineteenth century (see Elschek

1983 for a detailed description). However, the trend is that the gypsy music tradition is moving in the direction of folklore, identified with the music of the entire rural community.

In recent years social integration has led to many gypsies abandoning music. In their place, the peasant population has begun to show interest in playing in string ensembles, and has found a kind of moral value in setting up local village orchestras. In the 1940s, gypsy orchestras tried to play modern dance music instead, but it took a long time for the change to become well-established. Today, both older folk music orchestras and newer dance ensembles play both kinds of music. (Interview with Oskár Elschek in 1986, see also Elschek 1983.)

Just as in Hungary, Slovakia, and Romania, professional gypsy musicians were important as wedding musicians in Greece, Yugoslavia, and Bulgaria, thus serving as preservers and renewers of traditions to the extent that their audiences could tolerate change. On the significance of Jewish ensembles, see p. 216

Military Music as the Prototype for Folk Music Ensembles

The Zurla *and the* Tapan

The ensemble consisting of shawm (a folk oboe *zurla*) and double-headed drum (*tapan*) originated in the east but came to have its main center in

Serbia and Bulgaria. Sometimes bagpipes were added to the ensemble. The *zurla* and the *tapan* arrived in Europe as the Ottoman Empire spread. They were of low status but high popularity; played at weddings and festivities where they were appreciated for their penetrating sound. These instruments did not particularly change. They are very much like their Arab relations, and other members of their families played in countries where Arab immigrants have brought their culture with them. In Turkey the ensemble is known as *zurnadavul*, and is very important (see also Picken 1975).

Music for Wind Instruments Came, Saw and Conquered

Just as the piano revolutionized bourgeois music in home environments and gradually came to dominate the concert hall, wind instruments first became the domain of the peasants and later of the working classes, and ultimately came to dominate in outdoor music environments. The new wind instruments, with their brilliant systems of keys and valves, were introduced by the military bands. The wind instruments became popular in the villages via military music. This popularity came at the time when more and more people were learning to read music and more and more music education was available. In countries with established traditions (such as Hungary, Bohemia, Moravia, and parts of Austria), the older ceremonial melodies, dances, and folk songs were arranged for wind ensembles. Wind music did not, however, reach places where there was great isolation and poverty. The origins and spread of wind ensembles should be seen in conjunction with the growth of industrialism, spearheaded by Britain. In the beginning, in the 1810s, ensembles consisted of mixed woodwinds and brass instruments, but by the 1850s they were strictly brass bands. Interest was greatest in England between 1880 and 1890 and spread across Europe, taking on different forms depending on social structure, musical traditions, and the extent to which military musicians were available. Greger Andersson has described the organized creation of wind bands as having begun in earnest around 1830: "The wind ensembles in southern Germany and Austria today are, in many ways, comparable with Swedish country dancing ensembles and ensembles organized by fiddler's associations. The repertoire of these wind ensembles often contains older folk dances and adaptations of more and less authentic folk music.

Many of these groups also play in folk costume" (Andersson 1982, p. 19). Many of the more official wind and brass ensembles were established as parts of military organizations such as the Swedish Sharpshooters' Movement or the Swiss *Schützenwesen*. This official interest in wind and brass music, and the development of so many ensembles, often in the most unexpected places, also inspired the development of new folk ensembles with older dance melodies in their repertoire. In some parts of Europe, such as southern Germany, Austria, Switzerland, Slovakia, and Hungary, wind ensembles account for the majority of the ceremonial music today (see Suppan 1980, Sárosi 1967, Elschek 1983).

Folk Music Orchestras

In Russia, one of many efforts to bring folk music to life amongst the people in the late nineteenth century was the organization of different types of ensembles. These provided a basis for the development that accelerated after the October Revolution, when folk art became a matter of highest state concern. As early as at the Paris World Fair in 1884, a Russian instrumental ensemble with folk instruments performed. In orchestras in St. Petersburg in the 1890s, various shepherds' instruments such as the birch-bark clarinet were combined with the *domra* and the *balalaika*. Newer folk music instruments such as the accordion also came to occupy an important place in these folk music orchestras.

After the October Revolution professional state orchestras and dance music groups were organized, and amateur groups arose at factories, where *solkhozes* and *kolkhozes* competed to outdo one another in performance skill. Both types of ensembles later became obligatory aspects of culture in the Soviet Union and in neighbouring countries as well.

There is no doubt that these state ensembles achieved a great deal of popularity at home and abroad, and that they were greatly admired for their skill and virtuosity. They have also been criticized for their highly organized and disciplined performances, which are so far from the spontaneity and improvisation of the village ensemble. This also brought them into conflict with youthful folk music groups who sought their roots in the remaining fragments of rural tradition in the 1960s and 1970s. Revival groups were formed in the Soviet Union as well, and there, too, they based their music-making on remaining traditions and archival materials in order to achieve more "authentic" folk music than the popular folk music performed by state ensembles and amateur factory orchestras. Today, even in Western nations, folk music is often integrated into higher education programs in music and into official cultural policy. However, ensembles of the "orchestral" format, like those in the former Soviet Union and Bulgaria, will probably not come into existence in the west.

Scandinavian Fiddlers' Societies

In the late nineteenth and early twentieth centuries, many of the older folk ensembles died out as the new generations took over and lacked the burning interest of their forbears in old instruments and music. However, as mentioned above, new constellations did arise. For an ensemble to outlive the lifetimes of its founding members, there must be recruitment of new performers who gradually replace the old ones as they retire. This is an automatic process in a society in which children suceed their fathers and mothers, learning their occupations, customs and ceremonies. Things change radically when the fixed traditional structure is broken down and replaced with a freer choice of occupations and greater mobility of the population.

Folk ensembles in the Scandinavian rural areas generally consisted of two or three fiddlers. In the early twentieth century folk music meetings and competitions began to be organized, and the early fiddlers' societies formed. There were also professional musicians with an interest in folk music, who performed arrangements of folk music at concerts and, in the 1930s and 1940s, on the radio. The twentieth century also saw the rise of ensemble forms which are probably to be regarded as forerunners to the fiddlers' societies alongside the various wind ensembles and the various types of string orchestras. These orchestras played whatever was available, from salon pieces and simple classical music to arrangements of folk music.

In the 1940s these amateur orchestras suddenly split up into groups specializing in different kinds of music, including folk music. The Rättvik Fiddlers' Society was the prototype for many later societies. It began, as many such groups must have done, through the initiative of one man, Anders Sparf. He was familiar with the fiddling tradition, but he also wanted to break out of peasant society. He became a violin teacher, folk music scholar, and violin-maker. According to his description (see *Sumlen* 1984) a few fiddlers who played dance music together, along with an accordion player and a pianist at the outdoor summer dances in the park in Rättvik, founded the fiddlers' society (Figure 9.5). He illustrates what can provide impetus to a folk music ensemble.

> In my opinion, instrumental skill is not what counts. Interest is far more important, and skill can be acquired. These societies were to be democratic, in the sense that a desire to express oneself in music was the only eligibility requirement for membership. If I were to be the head of the society, my only task would be to tell people to give their all, not to tell them how to play, but to put their personalities into their playing. There were, of course, certain limits, because the group did have to be able to play together. We had Pål Olle to do the bottom parts, and he improvized them. We gave him free rein, and the others would just try to play along. Olle played the second part, and we also had a viola player, who played a third part. Then we had to find the mortar to cement it all into a whole, with the different tempos and all. From the beginning, this was not easy. We sounded, you might say, pretty awful. We got lost. But finally we started to be able to play together. We had to listen to each other, observe each other. Whenever I tried to give directions about nuances, things got worse. Their personalities didn't shine through. So we just had to go on playing, each man for himself, and stick to it so we could hear ourselves as part of a group, stick to it so each of us thought we were best and the others were just the background. (Ling/Ramsten 1984, pp. 50f.)

Thinking in terms of functional harmony arose with the introduction of such instruments as the cittern. This meant a notable difference in sound compared with many of the central European ensembles where, as described above, the rhythmic foundation lacks functional harmonies. Sweden, Norway, and Finland are also characterized by greater sensitivity to what scholars and experts regard as "folksy." The Rättvik Fiddlers' Society gradually became a group strictly for fiddles, under the influence of the belief of musicologists that the fiddle was the utmost in folk instruments. As R ttvik was also the place in Sweden where fiddle-playing had developed most strongly, this belief undoubtedly easily took root there. This ensemble

Figure 9.5. The Rättvik Fiddlers' Society, 1948. (Photograph: M. Berg, Rättvik, Sweden.)

gained great popularity, and many other local fiddlers' societies came into being modelled on their success.

In this case, too, then, tonal ideals can be traced to aesthetic or ideological beliefs to some extent *beyond* the intentions of both the musicians and the listeners. In some respect, fiddlers today have returned to the ensemble composition of the 1940s: the *old* fiddlers' society in Rättvik again contains an organist, an accordion player, and a guitarist along with the fiddlers, just as it did then, but there is also a *new* fiddlers' society in Rättvik today, composed strictly of violinists.

In a study entitled *Spelmän i lag* (Fiddlers in Societies) Gunnar Ternhag (1985), has described the organizational structure of Swedish fiddlers' societies, of which there are nearly three hundred. Many have been around since the 1940s, and were inspired by the Rättvik society and their theme song, *Gärdebylåten*. The growth of new societies increased steadily until 1967–1968 when it began a sharp rise that continued until 1980. That year saw the inception of no less than twenty-five fiddlers' societies. Fifteen percent of the associations have followed the new Rättvik model and use only violins, many are actually keyed fiddlers' societ-

ies, and many also have accordions. Ternhag gives an example of the skepticism that still marks the attitudes of many people toward the accordion, as well as the guitar, as a folk music instruments:

A society in the province of Halland stated: "We do not count the accordion, the guitar, or the bass amongst folk music instruments, nor have we yet begun to regard country dancing as folk music." A society from Dalacarlia has been equally firm in its statement: "We have not given the slightest consideration to mixing with tonal tools that are not at all inherent to Swedish folk music" [Ternhag 1985, p. 28].

Thus there is an awareness with regard to choice of instruments and folk music in these ensembles, indicating that they are not spontaneous groupings but rather ensembles with clearly formulated ideologies of folk music.

Alongside what Ternhag refers to as the Rättvik model are other less restrictive forms; ensembles with no aesthetic or orchestral ambitions. These include the community ensembles that have come into being as the result of study circles in instrumental music. These groups accept beginners and play another important social function of providing a forum for music-making without placing high demands on the performers. Often these community ensembles come into being after courses on keyed-fiddle-making, where the makers go on to learn to play the fiddles they have made in a study circle. Ternhag describes a third category, the country music fiddlers' society. Of course there are no sharply defined boundaries between these three categories. Indeed, there are societies based on the Rättvik model that have developed elements of the community and the country dancing model as well.

Internationalization of Ensembles

In the 1960s and 1970s, many ensembles were founded with the aim of renewing public interest in folk music. As it was felt that folk music had become antiquated, these ensembles represented a radical change. (For example, the Hungarian *Sëbo.*) Folk music clubs regained some popularity, and dance, again, became a mode of social interaction. These groups were trying to get away from the folk music "orchestras," by utilizing improvisation and combined, music-dance performances. At the same time, notions of nationalism diminished.

Today, there are French folk musicians trying out the Swedish keyed fiddle in their ensembles, German folk musicians playing Spanish music and Swedish ones playing German, Hungarian and Balkan music, all very skillfully, and with a sense both of tradition and renewal, as well as for both foreign and domestic ideals.

The new ensembles worked under different conditions in different countries. In some of the former socialist countries, in the 1970s and 1980s, groups performed for a special jury which either sanctioned their continued existence or rejected them in an "approval" procedure for performing at clubs, a source of income for many. In capitalist countries, there are cultural foundations and grants committees with a similar kind of power to determine the fate of ensembles. Alongside these official instruments, there is the tried and true method of letting the listeners be the judges. Only a combination of official public funding and audience approval enables the long-term survival of an ensemble.

The ensembles clearly reflect the different types of symbiosis between popular and folk music. They seldom rest on tradition. Instead, their music is oriented toward creating new sound combinations. Anything and everything is possible in a creative melting pot of folk traditions, jazz, rock, pop, etc.

The Jazz Ensemble in Sweden: The Starting Point of a New Wave of Folk Music?

It is possible that we may find the beginning of this movement in Sweden in the 1950s and 1960s, when jazz musicians like Jan Johansson (1931–1968), Lars Gullin (1928–1977) and Bengt-Arne Walling (b. 1926) combined two apparently irreconcilable things: the jazz ensemble and folk music.

Many musicians in folk-rock trace their interest back to Jan Johansson's many jazz records in Swedish, Russian, and Hungarian.

The Folk-Style Rock Ensemble

Folk music festivals in Europe reflect a wide variety of ensembles. To date it is probably valid to generalize that eastern Europe has been dominated by tradition and western Europe by folk-rock. Let us examine the relationships between this latter category and tradition. Ulf Gruvberg, a Swedish musicologist, has described folk-rock in relation to folk music.

> In the 1960s, Bob Dylan, the Beatles and Simon and Garfunkel were models for many kinds of vocal music groups, such as *Folk och Rackare* in Sweden and *Malicorne* in France. *Steeleye Span* is another of the many groups that have tried to combine English and American instrumental and vocal folk music, medieval and Renaissance music. All these groups are based on a duo. Trends have been somewhat different in the various countries. Norway was an early country, in addition to France and England. In West Germany there has been a great interest in Jewish music, with texts in Yiddish. In different parts of Spain, including the Basque region and Galicia, there are groups with strong senses of identity, picking up on the older traditions, and expanding on the unique cultural features that were taboo under the Franco regime. (Interview, 1987.)

Thus the new ensembles were based on both musical and ideological beliefs, both of which may have been rooted in the folk music tradition. Although the groups in various countries developed very different images, the trends from the 1960s

Figure 9.6. The folk music group *Groupa* offers a wide range and combination of instruments, here, the flute, recorder, triangle, guitar, viola d'amore, and accordion. (Photograph: Per-Ulf Allmo.)

and 1970s were very similar for folk music groups in different countries. They began with a duo, and their first focus was on popular songs. For one reason or another they found their way to folk music, sometimes in combination with an interest in the music of the Middle Ages or the Renaissance. The duo expanded, taking on more instruments, was reinforced with electrified instruments, and played more at festivals and less at clubs. After some time, a serious interest in exploring the "roots" of folk music arose.

There were also other reasons for forming folk music ensembles, of which some Swedish groups may stand as examples. The *Groupa* ensemble came into being in 1980. (See Figure 9.6.) Folk music from the province of Värmland was dear to the hearts of the founders, Leif and Inger Stinnerbom and Mats Edén. In the 1970s they had made extensive journeys for recording and collecting the vocal and instrumental music of folk musicians in Värmland. As students of music they then came into contact with a representative of very different traditions: Bill McChesney from the United States. He was a big band and marching band musician who later became a recorder player. He introduced them to the possibility of using the recorder and the bass clarinet as a folk music instrument. On the jackets of their discs, *Groupa* made their ideology manifest, taking a strong stand in favor of tradition. They expressed their awareness of the need for a sense of historicity. However, they simultaneously expressed the desire to associate with the branch of folk music that combined Swedish folk music with other influences. This is reflected in both the instrumental make-up and the performance style of the ensemble.

Groupa is an ensemble from western Sweden. As they developed, a group called *Filarfolket* came into being in southern Sweden. Early on, this group accepted a wealth of instruments and a mixture of styles of folk music from different countries as well as the influences of jazz and rock. The music of the following instruments could, for example, be heard on their second LP: flute, piccolo, baritone and sopranino saxophone, percussion, guitar, violin, cello, Hardanger fiddle, double bass, clarinet, bass and contrabass clarinet, Norwegian folk recorder (*spilopipa*), *bouzouki*, accordion, trumpet, bamboo flute, French horn, tin whistle, and harmonica. The group consisted of six musicians who, like the court jesters of the Middle Ages, mastered many instruments with great skill. Their greatest interest, however, proved to be in the Swedish folk music tradition; in its instrumental music and folk songs. This interest later embraced children's songs and nursery rhymes. Later the ensemble wrote more and more of its own music.

Northern Swedish groups, exemplified here by *Norrlåtar* and *J. P. Nyström's*, illustrate yet another aspect of the relationship between folk music and popular music. These groups arose with the awareness that the music of northern Sweden had not been documented. Like the members of *Groupa*, the members of *Norrlåtar* recorded and collected the dance repertoire of the older fiddlers. Using this material and the traditional dance instruments from the region—the accordion, the guitar, and the harmonium—they shaped a folk music tradition that became the musical identity of their region. What the folk music experts had previously classified as "old fashioned dance music" ensembles suddenly became folk music ensembles. They played for dancing and also gained high status as the musical symbols of their region.

Quantitatively speaking, this wave of folk music ensembles only accounts for one small aspect of contemporary European music. However, their strong profiles have probably had an impact on both popular music and art music. The ensembles consist of composers, instrumentalists who also teach their instruments, and intellectuals of other kinds as well. They have an extensive network of contacts through- out society, and surely as much influence as the collectors and composers had who began formal collection work and gave rise to the interest in folk music in the eighteenth century (see also Chapter 11).

Literature

This chapter is based on the modest amount of research which exists on folk music ensembles, particularly the contemporary ones. In this area, too, the most prominent source is *Handbuch der Europäischen Volksmusikinstrumente* (1967–) and Volume 2 of *Studia instrumentorum musicae popularis* (1972).

Ten

Movement and Dance,
Song and Instrumental Music

BACKGROUND

What Is Folk Dance?

Today we use the term *folk dance* to refer to all kinds of circle dances and games for couples and individuals, originating at any time from the Middle Ages to the present. Many of these folk dances were, in fact, created by collectors, who noted down certain elements from wedding ceremonial or seasonal festivities, describing them as "dances." Probably this description would have surprised many of the "dancers."

European peasants did, however, have many dances in the true sense of the word that were not integrated into ceremonies or rites but simply constituted holiday and evening entertainment for young people. One piece of historical evidence for this is that many dances were banned, a prohibition the peasantry delighted in violating.

Descriptions of dancing from the late Middle Ages are often quite contemptuous, and the dancers are described as awkward and clumsy. Collectors probably received this impression because they were outsiders, ignorant of the nature of the dances being performed, and usually with their own ideas that were influenced by bourgeois dance traditions. In this chapter, we will be using traditional terminology such as *wedding dance* or *women's circle dance*, despite the fact that the women in the circle may not have regarded themselves as dancing.

Song or Instrumental Music for Dancing

The different dances were accompanied by as many kinds of music, which could be described using various principles. I have chosen to classify them as vocal or instrumental accompaniment, but there was no strict barrier between the two–in many parts of Europe a young man would sing the melody to the musicians before asking a lady to dance, to ensure that the tempo would be to his liking. In some places dancing would be accompanied by singing or humming for want of instrumental musicians, for example, at times or in places where instrumental music for dancing was banned as sinful.

Many dancers and dance melodies were associated with short texts the subject matter of which could range from lyrical love songs to sexual innuendoes to jokes. The main thing was that the fiddlers be able to play the melodies. In Germany such more or less improvised short songs were referred to as *Schnadahüpferl* and can be traced back as far as the Middle Ages, when they were used to stamp the beat and get the dancing started (see Oetke 1982, p. 214). The tradition of the man asking the woman to dance has been around almost everywhere since time immemorial. This description from Austria in 1807 could just as well be from a folk dance festival today, except that the dancing might take place on a stage rather than at an inn:

> Let us imagine a great inn, on a holiday or at a wedding . . . in one corner the musicians have their special place, usually a huge chest of grain on which they stand . . . a dancer takes the floor with his partner, approaches the musicians and tosses his silver to them. This is known as 'ordering a dance.' When this takes place all the other dancers have to stand aside and allow the couple who ordered to dance it.

After dancing, the dancer raises his voice and sings his *Schnadahüpferl* to the tune of his choice. Most *Schnadahüpferl* are either erotic or satirical. (Oetke 1982, p. 218.)

There is a traditional belief that vocal dance music preceded instrumental. This is probably correct with regard to strictly instrumental music, but combinations of instrumental and vocal music appear to have been common for a very long time. If we examine paintings depicting dancing, we can often find someone sitting near the musicians singing (such as Pieter Bruegel's painting of a bagpipe player and a singer in the village, Figure 10.1). Dance melodies were also performed very differently on instruments than vocally. For example, the violin version of a *polska* from Rättvik, Sweden, after fiddler Höök Olof Andersson (1860–1936) is far more ornamented than the vocal version (Figure 10.2).

According to German musicologist Frans Magnus Böhme (1886) the shift towards more instrumental dance music can be dated to after 1500. It was not until the mid-seventeenth century, however, that purely instrumental dance music really broke through. This happened at the same time that instrumental art music also began life on its own. Thus dancing music "became mute" and was left to the instrumentalists (see also Oetke 1982, p. 14).

Unlike dance songs and danced games, instrumental dance music did not have texts relating to customs, ceremonies, or chores. When there were texts at all, they were simply for the purposes of making the dance and the melody identifiable. It is probable that instrumental dancing initiated a more comprehensive change which led, in the long run, to the liberation of dance as an independent form of expression. Loud instruments such as the hurdy-gurdy, the bagpipe, the shawm, the *rommelpott* (friction drum), and the xylophone were supplemented with dampers or plows and other tools transformed into instruments for dance music. However, the search had also begun for instruments that were loud, beautiful, and penetrating, and which also allowed for advanced technique. The violin satisfied many of theses demands, and its popularity as an instrument for dance music spread very quickly in rural cultures, often displaying special regional variations (see p. 159).

As long as dance, text, and melodies were one integrated unit, part of a rite or ceremony, the various components were not regarded as independent. As ceremonies began to dissolve, the aesthetic or comic effects of the dancing or entertainment were elevated at the expense of the ceremonial aspects, and the separate concepts of "dance" and "music" as we know them took root.

Dance from One Class to Another

In some contexts dance has been an extremely democratic cultural phenomenon: everyone danced together, especially at carnivals, markets and weddings, occasions on which age and class barriers were temporarily eradicated.

Dance has also transcended social class boundaries in another way: peasant circle and line dances were transformed into contredanses which, in turn, became folk dances. The skipping and hopping of dancing peasant couples was transformed into the allemands and minuets of the nobility. These dances, again, took on peasant variations of their own with time.

The dance melodies have their own patchwork history. Although it is possible to discern a few main stylistic categories, there are no rigorous ties binding given dances to specific melodies. Neither is it possible to set fixed dates to the categories of dance melodies. Thus it is not easy to give an overview of dance melodies in Europe: the material itself is endless and varied. I have taken my lead from dance research, and tried to provide a general picture of dance melodies using their traditional divisions of line and ring dances, couples' dances and solo dances.

LINE AND RING DANCES

Children's songs, seasonal songs, wedding songs, songs of work, and historical songs have all been performed to formalized movement, or "dances." "London Bridge," known to all in one version or another, can be danced to in many ways, depending on the story in the text.

Line and ring dances tend to be performed with everyone moving around a circle or in a line, performing very simple steps. Lisbeth Torp has systematized European line and ring dances, classifying them by formation, the way the dancers hold hands, the direction of movement, and the choreographic relationship of the individual dancer

Figure 10.1 Couples dancing in Poland to an ensemble including the suka, the bagpipe (*bock*) and the pipe and tabor. (Drawing from 1693, see also Dahlig 1985.)

to the collective. Torp goes on to categorize the dances by the groups of steps they contain as well.

Two of the main categories, in this work symbolized by the letters A and B, established themselves, due to the fact that the examples of dances based on these patterns were convincingly numerous, especially pattern B. In their simplest forms, they are easily recognizable and their structural make-up is clear, which makes the segmentation of the patterns into significant compositional units uncomplicated. Pattern A is simply based on the motif that we shall from now on designate by the generic term *traveling steps*, a term which includes walking or running steps.

Pattern B is based on a combination of two motifs and can be segmented as follows: two traveling steps followed by a hesitation step. *Hesitation step* will be used as the generic term for the motif described below. The *hesitation step* functions as a pausing step or hesitation, in that it creates a kind of break in the monotony of the progression of a series of *traveling steps*.

Traditional chain and round dances develop from a series of basic patterns ranging from a very simple motif, like the one based solely on the traveling step, to compound patterns consisting of a combination of several structural units, i.e., from simple motifs to complex motifs. (Torp 1990, pp. 69f.)

Her investigation gives the impression that the choreographic patterns of line and ring dances are far more pan-European than the melodies.

Polskan sjöngs med tillhörande text, och hade då denna lydelse:

In - te har jag pen-gar, in - te är jag pank, men en flic - ka har jag

som är rätt ga-lant, och hon går al - drig ur mitt sin - ne.

In - te ha vi nål och in - te ha vi tråd, men fan ge vi den som

lap - pen sät - ter på, och glas - su - pen ta vi al - la.

Ägg och fläsk i far, och gubb i juck i mor, soc-ker-sött i sys-ter och

dubb i subb i bror. Vi sk - - r i gam - la svär - mor.

Figure 10.2. *Polska* after Höök Olof Andersson (1860–1936), from the town of Rättvik in the province of Dalarna. Version played on the violin and sung. (*SvL Dalarna* IV 1926/R 1978 p.3.)

Some of these dances have been the movement parts of singing games that also included spoken dialogues, passing around an object, etc. Other dances, such as English Morris dancing, are associated with certain holidays or seasons. Cecil Sharp, a British folk music collector, assumes that Morris dances were of Moorish-Spanish origin. Today, this hypothesis has been abandoned in favor of interpreting *Morris* to mean *masking*, i.e., an attempt by the dancers to disguise themselves by blacking their hands and faces with soot. Like so many other dances, the Morris dance was originally very popular in central England. However, it was suppressed during the nineteenth century and only survived in a very limited area (Oxfordshire and Gloucestershire), where it did so because it was associated with a custom or tradition such as a fertility rite—in this case, taking down the May-

pole. When Sharp studied the Morris dance, it was no longer accompanied by the one-handed flute and drum, but instead by the violin or concertina. Many of the traditional dancers abandoned the dance because they did not like the sound of the new instruments, claiming that they took away the necessary rhythmic support for the dancing. New melodies then came onto the scene, and Morris dancing was increasingly performed as ring dancing or singing games. Only a few of the original Morris dance melodies were retained (Figure 10.3). Thanks to the educational books Sharp wrote on the Morris dance, and to a few faithful enthusiasts, it has remained in the repertoire of many dance societies, and is still performed at local spring and summer fêtes.

The formalized movements of many dances illustrate various tasks. There are also dances about courting, weddings, and family customs. Such dances are important to the passing down of traditions in society (see also p. 54). Some dances are also performed to ballads of love. Sometimes all the dancers sing all the verses, and sometimes the dancers divide into two choirs, of men and women or of lead and refrain, for example. The melodies are usually composed of one or two—seldom more—easily memorized melodic motifs in different combinations. Let us look at a few examples.

In Figure 10.4 three Russian ring dances are built up from combinations of different motifs: a) is one single repeated motif, b) is a repeated AB form, and (c) is an AABB form (Batjinskaja 1951). In Figure 10.5 we have a vocal (a) and an instrumental (b) Bulgarian dance melody based on the same type of descending call. Such melodies are common in the Balkans, not least in Greece. The vocal version consists, as is traditional, of two short repeated motifs. The instrumental version is considerably longer and more embellished, containing three eight-bar groupings, the second and third of which stand in contrast against the introductory descending formalized motif that consists of variations on melodic units.

Espelund (1979) described a similar structure of dance and melody patterns where the melody is in four and the movement is in six. This occurs in dances ranging from the medieval branle dances to dances from the Faeroe Islands to contemporary dances in Montenegro, Bulgaria, Greece, and Romania (see further details below).

The recent history of ring and line dances in

Figure 10.3. The cover of Cecil J. Sharp's booklet about Morris Dancing is a reproduction of the title page from *Kemp's nine daies wonder, performed in a daunce from London to Norwich*, 1600. In this, Kemp was said to have Morris danced his way from London to Norwich in nine days. He was a popular actor and performed with Shakespeare and others (see also Sharp 1912, p. 20f.). The dancer wears bells on his legs and is accompanied by pipe and tabor.

Figure 10.4. Melodies from N. Batjinskaja, *Russkie schorovodi i schorovodie piesni* (Russian Dances and Dance Melodies). (Moscow 1951, p. 58–63.)

Europe also indicates great similarities from place to place with a strong tradition of dancing while singing in unison. This was rooted in ceremonial and ritual traditions, often associated with labor, courting, or other aspects of family life, later transformed to ring or line dances with instrumental accompaniment, with increasing elements of choreographically sophisticated patterns. This development began in the eighteenth century. We can learn about the history of dance from art, as pictures of dancing also tell us a great deal about the environments in which dancing took place as well as about the way in which the painter interpreted dancing and dancers (Figure 10.6.)

How a Dance Acquires Its Identity

When we describe more recent couples' dances or ballroom dancing, we do so in terms of the structure of the melody or the steps of the dance. However, descriptions and identities within the category of ring and line dances can often better be distinguished in terms of social context. For these dances, the steps and melodies were of secondary importance, and could vary greatly within the loosely defined framework of the ring and line dance.

Based on the present comparative study of the comprehensive empirical material of chain and round dances the following conclusions can be drawn: (a) generally speaking, none of the various step patterns which form the basis of these dances, is itself exclusively connected to only one specific occasion; (b) when a dance is ascribed a certain significance or symbolic value, this particular characteristic is determined by the context in which the dance is employed, and not by the dance pattern itself. (Torp 1990, p. 47.)

Ring and line dances, associated with seasonal festivities and personal celebrations, usually had a ceremonial tone, and because they had been passed down from one generation to the next, they also contributed to the preservation of ancient traditions. This endowed them with a special social status and function. Couples' dances, in contrast, were generally regarded as mating games, and thus as lewd and offensive in societies where the parents decided who their children would marry. (Figure 10.7.)

Figure 10.5. Bulgarian (a) vocal and (b) instrumental dancing. *Narodni tanzi ot Srednogorieto* (Folk Dances from Srednogorieto). Publications from the Bulgarian Academy of Science, 1978, ed. Anna Ileva, pp. 409 and 238.

The *kvede* dances from the Faeroe Islands provide us with an example of line dances of the branle-type, traditionally performed from Christmas through Lent, dating back to the Middle Ages. In Sweden, branle type dances could mostly be found in the province of Dalacarlia, where they were known as *långdanser* (long dances). Linnaeus made the following journal entry after visiting Mora in Dalacarlia in 1734:

> The dancing in Mora was remarkable. It was known as the 'long dance.' There were four steps to each bar, the fourth of which was a loud stamp indicating that the circle was to be re-closed. In each measure, the dancers in the ring walked two steps out, expanding the circle, then two steps in, contracting the circle, as if everyone was gathering to stamp on one another's noses.

Slängrumpa

The *slängrumpa*, danced in Sweden at Christmas time, was a completely different kind of line dance. This primitive long dance is not very highly regulated, and could be danced to almost any popular melody at all. It was very common in old times, for instance at weddings in the Swedish-speaking parts of Finland:

> The 'long dance' [*langdansin* or *langnåoten*] was usually danced by the guests while they waited for a meal to be served, but the bride and groom did not participate. The fiddlers played a special melody known as the *fatifåglin*. The guests would form a ring, as large as there was room for. After some dancing both clockwise and counter-clockwise the leader would suddenly drop the hand of one of the people next to him, so the dancers would form a line, jumping to the beat, with the line twisting and twirling all around the house. No one was allowed to drop the hand of the dancers on either side of him. Finally, the entire troupe, with the *nåot-konin* (the king) at the head and the *sladdin* (the latecomer) bringing up the rear danced out into the garden, followed by the fiddlers, playing all the while. (*FSF Folkdans VI* p. LXXXII.)

The People Reclaim Line and Ring Dances

By the 1970s line and ring dances were mainly performed by folk dance performers, but around that time, in various parts of Europe from southern Italy to northern Sweden, they once again became functional and more or less improvised. For example, the text booklet to a Swedish disc entitled *Stamp, tramp och långkut* (KRLP2) (Stamp, Tramp, and Long Run) contains a detailed description of how to improvise a dance on the basis of a historical description or a melody annotated by a collector. The author, Anders Rosén, has tried to strike a balance between tradition and renewal, between fixed patterns and free improvisation:

> You may invent new steps if you like, but it is probably most important to retain the existing ones, because they often express a deeper content at the symbolic level. You can, of course, also invent variations on the steps. One thing we have found useful is to see what steps from the couples' dance can be taken out and made into a line dance. . . .

In the late 1970s, 140 women who were occupying a threatened building in Copenhagen performed a line dance, both to create a spirit of community and to demonstrate their collective unity against

Figure 10.6. Russian choral dancing to the popular song "Do Not Berate Me, My Love." Russian nineteenth-century broadside. (Batjinskaja 1951, plate 5.)

the authorities (Torp 1987). The future may also see new kinds of collective dancing arise as an alternative to couples' and solo dancing.

> Although the existing chain and round dances in many cases can be said to have lost their previous significance to the community in which they are now being performed, three basic functions of dancing in general, have been strengthened in modern society: the recreational function, the entertaining function, and the social function. This strengthening of function has taken place concurrently with society's rapid development, its still higher degree of specialization and individualization, and its continuous race for increased productivity. In addition, the participation in dance events is still valid for the purpose of matrimony, and probably always will be, due to the possibility of physical contact through dancing. However, today it is not necessarily limited to people of a specific age and social group such as the young unmarried people. (Torp 1990, p. 47.)

The Relationship between Melody and Dance in Line and Ring Dances

How are the melody and the dance steps related? There does not appear to be a general correlation, but in each individual combination of melody and dance there is a dialogue between the melodic and choreographic patterns of pulsation, each with its own structure. The melodies often have regional features. The only characteristics that always seem to distinguish line and ring dances is that they have a limited range and are based on a limited number of melodic units.

In folklore, dance and music are regarded as "complementary expressions" (Giurchescsu/Bloland 1987) that can be studied at the following levels:

1. a communicative level between dancers and musicians and, of course, also between dancers, musicians, and the audience; or
2. a structural level relating to the interplay between dance and music.

The first level assumes that dance is not only of interest to the dancers, but that the musicians and the audience also participate, to create an organic, dynamic whole. Researchers who study the structural level base their work on aspects including rhythm, meter, tempo, motif, phrase length and congruence, coupling, and internal organization. Giurchescsu/Bloland show, in their study of Romanian ring dances, that there is full agreement between dance and melody only in exceptional cases. Instead, any given melody can be used for different types of dances, and there is structural independence between dance and music. This is reinforced by the different types of improvisation used. Factors in agreement include tempo and dynamics, pulse and meter, while other, overarching levels such as the melody and dance motifs are often played off against one another. The melodies are divided into two motifs, and these prevail over the three-part motifs of the dance (see above). At the motif level, dance and melody may be brought into agreement through rehearsal. For instance, the dance motif may be divided into three parts (an introduction, a core, and a finale) that may be played off against the melody, which is divided into two motifs or periods.

In the attempts that have been made to study the structural interplay between music and dance, Owe Ronström (1986) has attempted to systematize dances on the basis of the demands placed on the individual dancer in terms of "subordinating himself to the collective in the dance." Some dances are far more demanding than others with regard to the ability of the dancers to work together and be disciplined. In other words, the collective dances are very different with regard to levels of individual expression.

There is also a difference between the lead dancer and the others in the ring: the lead dancer may allow himself to improvise, while the others in the ring have to keep more strictly to the basic pattern. The lead dancer also has opportunities to show his prowess in solo dancing, while the "refrain" dancers are more tightly bound to the structure (see also Espelund 1979).

The dance formations and melody types used in ring and line dances have moved throughout the course of history from more free improvisation to more strictly established patterns, when "peasant dancing" was replaced by dance performance, "peasant ballet on stage." With this development, certain melodies were inseparably linked to certain dances. This is often an indication of conscious cultural preservation, a symbol of the sense of community in dance and music. The formalization of ring and line dances we see today in folk dance societies in east and west took place in phases beginning in the eighteenth century. The first phase saw the transformation of ring and line dances to contredanses.

Torp emphasizes the importance of the melody as a "signal" for the dance: "In general, it can be said that, if people do not recall the melody, they usually cannot reproduce the dance, whereas a certain melody, or basic rhythmical accompaniment of a given dance, may signal a specific dance or dance type to the people concerned" (Torp 1990, p. 11).

FROM LINE AND RING TO TWO BY TWO

How are ring and line dances related to couples' dances and solo dances? Let us begin by examining the Hungarian dance tradition as studied by dance scholar György Martin. Hungarian girls' dance groups appear to be a surviving remnant of

Figure 10.7. Couples' dance performed by sixteenth century peasants. Copperplate from 1546 by Hans Sebald Beham. (*Volksmusik in Österreich* p. 56.)

medieval European dancing. In popular language, they are not referred to as dances at all (*tanc*) but rather as different versions of "circles." In the past, only girls of a marriageable age were allowed to dance. The young men would stand outside the ring observing while preparing to take the girl of their choice for a brief couples' dance. Martin has described the highly regulated structure of these ring dances. The order and divisions of the motifs are fixed, while the number of repetitions of steps and melodies is dependent on the spirit of the occasion. The rhythm and tempo of the melodies are fixed, and are known as *lépö* or walking step melodies, *csárdás*, and *fut* or running-step melodies. The structure may include walking and running steps or *csárdás* and running steps, or even all three (on the *csárdás* , see p. 190). According to Martin, the current form of ring dance for girls is a transition from old to new: "This transformation did not affect the substance, the circular form, or the singing, but the methods of performance, the motifs and various musical features were changed" (Martin 1974, p. 21). The *csárdás* is really a couples' dance, and its use in the ring dance has had the effect of transforming it to a dance with variations between slow and rapid tempos, making it more entertaining to watch and more complex, more like a dance than just circular movement (see p. 107 on the origins of the "new style" in Hungarian folk song).

Thus nothing is sacred in a folk tradition: almost everything but the basic form is subject to change, and melodies are extremely versatile and can be used interchangeably outside the ceremonial context as soon as dancers begin to dance for the fun of it.

Couples' dancing is generally regarded as having invaded the peasant environment from the aristocracy and the bourgeoisie. György Martin says, with regard to couples' dancing in Hungary:

> Late medieval and Renaissance Western couple dances took Hungary by storm, starting with the sixteenth century, in spite of the objections of Puritan Protestant preachers. The first seventeenth-century Hungarian dance music records already include the tunes of many fashionable European couple dances of the time, such as the gailliarde, courante, saraband. Polish (mazurka, polonaise) and German *(Ländler, Steirisch)* fashions gained ground in the seventeenth and eighteenth centuries.

Martin's observation is applicable to almost all of Europe, with the possible exception of areas where adjacent cultures offered alternatives (some Balkan areas, the Iberian peninsula, eastern Russia, or isolated areas such as the North Cape). However, I question the assertion that the peasantry always imported these dances from the upper classes. In a 1794 issue of his journal *Bragur*, David Friedrich Gräter describes a German gallop danced along with line dances. It seems to be the same kind of couples' dance that figures in medieval and Renaissance paintings of the peasantry (see Figure 10.7):

> All our German folk dances, however ancient, are of two kinds: either a "gallop" (*Schleifer*) or a line dance. The gallop is also known as the "German dance" and was divided by the people into two parts, a "wide" and a "narrow" passage, following the melody at a bright 3/8 beat or a rapid 2/4 beat. The dancing went round in a ring, quickly and energetically. What is the origin of the gallop, and what does it mean? Watching the dancing peasantry, it becomes obvious that the couples are portraying a love story. At the beginning, boy pursues fleeing girl. Soon he catches her and tries to keep her close, but she runs away from his embrace. He tries again, but as soon as he gets close she turns her back on him. However, he is stubborn and perseveres. Wherever she may turn he is there before her, begging for her favor, and it appears as if he would rather die than leave her. (Oetke 1982, pp. 213f.)

Couples' dances were probably not invented by the dancers. Rather, they seem to be rooted in the peasant couples' galloping and jumping, and in their courting games. Perhaps the growth of stylized couples' dancing should be regarded as a parallel to the growing interest among instrumental musicians in making use of peasant melodies in various contexts. Probably, too, the stylization to which the melodies were subjected by the composers who honed them affected the dancing: phrases and motifs were grouped into even periods, and conventions also arose with regard to the order of harmonies (see also Ländler, p. 237).

From the royal courts to the merchants' homes, couples' dances became serious competitors with line and ring dances. As described above, the changes took place all over Europe and in many different ways. Oetke (1982) gives many examples from the German cultural region at different points in time. The fashionable dances from elsewhere also hastened the stylization process with regard to the peasant gallops and courting games. Martin describes this process as follows:

> The present geographical distribution of types and their historical fashions are, of course, interconnected. It would appear that peasant dancing in various parts of Europe has preserved stages from various periods in the history of dancing, owing to the varying rate of development and to uneven social and historical progress. Dance types that dominated in particular ages have survived in particular territories with certain distortions and determined the way the peasantry danced almost to our own days. The nations of the Balkan Peninsula have preserved medieval chain and round dances and developed them to a high degree. The peasantry of western and central Europe, fast acquiring urban habits, has submitted to the fashion of regulated couple dances, country dances, and space-confined processional dances. The East-European dance dialect, on the other hand, has placed itself on the marches dividing these two styles or periods, and displays mainly the free dance forms that were taking shape early in the Modern Age. (Martin 1974, pp. 13f.)

The sixteenth century *pavane-galliard*, with its slow, stately introduction followed by a livelier section, provides an example of a basic dance pattern that recurs in many folk dances, such as the Hungarian *csárdás* and the Spanish *sardana*. In both of these, it appears that bourgeois couples' dances inspired the peasantry to formulate courting games into improvised dance steps and music.

The numbers and variations of couples' dances

are virtually impossible to count because of their widespread origins. We cannot possibly cover them all, and their infinite wealth of melodies from different epochs and styles. The following is simply a sampling of different couples' dances, spanning the spectrum from stylised forms to free improvisations.

Examples of Couples' Dances

The Mazurka: A Polish National Dance?

The *mazurka* is generally described as a Polish national dance with three beats to a bar and a strong accent on the second and third beats. This type of dance was very widespread even in the seventeenth and eighteenth centuries, perhaps because it was a variant on similar extant dances. There are many regional forms of the *mazurka*, originating at different times. They are different with regard to their patterns of stress and rhythm. In *Die Volkstänze in Österreich und verwandte Tänze in Europa* (1951), Richard Wolfram writes that "No Pole would recognise the *mazurka* in the rural Tyrolean *Massolkan* with its melodies in minor keys and with our German courting figures (p. 23). This also applies to melodies with regional and individual forms. Let us look at an example, the Nordic patchwork of melodies known as the *polska*.

The Polska: A Swedish National Dance?

In the late nineteenth century, the *polska* was regarded in Sweden as a Swedish national dance. Using various means, including the classic study of the Swedish *polska* published by Swedish musicologist Tobias Norlind in 1911, let us take a glimpse at the history of the Swedish *polska*, because, far from being unique, it is similar to that of many other national dances.

Swedish *polska* are part of a family tree composed of various popular dances with an epithet resembling the word *Polish* that began to be popular as couples' dances in sixteenth-century Europe. Like so many other combinations in couples' dances, these *polska* began with a slow introduction with an even number of beats per bar, followed by a more rapid running dance that changes to 3/4 time. In a late seventeenth-century dissertation from Uppsala University on rhythm in music (*De tacto musico* 1698), a distinction is made between the ways in which educated people and peasants performed the faster, later part of the dance (for further details, see Norlind 1911, p. 372).

In eighteenth- and early nineteenth-century Sweden, the *polonaise* appears to have been the educated, and the *polska* the popular, designation for one and the same dance. In 1812, when Afzelius published the text of "Djupt i havet" (Deep in the Sea) to a melody he had learned from a little peasant girl in 1810, he called the piece a Polonaise, although the melody itself was known as *Näckens polska* (The Sprite's Polska) (see Norlind 1911, p. 125). In his dictionary from 1802, Swedish lexicographer Envalsson defines a polonaise as *"alla Polacca. Pålska"* (p. 257), and states that the name "reveals its Polish origins." He goes on to say that the polonaise is played as a "concert and solo piece" and that the *polska* probably began to migrate into the consciousness of the people when popular texts were set to these melodies, thus becoming a national dance in popular musical performances.

The *polska* had one special characteristic which made it especially suitable as a national dance—it was regarded as powerful and virile. In 1711 Swedish author Johan Linder wrote: "For those who require more strenuous exercise and movement, riding, ball-playing, bowling, and Polish dancing are of use, while French compliments and minuets, gavottes, passepieds and such will do no good at all" (*Norlind* 1911, p. 370). The aristocratic minuet was relatively short-lived in Sweden—by the mid-nineteenth century it had vanished from the country, and lived on only in symbiosis with other dances in 3/4 time under the name of *polska*. Norlind shows how, as early as the early eighteenth century, the minuet and the *polska* began to form one indistinguishable unit. He provides the following hypothesis as to what happened to the *polska*, the polonaise, and the minuet:

> All descriptions of the *polska* indicate that during the period of the polonaise it became a dance with figures and turns like the minuet. Thus it was a dance performed by professional dancers, and only adopted by the people to a limited extent. The old seventeenth-century *polska* with its rhythmic final section was only temporarily set aside, and in the 1830s when there were no restricting factors, the old rhythmic *polska* danced by couples came into the limelight again. The *polska* became a highly

rhythmic, fast dance with sharp movements once again. The polonaise-*polska* had generally just been known as the *spin-polska*, a name undoubtedly older than the polonaise itself. There were special names for the different combinations of steps, including *ring-polska, four-step-polska, cross-polska, priest-polska* (for weddings), and *bride's polska.* (Norlind 1911, pp. 394f.)

After this point, a number of different types of dances became known as *polskas.* Nineteenth century scholars tried to categorize them. Adolf Lindgren (1893), for example, divided them into the *triplet polska,* the eighth-note *polska* and the sixteenth-note *polska,* depending on the type of melody.

Efforts were also made to determine which province and epoch each type of *polska* belonged to: the triplet *polska* was said to have emigrated from Norway, the sixteenth-note *polska* to have come from the eighteenth-century Polish polonaise, and the eighth-note *polska* to be either Norwegian or Swedish in origin once the possibility that it was a variation on the mazurka had been rejected (Figure 10.18).

Norlind provides a colorful historical review of existing theories, only to subvert them all by pointing out that the *polska* was also danced in Denmark. He goes on to presume that it had traveled via Germany to Denmark, and that the Germans unabashedly assume that their dance originated with the mazurka. Norlind's Danish guide through the jungle of *polskas* was the Danish cultural historian Troels-Lund. According to him, the *polska* was one of the first couples' dances to make its way to the Nordic region and it was popular in all classes of society until about 1650. French dancing then pushed it aside in the eighteenth century, after which it came into focus again and was generally accepted as a popular dance in the nineteenth century, when it also took on the character of a national dance. Variants (including acrobatics, for example) came to symbolize the strength of the nation. They were a part of nationalistic "folk dramas," such as *Jösseh radspolska* (The *Polska* from the Parish of Jösse), performed in *Wärmlänningarne* (The People of Värmland), a play from 1846 by Randel/Dahlgren.

Jösseh radspolska, like Schuhplattler and many other dances with a lot of jumping, is a couples' dance with many elements of acrobatics, requiring great agility on the part of the dancers. The following is a description from 1842:

Figure 10.8. Three *polskas. Eighth-note polska, sixteenth-note polska* (closely related to the *polonaise*), and the *triplet polska,* which has been compared with the Norwegian *springdansen.* (After Ermedahl 1980, p. 252 f.)

The *polska* from the parish of Jösse is distinguished from all the others both in that it contains so much turning and cart-wheeling, and in that part of the dance is reaching for the ceiling. The young male dancer from the parish places his left elbow in the bent arm of his young woman partner and, in this position and in close contact, with hands tightly intertwined, he gathers his strength, and raises himself, with the aid of the strong arms of the girl, which are vital to the completion of this manoeuver, high up towards the ceiling, which he usually manages to touch with both feet, and, alternately with his left hand. (Rehnberg 1966, pp. 31f.)

In the late nineteenth century, collectors began to systematically transcribe the *polska,* both the dance and the melody. In the twentieth century it became the emperor of Swedish folk music and dance, always a part of dance performances and competitions. Thus the *polska* not only traveled backward and forward throughout the social classes in Sweden, but also interacted with other kinds of music and became a national folk symbol despite the fact that many of its origins were not Swedish. Although we know this today, it is impossible to efface our canonized beliefs, rooted in the nineteenth century. (On the *polska* from an ethnological perspective, see Erkki Ala-Könnis' study, *Die Polska-Tänze in Finnland* [1956].)

The Hungarian Csárdás

How did the Hungarian *csárdás* originate, and what symbols are associated with this dance and its melodies? What process underlies its gradual development into an established dance with fixed melodies, which became part of the cultural heritage of the nation? One hypothesis is that the *csárdás* was an expression of the eighteenth- and nineteenth-century political situation in Hungary, in which the dancer used his body to express the strong emotions of the freedom fighter.

In 1869, Arthur Patterson gave a highly knowledgeable description of the *csárdás*:

> As far as I have seen, the genuine Magyar peasant never dances anything else than the *Csárdás,* but the style of its execution varies in different districts, and it contains so much variety that it never produces a sensation of sameness. Its name is the adjective form from *csárda*, which designates a solitary public house; ... The music of the *Csárdás* is at first slow, solemn, I may say melancholy. After a few bars it becomes livelier, which character it then keeps up, occasionally becoming very fast indeed, and at last ends in a delicious whirl of confusion. The movements, of course, correspond. The dance opens with a stately promenade; then as the music quickens, each couple take a twirl or two, and breaking away brusquely from one another, continue a series of pantomimic movements, now approaching coquettishly, like parted lovers desiring reconciliation then, as if the lady thought that she had given sufficient encouragement, she retreats with rapid but measured steps while her partner pursues, and gradually gaining on her, seizes her waist; they whirl swiftly round two or three times, and then, breaking away, recommence the pantomime as before. What makes the *Csárdás* unrivalled as a spectacle is its variety. One seldom sees two couples performing exactly the same figure at the same time. (Martin 1974, p. 43.)

As early as 1831, August Ellrich had emphasised this very improvisational element in the *csárdás* in his travelogue *Die Ungarn wie sie sind*, comparing it with the "monotonously rotating waltz" and the "empty minuet." He regarded the *csárdás* as poetry, but the waltz and the minuet as mechanical (see also Martin 1974).

What Patterson and Ellrich did not see was the highly-structured basic pattern on which the "step, turn, move, position" of the dancers was based. For this reason, they exaggerated the improvisational elements in their enthusiastic descriptions comparing the *csárdás* with the stiffness of the fashionable dances of the bourgeoisie. The *csárdás* provides us with an excellent example of how dance and music adopted from the aristocracy were not slavishly imitated by the peasantry. Rather, there was a strong creative potential in folk culture that absorbed stylistic elements of couples' dances from other environments, shaping them into their own mode of expression. This usually took place when there was an extant type of music or dance with certain similarities (compare with musical instruments, p. 159).

In this process, the folk environment was also subordinate to the prevailing taste and ideology, in this case the national romanticism that resulted in the *csárdás's* becoming a national symbol. It inherited many elements from the music of the soldiers' dances (see p. 194, Figure 10.12), with their forceful rhythms, and it is also an expression of the new style of folk music discussed above, which was characteristic in early nineteenth-century eastern Europe (p. 107). The *csárdás* was, moreover, not a strictly Hungarian dance. It appeared under different names in Slovakia, Romania, and Yugoslavia before it made its triumphal procession all over Europe and other parts of the world in dance performances (Figures 10.9).

The Austrian Ländler

The *Ländler* is another example of a couples' dance that spread widely in Europe. The name stresses that the *Ländler*, like the contredanse, had rural origins (see below). The rural connection is not surprising. As early as the start of the seventeenth century, certain dances began to be designated as "national dances," and being rural was an important element of this (see Oetke 1982, pp. 228f.). Thus these dances were not only performed spon-

Figure 10.9. (a) A slow *csárdás* from Szablocs-Szatmar. The figures in this dance are simple in comparison with (b) a fast *csárdas* from Zsere, Czechoslovakia. (Martin 1974, pp. 42 and 49.)

taneously by the peasants, but also in a conscious, stylized way by the bourgeoisie and nobility. The *Ländler* is a slow, stately dance, each couple turning around an axis of its own, with varying arm movements and ways of linking arms. The *Ländler*, too, is a kind of courting dance, and often includes singing and, in the Tyrol, yodelling. The *Ländler* is a relatively local dance with its center in the Alps, branching out to Bohemia and the German-language minorities in the Carpathians. Thus the designation *Ländler* is also applied to dances invented and performed outside of the environment

of origin. The musicians usually named their dances after the local community when they did not simply call each one a "dance." The form of the *Ländler* took shape in the mid-eighteenth century: a simple, symmetrical melody made up of eight-bar phrases in steady 3/4 time as its base. The monotony of the melody for a non-dancing listener is reinforced by the fact that the harmonies are strictly tonic and dominant, with only occasional variation in a subdominant chord. As with the Hungarian soldiers' dances, there are variations in which the male dancer provides extra accompaniment by striking the soles of his shoes, his heels, or his leather trousers in a more or less acrobatic way; one such dance is known as the *Schuhplatter* (Figure 10.10).

The Waltz

The *Ländler* was one of many German dances in turns with special sets of steps out of which the waltz gradually took shape as the tempo of the dance grew faster. The steps consequently had to be simplified. However, there are also other theories as to the origins of the waltz. Henry Sjöberg has established, through this satirical description from 1785 and elsewhere, that the waltz originated in the 1780s:

> this figure (the waltz) we have learned from our own peasant folk. Noone who has spent any time in the country can have missed seeing the peasants, particularly the young people, amuse themselves in the green grass, preferably along a hillside, by lining up two by two, couples holding tightly to one another's arms, and swinging their legs around one another. In this position they roll, or waltz, down the hill. This began as a game, but now the finer folk have made it a serious matter, introducing it into the contredanse, and putting music to it (Sjöberg 1988).

The Contredanse

The contredanse uses a restricted number of patters put together by trained choreographers who were inspired by the folk dance. This kind of dancing became an important expression of the social sense of community in the bourgeois environment. Their melodies were formed into binary motifs and periods. The contredanse was to be found, for example, in Playford's *The English Dancing Master* (1650), with detailed descriptions of the dance

Figure 10.10. One of the many local variants of *Ländler* is the *Wickler*, also known as the *Steirer* in the Steiermark region. *Steirische Volksliedwerk* publishes series of small dance booklets with melodies taken from old fiddling books. They are published in two parts, and intended to be arranged for whatever instruments are available. This is an attempt to retain the element of improvisation and the character of the dance music. (See, for example, Rudi Pietsch's foreword to *Musikantestückl'n herausgegeben zum Geigentag '83*, from which this melody (no. 20 in the collection) was taken.)

showing that, even at this time, the process of formalization had begun (Figure 10.11).

The name *contredanse* comes from the English "country dance," and, as with the *Ländler*, is a designation of its rural origins. The contredanse had spread to the Netherlands and above all to France as early as the 1680s, where it was given a detailed choreographic structure by court dancing masters who traveled specially to England to find new dances and to gather inspiration for variations of their own. The contredanse spread like wildfire over Europe. Any ball where the latest dances were performed would always begin with contredanses. However, they were not just an entertainment for the bourgeoisie and the nobility. At the height of their popularity in the late eighteenth century they were already danced by the peasants and the fishing folk. There were undoubtedly a large number of hybrids with older line and ring dances. In the bourgeois environment contredanses went their separate social ways, some became associated with popular songs, others with art music. Rameau, Haydn, Mozart, Beethoven and many others were inspired to borrow entire dances, or elements from them for their compositions.

The contredanse was a symbol of bourgeois society and its fixed norms. Later, when free dancing by couples had its breakthrough, they were disparaged as a sign of increasing moral decadence.

In *On the French* (1830), Danish dancing master O. Bagge wrote:

For a number of years I have observed finer social dancing gradually losing its foothold in high society. The minuet, the French country dance, the *allemand*, the English dance, the *Figaro*, the regular *Ecossaise* and *la Bateuse* have all disappeared, as light gives way to darkness: The Bohemian, the *Molinas*, the *Cotillon*, the *Cinque Pas*, and the *Rundsnurran* have taken their place. There has been an awful twisting and turning under the names of *Schwaber*, Viennese, Tyrol, *Hopsa*, Russian, 'Hungarian' and *Pirre-waltz*, rather like people being buried under a landslide. It was pathetic to see the dancers at rest, hear them heaving and sighing, see their panting chests and their bright red faces. It was enough to make one weep, that people were prepared so madly to put their lives and health at risk. (Grüner Nielsen 1920, p. 11.)

The Minuet: From the Peasant Cottage to the Salon

The minuet was danced both as ballet and as a social dance, with couples standing in a line. It also became an important musical form in the dance suite, and later in the symphony and the sonata. The minuet thus provides us with a fine example of choreographic and musical class circulation, the twists and turns of which were quite overwhelming. The minuet is regarded as being of rural origins, from Poitou in France, but after its success at the French court it quickly conquered most of the European nobility, bourgeoisie, and peasants in regions where the social distance between classes was not too great. It was not, however, accepted everywhere; in Austria where it became firmly

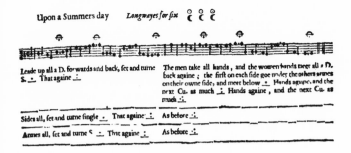

Figure 10.11. Country dance from John Playford, The English Dancing Master from 1651, with instructions. (Playford 1984, p. 1.)

anchored among the nobility as both light and art music, for instance, it never achieved popularity as a folk dance (Wolfram).

Among the peasantry, the minuet was danced mainly as part of the solemnity of marriage festivities. There are endless numbers of stories of elaborate minuets danced at weddings. Thus the minuet became the symbol of authority, a token of social status not unlike the way the peasantry copied the clothing fashions of the nobility. In the Nordic region the minuet was particularly cultivated and preserved in the Swedish-speaking parts of Finland. Ann-Mari Häggman filmed folk dancing in Finland from 1977 to 1981, and she noted from Munsala in western Finland:

> The Munsala region is known for its rich and varied minuet tradition. In the 1930s, villages still held minuet-dancing competitions. It bears witness to the dynamic nature of the minuet tradition today that it is still danced differently in the different villages, and among different age groups in the same village. In the late nineteenth century the minuet was danced by the people who held the canopy over the bride and groom, and it was not uncommon for the priest to dance the first minuet with the bride. However, there was a change after 1910. Anders Klockars (1897–1980) . . . described the weddings of the 1920s: 'The first dance was generally expected to be a wedding waltz, a rather calm, serious one . . . when all the guests joined in. The minuet and *polska* dominated, and the dancing lasted until dawn' (Häggman).

Anders Klockars goes on to explain that the popularity of the minuet was due to the fact that it was danced in a more orderly fashion (p. 178).

The minuet, too, was transformed when it ended up in the peasant environment, despite efforts to retain bourgeois and aristocratic ideals of style. Norwegian folk musician and musicologist

Ånon Engelund has studied minuets in the Norwegian fiddling books from the late eighteenth century (the first melody was noted down in 1758), based on tunes by Hans Nielsen Balterud. There were three types of minuets:

1. one with relatively long notes,
2. a simpler type of music, reminiscent of the polonaise, with a large number of sixteenth note figures, and
3. a third type containing triplets. This type indicates an influence from various stylistic elements from folk music, as does the fact that the name was changed by the peasants, for instance to *melevitt, munevitt*, etc. (Report from a seminar, 2, 1987, p. 37.)

Solo Dances

Solos danced by men often symbolize different occupations, and many can be traced to military activities. Gradually, their original roles faded, and they became strictly displays of dancing skill. For example, there are sword dances of all kinds from every corner of Europe, as well as later examples such as the Cossack dance and the Hungarian soldiers' dance, both of male warrior origin, but later transformed to more peaceful symbols of virility (Figure 10.12).

For various reasons, including the risk of the dancers' decimating one another during the performance, there is not much room for individual improvisation in group dances with swords. The development of solo performances, far from the previous ritual dance steps, left more space for improvisation. However, the solo dances too have begun to be more stabilized and formalized, with fixed steps and melodies that become part of the cultural history (see, for instance, the description

Figure 10.12. Hungarian soldiers' dance. (Martin 1974, p.39.)

of the Morris dance, above). The Greek *rebetiki*, the Spanish flamenco, and the Norwegian *halling* are all examples of dances displaying integration between the music, the social environment, and habitual behavior (see also Chapter 11). This very interplay is the context in which the dance must be seen and described. Similarly, the music in itself can hardly be described in a meaningful way without reference to its extramusical context–the sound structure or the steps of the dance have no meaning without the social context.

The Jig, the Hornpipe, and the Reel

The history of the British jig, hornpipe, and reel is complex and interwoven. The designation *jig* is regarded as being related to the old French word *giguer*, which means roughly "to jump" (see *New Grove*, vol. 9, p. 648). The dance itself has many steps and turns, all of which are performed with very difficult jumps. Ireland has come to stand out as its main center. There is a distinction between "regular" jigs, consisting of two eight-bar periods,

and "irregular" ones, varying in their numbers of bars. The jig can be found with time signatures of both 6/8 and 9/8. Jig melodies are played to some Morris dances. The hornpipe, named after an instrument of the horn family with a single or double reed, is very similar to the jig but played to different time signatures (see *New Grove*, vol. 8, p. 720). The hornpipe can be danced as a solo dance, a couples' dance, and a ring dance. Ireland was also important to the development of the hornpipe, and the Irish hornpipe has a profile of its own. The reel is regarded as a medieval dance. It came to Ireland in the late eighteenth century and, like the other two dances, it was greatly cultivated there. These dances were performed by adults and children alike, as entertainment on military crusades or as a social activity by the roadside (Figure 10.13).

More Recent Solo Dances

Similar dances come and go with time. Sometimes a relationship can be traced between them, at other times the dances appear to be independent of one another. For instance, when hip-hop dancing turned up in Scandinavia, this was not a revival of the Norwegian *halling* dance but an import from the United States. Likewise, popping and break-dancing began among the young people of Spanish and African origin in New York, but although their origins have been sought in Iberian and African folklore, it appears that the only close relatives are African-American show dances, including tap dancing.

These more recent dances give priority to strength and agility, like most of the European male dances. We have previously described these elements in the Hungarian soldiers' dances and the Austrian and Bavarian *Schuhplattler*. In her comparative study from 1986, Torp indicated that there is great agreement with regard to how these older and newer dances are learned and composed, how the groups stand, and how objects are used in the dance. Hip-hop dances probably serve the same function as earlier male dances, strengthening the masculine ego in fair competition with fellow males. Today's music is rock or rap, with the same steady beat as many of their predecessors in the genre of male dances.

What, then, is the relationship between the break-dance and the Norwegian or Swedish *halling* dance?

Figure 10.13. Newspaper sketch from the Afghan War, 1869. Two Scotsmen from the 72nd Highland Regiment dancing a reel. (From the *Illustrated London News*, 1869.)

Halling (Break) Dance

The name *halling* was first used to describe an acrobatic male dance in the second decade of the nineteenth century in Sweden and Norway (see Rehnberg 1966). Swedish author Fredrika Bremer describes these dances in detail in *Strid och frid, eller några scener i Norge* (Battles and Peace, or Scenes from Norway, 1840):

> There may be no other dance that describes the nature of the people who invented it than the *Halling*, which so well reflects the life and character of the Nordic inhabitant. It begins sort of low, down to earth, with small, heavy hops, legs and arms beneath, in which a great deal of force seems to be playing nonchalantly. There is something bearish, lethargic, awkward, somnambulant about it. But it wakes up, takes on a serious stance. The dancers rise and spread the wings of their power, apparently enjoying the opportunity to show their strength and prowess. After playing at being lethargic and awkward, they conquer these attitudes.
>
> Those very people who so recently seemed earthbound now run and somersault in the air, as if they had wings. An unaccustomed spectator cannot but feel this is breathtaking. Suddenly the dance takes on its early, carefree, lugubrious characters, ending as it began, down to earth [Rehnberg 1966, p. 9].

A magazine illustration from 1860 (Figure 10.14), provides an excellent supplement to Fredrika Bremer's romantic description of the dance that "portrays the *joie de vivre* of the Nordic inhabitant, showing mad joy in the dance." This "mad joy" characterizes many male dances, with two antago-

nists threateningly facing one another but turning somersaults and cartwheels instead of fighting. The *halling* was very popular during the nineteenth century, not least as a soldiers' dance.

It is difficult to know how old the *halling* really is and where it originated, because the name of a dance often changed over time and many dances often had similar names in an effort to make them as popular as the original dance. Rehnberg, for instance, points out that there were seventeenth-century dances requiring acrobatic skill in Sweden and that they had elements in common with English Morris dancing:

> The comparison between the halling and the English Morris dance is justified, as Morris dancing is also exclusively performed by men, and is also a dance performed for show, like the *halling*. Moreover, Morris dancing is marked by extreme masculinity and power. When two Morris dancers perform face to face, they may look rather like two *halling* dancers, although much of the similarity ends at appearances. . . . According to Norlind (1916) the *halling* had developed in Norway as a variant on the English reel, which he says came to Norway in the eighteenth century. (Rehnberg 1966, p. 45.)

There are other indications that the *halling* may have been related to English dances, such as the jig (see Rehnberg 1966, p. 42) but this hypothesis of diffusion is difficult to pin down.

The *halling* died out in the late nineteenth century, only to reappear in the 1940s. Today it is danced in both Norway and Sweden in competitions and for pleasure. It has been preserved thanks

Figure 10.14. *Halling* dance illustrated in a magazine from 1860.

to the efforts of enthusiasts such as Sverre
Halbakken and Gullik Kirkevold in Norway and,
in addition, to the fact that their music continued
to be played even during the period when the dance
was not performed. Leif Stinnerbom, himself a folk
musicologist, a fiddler, and a dancer, describes the
halling as follows:

Just as in the Cossack dances, a sitting position and
kicking legs are in focus. The Norwegians say that
the halling is not danced to 2/4 time but rather is
danced to the beat. When the 2/4 time shifts into 3/4
this does not disturb my dancing. The fundamental
step is the walking step. Older dancers have a natural movement, their arms swinging to the beat, hanging down loosely during the introductory march.
Today, dancers move their arms and legs in time.
The movement of the older dancers is as organic as
the movement of young people today doing the electric boogie, and their bodies move in waves of
rhythm.

The dance begins with small jumps, stressing
every step evenly. I then move backwards in 2/4 time,
may suddenly put in a knee bend in 3 with no
change in the music—its only function is to provide
the pulse. Because we do not have special *halling*
melodies in Vä rmland [Sweden] as they have in
Hallingdal, Valdres or Telemark [Norway], we can
just as well dance to a *schottische* or a march.

Every new age requires a new dance to perform,
although they are often much alike. Today it is break-
dance and electric boogie. The best break-dancers
perform on the dance floor with many movements
like those of a *halling* dancer, although the boogie
also appears to be rooted in African-American show
dancing. Electric boogie, like robot dance, is a way
of making the body appear to be a sort of machine,
and thus to express the most common set of movements of the modern age. The most common music
for these dances is 'artificial' music, on the synthesiser.
Soon there will probably be a new couples' dance
with acrobatic elements, or a new fifties swing with

Figure 10.15. "Peasant ballet" from Belarus. (Photograph: APN.)

rock 'n roll. When the new dances arrive, the older ones will surely try to oppose them, not least in the traditional way, by predicting that they will have negative 'medical consequences.' (Interview, 1987.)

Dances Become Folk Dances

In the nineteenth century, more and more choreographically composed dances in the form of folk dances began to be performed by groups like *Philochoros*, the university student's dance society in Uppsala in 1884. The folk dance movement began to pick up speed once these prototypes were established, not only in Sweden, but in a large number of European countries. Today the dances have international conventions and competitions. However, many folk dances survived on their own, despite the competition from the polka, the waltz, the *schottische* and later the shimmy, one-step, and two-step of the dance halls.

This strange folk dance revival movement occurred at a time when many people probably regarded the time of the social phenomena of folk dance and folk music as having died out. This revival movement integrated not only music and dance but also tried to interweave whole life patterns. The movement was especially strong in countries like Sweden and Hungary, where there was a dormant folk music tradition that, in the case of Hungary, strongly emphasized the "peasants' ballet"-type of performance, and where there was a vast amount of unexplored archived material. In the 1960s in Sweden, the conflicts between the established folk dance movement, the Swedish Youth

Ring, and the new movement spearheaded by Henry Sjöberg, had to do with both a generation gap and different ideologies and dance styles. In both cases, the trends have been constructive. The "peasants' ballet" has clearly been enriched by the freedom of the new youth dancers and their desire to improvise. The new movement, in turn, has come to understand the historic importance of the peasant ballet and its function as a spectacular show for uninitiated audiences. Perhaps, in fact, the development of new forms on the basis of variations of old formulas is the core of folk dance and the question of origins is of secondary importance (Figure 10.15).

The Unexplored No-man's Land Between Dance and Music

The area between dance and music is surprisingly unexplored. From the attempts that have been made, we may conclude that the complex problems generated by dance and music must be studied either at the level of basic signs, a sort of semiotic means of observation, or at the level of communication of bodily movements between dancers and musicians (see Blom 1978, 1981, 1986). It is possible that, in the long run, a kind of "generative grammar of dance" will be developed, analogous to the efforts of linguists and to certain other work in musicology. It is difficult to say whether this will bring us to a closer understanding of the interplay between dance and music.

There are clearly differences of principle between dances and melodies that are composed and learned, and improvised ones with no canonized prototype. However, just as prototypes may be broken down into improvised variations, spontaneously created dances and melodies may gradually become canonized styles. Perhaps it is this very interchange between freely improvised chaos and rigorously structured order that makes dance so exciting to study.

Literature

Folkdanser 1, Norden (1981) by Dagmar Hellstam provides a survey of folk dances from the Nordic countries, as well as a bibliography of studies of folk dance all over Europe. *Dance: A Multicultural Perspective*, edited by Janet Adshead, and *To Dance is Human, A Theory of Nonverbal Communication* (1977) by Judith Lynne Hanna address general problems relating to dance. Anca Giurchescu has written methodological articles of interest to musicologists, including "The process of improvisation in folk dance," in *Dance Studies*, 7:21–50. Lisbeth Torp's dissertation, "Chain and Round Dance Pattern" (1990) has a structural approach which will be seminal for future research on problems of dance studied from a musicological perspective.

Eleven

Folk Music Between Town and Country

FOLK MUSIC AS ART MUSIC AND POPULAR MUSIC

Some of the songs and melodies, songs of work, and dances transcribed by collectors were transformed in the nineteenth century into either popular music or art music or both. Composers of popular and art music arranged or adapted the melodies or applied the standard stylistic features of folk music to their own compositions. In addition, many composers with a genuine interest in folk music were in direct contact with the people who performed it. Examples are to be found among Russian nineteenth-century composers such as Glinka and Mussorgsky, who grew up in the company of nurses and servants who loved to sing folk songs. Other composers, such as Kolberg and Lindeman, knowingly or unknowingly followed the advice of Dybeck and journeyed to the mountain pastures or farmers' fields themselves in order to listen to the music of the people and then interpret it themselves. Such composers worked rather like the artists of their generations, who rendered sketches, water colors, and oil paintings with folk-life motifs.

Nineteenth-century rural music was also very much influenced by the popular and art music of urban areas. Many new forms of music arose, comprising a kind of "urban folklore" of new styles of folk songs, dances and instrumental melodies that gradually gained widespread popularity (see p. 212).

The terms *popular music* and *art music* are at least as problematic and ambiguous as *folk music*. Let us therefore begin by defining them for our purposes, while still keeping a focus on folk music.

Using Folk Music for Greater Popularity

In his book *Populär musik under 1800-talet* (Nineteenth Century Popular Music) (1986), Martin Tegen establishes criteria for defining popular music. One of them is that "a piece of popular music must possess stylistic traits which make it entertaining and comprehensive to a large audience. This includes its being useful in social activities such as dancing and parading, as well as in the theater, at cafés and restaurants, etc." (p. 15). According to Tegen, the music must also be appreciated by a large proportion of the general public and be "in the hands of one or more music publishers," who ensure the availability of different arrangements. This definition, of the kind used by sociologists of music, reflects the encounter between the music and its contemporary consumers. Most music albums, printed or handwritten, from the eighteenth century through the first two decades of the twentieth century, contain one or more arrangements of folk music pieces alongside known and unknown music or "classical evergreens."

Eighteenth-century composers were not embarrassed about being popular—they thrived on it. For the purpose of achieving popularity, they attempted to write their pieces in a way that provided plenty of familiar signals to the listener, facilitating the acceptance of the more erudite features. This was one of the reasons they borrowed so heavily from folk music. George Philip Telemann (1681–1767) provides us with an excellent example in his description of a visit he made to Poland in his capacity as *Kapellmeister* to Count Erdmann von Promnitz:

There (in Plesse), as in Krakow, I learned how to recognise Polish music in its true barbarian beauty. At an ordinary inn, the musicians would consist of a fiddler, his violin, tied round his waist, tuned a third higher than usual, and which could therefore shout louder than half a dozen normally tuned ones together; a Polish *bock* [bagpipe], a bass viol and a *regals*. In larger towns, the *regals* was not included. Instead, there would be more of the high-tuned violins. Once I heard an ensemble of 30 *bocks* and 8 violins altogether. One can hardly believe one's ears when listening to the spontaneous music-making of these pipers and fiddlers as they improvise together while the dancers are at rest. A week of listening to such music would give the attentive listener enough musical material for a lifetime. . . . I have written any number of concertos and trios of this kind over the course of the years, incorporating them into the Italian style and alternating adagio and allegro movements [Fleichhauer 1981, p. 7].

As Fleichhauer points out in his study, Telemann was inspired by these Polish musicians in other places than his chamber music, for example, in his keyboard pieces, where the sounds of thirds and sixths as well as the drones are sometimes very much like the original folk music.

Joseph Haydn also felt an affinity with popular folk music and, like Telemann, had an ambition to please his audience. His symphonies are woven across the weft of contredanses.

The correspondence between Wolfgang Amadeus Mozart and his father, Leopold, is often quoted in contexts relating to popular music. On 13 August 1778, Leopold wrote to Wolfgang recommending that he write something easy and popular. Leopold himself clearly had nothing against popular pieces such as *Die Schlittenfahrt*, *Sinfonia burlesca* and *Divertimento militaire* (see Einstein p. 121f.).

One way of becoming popular was to make use of familiar melodies, incorporating them into one's own special language. Thus folk or popular elements were readily integrated into the language of the music of the classical period, which was often rooted in rural folk song and dance or in the calls and marches of the city streets.

Folk Music Becomes Exclusive

As described above, the eighteenth and early nineteenth centuries were not periods in which exclusivity was considered the most important attribute

of music. This was a nineteenth-century phenomenon, that became the golden standard for music after the middle of the century. At that time folk music became a special aesthetic category; art music had separated from it and from the idea of popularity. This trend can be followed, beginning in the late eighteenth century until it was firmly established during the nineteenth century. Philosophers including Kant, Fichte, and Hegel and music critics such as A. B. Marx, Wendt, and Schumann all contributed to the idea that certain types of music, written in accordance with particular aesthetic ideals, should be elevated to the category of "poetic music" while other types were regarded as "mechanical". The idea of music as works created by composers who were regarded as geniuses and whose creations were therefore virtually sacrosanct, reinforces the view of music being in a world of its own, a world of sound to which only the elite have access. Folk music had to struggle for validity. Instead of being simple and unproblematic, providing material from which composers could borrow, it was now subject to the same kind of aesthetic assessments as the "finer" arts. Thibaut distinguishes between street songs, which were "short-lived," and folk songs which "go on flourishing amongst the people" (see also Dahlhaus 1980, p. 87) (Figure 11.1).

The shorter-lived category of folk music was referred to not only as "street songs" but also as "rubbish" and "drivel" (*Wiede* in Sweden) or "plebeian" (*Lessing* in Germany). Dahlhaus (1980) shows how the folk song became a normative concept based on the "idea of that which was truly human, and common to Romanticism and the Enlightenment." This was associated with the idea that "what is of value will survive."

As a folk song could either be created by "the people" or created by a composer and accepted by "the people," pastiches were also originally considered folk songs. Florentin von Zuccalmaglio (1803–1869), for example, gave German folk song melodies his own considerable personal and romantic touch before publishing them.

At this time, a distinction between good and bad folk music also arose. One symptomatic example is found in a letter from Brahms to musicologist Philipp Spitta, complaining that Böhme did not make an aesthetic selection when publishing his German folk songs: what Brahms refers to as *Dreck* (rubbish) in the Böhme selection are sim-

Figure 11.1. The opening of Anton Friedrich Justus Thibaut's arrangement of an Irish folk song from a collection of old national anthems.(Thibaut 1824/R 1907.)

ply the songs that do not fall within Brahms's values encompassing art music (see quotation p. 18).

Let us now devote some thought to an article from 1849 on "Folk Music and the New Music" before going on to consider the route taken by folk music from the world of popular to that of aesthetic music. The anonymous author claims that:

Today [in the mid-nineteenth century] music has developed so as to make it irreconcilable with the naive, primitive, means of expression of folk music. In his opinion, this development was both conscious and unconscious. He states that it is vital to acknowledge the differences between the music of different nations, music of German, Italian and French masters. Very little interest has been shown to date in the interplay between folk music and art music. While the operas of Hasse rest on the erudite aria system of the Italians, the operas of Mozart rest on—the folk song. His 'brilliant naturalism' is drawn directly from the 'sparkling well water of folk music.' The folk song also appears hundreds of times in the

oratorios of Handel, although not in his operas. Are not the victory chorale in *Judas Maccabeus* and the pastoral in the *Messiah* living folk music? One need not change more than three notes to be able to hear the peasants today singing such songs under the lime trees in the evenings.

After this first victory for the new music, rooted in folk music, battles were easily won: Bach's sons provided a German alternative to the Italian folk song, and Mozart continued the tradition. This style contained the basis of musical naturalism, making art accessible to the people, unlike Johann Sebastian Bach and his followers, who were considered representatives of the 'clerical style' which had no future, but was "buried with Johann Sebastian Bach."

This author wishes to introduce the terms 'naturalist' and 'idealist' to replace 'classical' and 'romantic' composers. Mozart, Haydn, and C. M. von Weber were naturalists, basing their compositions on folk music, while Bach, Beethoven, Cherubini, and Spohr were idealists. J. S. Bach, Beethoven, and Cherubini were regarded as loners who did not take their audiences into account while Mozart, and even more so Haydn, wrote music for the people who, in turn, hummed and sang in their styles. Mozart and Haydn retained and developed the folk music heritage, while Beethoven lost his, and particularly in his late works sank deep into his abstract-idealistic composition, making his last works virtually incomprehensible to the layman. The final works of Mozart and Haydn, on the other hand, were characterized by the most childlike of harmonies, which could be taken to heart by nearly anyone. ("Das Volkslied in seinem Einfluss auf die Gesammte Entwicklung der modernen Musik," *Die Gegenwart eine encyklopadische Darstellung der neuesten Zeitgeschichk für alle Stände.* Leipzig 1849, vol. 3, pp. 667ff.)

The author of this article was not very fair to Beethoven, who was certainly popular in his own right. Moreover, Beethoven was extremely interested in folk music of many nations, using Herder as his model. This interest showed in his compositions. He also wrote popular variations and folk music arrangements, as well as using the stylistic tools of folk music, for instance, in his sixth and seventh symphonies.

Clearly the author of this article wished to defend popular music at any price, and did so by tracing it back to folk music. The ideals represented by the author remained dominant through 1850.

The article also indicates the representatives of the new ideals that would gradually demolish these idyllic views. One was Beethoven, who represented the language of individuality and compositions that placed demands on the listener, who had to be constantly receptive to new and original music. Another was Bach, who represented historical music that would be integrated into the realm of art music, which was newly composed and really intended for an exclusive segment of listeners. Folk music took its place in this realm thanks to the discovery of its specific aesthetic qualities and the ability of composers to integrate it into their personal, individual musical languages.

Popular Versions and Arrangements of Folk Music

The ambition of the transcribers of folk songs and music was to polish and harmonize the songs, melodies, and dances of the peasants so as to be suited for performance in the salons of the bourgeoisie. This folk music was, therefore, chiefly material for music-making in the home, and very few of these songs reached the concert hall until the time when Jenny Lind and Christina Nilsson introduced them as part of their standard repertoire. The arrangements for the bourgeoisie changed in style and character during the nineteenth century, from simple, idyllic melodies with a chorale-like style to arrangements with more demanding piano accompaniments and individual styles of composition (see Ling 1978).

Beethoven's version of Scottish folk songs that he, in turn, had heard only as arrangements of the originals, shows all this in a nutshell. The melodies of his Scottish folk songs might have been folk melodies, but they could just as well have been melodies composed in folk style and later adopted by "the people." The latter type of song was also considered to fulfil the criteria for a folk song, and was accepted as such just as much as any song transcribed by a collector. Such a song was first given a simple continuo accompaniment. Beethoven—who probably never had the opportunity to listen to a folk song performed by a Scotsman—used the melody as the raw material for his composition. In this case, Beethoven had a patron, George Thomson, who commissioned the work and provided him with suitable melodies. In other cases Beethoven adapted folk melodies he himself found in *Allgemeine Musikalische Zeitung*. Beethoven can hardly be said to have thrown himself at the feet of the "glorious being" of folk music. Rather, he can be described as having tested the composi-

tional potential of folk melodies, applying his own artistic temperament to them (Figure 11.2).

The same may also be said of the versions of German folk music or the arrangements of Hungarian dances composed by Johannes Brahms. As mentioned above, Brahms was entirely disinterested in whether or not the folk music he used was 'authentic.' All he cared about was that he could use this material to create his interpretation of a romantic folk atmosphere, albeit one that probably had very little to do with the place from which that particular folk song originated. In addition to his *Deutsche Volkslieder* from 1894, which were a musical reply to what he considered Böhme's "miserable" Liederhort, he had previously published *Volks-Kinderlieder* in 1858 and German folk songs in several voices in 1864. Schmidt (1983) has shown how Brahms works with folk songs and "folk tone" in many ways. For instance, in his famed "*Wiegenlied*" op. 49, no. 4 (better known in English as "Brahms's Lullaby"), he uses an 'authentic' folk song as treble accompaniment. He adapts a simple *Ländler* melody in the third movement of the Clarinet Sonata, op. 120, and uses a folk song pastiche to create an exciting polyrhythm (see also Schmidt 1983, pp. 133–42). It is not impossible that Brahms's own experience with dance music in his youth gave birth to the rhythmic versatility of his music that stands out in the performances of skilled musicians (Figure 11.3).

The tradition of arranging folk songs continued well into the twentieth century, although the pace slowed somewhat. In 1906 Béla Bartók published a collection of folk melodies, writing in the preface, "We must put a dress on it, when we move it from meadow to town. But in city finery, it feels awkward and anxious. The dress must be cut so as not to inhibit the breathing. Whether we are working for choir or for piano, the accompaniment must attempt to replace the lost meadow and village" (Ujfalussy 1981, pp. 62f.). In their magnificent monograph on Grieg, Benestad/Schjeldrup-Ebbe (1980) compared Grieg's harmonization of a folk melody with those of two of his countrymen, Lindeman and Kjerulf. Grieg's was the least respectful of the original style. While the other two are satisfied with simple harmonies and appropriate drones, Grieg paints with bold colors. Grieg's way of working can be compared with the artists who portrayed folk life in the nineteenth century, using "the people" as a motif. Kjerulf's and Lindeman's style was more cautious, perhaps comparable to that of

Figure 11.2. The opening of Beethoven's arrangement of a Scottish folk song, "Charlie is my darling" for soprano, alto, bass, violin, cello, and piano. This was Beethoven's contribution to Scottish romanticism, dedicated to Charles "Charlie"Edward Stuart, pretender to the throne, who was conquered and forced to flee Scotland in 1745.

the peasants' own tapestries rather than of more sophisticated oil paintings (Figure 11.4).

There are endless numbers and varieties of folk song arrangements from all over Europe, and the genre is still very much alive. Lennart Hedvall has written an interesting portrait of Swedish composer Hugo Alfvén, explaining the artistic, national and financial reasons for his having devoted so much time to arranging folk music. Alfvén regarded his arrangements of existing melodies as the most significant part of his work, the core of his oeuvre as a composer (see Hedvall 1973, p. 367). In a long letter to publisher Einar Rosenborg dated 23 October 1936, Alfvén presented his views on the harmonization and arrangement of Swedish folk melodies. He reflected a furthering of the ideology of the nineteenth century, of using the melody as raw material:

We can compare the melody with the lines in a painting and the harmony with its colors. What good do the loveliest lines do, if the colors are monotonous, banal, insensitive, and sloppily applied? I can just imagine the famous painting by Zorn of the milkmaid, standing in the mountain pasture blowing her ancient horn to call the cows. The painting is spellbinding, and

what is decisive is the nuances of the colors. . . . What I am trying to say is that the harmony is extraordinarily important in the adaptation of a folk melody. The composer re-composes the little piece, giving it his personal touch. The melody and the harmony become indissolubly intertwined in a new creation—for better or for worse [Hedvall 1973, p. 368].

Alfvén's arrangements of folk songs have become national symbols, reflecting the essence of Swedishness as much as Zorn's milkmaid.

There are also examples of composers who have internationalized arrangements of folk songs. For instance, Luciano Berio's *Folk Songs* from 1969 contains an inseparable medley of songs from the United States, Armenia, France, Italy, and Azerbaijan. Berio highlights the idioms of the different songs, but all within an artistic framework that releases each style from the glue of its country's label, to which folk songs and melodies so readily adhere.

Variations on Folk Melodies

Titles beginning with the words "Variations on" followed by "a Russian, or German, English, Scot-

Figure 11.3. Johannes Brahms' *Wiegenlied* op. 49, no. 4 with an Austrian folk song as the treble accompaniment in the piano part.

tish, Spanish, etc. Folk Song" can be found virtually everywhere. These are not always true folk songs: many new compositions can be found among them, and it is not always easy to separate the sheep from the lambs (Figure 11.5).

As the structure of theme and variations belongs to a sphere of music beyond that of folk music and is not only associated with the melodies of folk songs, we will devote no particular attention to it but go on to examine the melodies used as themes for variations and referred to as folk songs or folk melodies. Many of the songs referred to by these names are not rural songs at all, but simply popular melodies of their time.

Thus these songs more often tend to fall into the category of "everyone's favorites." Songs used as themes for variations are intended to reflect rural, idyllic music, although there are certainly also a fair share of parodies. As mentioned above, the composer uses these melodies as raw material, either for the pleasure of musical amateurs or to give the professional artist the opportunity to display his virtuosity.

We can draw a parallel between the use of variations and folk music as it was performed. The variations can be seen as a kind of "frozen" set of improvisations. Ever since the Middle Ages, the ability to embellish on a melody has been the trademark of any good instrumentalist. This was no less true for the virtuosos of the eighteenth and nineteenth centuries who, in their desire to achieve popularity, often chose to improvise either on a folk song or some other melody dearly loved by the people. The structure tended to be a spectacular stylistic pastiche, creating a sensation by constant shifts in register from soprano to bass or by a gradual virtuoso build-up.

A composer had to be careful to select a suitable folk melody for the context. Mozart's *Rondo alla Turca*, in the "Paris" sonata 1778 (K. 331), like many of his other Turkish borrowings (which may actually be more Hungarian than Turkish, see Barta 1956), were acceptable as long as the Ottoman and Habsburg empires were at peace.

The national affinity of the melodies used for these themes and variations was so important that it even received a comment in *Allgemeine musikalische Zeitung*. Friedrich Rochlitz gave composers wishing to try their hand at the task, the following clue on 28 May 1800: "every nation depicts itself, ruthlessly, and thus all the more pointedly, in its dances, its music and its folk songs. The first of these sources may be the most reliable." He goes on to characterize the different dances, from the gallant

Figure 11.4. Arrangements of the folk melody *jölstring*. (After Benestad/Schjelderup 1980, p. 120 f.) (a) Lindeman, (b) Kjerulf, and (c) Grieg.

Figure 11.5. The theme and the first four variations of Trutovsky's Variations on a Russian Folk Song, 1780. (Leningrad City Library.)

minuets of the French to the moderate excesses and wealth of variation of the British to the wild, stormy, and yet dryly dull dances of the Scots to the fiery, rapid fandango and bolero of the Spanish. He recommends them all as a basis for variations.

When a composer borrowed a melody, it often retained its original rhythm in the first variation. It would certainly also be structured so as to be suited to the lengths of classical periods. Many folk melodies have been handed down to us as variations thanks to the adaptations of the melodies made by the collectors who transcribed them. Because they adapted them to the prevailing taste in art music, they became easy prey for the interested composer (cf. Zuccalmaglio-Brahms). Since composers tended to take their folk music themes from transcriptions made by collectors, they had seldom if ever heard the original. Naturally, there were

exceptions, such as Haydn, who worked as a dance musician, or Ralph Vaughan Williams, who collected folk melodies himself and then used them in his variations, fantasies, and symphonies. *Five Variants of "Dives and Lazarus"* (1939) may be the most interesting from the point of view of the interplay of folk and art music. In this piece, the composer "recalls" variations of the folk song, from the first time he heard it in 1893 through many subsequent versions until the time of composition.

There are, in other words, endless types of variations on folk songs. Some composers, such as Beethoven, used them to flirt openly with their audiences, basing their work on a transcribed folk song for which they had no more feeling than for any other series of notes. Other composers such as Vaughan Williams, felt deeply committed to the songs as well as the singers who passed them down. Variation has remained a popular genre.

FOLK MUSIC TRANSFORMED TO THE COMPOSER'S PERSONAL STYLE

Arrangements of folk songs or variations on folk melodies have their limitations. With the exception of Vaughan Williams and a few others, it appears as if the form itself places the composer at a distance from the distinguishing marks of folk music, resulting in general music in a folk music style. This gradually developed into a genre of its own, not unlike the Eurovision Song Contest melodies of today. This folk style has remained surprisingly constant since the early nineteenth century from country to country because it is based on the ideals of the Classical period and those of Mendelssohn, which came somewhat later (Figure 11.6).

At the same time, another, more intimate relationship between folk music and composers developed, with completely different artistic results. In the late eighteenth century, Vienna was one of the European centers of music, a place where different musical impulses from all directions met: from Italy to the southwest, France to the west, Germany to the north, Bohemia and Moravia, Slovakia, Hungary, and the Balkans to the southeast. This melting pot of musical styles, musical functions, and social classes provided the point of departure not only for the development of the Classical style but also for different national styles of folk music. Haydn played a special role in this process, although we can see a similar development in the work of Mozart, Beethoven, and Schubert. Haydn was the product of a combination of musical environments: he spent thirty years in Hungary, and many of his movements bear witness to the influence of Hungarian and gypsy folk music. There are examples of movements with simple variations, but the most interesting aspect of his work to examine in this context occurs where the folk music was not simply borrowed and inserted, but integrated into the personal style of the composer. Haydn does not hesitate to take a simple folk song and make it part of an artistic context, stripping it of its social background and simplicity and clothing it in the drapings of universally accepted norms (see also Sárosi 1970, pp. 199f.).

The Composers and National Identity

During the nineteenth century, "national identities" became a sort of line of demarcation in rela-

Figure 11.6. Extract from *Volkslied, Lieder ohne Worte* for piano by Felix Mendelssohn-Bartholdy op. 53 no. 23.

tion to that which was considered universal, for example, Beethoven's use of folk style in his symphonies. Frédéric Chopin is an excellent example of a composer with national identity. He used the dances that were popular in his day—the mazurka, the waltz, and the more military polonaise—as the molds for his music. However, he transformed the content, despite the fact that the rhythmic and the melodic forms of his music contain many of the stylistic elements of folk music. In this way, Chopin paints a folk atmosphere in his music reminiscent of the canvases of the nineteenth-century painters, and he also uses sound as a living model for his musical tableaux. He often makes use of drones or melodic motifs that break the conventions of major and minor, and he also uses rhythmic variability in several dimensions. The left hand in his piano scores may also render the broken chords of the fiddles playing dance music. There may be a sudden shift to the salons of Paris, bringing with it a wave of sentimental music far from Polish soil (Figure 11.7). In the same way, Chopin transforms the polonaise to a work of sophisticated musical art without losing contact with the military roots of the dance.

Liszt, too, attempted to write "Hungarian music" with the aid of popular gypsy melodies. His music therefore became a variation on bourgeois popular music "in the folk style" that appeared in the early nineteenth century. In his *Csárdás* (cf. R 45 no. 1-2, *Csárdás macabre* R46), moreover, Liszt also approached transformation: these are far from audience-enticing rhapsodies. Instead, they appear to be forerunners of Bartók's style, in which the stylistic tools of folk music are personally transformed (Figure 11.8).

In many cases, this transformation began with a national consciousness, which made folk music particularly attractive to individual composers' styles. In a historical perspective, such national consciousness often appears quite comical. In his *History of Music* from 1864 (in Swedish), Abraham Mankell wrote a very typical piece about the unrivalled nature of Swedish folk music:

> Let us allow a man of the south, and one of the most highly gifted inventors of melodies of his time, to describe for us the value of some of our folk songs. At one of the evening entertainments Baron Rothschild, who lived in Paris, arranged for Rossini, he was to be honored with an evening of *his own* music. By chance, Rossini heard that one of the women who was present was Swedish. This was a woman no longer young, not beautiful, and certainly not sylphidic. However, she was *Swedish*, and Rossini had his more or less vague ideas about the Nordic folk melody. He persuaded the host to encourage her to sing what he imagined would be a 'true Scythian' barbarism. She performed a simple version of *Näcken's Polska* (The Sprite's Polska), with Afzelius's indescribably beautiful text. After a long silence, he (Rossini) burst out with: 'Ah, such a melody I cannot write.' (Mankell 1864, p. 216f.) (Figure 11.9.)

A great deal of this nationalism also took place in the Slavic regions under Smetana and Dvořák in Bohemia and Glinka and Mussorgsky in Russia.

Folk customs were, of course, important here: the Russian wedding has been described musically by both Rimsky-Korsakov (*A May Night*, 1880) and Stravinsky (*The Wedding* 1914–1917), and in Sweden and Norway there are parallel phenomena such as Söderman's *Peasant wedding* (1868) and Grieg's *Peer Gynt* (1874–1908).

However, patriotism is not the main criterion for composing national music: German composer Fredrik Pacius (1809–1891) initiated the national orientation in the Finnish music tradition, even attempting to render elements of Finnish folk song in musical theater. Thus this German created the first in a line of compositions based on extracts from the *Kalevela*, which in turn led to the composition of nationalistic music of the most unique and outstanding quality in Europe.

Edvard Grieg stands as an example of the many composers who gradually moved on from arranging folk songs to a more personal musical style. Grieg was of the opinion that the art of every nation could be characterized by the transformation of folk songs from smaller forms to larger and finer ones. He, too, began with the small form: *Norske folkeviser och dandse* (1869), op. 17 (Norwegian Folk Songs and Dances). This was the first of a very large collection of arrangements of folk songs and dances. Grieg attempted to bring forth harmonies he considered to be latent in the songs and melodies. He found that Norwegian folk music had an unexplored potential of harmony; the melodies inspired him to use a colorful spectrum of harmonies that first shocked and later enraptured his contemporaries. The chromatic elements were particularly inspiring to Grieg as points where harmony could come into play. Grieg could produce *halling* and running-dance melodies of his own that could easily be taken for genuine Norwegian folk music. His knowledge of the playing style of the Hardanger fiddle was so intimate that he became a renewer of the folk music tradition. Grieg was not a collector. He often picked up melodies from good friends and in other collections, and of course he also listened to folk music himself.

One outstanding example is the origin of his *Norwegian Peasant Dances* (1902–1903). A Norwegian fiddler, Knut Johanessen Dahle from Telemark, a student of the legendary Myllarguten, decided that it was time to see his musical heritage transcribed. He wrote to Grieg and asked him to come and see him for this purpose, but was re-

Figure 11.7. Opening of Frederic Chopin's *Mazurka* op. 7 no. 3.

ferred by Grieg to his good friend Johan Halvorsen. Grieg later published both Halvorsen's and his own versions of the songs. This publication is regarded as one of the sources of inspiration for Bartók's folk music collection and his compositions in the Hungarian tradition (Figure 11.9).

Putting the Myths of the People into Music: Stravinsky's *Rite of Spring*

On 28 May 1913, at the Théâtre des Champs Élysses in Paris, Stravinsky's *Rite of Spring* was performed for the first time. It was a public scandal of vast proportions. Two years earlier, Russian folk music collector Mitrofan Pianitsky had shocked concertgoers in Moscow by bringing a peasant choir on stage (Figure 11.10, p. 211). Both Stravinsky's *Rite of Spring* and Pianitsky's ensemble played decisive roles, although in different ways, with regard to the reception of folk music in the twentieth century.

In his *Poetics of Music* (1950) Stravinsky sets out a line of demarcation between his own use of folk music in Russia, and the uses of Glinka, who, he says, "takes folk motifs as his raw material and uses them purely instinctively, with his eye on the Italian music that was in fashion" (p. 81); the *Mighty Five*– Balakirev, Mussorgsky, Borodin, Rimsky-Korsakov and Cui, who tried to "graft folk style onto art music" (p. 82); and all the efforts after the October Revolution to make use of various collections of folk music. However, paradoxically, Stravinsky came to play a decisive role for many younger Soviet composers, despite the fact that they did exactly the opposite of what Stravinsky favored, mixing "the problems of culture and musical composition" (p. 95).

Although Stravinsky was not a collector of folk music, there are photographs of him transcribing the songs of a blind singer (see Danuser 1984, p. 53), a piece of evidence that his sources were not only the published collections by Rimsky-Korsakov and others, but also live performances of folk music. This also explains why the *Rite of Spring* provides a sort of artistic quintessence of Russian and Ukrainian folk music. It contains many melodies that can be found in collections, but they are rendered in the free improvisational artistic form we find in the best performances of folk music. Moreover, the sound is far from the orchestral palate of late Romanticism, making the orchestral music of Hugo Alfvén a "country relation dressed up to come to town." Stravinsky did not borrow from one distinct tradition, nor did he use the transcriptions of others as they existed. Instead, he selected ingredients from the wealth of Russian folk music and put them into spontaneous free play with one another. They are bound together by the general extramusical idea of the piece: an incantation on life and death. The music reveals a primitive human force instead of concealing it within a conventional artistic framework, as was the case in many previous versions of folk music. Without the traditions handed down by Rimsky-Korsakov and Mussorgsky, the revolutionary symbiosis between rite and art music brought about by Stravinsky would not have been possible. Earlier attempts had been made to mix ingredients from dance music and laments, Christmas begging songs and spring songs into a sort of national symbolic language which could be regarded as a special Russian national substance. Stravinsky peeled away the remains of nineteenth-century art-music aes-

Figure 11.8. Franz Liszt was interested in many things, including the potential of the *cimbalom* as the source of the sound of Hungarian national music. In *The Rákóczy March* (R 439, 1865), he tried to reproduce the sound of the *cimbalon*, using parallel octaves and full harmonies.

thetics, which was probably a prerequisite for the possibility of folk music gaining a platform in twentieth century musical society. He was not alone, nor was he the first. His predecessors included Claude Debussy, who provided him with support when he was writing the *Rite of Spring* (see Stravinsky 1962, p. 142n.).

Folk Music Flavor Without Folk Music

In the search for new means of expression, many twentieth-century composers entered the domain of folk music. Some basically followed the nineteenth-century tradition of borrowing raw materials; others have developed different variants that often lead to the dissolution of the elements of folk music into a personal style. One might say that the composer himself becomes the last outpost in a long musical tradition rooted in the rural areas.

Claude Debussy's musical exoticism had a great impact on his contemporaries. Debussy came into contact with *gamelan* music as well as with Spanish folk music at the Paris World Exhibition in the late 1800s, but this could hardly have been his only source of inspiration. Debussy was familiar with many previous composers who were partial to a Spanish flavor in their music, such as Bizet, Rimsky-Korsakov and Ravel. Debussy was never in Spain, but he still managed to create his own kind of Spanish style. Manuel de Falla, an expert on the Andalusian *cante jondo (or hondo)*, praised the "intuition" of Debussy and Ravel in composing a "true" if not "genuine" musical impression of Spanish folk music.

Debussy often used the typical sound idioms of the Spanish folk guitar in the same way that Grieg used the idiom of the Hardanger fiddle in his peasant dances. Perhaps this provides an explanation of Debussy's Spanish sound, see, for example, "La sérénade interrompue," in the first volume of the *Preludes* (1910). Debussy's own national interest may have been related primarily to his love of the French language, which he uses to its full range in his vocal works. At any rate, he does not seem to refer directly to the music of the people of France in any way.

It is possible that efforts to render language in music is one of the keys to the folklorism in music, which sounds national without being directly rooted in the folk music tradition. Perhaps, too, it is in this linguistic field of intonation that the meeting takes place between art and folk music, even in scholars such as Bartók and Kodály, whose "mother tongue" was folk music. The goals of the first composers of opera in the early sixteenth century were to achieve this in the speech of the dramatic recitative (see the letter from Pietro Bardi to G. B. Doni, in Strunk 1950, pp. 363f.). We can surely learn a great deal from Italian folk music by listening closely to the popular market scenes in seventeenth-century opera such as Vittorio Loreto's *La Galatea* (1639) and Jacob Melani's, *Tancia* (1657). The operas of Mozart also contain many such descriptions. This close-up of the people then became a central emphasis in the works of many nationalistic composers. Mussorgsky's letters contain lively descriptions of his attempts to render the speech of different people exactly in his music (Asafjev 1965, p. 7). Leo Janácek studied language motifs in order to render rhythmic and melodic structures from folk dialects exactly. Stravinsky uses Russian accents in *Svadebka, The Wedding,* and elsewhere.

Figure 11.9. Edvard Grieg's interpretation of *Jon Vestafes Springar* after Johann Halvorsen's transcription of Knut Johannesen Dahle's (1834–1921) playing.

A letter from Grieg to Halvorsen dated 18 October 1901: "However, it is now clearer to me that only a fiddler with a feeling for Norway would be able to transcribe it like this .... We must not wait a single day to get Myllarguten's *Peasant Dances* on paper, as Knut Dahle is an old man. I would prefer to see *you* take over the assignment. Just imagine if you could do it and then I could arrange the piece for keyboard, and we could bring them to world renown via Peters (publishing house) right in front of the nose of the Norwegian Parliament, as non-national as anyone could be out of pure nationality." (Quoted after Benestad/ Schelderup-Ebbe 1980, p. 309.)

Jon Væstafæ's Springdans.

Grieg and Debussy contributed, each in his own way, to the birth of the new Spanish dynasty of composers, beginning with Manuel de Falla (1876–1946). In 1893 de Falla heard the work of Grieg played in concert, and was seized with a burning interest to try to use the music of his own country in a similar way. In 1907 he arrived in Paris where he came into contact with Debussy and Ravel. In his *El amor brujo*, the *cante hondo* served as the point of departure for the melody, sound, and rhythm. Thus composers have discovered the music of their own countries and its artistic potential via their colleagues in other countries.

"If the Land, the Earth, and the Soil Could Compose Music, I Believe They Would Do So like Béla Bartók"

(Erik Lindegren, Swedish poet)

Béla Bartók and Zoltan Kodály, both composers, scholars, and educators, paved the way for a Hungarian national music culture, at the same time as they created works of art and established scholarly and educational models of great international renown. We will now focus on the artistic symbiosis that arose between folk and art music, mainly in the work of Bartók, whose musical language can be regarded as a true integration of art and folk music. The burning interest in folk music displayed by both Bartók and Kodály is rooted in a sense of patriotism. Bartók's Symphonic Poem *Kossuth*, written in 1903, when the composer was twenty-two years old, is dedicated to Lajos Kossuth, the revolutionary hero, and his heroic struggle against Austria and the Russians in 1849. The ten programmatic musical pictures presented by Bartók use a tonal language inspired by Richard Strauss's orchestral apparatus, with some additions from nineteenth-century Hungarian folk music. It even includes a distorted version of the Austrian national anthem to illustrate the enemy troops.

Bartók had now begun to discover a whole new kind of expressive potential:

Figure 11.10. The introduction to Igor Stravinsky's *The Rite of Spring*, based on a Lithuanian melody. See also Golovinsky 1981, p.156 ff., who has also studied how Stravinsky carried out his process of transformation, by examining the drafts of *The Rite of Spring*.

For me, the study of all this peasant music was decisive, because it helped me to liberate myself from the prevailing system of major and minor keys. The majority of the wealth of melodies I had discovered while collecting—and certainly the most valuable ones—were in the old church modes, i.e., the ancient Greek keys, and some were even more primitive (pentatonic). They also displayed free and greatly varied rhythmic forms, as well as shifts in tempo, both in rubato and in *tempo giusto*. . . . The use of the diatonic scale led to a liberation from inflexibile major-minor scales, the ultimate consequence being that we are completely free to pick and choose among all the notes of the twelve-tone chromatic system. [. . .] (Ujfalussy 1981, p. 57.)

It was not always so easy to gain the trust of the peasants: gentlemen dressed in the bourgeois fashion of the city and bearing phonographs aroused suspicion and were identified with the upper classes (see figure 1.9, p. 18). But Bartók and Kodály were accepted, probably due to the fact that the singers and fiddlers saw the composers' genuine interest in their art. Bartók considered the time he spent among the peasants to be the happiest of his life, as Dybeck did of his corresponding experience in Sweden. It was also a decisive period for him as an artist and a scholar, and he repaid the Hungarian

people many times over in compositions and scholarship, creating a breeding ground for the international reputation of Hungarian music both as folk and art music. From the very beginning, Bartók, and above all Kodály, had pedagogical ambitions, and Kodály's accomplishments as a pedagogical pioneer and popular educator were unique. In the preface to their joint edition of *Hungarian Folk Songs* from 1906, Bartók described his pedagogical aims, leaving his scholarly ambitions by the wayside:

The first objective is for all songs emanating from the people to be gathered together, and the only important perspective is the ambition to be exhaustive. The greater or lesser value of particular songs is not to be taken into consideration. The second objective is for the general public to become acquainted with and get to like folk music. The very best of it must be selected, somehow revised and brought closer to the taste of the people. (Ujfalussy 1981, p. 62).

In Bartók's own opinion, his art was a product of Western classical music with regard to compositional techniques, and also a product of the beauty and perfection of peasant music, which bear forth spirituality. It was the spiritual content of this music he wished to render (see Antokoletz 1984). His study of peasant music was important in helping him find ways around major-minor tonalities. His discovery of scale structures related to the church modes or pentatonic scales that were the building blocks of the melodies, was inspiring to this musical pioneer. He was also inspired by the different rhythmic forms, the time changes in the more rhythmic melodies and the free rhythmic structure he experienced in laments and narrative songs, for example. Bartók credited his shift away from conventional scales and time signatures to peasant music, which helped him to use the twelve notes of the chromatic scale with the same freedom as Schönberg did through a logical development of the German classical tradition (Figure 11.11).

Bartók was also greatly influenced by Debussy, who was also moving in the same direction and also carried forward by folk music. Bartók later, like Stravinsky, used folk music material to develop his own personal style of composition. However, while for Stravinsky this was just a short, youthful detour, for Bartók it became a life-long process.

In his article *Einfluss der Bauernmusik auf die Musik unserer Zeit* (1931), Bartók discusses three different ways in which composers can approach folk music:

1. through harmonization or adaptation of given folk songs using modern harmonies;
2. through imitation of peasant melodies;
3. through the development of a common bond between art and peasant music.

Bartók wrote, for example, of Zoltan Kodály's *Psalmus hungaricus*, op. 13 (1923). "At a time like this one can say: the composer has learned the musical language of the peasants, and has mastered it as completely as a poet has mastered his mother tongue (Ujfalussy 1981, p. 301). While Bartók devoted himself primarily to instrumental music, Kodály had a preference for vocal forms of expression. His works for choir may thus have done more than Bartók's instrumental pieces to spread interest in Hungarian folk songs and to keep them alive.

Popular Composers and the Urbanization of Rural Folklore

Urbanization meant that more and more people abandoned the countryside. A kind of urban musical folklore arose, rooted in older traditions but shaped according to new functions and demands

and adapted to new instruments, or adapting new instruments to its needs. Gradually anonymous composers were replaced by well-known, popular ones.

The Russian Chastushka

The Russian *chastushka* is closely associated with the Russian accordion, the *bajan,* and the balalaika, as well as with Cossack dancing and other acrobatic folk dances. The *bajan* and the balalaika became popular just at the time when rural and urban cultures were in confrontation, and became the favorite instrument of male domestics such as butlers and coachmen. Today the composers and lyricists of *chastushki* are well-known, established popular composers (see p. 107, Figure 5.9), and *chastushki* are also freely improvised at organized or spontaneous folk festivals popular in Russian cities today (Alexeyev 1988).

The Greek Rebetiko

The Greek *rebetiko* is dance, song, instrumental music, and lifestyle woven into an indissoluble unit, and embodies exactly all that appears to distinguish the culture of the people. Various aspects of this art form crystallize as separate artifacts, and begin to live their own lives, re-integrated into new social contexts. The *rebetiko* is part of urban folklore. The history of the dances makes it possible for us to discuss some general aspects of how dance, music, and song come into being outside the bounds of established social norms. This was also the case in rural areas, where gypsies, beggars, and other social outcasts were often the local musicians and composers.

Ted Petrides describes the *zeybekiko*, one of the two dances of the *rebetiko*, (the other is the *Khasapiko*).

Envision a small smoke-filled room late at night, the neighborhood hangout, a dozen or more *manges* and perhaps some of their women seated at tables around a small space for dancing. At one end of the room, or at one of the tables, are seated the musicians, apparently tuning their instruments: a *bouzouki*, a guitar, and a *baglamas* (4–6 stringed tambour instrument). The aimless strumming and picking gradually leads into something more recognizable—a *taxim*, an arhythmic instrumental introduction which draws the *manges'* attention. They try to follow the course of the improvized melody in their minds, murmuring

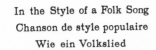

Figure 11.11. The openings of two piano pieces by Béla Bartók from *Mikrokosmos IV* and *VI*. Note that Bartók designates the former "In the Style of a Folk Song." It (a) is a lyrical melody of the type one might regard as more or less "pan-European." However, Bartók's passacaglia-like bass line, with its introductory leap of a seventh makes it sound far more biting than the conventional folk song arrangement. When the melody is presented in the bass, the top part responds, predominantly using leaps of fourths and fifths. In the second example (b), the fourth of six dances in a Bulgarian rhythm, the melody is pentatonic. It was through struggling with such melodies that Bartók's special world of harmonies developed. His development from harmonisation to transformation of folk modes has been studied by Antokoletz 1984 (Chapters II and III).

satisfaction at an unexpected turn, or disappointment at the insufficient development of a theme. Gradually the *taxim* builds to a climax and the tension mounts as the rhythm of the *zeybekiko* is introduced. Now one of the *manges* pushes back his chair and gets up. Putting his lit cigarette between his lips, eyes on the floor, body tense and slightly crouched, arms loosely out to the sides, he begins to move slowly, deliberately around some fixed imaginary point on the floor. Snapping his fingers to the rhythm, he elaborates his steps, occasionally doubling a step or holding a step for two beats, always circling round the point on the floor which is the unwavering focal center of his intense concentration, now and then breaking the heavy tension of the dance with explosive outbursts of energy as in sudden leaps, hops, turns, squats. No one else gets up to dance; it would be an insult and a trespass on his impending emotional release. Oddly enough this moment may come at any time, and he may decide to sit down again in the middle of the song; he is satisfied, he is released. No one cheers, no one claps. Perhaps another *mangas* who was able to project himself into the dancer's mood has a carafe of wine quietly sent to the man's table. But nothing more. The man danced for himself.

The *rebetiko* was long regarded as a form of vulgar entertainment. Gail Holst (1975) describes her

encounter with the *rebetiko* and how she was forced
to reappraise her snobbish attitude toward the juke
box when she heard it functioning as the "musician" playing the *rebetiko.* Young men would come
into a tavern, feed the jukebox a handful of coins,
and start to dance. Holst distinguishes between the
rebetiko danced at the hashish cafés and the *rebetiko*
as it was danced at professional *bouzouki* clubs. At
the latter, a frozen, commercialized form of the
rebetiko developed. The *rebetiko* originated in Piraeus
in the 1920s among Greeks who had fled from
Smyrna in Turkey, bringing with them both instruments and music of Ottoman origin. It took
time for the *rebetiko* to win approval as Greek folk
music, not only because of its lowly social origins
and its association with hashish cafés, but also
because it had a Turkish flavor. The *baglama* and
the *bouzouki,* instruments closely related to the Turkish *saz*, were even banned, as were the songs sung
to their accompaniment. These banned items had
been the consolation of many prisoners. This art
form of the underground was influenced by a wide
variety of contemporary styles. Holst mentions a
special kind of café music that originated in
Smyrna, for example. The establishment of the
rebetiko as accepted entertainment music went hand
in hand with its adaptation to the style and instruments of Western music. At this point, the names
of the writers of *rebetiko*s also became commonly
known.

The Spanish Flamenco

The Spanish flamenco is of special interest, owing
to its multicultural origins, rooted in Indo-Paki-
stani (gypsy), Muslim, Jewish, and Greek cultures.
Amongst the many wild theories about the origins of the flamenco, the following (by D. E.
Pohren) appears to be the most probable. The
Spanish Inquisition brought Jews, Muslims, and
gypsies together during the Middle Ages. Along
with persecuted Christians, they established refugee camps in the mountains, where a special culture arose and provided the soil in which the flamenco took root. In Arabic, *peasant refugee* is *felag
mengu,* and it is very likely that this is the origin of
the word flamenco. A flamenco of the old style,
associated with gypsy culture, is known as *cante
jondo,* and expresses the suffering of this oppressed
and yet paradoxically free people. The flamenco
consists of song (*cante*), dance (*baile*), guitar play-

ing (*toque*), rhythmic accentuation, (*jaleo*), and recitation (Figure 11.12). When the flamenco is performed, the singing, dancing, and guitar playing
must be fused into a whole.

The guitarist must know all the dances and
songs as well as if he were to dance or sing them
himself. Because the text is constantly broken up
by periods of improvisation, and the dance can
change faster than one can blink an eye, the guitarist must be instantaneously flexible, continually
adding interludes (*falseta*) to give the dancer and
the singer breathing space. While the tempo and
rhythm shift, he must maintain an inexorable pulse,
which he marks with his foot. A third, sometimes
extremely free rhythmic element, sometimes used
to mark the pulse as well, is finger-snapping or, in
commercialized contexts, the use of castanets.

The flamenco has gone through any number
of phases, beginning as an improvised dance in
the ceremony of the Spanish gypsy wedding, and
finally becoming a stereotyped dance for restau-
rant entertainment. It has also shifted back and
forth between being a form of art dance to a kind
of popular dance. According to Pohren the singing and guitar-playing have survived this transformation far better than the dance, which degener-
ated to acrobatic ballet exercises somewhere along
the route from the Andalusian caves to the Grand
Hotel in Barcelona. Along the way, there are flamencos, created by various categories of working
people outside the world of the gypsies, which reflect various social environments and contexts in
song, accompaniment, and dance style. Of course
the dance cannot be seen alone but is intertwined
with its social environment, the music, and customary behaviour patterns. Both the dance and
the music must be examined in this interplay and
are hardly meaningful outside this entire context.

The Portuguese Fado

The *fado*, like the *rebetiko*, is café and nightclub
music. There is a great deal of uncertainty about
its origins, for example, whether a rural version
preceded the urban one, and whether it may be
Moorish or Arabian in origin. The *fado* is a strophic type of song, associated with Portuguese
broadsides, the *literatura de cordel.* The songs are
sung to the accompaniment of a *viiola* (a 4–6
stringed guitar) or a Portuguese guitar (a cithern-
like instrument). The *fado* occurs in many literary

SANTUARIO
(SOLEARES)

Figure 11.12. The introduction to a *soleares* or *soleá*, sometimes known as *la madre del flamenco*. (Paco Pena, Toques flamencos 1976, p. 36.) It is a *Cante Jondo*, (great or deep song), one of the oldest types of the flamenco. *Soleares* is played as an improvised interchange between instrumentalist and singer/dancer, after a given form. This example renders the introduction and one of the following sections, the *rasgueado*, played rhythmically, with accented chords and the designation *llamada* the accented chords of which signal the dancer or singer, or begin the instrumental passage, known as the *falseta*. (Summary of information from manuscript by Mats Grundberg 1987, *A Study of the Flamenco*).

and musical forms, adapted to different environments and contexts from spontaneous folk to professional, from the street to fashionable *fado* clubs. It is also associated with the names of well-known artists and composers.

The Swedish Gammaldans

All over Europe, an abundance of social dances has developed, rooted in traditional folk dances and in dances fashionable among the bourgeoisie beginning in the eighteenth century. These include the waltz, the mazurka, the polka, the gallop, etc. (See Chapter 10 for more details on some of them.) These dances comprise a kind of urban folklore, most readily accessible in the city dance halls where young manual laborers and craftsmen met. These dances eventually also spread back to the coun-

tryside. During the nineteenth century, this genre became a global dance repertoire. Strauss, and Lanner, kings of the waltz, were among its best-known proponents. different regional styles and schools arose. Twentieth-century Sweden provides an example of a particularly Swedish style, the big names of which were Calle Jularbo, Andrew Walter, and Gnesta-Kalle.

Thus urban folklore became less and less anonymous and was increasingly attributed to established popular composers. At the same time, we can see the stylistic tools becoming increasingly universal and losing the power of their original association with social and functional contexts. In other words, we can see a parallel development with what happened when composers took up laments or folk dances as neutral stylistic tools in the nineteenth century.

Jewish Folk Music in Europe: Links between East and West, between Urban and Rural

According to Idelsohn (1948), secular folk music in Jewish culture originated at the time of the raising of the walls around the ghettos, i.e., when Jewish culture was prevented from becoming an organic part of the world around it. Jews living in or descended from the Jews of western, central, and eastern Europe are referred to as *Ashkenazim*. Beginning in the ninth century and until the songs of the synagogue were banned in the thirteenth century, there was considerable interplay between the songs of the synagogues and the Christian church. There was also interplay between secular music and the music of the synagogues, although such interplay was looked down upon by Jews and non-Jews alike. It was the obligation of Jewish cantors to preserve the traditional songs, the melodic principles of which were identical with those of other eastern cultures. At the same time, cantors were also interested in renewal and change, and in the impulses coming from the Christian musical environment. Oppression and suspicion led to periods of musical isolation and sometimes to musical silence. Alongside the music of the synagogues, instrumental music grew up among the Jewish urban population, and there were Jewish orchestras that attracted considerable attention as early as the sixteenth and seventeenth centuries. These musicians, known as *klezmorim*, played at Jewish weddings, the ceremonies of which are closely associated with very special instrumental music. They also made their livings as musicians in non-Jewish contexts. They became "transit musicians," moving impressions from one musical culture to another, not unlike the role of the gypsies mentioned above. However, according to Idelsohn, who refers to the distinction made by Liszt and others between gypsies and Jews, Jewish music has its own types of scales and structuring principles, and reflects a different attitude. Still, it is not easy to know where the boundaries go between these musical cultures.

It is equally difficult to distinguish between Jewish elements and folk music elements, and to determine the roots of the different elements of music. Ukrainian musicologist Moshe Beregovsky (1892–1961) made extensive collections of Jewish and Ukrainian folk music and found great similarities in both melody and expression (Figure 11.13). We cannot generally say who borrowed from whom; some traditional Yiddish songs have become popular in the Ukraine, and some Ukrainian songs have been translated into Yiddish and adopted into that culture. However, Beregovisky also points out fundamental differences. The two-line Ukrainian folk song corresponds to an expanded four-line one in Yiddish. There are also notable deviations in performance technique and ornamentation. The Yiddish music is far from the gentle means of expression that characterizes the music of the synagogue. It also includes more highly ornamented melodic material and gives more emphasis to textual interpretation. Yiddish songs are more often set in a minor key, with elements of the Phrygian mode and the unusual tonality known as the altered Dorian scale. According to Idelsohn, this is very different from the gypsy scale, with the main difference being the placement of the interval of the augmented second.

The fusion of folk music and Jewish music took place after 1700, primarily in the easternmost parts of Europe. The Jews in Germany, on the other hand, strove to provide their children with classical musical training. Many outstanding Jewish musicians in nineteenth-century Europe were descended from musicians in the above-mentioned instrumental orchestras, which generally consisted of two violins, a double bass, and sometimes a clarinet and horn or dulcimer. As in the gypsy orchestras, the musicians had varying abilities when it came to reading music. The violin was the instrument of the people, and it was said that one could count the number of men living in a household by the number of violins hanging on the wall. In the nineteenth century some Jewish musicians devoted themselves to popular music while others were classically oriented, and so their folk music style and the very special Yiddish heritage was also spread to both these fields.

Research into Jewish folk music has increased in recent years, thanks to the work of U. S. musicologist Mark Slobin, who bases his research on the scholarship that existed in the archives of eastern Europe before they were destroyed by the Nazis.

Many of the keys to the history of European folk music, with its many eastern elements, are

Figure 11.13. A Jewish and Ukrainian version of the same folk song. (*Old Jewish Folk Music* 1982, ex. 18, p. 517.)

surely concealed behind the search, within national folk music research, for a music of one's own, for what is "genuine." This clearly limits the perspective of many scholars, preventing them from seeing the contributions of itinerant musicians from various foreign countries and ethnic origins.

Music, Popular Music, and Dance Music: New Folk Music Groups and Young Composers Bridge the Gaps

Chapter 9 provided examples of folk music groups of differing origins and playing in different styles, from jazz to rock to folk music to medieval and Renaissance music. The instruments used by these musicians contradict all traditional notions of folk music. One additional example is the English group *Pyewackett*, in which the musicians play many instruments, including the bassoon, the dulcimer, the electric violin, the viola, and the accordion, as well as the synthesizer. "Early on, Puritan audiences reacted against Bill's synthesizers. People would sometimes come into the room where we had a gig, see the synthesizers, and leave before we started to play. Now, however, our audiences are really

interested in them" (Hansson/Fahlin 1987, p. 15).

The performance style of today's groups also varies from historicism to new attempts at coalescence. Some groups that began as "puritan" revival groups making demands in terms of folk authenticity have later gone on to compose their own pieces.

Can the music of revival groups be considered folk music or is it a kind of art music performed by collective composers who, like Grieg and Chopin, use some of the ingredients of folk music to develop a common style of composition? Groups searching for authentic folk music also base their work on a philosophy we recognize from Mendelssohn or Brahms, a striving for classical ideals of style, using the works of older composers as their model. The way in which hard-rock groups borrow folk melodies for their intros is not unlike the way in which nineteenth-century composers borrowed folk melodies for their variations. Between the search for the roots of folk music and superficial borrowing, there is a whole spectrum of ways of using folk music that, to date, has hardly been explored.

Today, folk music is in a new stage in its en-

Figure 11.14. The beginning of Karin Rehnqvist's composition *David's nimm* (1984). In a letter, she wrote: *"Davids nimm* (1984) is the clearest example of, and the first piece in which, I use folk music. The piece is based on a *polska* sung onto audio tape and then played backwards. Soprano 1 has an exact steal of the polska, the mezzosoprano sings the *polska* in inverted form (with the intervals reversed) and backwards. Soprano 2 is the only freely composed part, moving from an introverted pianissimo which hardly leaves her mouth, to a dramatic fortissimo. Soprano 1 and the mezzosoprano simply repeat the same thing louder and faster –cf. the tape recording technique à la Donald Duck. Playing the text backwards reinforces the 'm' and 'n' sounds and other consonants, which is also a technique used in folk music performed in the right direction. Backwards articulation suits me, and it isn't actually very backwards, but rather it is most certainly forwards, for instance when used in violin folk music" (dated 23 February 1988).

DAVIDS NIMM
[Davɪds nɪm]

counter with art music, which is far more naturally melodic and lighthearted than most music written in recent decades. Sweden provides a couple of examples. Mats Edén, a young composer, was originally a folk musician in a group known as Groupa, and uses both art and folk music traditions in his compositions. In 1984 Karin Rehnqvist began testing the use of material for folk music (a vocal *polska* on audio tape) in "David's nimm" (Figure 11.14). Rehnqvist cooperates very closely with folk musicians, developing new musical forms of expression from traditional improvisation techniques in her compositions.

Using folk music in popular music contexts seldom results in great hits today. Folk music-style contributions to the Eurovision Song Contest, for example, often wind up at the bottom of the juries' ranking scales, probably because they stand out and run against the grain of the international popular song style (see Björnberg 1985). However, popular music today appears to be in a serious crisis: no new dances and no special new musical styles are coming to light. We can follow how musicians of popular music instead consider more

collaboration with fiddles and folk singers. Benny Andersson (composer and musician in the former Swedish group *ABBA*) has discovered the potential of folk music, and initiated cooperation with the fiddlers' society from Orsa.

Perhaps, in fact, the terms art *music, folk music,* and *popular music* are becoming obsolete. There is certainly no question that the musical antagonism that marked the 1960s and 1970s has been followed by a phase of reconciliation, in which individual musicians are free to browse through the entire library of music, uninhibited by the labels of the past.

Literature

There are many articles on the relationship of individual composers to folk music. Many biographies have separate chapters on this subject. What is lacking is a general analysis. Interesting pioneering works include Helmer (1972), where one chapter is devoted to folk sound in art music, and a dissertation by Huldt-Nyström from 1966 that attempts to define the Norwegian "national sound." Soviet musicologist G. Golovinsky is the author of *Kompozitor i fol'klor* (1981), which has both an English summary and an extensive bibliography, primarily of Russian works. In his study of tonality and progress in twentieth century music, Elliot Antokoletz provides a detailed analysis of the route taken by Béla Bartók from major and minor to his own personal tonalities based on folk music modes (*The Music of Béla Bartók* [1984]). This is an extremely complex problem because some composers who were not interested in folk music also found similar routes. Thus there may have been some kind of general *Zeitgeist*.

Twelve

European Folk Music:
A Uniform Diversity

CONCLUDING REMARKS

The period of European folk music in focus in this book, from the late eighteenth century until the early 1990s, includes the period of transition from agrarian to urban industrialized society. This was a time of revolutionary change in all countries of Europe in terms of living conditions and lifestyles. These changes also explain why the map of European folk music contains such a mixture of old and new. Until about 1600, most of the inhabitants of Europe were peasants, and there were relatively few large cities. Then a new demographic structure began to develop as cities grew in size and became dominant at the expense of the countryside. Urban culture thus also came to dominate while simultaneously assimilating many of the rural cultural traditions. We have followed these changes in song, instrumental music, and dance.

When urban cultures and industrialization took the stage, attention ceased to be paid to preserving the songs, melodies, and dance traditions associated with a cyclic view of time reflecting the changes in agricultural seasons and the life cycle. Instead, people began to strive for constant renewal, greater entertainment, and the unknown in music, performed by professional or semi-professional musicians. New songs and instruments, of course, had also developed in agrarian society, which had also tried to incorporate new developments from outside, but this was always within the framework of the given traditions, a code which was not to be violated.

The regional folk music styles that developed in the musical cultures of peasant society were also the products of the creativity and efforts of indi-

vidual artists. There were masters and apprentices, just as in art music. But the work of these musicians, singers, and instrument makers was regulated by functions and traditions. Probably, most of them regarded themselves more as musical craftsmen than as "artists" in accordance with the bourgeois ideology of the nineteenth century.

Folk Music Explorers from the European Viewpoint

The explorers and advocates of folk music have appeared in the wake of the collectors of folk literature, ballads, and songs. They were part of the same cultural national movement. This movement began early in England, Germany, and Russia, although for somewhat different reasons. The people who discovered the Nordic *jojk* and runic songs were also early explorers, searching for exotic cultural game. The interest in the Scottish folk song as a song of the people was also an eighteenth-century phenomenon as well as a manifestation of nationalism. Elsewhere, it was the early nineteenth century that saw the most activity in terms of discovery and collection of folk music. One exception is the countries where Romance languages are spoken, although not France, where such activity did not pick up speed until the late nineteenth century. The reasons for this delay were related to the fact that nationalism was not a general phenomenon in either Italy or Spain, for example, where there are both linguistic and cultural boundaries within each country, not to mention economic and social regionalization.

What, then, were the implications of the activities of the collectors, seen in a holistic European perspective, beyond the fact that they preserved the compositions, like flowers in a herbarium, for the future? First, their activities were important to the development of art music. Nineteenth-century art music is inconceivable without its foundation in folk music. As mentioned above, there had been a dialogue between art and folk music even earlier, but when music-lovers began to express an interest in the unique qualities of folk music, folk music could begin to take a more active and conscious part in shaping trends in art music as well. Exchange between countries was another important ingredient. Trying to understand the peculiarities of the folk music of another country than one's own encouraged respect and understanding for other cultures, even in times when any true patriot was required to regard the folk music of his own nation as best. In the late nineteenth century, collection began to take more conscious shape as scholarly preservation for the future. Many of the archives that developed at this time were based on the work of a small number of collectors, who devoted their lives to the task. The groundwork they laid later took on different superstructures depending on the intentions of the scholars who succeeded the original collectors, and on the objectives of the prevailing cultural policy in each country.

During the twentieth century, the dialogue between composers and European folk music has faded, particularly in the wake of the philosophy of art music coined by Arnold Schönberg and continued by the representatives of the Darmstadt school. The various waves of folk music revival in the twentieth century have undoubtedly been a reaction to this change. The work of the collectors has been honored in these movements, and the dried flowers of written music and transcribed melodies in collections have been transformed to a dynamic culture with both functional and aesthetic aspects. Throughout the life of folk music as an independent category of music, there has been tension between it and the artistic ideals developed in the late eighteenth and early nineteenth centuries, which emphasized the creative genius of the composer. Scots folk musician Hamish Imlach is said to have claimed that "music which fills large rooms and costs nothing in subsidies and which also helps people enjoy themselves can hardly be an art" (Frey/Siniveer 1987, p. 9). This expresses something of the contradiction that still exists today but appears to be weakening.

Using Sound at Work

We can unreservedly state that "music at work" has been a pan-European phenomenon. But the music which remains indicates that the phenomenon was strongest in countries with an active, independent herding or farming culture where song, instrumental music, and instruments have developed artistic profiles far beyond their functions at work. Above all, there is a wealth of material to study in Scandinavia and eastern Europe. The songs and shouts of work from Italy, Spain, and Portugal are at least as interesting from aesthetic and ethnological points of view, but the amount of material available in print and on disc is relatively limited.

Songs in the Life Cycle and the Annual Cycle

There have always been and will always be lullabies, despite the fact that the first decades of mass media made them somewhat less prevalent. Wedding songs, from both singing and weeping weddings, were so intimately intertwined with an older way of life and thinking that it is perfectly natural for them to have lived on only where the tradition was strongest—in the Baltic countries, Russia, the Ukraine, Belarus, Poland, Romania, Hungary, and the Balkans. Instrumental wedding marches are a clear indication of the way in which bourgeois festivities have replaced ancient agrarian family ceremonies. It is noteworthy that laments are still sung at funerals in Karelia, along a belt south of Greece, and parts of the Mediterranean (Corsica and Sardinia). Like wedding laments, this is territory for female singers, deeply emotional and rooted in the fundamental human experience of life and death. Thus it is no coincidence that lullabies and funeral laments have both survived.

Song

Although the *jojk* is probably the most unique of the many kinds of songs in Europe, it is still not so different from a yodel that one might not confuse the two. The *jojk* is actually rooted in the culture of the nomadic peoples of the Siberian tundra, and is also associated with the striking songs of the American Indians. Other very special types of song include the runic song and the *bïlïnï*, the Balkan heroic songs, the Irish *sean-nós* and the Icelandic *rímur*. All these types of song prioritize the text over musical expression, and the singers appear to work with a set of fixed melodic elements and rhythms used in accordance with a special structure. Thus we might say that these types of song, including the *jojk*, are not really music as we define it, but rather a kind of elevated speech in which the musical dimension has a distancing poetic effect.

There were similar kinds of narrative song in Europe earlier in time as well, such as the French *chanson de geste*. These disappeared, particularly in conjunction with the advent of written culture. Only where writing remained of secondary importance have these types of vocal narrative art been able to survive and develop.

With regard to the ballad and lyric song, these seem to have been found all over Europe and in healthy interplay with the song traditions that preceded and succeeded them. The melodies, which lived their own separate musical life, also display influences from the styles of different periods (Vargyas 1983). The singers appear to have cared very little about categorizing their songs, having simply sung and preserved the songs they personally preferred. The ballad, lyrical song, and chorale show us three stages along the way to the normative influence of written culture. With regard to the ballad, forms are used, as described above, which are related to the bïlïnï, the *sean-nós*, and the *rímur*. However, it is also possible to follow how melodies are borrowed, not only from one ballad to another, but also from hymns, dance melodies, etc.

The subject of hymns is an exciting one, where popular creativity confronted an increasingly rigid set of norms. The many existing variants show strong artistic, individual influence, constantly in confrontation with the schooled organist or cantor and his unrelenting ideas. This kind of popular song developed primarily in Protestant countries. The same battles were fought there as earlier, in the Middle Ages, when efforts were made to develop a kind of liturgical song that was generally accepted, when personal creativity had to give way to the central powers that wanted conformity to certain established aesthetic ideals. Singing in unison in church is a musical expression of the victory of centralism, not unlike the way in which the military uniform shaped individuals into a collective expression of the pursuits of war.

Instruments

Different kinds of spontaneous instruments have been discovered and new ones developed in every generation, utilizing the new materials and tools of their times (plastics and personal computers are examples from our own times). With regard to medieval instruments, the bagpipe, hurdy-gurdy and Jew's harp appear to have been pan-European, while the keyed fiddle and other regional types of fiddles, the bowed harp, and the Hardanger fiddle provide examples of local between older kinds of stringed instruments and the violin. Flutes and horns are the instruments of herding cultures and were generally restricted to herding areas. There are any number of types of flutes, from medieval bone flutes to various kinds of wooden ones, which also became part of a symbiosis with the instruments of art music, for example the Norwegian *tusseflöjt* or *sjöflöjt*.

Beginning in the seventeenth century, we see the spread of art music instruments to rural areas and to urban artisans and manual laborers. These instruments, primarily the violin, but also the clarinet and the oboe, contributed to an intensification of the dialogue between folk and art music on the one hand and between folk and popular music on the other, and gave rise to mixed forms of instruments, music, and performance. Later, different brass instruments were added, and these impacted on the wooden trumpets and long horns from the shepherd cultures. The bassoon and the dulcimer, in turn, inspired the development of the Slovakian *fujara*.

Ensembles

The development of ensembles made it possible to introduce a polyphony based on traditional harmonies, but not always like that of art music (for example, Hungarian dance orchestras). Gradually, very different kinds of folk music orchestras developed all over Europe, some hastened by national policies that encouraged this kind of folk art, for example, in many of the former socialist countries, others developing more spontaneously on the basis of functional needs.

Dance

Scholarship in the past has stressed the difference between ring and line dances, which developed in the east, and couples' dances, which developed in the west. The former were claimed to be a sort remnant of residue of the Middle Ages, the latter to have come into being during the Renaissance. However, the line of demarcation has proven to be far more complex and fluid; this applies to the melodies and rhythms as well. This is a research field which will undoubtedly come to be very important with regard to an understanding of regional cultural differences in Europe.

The Composer and Folk Music

The ambition of composers to utilize folk music as one of their sources can be explained in many ways. Many composers grew up in regional folk music cultures, and it was natural for them to use their musical mother tongue in artistic contexts. Others were inspired by a national-ideological philosophy, or discovered the music of "others" and tried to make it their own. Italian composers are among those who have expressed the least interest in their local folklore, yet it may be reflected all the more directly in their compositions, which may account for its being difficult to distinguish as a separate ingredient.

What Is Shared, and What Distinguishes Individual Regions?

Is it possible to determine separate musical layers in European folk music which, like layers in bedrock, may have been protected and retained in some parts of Europe and eroded in others by processes of cultural, political, and social weathering? The examples we have seen from the diversity and wealth of folk music cultures in Europe are, of course, too few and too randomly selected to allow us to draw conclusions about the whole. We have also tapped sources stretching over three centuries, with all the problems of interpretation this entails.

In certain regions, song, dance and instrumental music have been, and remain, integral parts of ceremonies and customs. In others, there was a gradual transition beginning in the eighteenth and nineteenth centuries toward assimilation with the growing urban popular and art music cultures. Gradually, folk music was rediscovered, and efforts made to revitalize it, with the realization that it would otherwise soon be extinct.

Without these preservation efforts of different kinds, folk music as a musical treasury and a source of historical documentation would probably have been lost. The late 1960s saw veritable waves of folk music all over Europe, different in each country, depending on what the basic traditions and academic situation were, and not least depending on different political ideologies. From that point on, we may say that folk music had begun its gradual entrance into the phase of historicism. It was transformed into part of the cultural heritage, just as music from older epochs was canonized and took on designations such as "Renaissance music" and "Baroque music."

Today, then, folk music is very different from what it was when collectors in the eighteenth and nineteenth centuries first began transcribing folk music that until then had existed only as oral tradition.

Many different methods of scholarship have been applied to the study of folk music, using both historical and sociological approaches, and via studies of performance practice and detailed analyses of various musical structures. Perhaps in the future it will be possible to provide the concept of folk music with deeper implications and a deeper meaning when we learn more about the impact of this powerful movement on the enrichment and democratization of musical culture. Without folk music we would have neither art nor popular music.

Literature

The literature on the genesis of folk music includes Alan Lomax's *Folk Song Style and Culture* (1968) and *Cantometrics* (1976), which is an approach to the anthropology of music. These are basic books, tackling the connection between song style, lifestyle, and cultural, economic, and sexual factors. Lomax works with studies of statistical data collected from scholars all over the world. His methods have been criticized, especially by scholars such as Zemtovsky, who advocate the deductive approach. But the theory of intonation, which provides Zemtovsky's theoretical foundation (see Chapter 3) has also been subject to criticism. However, there are also interesting new spinoffs. The Yakut folk musicologist Edward Alexeyev has written a book continuing the work of Zemtovsky, entitled *Early Folklore Intonation* (1986, in Russian with summaries in English, German, and French). In this work he has attempted to provide a general system of pitch analysis by establishing a hierarchy of different modes of singing. In the future, perhaps a fruitful connection will be made between the work of Lomax and Alexeyev.

Doris Stockmann has written a number of articles discussing fundamental problems in the field of folk music and applying an interdisciplinary approach. Among her many works (see the bibliography in the *Yearbook for Traditional Music 1987*, vol. 19, pp. 182ff.), I would like to mention *Zur Analyse schriftlos überlieferte Musik* (1976), *Die sthetisch-Kommunikativen Funktionen der Musik unter historisch, genetischen und Entwicklungs-Aspekten* (1980), *Musik-Sprache-Biokommu- nikation und das Problem der musikalischen Universalien* (1982), and *Tonalität in*

europäischer Volksmusik als historisches Problem. A regular source of information on the latest research can be found in the following journals: *Yearbook for Traditional Music* (1981–), which is the continuation of *Yearbook of the International Folk Music Council* (1969–1980) and *Ethnomusicology* (1965–).

An interesting attempt is made to delineate cultural regions in European folk music by James Poster and A. L. Lloyd in their article "Europe" in *New Grove*, vol. 6, pp. 295–312. Their article also provides a review of the early history of folk music and its connections with non-European cultures.

Bibliography

Abbreviations used

Bzm = Beiträge zur Musikwissenschaft.
CPA = Culture populaire albanaise.
Dfg = Danmarks gamle Folkeviser.
DJbf Vk = Deutsches Jahrbuch für Volkskunde.
DMT = Dansk musiktidssknft.
EM 1 = Ling, Jan. Europas musikhistoria 1.
FSF = Finlands svenska folkdiktning.
ICTM = International Council for Traditional Music.
Jb Volksliedf = Jahrbuch für Volksliedforschung.
JIFMC = Journal of the International Folk Music Council.
MGG = Musik in Geschichte und Gegenwart.
NG = The New Grove Dictionary of Music and Musicians.
SIMP = Studia instrumentorum musicae popularis.
SMASH = Studia musicologica Academiae Scientiarum Hungaricae.
SMB = Sveriges medeltida ballader.
STM = Svensk tidsknft för musikforskning.
Sohlex = Sohlmans musiklexikon.
SvL = Svenska låtar.
ULMA = Dialekt och folkminnesarkivet i Uppsala.
YIFMC = Yearbook of the International Folk Music Council.
YTM = Yearbook for traditional music.

Journals

Acta musicologica. Basel, 1928–.
Allgemeine musikalische Zeitung. Leipzig, 1798–1882/rptd. 1964–69.
Antropologiska studies published by Antropolog-föreningen vid Socialantropologiska institutionen, Stockholm University, Stockholm, 1971.

Baessler Archiv. Beiträge zur Völkerkunde. Berlin, 1910.
Beiträge zur Musikwissenschaft. Verband deutscher Komponisten und *Musikwissenschaftler.* Berlin, 1959. After 1972: Rom Verband der Komponisten und Musikwissenschaftler der DDR.
Bellmanstudier. Published by Bellmanssällskapet (The Bellman Society). Stockholm, 1924–.
Brussels Museum of Musical Instruments Bulletin.
Budkarlen. Organ for the Brage section for Folklore Research and the Institute for Nordic Ethnology at the Academy of Tuurku. Tuurku, 1922–.
Common Stock. (The journal for the Bagpipe Society of the Lowlands and Borders.)
Culture populaire albanaise. Académie des sciences de la République d'Albanie. Tirana.
Dagens Nyheter. (Swedish daily newspaper.)
Dansk musiktidskrift. Published by the Danish Young Composers' Association. Copenhagen, 1925–70.
Deutsches Jahrbuch für Volkskunde. Institut für deutsche Volkskunde an der Deutschen Akademie der Wissenschaften zu Berlin durch Wilhelm Fraenger. Berlin, 1955–1969.
Ethnomusicology. Journal of the Society for Ethnomusicology. Ann Arbor, Michigan 1953–.
Fataburen. Yearbook of the Nordic Museum. Stockholm, 1906.
Finnish Music Quarterly. Helsinki. Sibelius Academy, 1985–.
Folkminnen och folktankar. Lund 1914–24, Stockholm, 1924–44.
Folk Roots. London 1978–.
Hembygden. Swedish Youth Circle for Rural Culture. Stockholm, 1922–.
Idun. Praktisk veckotidning för kvinnan och hemmet (The practical weekly for women and the home). 1885–1963.
Italian Quarterly. Riverside, California

Jahrbuch des österreichischen Volksliedwerkes. Vienna, 1952–.

Jahrbuch für Volkskunde und Kulturgeschichte. Berlin, 1973–. (continuation of *Deutsches Jahrbuch für Volkskunde*).

Jahrbuch für Volksliedforschung. Deutschen Volksliedarchiv. Berlin, 1928–.

Journal of the Folklore Institute. Indiana University, Bloomington, 1964–82.

Journal of Folklore Research. Bloomington, 1983–. (continuation of *Journal of the Folklore Institute*).

Journal of the International Folk Music Council (1949–1967).

Die Karawane. Vierteljahreshefte der Ges. für Länder und Völkerkunde. Ludwigsburg, 1955–.

Musikens makt. Vaxholm, 1973–.

Musikethnologische Jahresbibliographie Europas. Eds. Erich Stockmann, Oskar Elschek & Ivan Mačak. Bratislava, 1967–.

Musikethnologische Sammelbände. Institut für Musikethnologie. Graz, 1977–.

Narodna tvorcist' ta etnografya (Ethnography of popular/folk art). Kiev, 1957–.

Nord Nytt. Published by the Institute for European Folklore Research. Lyngby, 1967–.

Norveg. Tidskrift for folkelivsgransking. Oslo, 1951.

RILM Abstracts. Répertoire international de la littérature musicale. Flushing, New York, 1967–.

Russky fol'klor (Russian folklore). Materialy i Issledovanya. Ed. A.M. Astachova . . . Moscow and Leningrad, 1956–.

Slavia. Prague, 1922.

Sovetskaja étnografya. Moscow, 1932–.

Spelmannen. Published by Swedish Folk Musicians' National Council (continuation of *Spelmansåret* (Folk Musicians's Yearly)), 1978–.

Spelmansbladet. Published by Swedish Folk Musicians' National Council. 1959–1962.

Spelmansåret. Published by Swedish Folk Musicians' National Council. 1965–1977.

Studia musicologica Academiae scientiarum Hungaricae. Budapest, 1961.

Südtiroler Volkskultur.

Sumlen. Svenskt visarkiv och Samfundet för visforskning. Stockholm, 1976–.

Svensk tidskrift för musikforskning. Published by Swedish Society of Musicology. Stockholm, 1919–.

Svenska Familjejournalen, 1863–87.

Svenska Familje-vännen. Illustrated magazine for the home, 1879.

Western Folklore. Berkeley and Los Angeles: California Folklore Society, 1968–.

Yearbook for Traditional Music, 1981–, (continuation of *Yearbook of the International* . . .).

Yearbook of the International Folk Music Council. 1969–1980, (continuation of *Journal of the International* . . .).

Zeitschrift für Ethnologie. Organ der Deutschen Gesellschaft für Völkerkunde. Braunschweig, 1869–.

Music Dictionaries

Die Musik in Geschichte und Gegenwart. Ed. Friedrich Blume. Kassel, 1949–68. Suppl. 1969–.

The New Grove Dictionary of Music and Musicians. Ed. Stanley Sadie (new edition) London, 1980.

The New Grove Dictionary of Musical Instruments. Ed. Stanley Sadie. London and New York, 1984.

Sohlmans musiklexikon. 1st edn. (Gösta Morin, ed.). Stockholm, 1948–52.

Sohlmans musiklexikon. 2nd edn. (Hans Åstrand, ed.). Stockholm, 1975–79.

Books by Composers Cited Herein

Balakirev, Mily. *30 russkich narodnich pesen.* Leipzig, 1898. (Arrangement for piano duet, 1898).

Balakirev, Mily. *Sbornik russkikh narodnikh pesen.* St. Petersburg, 1866.

Bartók, Bela. *Kossuth,* Symphonic Poem. 1903.

Beethoven, Ludwig van. *Twenty-four Foreign Melodies.* 1815.

Beethoven, Ludwig van. *Scottish Lieder* WoO 156. 1822–41 (translated from English).

Beethoven, Ludwig van. *Twenty-three Songs of Various Nationalities* WoO 158 a. Leipzig, 1943.

Beethoven, Ludwig van. *Tyroler Arien.* 1816.

Berio, Luciano. *Folk Songs.* 1964.

Brahms, Johannes. *Deutsche Volkslieder.* 1894.

Brahms, Johannes. *Deutsche Volkslieder* (arrangement for four unaccompanied voices). 1864.

Brahms, Johannes. *Wiegenlied* op. 49:4. 1868.

Brahms, Johannes. *Volks-Kinderlieder.* 1858.

Brahms, Johannes. Sonata for clarinet and piano op. 120:1 f-minor. 1894.

Chopin, Frédéric. Mazurkas and Polonaises.

Dahlgren, E.A., see Randel, A., & Dahlgren, F.A.

Debussy, Claude. *Soirée dans Grenade* (from *Estampes*). 1903.

Dvořák, Antonin. 4 Songs, op. 6. on Serbian folk lyrics/poems, 1872.

Enström, Rolf. *Tjidtag och tjidtjaggaide.* 1987, (Prisvinnare, Prix Italia, 1987.)

Falla, Manuel de. *El amor brujo.* 1914–15, (concert version. 1916).

Gleisman, Carl Erik. *Den fromma fru Signild* (in Olof Åhlström, *Skaldestycken satte i musik,* 1794–1823).

Gliére, Reinhold. Symphony no. 3 op. 42 "Ilja Muromets." 1909–1911.

Glinka, Mikhail. *Ruslan and Lyudmila.* 1837–42.

Grieg, Edvard. *25 Norske folkeviser og dandse för piano* op. 17. 1869.

Grieg, Edvard. *Peer Gynt* op. 23 (Ibsen). 1874–1908.

Grieg, Edvard. *Slåtter for klaver* op. 72. 1902–03.

Hiller, Johann Adam. "Ohne Lieb und ohne Wein" (from the Singspiel *Der Teufel ist los*, Leipzig, 1766).

Janácek, Leo. Edited and arranged Moravian and Slovakian folk songs.

Janácek, Leo. *Kytice z národnich pisni moravskych.* Collection of 174 Moravian folk songs (1890 and 1901).

Johansson, Jan. *Visa från Utanmyra.* 1963.

Koch, Erland von. *Oxberg-variations.* 1956.

Kodály, Zoltán. *Balmus hungarics* op. 13. Budapest, 1923.

Lidholm, Ingvar. *Riter* (Ballet after an idea of E. Lindegren), Stockholm, 1960.

Lissenko, Nikolai. see Lysenko, N.

Liszt, Franz. *Rákóczymarsch.*

Liszt, Franz. *Csárdás obstiné* rptd. 45:2. 1886.

Liszt, Franz. *Hungarian Rhapsodies.*

Lysenko, Nikolai. *Ukrainian Folk Songs.* 7 vols. (for voice and piano) and 12 vols. (arrangement for choir) (1886–1903).

Mahler, Gustav. *Lieder aus Des Knaben Wunderhorn.* 1888–1899.

Mahler, Gustav. Symphonies nos. 2–4. 1888–1892 (text from *Des Knaben Wunderhorn*).

Mozart, Leopold. *Die Bauernhochzeit.* 1755.

Mozart, Leopold. *Divertimento militare.*

Mozart, Leopold. *Die Jagd.*

Mozart, Leopold. *Musikalische Schlittenfahrt.* 1755.

Mozart, Leopold. Sinfonia burlesca G-major.

Mozart, Wolfgang Amadeus. *Don Giovanni* K. 527. 1787.

Mozart, Wolfgang Amadeus. *Le nozze di Figaro* K. 492. 1786.

Mozart, Wolfgang Amadeus. Sonata for piano. KV 331 A-major "Rondo alla Turca".

Musorgsky, Modest. *Kalistratushka* (Song). 1864.

Musorgsky, Modest. *Intermezzo i modo classico.* 1861.

Randel, A. & Dahlgren. F.A., *Värmländningarna.* Stockholm, 1846.

Ravel, Maurice. *Habanera* (from *Rapsodie espagnole*). 1908.

Rehnqvist, Karin. *Davids nimm,* for 3 ladies voices. 1984.

Riedel, Georg. *En visa vill jag sjunga* (Pippi Långstrumpsvisa. Text: Astrid Lindgren).

Rimsky-Korsakov, Nikolai. *Mayskaja noch',* (A May night). 1880.

Rimsky-Korsakov, Nikolai. *Noch, pered rozhdestvom* (Christmas Night) 1894–95.

Rimsky-Korsakov, Nikolai. *Sbornik 100 russkikh narodnikh pesen* op. 24. 1875-76.

Rimsky-Korsakov, Nikolai. *40 narodnikh pesen.* 1882.

Schubert, Franz. *Am Brunnen vor dem Tore,* see Schubert, *Der Lindenbaum.*

Schubert, Franz. *Der Lindenbaum* D 911:5 (from *Winterreise.* 1827. Text Wilhelm Müller).

Schulz, Johann Abraham Peter. *Der Mond ist aufgegangen.* (Text: Matthias Claudius, from *Lieder im Volkston.* Berlin, 1792–90).

Söderman, August. *Ett bondbröllop.* 1868.

Stravinsky, Igor. *Le sacre du printemps* (The rite of Spring). 1911–13.

Stravinsky, Igor. *Svadebka* (Les noces). 1914–23.

Tchaikovsky, Peter. Arrangement of folk songs from the Balkirev collection.

Tchaikovsky, Peter. Concert for piano and orchestra no. 1 B♭-minor op. 23. 1874–75.

Vaughan Williams, Ralph. *Five Variants of "Dives and Lazarus."* 1939.

Weyse, Christoph Ernst Friedrich. *Vermischte Compositionen.* 1799.

Other literature quoted

This bibliography contains references to collections of folk music quoted and to collections about folk music quoted. All compact discs quoted contain cover text or illustrations used in the text.

Acerbi, Guiseppe. *Travels through Sweden, Finland and Lapland to the North-Cape in the Years 1798 and 1799.* London, 1802.

Adorno, Theodor W. *Philosophie der Neuen Musik.* Tübingen, Mohr, 1949.

Ældre og nyere norske fjeldmelodier. Saml. og bearb. for pianoforte af Ludvig M. Lindeman. Oslo, 1853–1867/ rptd. 1963 (Norsk musikksamling. Publikasjon 3).

Afzelius, Arvid August. see Geijer. E.G. and Afzelius, A.A.

Afzelius, Arvid August and Åhlström, Olof. *Traditioner af swenska folkdanser.* H. 1–4. Stockholm, 1814–15; rprd 1972.

Afzelius, Nils. "Bellman som folklig författare" (*Bellmanstudier* 16. Stockholm, 1970, p. 9–35).

Ahlbäck, Gunnar. *Nyckelharpfolket.* Stockholm, 1980.

Ala-Könni, Erkki. *Die Polska-Tänze in Finnland: Eine ethno-musikologische Untersuchung.* Thesis. Helsinki, 1956 (Kansatieteellinen arkisto 12).

Albanische Volksmusik=Muzika popullore shqiptare. Eds. Doris Stockmann, Wilfried Fiedler, Erich Stockmann. Berlin, 1965 (Deutsche Akademie der Wissenschaften zu Berlin. Veröffentlichungen des Instituts für deutsche Volkskunde 36).

Alexandre, Charles. "La cornemuse dans les Pyrénées françaises." *The Brussels Museum of Musical Instru-*

ments Bulletin, Ed. René de Maeyer. Vol. VI–1/2, 1976, p. 16–31.

Alexandru, Tiberiu. *Romanian Folk Music*. Translated from Romanian. Bucharest. 1980.

Alexandru, Tiberiu. *Muzica popular ă românească*. Bucharest, 1975.

Alexgev, Eugen. *Rannefolklore intonirovanje* (The pitch nature of primitive singing). Moscow, 1986.

Alexiou, Margaret. *The Ritual Lament in Greek Tradition*. London, 1974.

Alimos, Toma. *Meşterul Manole: Balade populare românesti*. Bucharest, 1967.

Allardyce, A. see *Scotland and Scotsmen in the Eighteenth Century*.

Allmo, Per-Ulf & Winter, Jan. *Lirans hemligheter*. Stockholm, 1985.

Allmo, Per-Ulf & Winter, Jan. *Säckpipan i Norden*. Från änglars musik till djävulens blåsbälg, MS (manuscript). 1988.

Alver, Brynjulf. see Bjørndal, Arne & Alver, Brynjulf.

Andersson, Greger. *Bildning och nöje*. Bidrag till studiet av de civila svenska blåsmusikkårerna under 1800-talets senare hälft. Stockholm, 1982 (Studia Musicologica Upsaliensia Nova Series 7) Thesis. Uppsala University.

Andersson, Nils. see *Svenska låtar*.

Andersson, Otto. "Bröllopsmusik på säckpipa" (*STM* 43, 1961, p. 17–36).

Andersson, Otto. see *Finlands svenska folkdiktning*.

Andersson, Otto. *Spel opp, I spelemänner Nils Andersson och den svenska spelmansrörelsen*. Stockholm, 1958.

Andersson, Otto. *Stråkharpan*. En studie i nordisk instrumenthistoria. Thesis. Helsinki, 1923.

Andreassen, Eydun. "Dansens og arbejdets vise–samme vise med forskellig form?" (*Sumlen*, 1979, p. 39–50).

Anoyanakis, Fivos. *Greek Popular Musical Instruments*. Aten, 1979.

Antokoletz, Elliott. *The Music of Béla Bartók*. A study of tonality and progression in twentieth-century music. Berkeley, California, 1984.

Apkalns, Longins. *Lettische Musik*. Wiesbaden, 1977.

Arbeit und Volksleben. Deutscher Volkskundekongress 1965 in Marburg. Göttingen, 1967 (Veröffentlichungen des Instituts für mitteleuropäische Volksforschung an der Philipps-Universität Marburg-Lahn. Allgemeine Reihe. 4).

Arkkiveisuja [Skillingtryck]. *Suomalaista kansanmusiikkia 2*. (Finnish folk music 2.) Phonograph record. Booklet by: Anneli Asplund Finnlevy SFLP 8566.

Arnberg, Matts, Ruong, Israel, & Unsgaard, Håkan, Joik. *Yoik*. Stockholm, Sveriges Radio, 1969.

Arnberg, Matts. see Jansson, Svea.

Arnim, Ludwig Joachim von & Brentano, Clemens. *Des Knaben Wunderhorn. Alte deutsche Lieder. Vollst. Ausg. nach dem Text der Erstausg. von 1806–1808 . . .* Munich, 1957.

Arwidsson, Adolf Iwar. *Svenska fornsånger. En samling af kämpa-visor, lekar och dansar, samt barn- och vall-sånger*. 1–3. Stockholm, 1834–42.

Asaf'ev, Boris. *Izbrannye stat'i o muzykal' nom prosvecenii i obrazovanii*. Leningrad, 1965.

Asplund, Anneli. see Arkkiveisuja (Skillingtryck).

Asplund, Anneli. *Kantele: Suomalisen Kijalisuu den Seuran toimituksia 390*. Forssa, 1983.

Asplund, Anneli. See *Kansan Musiikki*.

Asplund, Anneli. *Kantele*. Helsinki, 1983.

Asplund, Karl. See *Brittiska ballader och visor*.

Astachova, A.M. Bylini. *Itogi i problemy izučenija*. Moscow & Leningrad, 1966 (Akademija nauk SSSR) (Institut russkoj literatury (Pukinskij dom)).

Astachova, A.M. See Bylini. Severa. Zapisi . . .

Atanassov, Vergilij. "Der Gadulkaspieler und die Multifunktionalität seines Instruments" (*SIMP 7*, 1981, p. 120–126).

Atanassov, Vergilij. "Gaida (Dudelsack)." *The Brussels Museum of Musical Instruments Bulletin*, Ed. René de Maeyer. Vol. VI–1/2, 1976, p. 37–46.

Atlas musikalnisch instrumentov narodov. SSSR Ed. K.A. Vertkov . . . Moscow, 1963.

Åhlström, Olof. *Skaldestycken satte i musik (1794–1823)*.

Åhlström, Olof. See Afzelius, A.A. & Ahlström, O.

Das Akkordeon (Autorenkollektiv). Leipzig, 1964.

Bacer, D. & Rabinovic, B. *Russkaja narodnaja muzyka. Notograficeskij ukazatel, (1776–1983)*. Moscow, 1981.

Bachmann-Geiser, Brigitte. *Die Volksmusik instrumente der Schweiz*. Leipzig, 1981 (*Handbuch der europäischen Volksmusikinstrumente* ser. 1 vol. 4).

Bacinskaja, N. *Russkie chorovody i chorovodnye pesni*. Moscow, 1951.

Baines, Anthony. *Bagpipes*. Oxford, 1960.

The Ballad Image: Essays Presented to Bertrand Harris Bronson. Ed. James Porter. Los Angeles, 1983 (Center of the Study of Comparative Folklore & Mythology. University of California).

Balys, Jonas. *Lithuanian Narrative Folksongs*. A description of types and a bibliography. Washington, 1954 (A treasury of Lithuanian folklore 4.).

Bartha, Dénes. "Mozart et le folklore musical de l'Europe Centrale" (*Les influences étrangères dans l'uvre de Mozart*. CNRS, Paris, 1958).

Bartók, Béla. *Béla Bartók . . . ur folkmusikens källa*. Brev, artiklar, dokument. Sammanst. av József Ujfalussy. Translated from Hungarian. Uddevalla, 1981 (Original title: *Bartók-brevárium*).

Bartók, Béla. *Ethnomusikologische Schriften*. Berlin . . . ,

1913–25/R 1965–68. (I. Das ungarische Volkslied, 1965; II. Volksmusik der Rumänen von Maramures, 1966; III. Rumänische Volkslieder aus dem Komitat Bihar, 1967; IV. Melodien der Rumänischen Colinde (Weihnachtslieder), 1968.)

Bartók, Béla. *The Hungarian Folk Song*. Ed. Benjamin Suchoff. New York, 1981.

Bartók, Béla. See *Magyar Népdalok*.

Bartók, Béla. See *A magyar népzene tára*.

Bartók, Béla. See *Népdalok*.

Bartók, Béla. See *Rumanian Folk Music*.

Bartók, Béla. See *Serbo-Croatian Folk Songs*.

Bartók, Béla. See *Slovenské l'udové piesne*.

Bartók, Béla. *Das ungarische Volkslied. Versuch einer Systematisierung der ungarischen Bauernmelodien* (Ungarische Bibliothek für das Ungarische Institut an der Universität Berlin; 1:11) Berlin and Leipzig 1925.

Batjinskaja. See Bacinskaja.

Baumann, Max Peter. *Musikfolklore und Musikfolklorismus. Eine ethnomusikologische Untersuchung zum Funktionswandel des Jodels, mit einer Zusammenstellung der gedruckten Quellen und einer Bibliographie zur musikalischen Volkskunde der Schweiz*. Thesis. Bern, 1974. Winterthur, 1976.

Baumann, Max Peter. "Funktion und Symbol. Zum Paradigma 'Alphorn'" (*SIMP* 5, 1977, p. 27–32).

Bayard, Samuel P. "Prolegomena to a Study of the Principal Melodic Families of Folk Song" (*The Critics and the Ballads*. 103–150, 1961).

Beeking, G. "Der musikalische Bau des Montenegrinischen Volksepos" (*Proceedings of the International Congress of Phonetic Sciences. Amsterdam*, 3–8 July, 1932, p. 144–153; tr. 1933).

Bellman, Carl Michael. See Afzelius, Nils.

Belonenko, A.S. *Problemy russkoj muzykal'noj tekstologir*. Leningrad, 1981.

Bene Bohuslav, *Die Bänkelballade in Mitteleuropa*. Ein Beitrag zur morphologischen Typologie Jb Volkslied 16, 1971 p. 9–41).

Benestad, Finn & Schjelderup-Ebbe, Dag. *Edvard Grieg*. Mennesket og kunstneren. Oslo, 1980.

Bengtsson, Ingmar, Tove, Per-Arne & Thorsén, Stig-Magnus. "Sound Analysis Equipment and Rhythm Research Ideas at the Institute of Musicology in Uppsala" (*SIMP* 2, 1972, p. 53–76).

Bentzon, Andreas Fridolin Weis. *The Launeddas: A Sardinian Folk Music Instrument*. Thesis. Copenhagen, 1969 (Acta Ethnomusicologica Danica 1).

Beregovski. See *Old Jewish Folk Music*.

Berg, Göran. See Norinder, Johan & Berg, Göran.

Bergelt, Styrbjörn. *Stråkharpans spelteknik*. MS Stockholm, 1977.

Bergendal, Göran. *Isländsk musikhistoria* (MS, 1986).

Berlioz, Hector. *Mémoires de Hector Berlioz*. Ed. P. Citron, Paris, 1969.

Bernskiöld, Hans. *Sjung, av hjärtat sjung. Församlingssång och musikliv i Svenska Missionsförbundet fram till 1950-talet*. Thesis. Göteborg, 1986 (Skrifter från Musikvetenskapliga institutionen, Göteborg 11).

Bettencourt da Cāmara. *José Manuel, Música tradicional açoriana–a questão histórica*. Lisbon, 1980.

Bielawski, Ludwik. "Instrumentalmusik als Transformation der menschlichen Bewegung. Mensch–Instrument–Musik" (*SIMP* 6, 1979, p. 27–32).

Bielawski, Ludwik. *Rytmika polskich piésni ludowych*. Krakow, 1970.

Bjørkvold, Jon-Roar. *Den spontane barnesangen–vårt musikaliske morsmål*. Oslo, 1985.

Björnberg, Alf. *En liten sång som alla andra. Melodifestivalen 1959–1983*. Thesis. Göteborg, 1987 (Skrifter från Musikvetenskapliga institutionen, Göteborg 14).

Bjørndal, Arne & Alver, Brynjulf.–og fela ho lét. Oslo, 1966.

Blom, Jan-Petter. "Hvor gammel er fela?" (*Arne Bjørndals hundreårsminne*, Bergen, 1985, p. 191–208).

Blom, Jan-Petter. See *Norsk folkemusikk*.

Blom, Jan-Petter & Kvifte, Tellef. "On the Problem of Inferential Ambivalence in Musical Meter" (*Ethnomusicology* 30, 1986, p. 491–517).

Blom, Jan-Petter. "Principles of Rhythmic Structures in Balkan Folk Music" (*Antropologiska studier* 25–26, 1978, p. 1–11).

Bogatyrev, P. *Nekotorye zadaci sravnitel'nogo izucenija èposa slavjanskich narodov*. Moscow, 1958 (Akademija nauk SSSR) (Sovetskij komitet slavistov).

Boswell, James. *Boswell's Journal of a Tour to the Hebrides with Samuel Johnson, LLD*. 1773. Eds. Frederick A. Pottle & Charles H. Bennett. Melbourne, 1963 (The Yale editions of the private papers of James Boswell).

Boydell, Barra. *Music and Paintings in the National Gallery of Ireland*. Dublin, 1985.

Böhme, F.M. *Deutsches Kinderlied und Kinderspiel*. Leipzig, 1924.

Böhme, EM. See Erk, Ludwig Christian.

Brandl, Rudolf Maria. "Musiksoziologische Aspekte der Volksmusikinstrumente auf Karpathos" (*SIMP* 5, 1977, p. 131–138).

Brandl, Rudolf Maria. "Zur pragmatischen Dimension des musikalischen Hörens: Individualstil und Instrumentalstil eines griechischen Geigers" (*SIMP* 7, 1981, p. 86–94).

Braun, Hartmut. *Tänze und Gebrauchsmusik in Musizierhandschriften des 18. und frühen 19. Jahrhunderts aus dem Artland* (Materialien zur Volkskultur, nordwestlisches Niedersachsen Heft 19, 1984).

Braun, Maximilian. *Das serbokroatische Heldenlied.* Göttingen 1961 (Bilaga med originaltexter, 1963) (Opera Slavica 1).

Brăiloiu, Constantin. *Problèmes d'ethnomusicologie.* Textes réunis et préfacés par Gilbert Roguet. Geneva, 1973.

Breathnach, Breandan. *Folk Music and Dances of Ireland.* Dublin, 1971. Rev. Edn. 1977.

Brentano, Clemens. See Arnim, Ludwig Joachim von & Brentano, Clemens.

Brittiska ballader och visor. I svensk tolkning av Karl Asplund, Stockholm, 1972.

Brockpähler, Renate. "Bastlösereime in Westfalen" (Jb Volkslied 15, 1970, p. 81–135).

Bronson, Bertrand Harris. *The Ballad as Song.* Berkeley and Los Angeles: University of California Press, 1969.

Bronson, Bertrand Harris, "The Interdependence of Ballad Tunes and Texts" (*The Critics and the Ballad,* 1961).

Bronson, Bertrand Harris. See *The Traditional Tunes of the Child Ballads . . .*

Bröcker, Marianne. *Der Drehleier: Ihr Bau und ihre Geschichte.* Thesis. Düsseldorf, 1973.

The Brussels Museum of Musical Instruments Bulletin, Ed. René de Maeyer. The bagpipes in Europe (Part 1). Vol. VI–1/2, 1976.

Buchan, David. *The Ballad and the Folk.* London and Boston, 1972.

Buchan, David. See *A Scottish Ballad Book.*

Bücher, Karl. *Arbeit und Rhythmus.* Leipzig, 1896/9.

Buckley, Ann. "Considerations in a stylistic analysis of uilleann piping" (*SIMP* 6, 1979, p. 120–125).

Bunting, Edward. *The Ancient Music of Ireland.* Comprising the three collections by Edward Bunting originally published in 1796, 1809 & 1840. Dublin, 1969.

Bunting's Ancient Music of Ireland. From the original manuscript by Donald O'Sullivan & Micheal O'Sulleabhain. Cork, 1983.

Burke, Peter. *Folklig kultur i Europa 1500–1800.* Stockholm, 1983.

Burke, Peter. *Popular Culture in Early Modern Europe.* London, 1978.

Burney, Charles. *Music, Men, and Manners in France and Italy 1770.* London, 1980.

Burns, Robert. See *The Scots Musical Museum.*

Butterworth, Katherine. See *Rembetica.*

Bylini. *Archangel'skija byliny i istoriceskija peni, sobrannyja A.D. Grigor'evym v 1899–1901.* Prague. 1939.

Bylini. *Itogi i problemy.* See Astachova, A. M.

Bylini. *Pecory i Zimnego Berega.* (Bylini from Petjora-området and Zimin-Bereg.) Ed. A.A. Astachova m.fl., Institutet för rysk litteratur, Sovjetiska vetenskapsakademien. Moscow and Leningrad 1961.

Bylini. *Severa.* Zapisi, vstupitel'naja stat'jaxu i kommentarij A.M. Astachovoj. Moscow and Leningrad, 1938–51 (Akademija nauk). SSSR. Folklornaja kommissija pri Institute etnografii.

Bylini v dvuch tomach. Podgotovka teksta, vstupitel'naja stat'ja i kommentarii. Eds. Ja. Proppa and B. N. Putilova. Moscow, 1958.

Byliny v. zapisjach i pereskazach XVII–XVIII vekov. (Bylinor i 1600-talet och 1700-talets anteckningar och berättelser) Ed. A.M. Astachova m.fl. Moscow and Leningrad, 1960.

I canti popolari italiani 120 testi e musiche. Ed. Roberto Leydi. Milan, 1973.

Carson, Ciarán. *Irish Traditional Music.* Belfast, 1986.

Celander, Hilding. "Staffansvisorna" (*Folkminnen och folktankar* 14, 1927, p. 1–55)

Chavarri, Eduardo Lopez. *Musica popular española.* Barcelona and Buenos Aires, 1927.

Chikvadse, see Čikvadse.

Čikvadse [Chikvadse, Tschschikwadse], Grigol, *Grundtypen der Mehrstimmigkeit im grusinischen Volkslied* (*BzM* 10:3, 1968, p. 172-188).

Ciobanu, Gheorghe. *Național și universal în folclorul muzical românesc* (National și universal în musica. Ed. Florin Georgescu. Bucharest, 1967).

Clausen, Karl and Marianne. *Åndelig visesang på Færøerna.* Fra Færøerna VI–VII. Dansk-Færøsk samfund. Copenhagen, 1975.

Cocchiara, Giuseppe. *Storia del folklore in Europa.* Turin, 1954.

Coffin, Tristram P. See *The Critics and the Ballad.*

Coirault, Patrice. *Recherches sur notre ancienne chanson populaire traditionnelle.* Paris, 1927–33.

Collaer, Paul. *La musique populaire traditionnelle en Belgique.* Brussels, 1974 (Académie Royale de Belgique. Mémoires de la classe des Beaux-Arts 2).

A Collection of Highland Vocal Airs Never Hitherto Published. Coll. Joseph McDonald 1784.

Collinder, Björn. *Finnarnas folkliga kväden.* Stockholm, 1970 (K. Gustav Adolfs akademiens småskrifter 7).

Collinder, Björn. *Det finska nationaleposet Kalevala.* Stockholm, 1951 (K. Gustav Adolfs akademiens småskrifter).

Collinson, Francis. *The Bagpipe: The History of a Musical Instrument.* London, 1975.

Collinson, Francis. *The Traditional and National Music of Scotland.* London, 1966.

Les colloques de Wégimont 4 1958–1960. Paris, 1964 (Ethnomusicologie 3). (Bibliothèque de la Faculté de philosophie et lettres de l'Université de Liège 172.) (See Comişel, Nataletti, Stockmann.)

Comişel, Emilia. La musique de la ballade populaire roumaine (*Les colloques de Wégimont 4*, 1958–1960, p. 39–73).

Cooke, Peter. See *Pibroch*.

Cooke, Peter. See *Waulking Songs from Barra*.

Corpus musicae popularis Hungaricae. See *A magyar népzene tara*.

Corrette, Michel. *Les dons d'Apollon, méthode pour apprendre facilement àjouer de la guitarre*. 1762.

Corrette, Michel. *La belle vielleuse, méthode pour apprendre facilement à jouer de la vielle*. 1783/rptd. 1977.

Crannitch, Matt. *The Irish Fiddle Book. The Art of Traditional Fiddle Playing*. Cork and Dublin, 1980.

The Critics and the Ballad. Eds. MacEdward Leach & Tristram P. Coffin. Carbondale, 1961 (see Bayard, Bronson).

Cvetko, Dragotin. *Histoire de la musique slovène*. Maribor, 1967.

Cvetko, Igor. "The Instrumental Musical Creativity of Children in Slovenia" (*SIMP* 8, 1985, p. 38–42).

Czekanowska, Anna. *Features of old-slavic folk music. State of research and attempt at chronologisation* (Stencil MS).

Czekanowska, Anna. "The importance of Eastern religions, calendars for the rhythm of annual folk songs in Slavic countries" (*Baessler-Archiv Beiträge zur Völkerkunde* 23:1, 1975, p. 239–255).

Czekanowska, Anna. *Signal Versus Aesthetic Function*. MS, 1985.

Dahlhaus, Carl. *Die Musik des 19 Jahrhunderts*. Wiesbaden, 1980 (Neues Handbuch der Musikwissenschaft).

Dahlig, Ewa. "Intercultural Aspects of Violin Playing in Poland" (*SIMP* 8, 1985, p. 112–116).

Dahlström, Greta. See *Finlands svenska folkdiktning*.

Dahlström, Greta. "Staffan och Herodes-visans melodi" (*Budkavlen* 14:2, 1935, p. 66–67).

Daja, Ferial. "Le caractère des gammes du chansonnier épique héroïque-lègendaire" (*CPA* 1983, p. 151–159).

Dal, Erik. *Nordisk folkeviseforskning siden 1800*. Copenhagen, 1956 (Universitets-Jubilæets danske Samfund 376).

The Dance Music of Ireland. Ed. Francis O'Neill. Dublin, MS/rptd. 1986.

Danckert, Werner. *Das europäische Volkslied*. Berlin, 1939.

Danmarks gamle Folkeviser. Ed. Svend Grundtvig. Copenhagen, 1953–1965.

Danmarks gamle Folkeviser: XI. Eds. Thorkild Knudsen, Svend Nielsen and Nils Schiørring, Copenhagen, 1976.

Danuser, Hermann. *Die Musik des 20: Jahrhunderts*. Regensburg, 1984 (Neues Handbuch der Musikwissenschaft. Ed. Carl Dahlhaus 7).

Dencker, Nils. See Tillhagen, C.H., & Dencker, N.

Derschmidt, Hermann. "Landlergeigen. Die Geige in der oberösterreichischen Volksmusik" (*Die Geige in der europäischen Volksmusik*. 161–175, 1975).

Deutsch, Walter. See *Die Geige in der europäischen Volksmusik*.

Deutsch, Walter. "Volksmusiklandschaft Österreich" (*Volksmusik in Österreich*, p. 9–44).

Deutsche Volkslieder mit ihren Melodien. Ed. Deutschen Volksliedarchiv. Berlin and Leipzig, 1935.

Dević, Dragoslav. "Cevara, ein Kernspalt-Längsflötentyp in Ostserbien" (*SIMP* 8, 1985, p. 122–125).

Dević, Dragoslav. "Porträt eines Flötenensembles in Nordostserbien" (*SIMP* 7, 191, p. 153–157).

Dević, Dragoslav. "Hirtentrompeten in Nordostserbien" (*SIMP* 5, 1977, p. 76–80).

Dillner, Johan(nes). *Melodierna till swenska kyrkans psalmer, noterade med ziffror för skolor och menigheten*. 1830.

Din don deine: Lieder der Völker Europas. Leipzig, 1978.

Dorson, Richard M. See *Folklore and Folklife* . . .

Dundes, Alan. See *The Study of Folklore*.

Dybeck, Richard. *Svenska folkmelodier*. Stockholm, 1853–56.

Dybeck, Richard. *Svenska gång-låtar*. Stockholm, [1849].

Dybeck, Richard. *Svenska vallvisor och hornlåtar, med norska artförändringar*, Stockholm, 1846/rptd. 1974. Efterskrift Märta Ramsten.

Dybeck, Richard. *Svenska wisor*. I–II. Stockholm, [1847–48].

Dybeck, Richard. *Runa*. 1865–76.

Dzieje muzyki polskiej w zarysie. Ed. Tadeusz Ochlewski. Warsaw, 1977.

Edström, Karl-Olof. *Avspeglar den stilistiska skillnaden inom jojken samernas förhistoria?* Thesis, Musikvetenskapliga institutionen i. Göteborg, 1988.

Edström, Karl-Olof. *Den samiska musikkulturen. En källkritisk översikt*. Thesis. Göteborg, 1977. (Skrifter från Musikvetenskapliga institutionen, Göteborg 1.)

Eeg-Olofsson, Leif. *Johan Dillner: präst, musiker och mystiker*. Stockholm, 1978.

Eeg-Olofsson, Leif & Ostenfeld, K. *Förteckning över psalmodikonnoter*. Stockholm, 1978.

Eesti rahvalaule viisidega. Ed. H. Tampere. Tallinn, 1956–65 (Eesti NSV teaduste akadeemia Fr.R. Kreutzwaldi nim Kirjandusmuuseum).

Eggen, Erik. *Skalastudier Kristiania*. Oslo, 1923.

Eibner, Franz. "Geigenmusik in Vienna" (*Die Geige in der europäischen Volksmusik*, p. 129–160).

Eibner, Franz. "Die musikalischen Grundlagen des volkstümlichen österreichischen Musiziergutes" (*Jahrbuch Österreich Volksliedwerkes* XVII, 1968, p. 1–21).

Eighteen Hundred and Fifty Melodies. Ed. Francis O'Neill. Ho-Ho-Kus NJ, 1903/rptd. 1979.

Einstein, Alfred. *Mozart, sein Charakter, sein Werk*. Frankfurt/Main, 1973.

Elschek, Oskar. See *Methoden der Klassifikation* . . .

Elschek, Oskar. See *Musikethnologische Jahresbibliographie Europas*.

Elschek, Oskar. *Die slowakischen Volksmusikinstrumente*. Leipzig, 1983 (*Handbuch der europäischen Volksmusikinstrumente* ser. 1 vol. 2).

Elschek, Oskar. See *Slovenské l'udové piesne*.

Elschek, Oskar. See *Slovenské l'udové piesne a nástrojová hubda*.

Elschek, Oskar. "Typologische Arbeitsverfahren bei Volksmusikinstrumenten" (*SIMP* 1, 1969, p. 23–40).

Elschek, Oskar. "Volksmusik und Volksmusik-instrumente der Karpaten und des Balkans–Prinzipien eines interkulturellen Forschungsprojekts" (*SIMP* 8, 1985, p. 63–66).

Elscheková, Alica. See *Slovenské l'udové, piesne*.

Elscheková, Alica. See *Slovenské l'udové piesne a nástrojová, hubda*.

Elscheková, Alica. "Stilbegriff und Stilschichten in der slowakischen Volksmusik" (*SMASH* 20, 1978, p. 263–303).

Elscheková, Alica. "Slowakische Volksmusikinstrumente in den weihnachtlichen Hirtenliedern des 17.–19. Jahrhunderts" (*SIMP* 5, 1977 p. 96–105).

Elscheková, Alica. See *Stratigraphische Probleme der Volksmusik* . . .

Elscheková, Alica. *Technologie der Datenverarbeitung bei der Klassifizierung von Volksliedern*. (*Methoden der Klassifikation* . . .) Bratislava, 1969.

Elscheková, Alica. "Vergleichende typologische Analysen der vokalen Mehrstimmigkeit in den Karpaten und auf dem Balkan" (*Stratigraphische Probleme der Volksmusik in den Karpaten* . . . p. 159–256. 1981).

Emsheimer, Ernst. "Art: Georgische Volksmusik" (*MGG Supplement*, p. 448–455).

Emsheimer, Ernst. "Georgian Folk Polyphony" (*JIFMC* 19, 1967, p. 54-57).

Emsheimer, Ernst. "Gedanken zur Welt der Kinderinstrumente und ihrer Beziehung zur Erwachsenenkultur" (*SIMP* 8, 1985, p. 10-17).

Emsheimer, Ernst. See *Handbuch der europäischen Volksmusikinstrumente*.

Emsheimer, Ernst. "Knallbüchse und Weidenpfeife. Zwei traditionelle Kinderklanggeräte in Schweden" (*SIMP* 8, 1985, p. 52–60).

Emsheimer, Ernst. "Koskällan–magiska föreställningar och bruk kring ett klangredskap" (*Sumlen*, 1979, p. 11–24).

Emsheimer, Ernst. "Zur Typologie der schwedischen Holztrompeten" (*SIMP* 1, 1969, p. 87–97).

Emsheimer, Ernst & Stockmann, Erich. "Vorbe-merkungen zu einem *Handbuch der europäischen Volksmusikinstrumente*" (*Acta musicologica* 32, 1960, p. 47–50).

Entwistle, William J. *European Balladry*. Oxford, 1959.

Envallsson, Carl Magnus. *Svenskt musikaliskt lexikon, efter grekiska, latinska, italienska och franska språket*. Stockholm, 1802.

Das Erbe: Deutsche Volkslieder aus Mittel- und Osteuropa, Quellen und Dokumentation. Ed. Hermann Wagner. Bonn-Bad Godesberg, 1972.

Erhardt, Ludwik. *Music in Poland*. Trans. from Polish. Warsaw, 1975.

Eriksson, Leif & Gudmundson, Per. *Säckpipan i Dalarna*. Falun, 1981 (Dalarnas museums serie av småskrifter 25).

Erk, Ludwig Christian. *Deutscher Liederhort*. Berlin, 1856. Revised 2nd edn. Ed. F.M. Böhme Leipzig, 1893–94. (3rd edn., 1925.)

Erk, Ludwig Christian. *Singvöglein*. 1842–48.

Ermedahl, Gunnar. "Spelmannen stryker på Violen up: Om spelmannen och hans musik." *Folkmusikboken*, 1980, p. 232-262.

Espelund, Arne. "Strukturelle trekk i levende middelalderdans" (*Sumlen*, 1979, p. 25–38).

Ethnomusicologie 3 (Les colloques de Wégimont). See Comişel, Nataletti, Stockmann.

European Folk Ballads. Ed. E. Seemann. Copenhagen, 1967.

Ewald, Z.V. "Die soziale Umdeutung von Ernteliedern im belorussischen Poles'e" (*Sowjetische Volkslied- und Volksmusikforschung*. Berlin, 1967 p. 259–291).

Fahlin, Lars. See Hansson, Nils & Fahlin, Lars.

Falla, Manuel de. *Escritos sobre música y músicos*. Ed. F. Sopena. Madrid, 1950, 3/1972.

"Fäbodmusik i förvandling." Report from an excursion in the summer of 1977 by Anna Johnson. (*STM* 60:2, 1978, p. 5–39).

Festschrift für Karl Horak. Ed. Manfred Schneider. Innsbruck, 1980. (Inst. für Musikwissenschaft der Univ. Innsbruck) (See Geiser; Haid; Petermann; Salmen; Schmidt; Suppan; Kumer; Wolfram; Hermann-Schneider).

Festschrift für Walter Wiora zum 30, December 1966. Ed.

Ludwig Finscher & Christoph-Hellmut Mahling. Basel, 1967.

Fiedler, Wilfried. See *Albanische Volksmusik.*

Filikromen: Hittills otryckta skämtsamma sånger. Ed. Axel I. Ståhl. Stockholm, 1850–77/rptd. 1973.

Finlands svensta folkdiktning: 5 [Folkvisor] 3 Sånglekar. Ed. Otto Andersson, Greta Dahlström & Alfhild Forslin. Helsinki, 1967 (Collected and edited by Svenska Litteratursällskapet i Finland 423).

Finlands svenska folkdiktning: 6 Folkdans, A. 3 Bröllopsmusik. Ed. Otto Andersson. Helsinki & Copenhagen, 1964 (Collected and Edited by Svenska Litteratursällskapet i Finland 402).

Finno-ugorskij muzykal'nyj fol'klor i vzaimosvjazis sosednimi kul'turami/ Soome-ugrilaste rahvamuusika ja naaberkultuurid. Ed. Ingrid Rüütel. Tallinn, 1980.

Finscher, Ludwig. *Studien zur Geschichte des Streichquartetts 1, Die Entstehung des klassischen Streichquartetts: Von den Vorformen zur Grundlegung durch Joseph Haydn.* Kassel, 1974 (Saarbrücker Studien zur Musikwissenschaft 3).

Fleischhauer, Günter. "Polnische Einflüsse und ihre Verarbeitung in der Klaviermusik Georg Philipp Telemanns" (*BzM* 23: 1, 1981, p. 6–19).

Folkdanser i Norden. Ed. Dagmar Hellstam. Falköping, 1981.

Folkevisen i Danmark: Efter optegnelser i Dansk folkemindesamling. Ed. Thorkild Knudsen & Nils Schiørring. Copenhagen, 1959–[1968?]

Folkliga koraler. Collected by Anders Lindström & Gunnar Ternhag. Älvsjö, 1985.

Folklore and Folklife: An Introduction. Ed. Richard M. Dorson. Chicago & London, 1972.

Folk Music and Poetry of Spain and Portugal. Collected by Kurt Schindler. Olms, 1979.

Folkmusikboken. Ed. Jan Ling. Stockholm, 1980.

Folkmusikvågen. Ed. Birgit Kjellström. Stockholm, 1985.

Folksongs of Britain and Ireland: A Guidebook to the Living Tradition of Folksinging in the British Isles and Ireland. Eds. Peter Kennedy & Allison Whyte. London, 1975.

Folk Songs of Europe. Ed. Maud Karpeles. London, 1956.

Forslin, Alfhild. See *Finlands svenska folkdiktning.*

Fortis, Alberto. *Viaggio in Dalmazia (1774).* Ed. Johan Vokovic. Munich, 1974.

Fra Færøerne: "Ur Føroyum". Copenhagen, 1973.

Från skrapare till hackare. Eds. Jan Ling & Sture Olofsson. Stockholm, 1972.

Fredin, August. See *Gotlandstoner.*

Frey, Jürgen & Siniveer, Kaarel. *Eine Geschichte der Folkmusik.* Hamburg, 1987.

Friedman, Albert B. "The Oral-Formulaic Theory of Balladry: A Rebuttal" (*The Ballad Image*, 1983, p. 215–240).

Frye, Ellen. *The Marble Threshing Floor: A Collection of Greek Folk Songs.* Austin & London, 1973. (Publications of the American Folklore Society. Memoir series 57.)

Den fynske sang. Ed. Ole Heyde. Odense, 1984.

Gabrielsson, Alf & Johnson, Anna. "Melodic Motion in Different Vocal Styles" (*Analytical Studies in the Description and Analysis of Music.* Ed. Anders Lönn & Erik Kjellberg. Uppsala, 1985, p. 277–99).

Galilei, Vicenzo. *Fronimo. Dialogo . . . sopra l'arte del bene intavolare, et rettamente sonare la musica negli strumenti artificiali si di corde come di fiato, & in particulare nel liuto.* Venice, 1584/rptd. 1969.

Gauthier, André. *Les chansons de notre histoire.* Paris, 1967.

Die Geige in der europäischen Volksmusik. Bericht über das 1. Seminar für europäische Musikethnologie. St. Pölten, 1971. Ed. Walter Deutsch & Gerlinde Haid. Vienna, 1975 (See Derschmidt;Eibner; Sarosi; Sevåg; Steszewski; Thiel).

Geiger, Paul. *Volksliedinteresse und Volksliedforschang in der Schweiz vom Anfang des 18: Jahrhunderts bis zum Jahre 1830.* Thesis, Bern, 1911.

Geijer, Erik Gustaf & Afzelius, Arvid August. *Svenska folk-visor från forntiden.* 1st edn. 1814–17, 2nd edn. 1880, 3rd edn. 1957–60.

Geiringer, Karl. *Joseph Haydn.* Potsdam, 1932 (Die grossen Meister der Musik 3).

Geiser, Brigitte. "Die Maultrommeln in der Schweiz" (*Festschrift für Karl Horak*, p. 95–103).

Geiser, Brigitte. "Schellen und Glocken in Tierhaltung, Volksbrauch und Volksmusik der Schweiz" (*SIMP* 5, 1977, p. 20–26).

Gestrein, Rainer. *Aspekte der Tanzmusik in Österreich im 19: Jahrhundert.* Innsbruck, 1984.

Giacometti, Michel & Lopes-Graça, Fernando. *Cancioneiro popular português.* Lisbon, 1981.

Gil Garcia, Bonifacio. *Cancionero del campo.* Madrid, 1966.

Ginsburg, Råland. See *Jugoslavien. . . .*

Giurchescu, Anca. "The Process of Improvisation in Folk Dance" (*Dance Studies*, 1983, 7:21-50).

Giurchescu, Anca & Bloland, Sunny. *The Romanian Folk Dance* (MS, 1987).

Gjertsen, Ingrid. "Vokal folkemusikk på Vestlandet" (*Arne Bjørndahls hundreårsminne.* Bergen, 1985, p. 211–221).

Gjertsen, Ingrid. "Religiøs folkesang: Belyst ur fra to lokalmiljøer i Norge" (*Nord Nytt* 24, 1985, p. 17–24).

Goldschmidt, Aenne. *Handbuch des deutschen Volkstanzes.* Berlin, 1967.

Golovinskij, Grigorij. *Kompozitor i fol'klor. Iz opyta masterov XIX–XX vekov.* Moscow, 1981.

Gordijtjuk, M. *Folklore i folkloristiska.* Kiev, 1979.

Gosovskij, V.L. *Ukrainskie pesni Zakarpat'ja.* Moscow, 1968.

Gotlandstoner. Collected by August Fredin. Stockholm, 1909–33.

Grajcie dudy, grajcie basy: Texthäfte till Polish Folk Musik by Jadwiga Sobieska. Phonograph record. 1976. Polskie Nagriana Warszawa SX 1125–26.

Green, Archie. "A Folk Music Exhibition" (*The Ballad Image,* p. 97–130) Los Angeles, 1983.

Greni, Liv. "Bånsuller i Setesdal. Om bruken av tradisjonelle melodiformler" (*Norveg* 7, 1960, p. 13–28).

Griechische Musik und Europa: Antik–Byzanz–Volksmusik der Neuzeit. (Ed. R.M. Brandl and E. Konstantinou.) Aachen, 1988.

Grigor'ev, Aleksandr D. See *Byliny: Archangel'skija byliny....*

Grigorjev, A.D. See Grigor'ev, A.D.

Grinde, Nils. *Norsk musikhistorie. Hovedlinjer i norsk musikkliv gjennom 1000 år.* Revised 3rd edn. Oslo, 1981.

Groupa: Av bara farten. Inger & Leif Stinnerbom . . . Phonograph record. 1983. AMIGO AMLP 709.

Groven, Eivind. *Naturskalaen: Tonale lover i norsk folkemusikk bundne til seljefløyta.* Skien, 1927.

Grundtvig, Svend. See *Danmarks gamle Folkeviser.*

Grüner, Nielsen. *Hakon, Folkelig vals.* 1920.

Gudmundson, Per. See Eriksson, Leif & Gudmundson, Per.

Guilcher, Jean-Michel. *La tradition populaire de danse en Basse-Bretagne.* Thesis, Paris, 1963.

Guizzi, Febo & Leydi, Roberto. *La zampogne in Italia. Strumenti musicali popolari no. 1. vol. 1.* Milan, 1985

Guizzi, E. See *Strumenti musicale . . .*

Gurvin, Olav. *Norsk folkemusikk.* Hardingefeleslåttar 1/1. Oslo, 1958.

Habenicht, Gottfried. "Ein rum nischer Sackpfeifentyp" (*SIMP* 3, 1974, p. 68–74).

Habenicht, Gottfried. "Kastenratschen in Ebnet bei Freiburg: Instrument und Brauch im Spannungsfeld der Generation" (*SIMP* 8, 1985, p. 43–51).

Habenicht, Gottfried. "Die rumänischen Sackpfeifen" (*Jb Volksliedf* 19, 1974, p. 117–150).

Habenicht, Gottfried. "Die Musik der rumänischen Hirtentrompeten" (*DJbf Vk* 13, 1967, p. 244–259).

Haeger, Ellika. "Om de första jojkningsuppteckningarna i Sverige" (*STM,* 1955, 37, p. 147–155).

Haid, Gerlinde. See *Die Geige in der europäischen Volksmusik.*

Haid, Hans. "'Tanzn ist kindisch, tanzn tuat man nit': Quellen zur Volksmusik im Oberinntal" (*Festschrift für Karl Horak,* p. 229–44).

Hako, Matti. See *Kansan Musiikki.*

Hammarlund, Anders. *Kaval. Ett bulgariskt folkmusikinstrument.* Stockholm, 1983 (Skrifter från musikvetenskapliga institutionen, Stockholms univ. 2).

Handbuch der europäischen Volksmusikinstrumente Hrsg. Institut für deutsche Volkskunde Berlin in zusammenarbeit mit dem Musikhistorischen Museum Stockholm durch Ernst Emsheimer & Erich Stockmann. 1967– (see Bachmann-Geiser; Elschek; Kumer; Kunz: Sárosi).

Hanna, Judith Lynne. *To dance is human: A theory of nonverbal communication.* Austin, Texas, 1979.

Hansson, Nils & Fahlin, Lars. "Spelar popmusik från fem århundraden" (*Dagens Nyheter* 199, 26 July 1987, p. 15).

Harker, Dave. *Fakesong. The Manufacture of British Folksong, 1700 to the Present.* Philadelphia, 1985.

Havanna Club: Orientexpressen med gäster. Phonograph record. Origo 1007 (LC 8433).

Haxhihasari, Quémal. "Le chansonnier éique populaire sujet historique" (*CPA,* 1982, p. 3–23).

Häggman, Ann-Mari. "Filmen återger glädjen i dansen. Fynden och forskning till Ragna Ahlbäck 17.7.1981." *Meddelanden från folkkulturarkivet* 7, Svenska litteratursällskapet i Finland, p. 157-182.

Hedwall, Lennart. *Hugo Alfvén: En svensk tonsättares liv och verk.* Stockholm, 1973.

Helg och söcken: Bilder ur svenska folkets liv och arbete vid mitten av förra seklet. Ed. Mats Rehnberg. Stockholm, 1973.

Hellgren, Otto. See *Sånglekar från Nääs.*

Helmer, Axel. *Svensk solosång 1850–1890.* Thesis, Uppsala. Stockholm, 1972.

Helmer, Robert Herman Paul. *European Pastoral Calls and Their Possible Influence on Western Liturgical Chant.* Thesis, Columbia University, 1975. Ann Arbor, Michigan, 1978.

Herder, Johann Gottfried von. *Alte Volkslieder.* 1773.

Herder, Johann Gottfried von. *Volkslieder.* 1778–1779.

Hermann-Schneider, Hildegard. "'Alpenscene,' und 'Ländliches Charakterbild' im kompositorischen Schaffen des Münchner Hofmusikdirektors Ignaz Lachner" (*Festschrift für Karl Horak,* p.245–304)

Hernes, Asbjörn. "Salmetone og menighetssong" (*Kultur og Kirke,* 1940, p. 174–187).

Herzog, George. "Stability of Form in Traditional and Cultivated Music" (*The Study of Folklore,* p. 170–174).

Heyde, Ole. See *Den fynske sang.*

Hobsbawn, Eric. See *The Invention of Tradition.*

Hofer, Tamas. "The Perception of Tradition in European Ethnology" (*Journal of Folklore Institute*, 21: 2–3, 1984, p. 133–147).

Holst, Gail. *Road to Rembetika: Music from a Greek Sub-Culture. Songs of Love, Sorrow, and Hashish.* Athens, 1975.

Holzapfel, Otto. *Det balladeske: fortællemåden i den ældre episke folkevise.* Odense, 1980 (Ed. Laboratorium for folkesproglig middelalderlitteratur, Odense).

Honko, Lauri. See Kuusi, Matti & Honko, Lauri.

Horak, Karl. "Ländler" (*Volksmusik in Österreich*, p. 55–70).

Horak, Karl. See *Festschrift für Karl Horak.*

Hornbostel, Erich M. von & Sachs, Curt. "Systematik der Musikinstrumente: Ein Versuch" (*Zeitschrift für Ethnologie*,1914, p. 553-590).

Hornbostel, Erich M. von. *Tonart und Ethos. Aufsätze zur Musikethnologie und Musikpsychologie.* 1st edn. Leipzig, 1986 (Reclams Universal Bibliothek 1169).

Hoschkowsky. See Hoškovs'kyj.

Hoškovs'kyj, Volodymyr. "Ein ukrainisches Räuberlied der Ostkarpaten" (*BzM* 11:2, 1969, p. 81–90).

Hugill, Stanley J. See *Shanties from the Seven Seas . . .*

Hugill, Stanley J. *Shanties and Sailors' Songs.* London, 1969.

Huldt-Nyström, Hampus. *Det nasjonale tonefall.* Oslo, 1966.

Huldt-Nyström, Hampus. "Polsdanser og hallinger fra gamle norske noteböcker" (*Sumlen*, 1978, p. 24–39).

Hungarian Folk Music from the Collection of the Hungarian Academy of Sciences and the Hungarian Ethnographic Museum. Ed. Benjamin Rajeczy. Phonograph record. 1982. Vol. 3 Hungaroton LPX 18050-3.

Hungarian Instrumental Folk Music from the Collection of the Hungarian Academy of Science. Ed. Bálint Sárosi. Phonograph record. 1980. Hungaroton LPX 18045-47.

ICTM. See International Council for Traditional Music.

Idelsohn, A.Z. *Jewish Music in Its Historical Development.* New York, 1948.

Ileva, Anna. See *Narodni tanzi ot Srednogorieto.*

"L'instrument de musique populaire. Usages et symboles." Exhibition at Musée National des Arts et Traditions Populaires. Paris, 28 November 1980 to 19 April 1981.

International Council for Traditional Music. See *Journal of the International Folk Music Council* (1949–1967); *Yearbook of the International Folk Music Council* (1969–1980); *Yearbook for Traditional Music* (1981–).

The Invention of Tradition. Ed. Eric Hobsbawn & Terence Ranger. Cambridge, 1983.

Istorija ukrainskoj muzyki. Ed. A.Ja. Šreer-Thacenko. Moscow, 1981.

Jakobson, Roman. "Über den Versbau der serbokroatischen Volksepen" (Proceedings of the International Congress of Phonetic Sciences, Amsterdam, 3–8 July 1932. *Archives Néerlandaises de phonétique expérimentale* 8–9, Haag, 1933, p. 135–144).

Janácek, Leoš. *Arrangements of Moravian and Slovakian Folksongs.*

Jansson, Svea. *Svea Jansson sjunger visor från Åbolands skärgård Insp. Matts Arnberg 1957–61.* Phonograph record. 1978. Caprice CAP 1156 (Folkmusik i Sverige 13. Traditioninspelningar från Sveriges Radio).

Jeanson, Bo Gunnar. *Gunnar Wennerberg som musiker: En monografi.* Ed. Gunnar Wennerberg-Sällskapet. Stockholm 1929.

Jersild, Margareta. *Skillingtryck: Studier i svensk folklig vissång före 1800.* Stockholm, 1975. Thesis, 1975 (Svenskt visarkivs handlingar 2).

John, Otto. "Två Staffans-visor" (*Folkminnen och folktankar* 3, 1916, p. 14-18).

Johnson, Anna. See "Fäbodmusik i förvandling."

Johnson, Anna. See Gabrielsson, Alf & Johnson, Anna.

Johnson, Anna. Sången i skogen. *Studier kring den svenska fäbod-musiken.* Thesis, Uppsala, 1986 (Institution för musikvetenskap. Uppsala University). Stencil.

Johnson, David. *Scottish Fiddle Music in the 18th Century.* Edinburgh, 1984.

Johnson, Geir. *Norge i melodi Grand Prix.* Oslo, 1986.

Johnson, James. See the Scots Musical Museum.

Johnson, Samuel. *A Journey to the Western Islands of Scotland.* 1775/rptd. 1968.

Jonsson, Bengt R. *Svensk balladtradition, 1: Balladkällor och balladtyper.* Stockholm, 1967 (Svenskt visarkivs handlingar 1).

Josep, Crivillé i Bargalló. *El folklore musical.* Istoria de la música española nr 7. Madrid, 1983.

Jugoslavien: Folklig dans, musik och konst. Ed. Råland Ginsburg. Stockholm, 1979.

Kaculev, Ivan. "Zweistimmige Volksmusikinstrumente in Bulgarien" (*SIMP* 1, 1969, p. 142–158).

Kaden, Christian. *Hirtensignale-musikalische Syntax und kommunikative Praxis.* Leipzig, 1977 (Beiträge zu musikwissenschaftlichen Forschung in der DDR 9).

Kaden, Christian. "Utilitäres und Ästhetisches in der Struktur instrumentaler Arbeitssignale der Hirten" (*SIMP* 5, 1977, p. 51-60).

Kaivola-Bregenhøj, Annikki. *Bondebryllup: Optegnelser i Dansk Folkemindesamling.* Copenhagen, 1983 (Foreningen Danmarks folkeminders dokumentationsserie 2).

The Kalevala or Poems of the Kaleva District. Ed. Fr. Peabody Magoun, Jr. Cambridge (Mass.), 1963.

Kalevipoeg. Ed. Friedrich Reinhold Kreutzwald. Tallinn, 1953.

Kalewala taikka Wanhoya karjalan runoja suomen kansan muinosista ajoista. Ed. Elias Lönnrot. Helsinki, 1835/ rptd. 1930, 1935.

Kansan Musüikki. Ed. Anneli Asplund & Matti Hako. Helsinki and Vasa 1981 (Suomalaisen Kirjallisuuden Seuran toimituksia 366).

Karadžič, Vuk Stefanovic. See *Serbische Volkslieder.*

Karłowicz, Jan. "Narzędzia ludowe na wystawie muzycznej w Warszawie na wiosnęr, 1888." *Wisla*, 1888, p. 434.

Karpeles, Maud. "Definition of Folk Music" (*JIFMC* 7, 1955. Proceedings of the seventh conference of the International Folk Music Council. São Paulo, 1954, p. 6–7).

Karpeles, Maud. See *Folk songs of Europe.*

Kaufmann, Nikolaj. "Die Mehrstimmigkeit in der Liedfolklore der Balkanvölker" (*BzM* 9, 1967, p. 3–22).

Kealiinohomoku, Joann Wheeler. "Folkdance" (*Folklore and Folklife*, p. 381–404).

Kennedy, Peter. See *Folksongs of Britain and Ireland.*

Kerfstedt, Amanda. "En sångare och en sång" (*Idun*, 27 February 1908, p. 107–108).

Ketlewell, David. *The Dulcimer.* Thesis, Loughborough University, 1973.

Kjellberg, Erik. "Musiklivet i stormaktstidens Västergötland" (*Vi äro musikanter alltifrån Skaraborg.* Ed. Jan Ling. Skaraborgs länsmuseum 1983, p. 97–128).

Kjellström, Birgit. *Dragspel, Om ett kärt och misskänt instrument: Under medverkan av K. G. Andersson och Mogens Ellegaard och i samarbete med Musikmuseet, Stockholm.* Stockholm, 1976.

Kjellström, Birgit. See *Folkmusikvågen.*

Kjellström, Birgit. "Hembyggt: Instrumenttillverkning speglad i pressen" (*Folkmusikvågen*, p. 77–113).

Kjellström, Birgit. *Spelpipan i Dalarna* (Musikmuseet, 1964). Stencil.

Kjellström, Birgit. "Zur schwedischen Spilopipa" (*SIMP* 5, 1977, p. 39–44).

Klusen, Ernst. (Ed.) *Volkslieder aus 500 Jahren.* Frankfurt am Main, 1978.

Des Knaben Wunderhorn in den Weisen seiner Zeit. Ed. Erich Sockmann. Berlin, 1958 (Deutsche Akademie der Wissenschaften zu Berlin. Veröffentlichungen des Instituts für deutsche Volkskunde 16).

Knight, Frida. *Beethoven and the Age of Revolution.* London, 1973.

Knudsen, Thorkild. *Arbejdsvise og dansevise* (Nordisk seminar i folkedigtning 1, 1961).

Knudsen, Thorkild. See *Folkevisen i Danmark.*

Knudsen, Thorkild. "Model Type of Variant" (*DMT* 1961:3, p. 79-92).

Knudsen, Thorkild. *On the Nature of Ballad Tunes* (DFS-Information, 1967:1).

Kodály, Zoltán. *Folk Music of Hungary.* Revised 2nd edn. Lajos Vargas. London, 1971.

Kodály, Zoltán. see *Magyar Népdalok.*

Kodály, Zoltán. *A magyar népzene.* Budapest, 1937.

Kodály, Zoltán. See *A magyar népzene tára.*

Kodály, Zoltán. See *Népdalok.*

Kolberg, Oskar. *Piésni ladi polskiego: Zebrał i wyd.* Warsaw, 1857/rptd. 1961 (Dzieła wszystkie 1).

Kolessa, Filaret. "Das ukrainische Volkslied, sein melodischer und rhytmischer Aufbau" (*Österreichische Monatschrift für den Orient* 42, 1916, p. 218–233).

Kopec, Anna. "Zur Geschichte der Drehleier in Polen" (*SIMP* 6, 1979, p. 142–145)

Kortsen, Bjarne. *Tonal and Formal Structure of Norwegian Religious Folk Tunes.* Bergen, 1969.

Kortsen, Bjarne. *Tonality and form in Norwegian springleiks.* Bergen, 1969.

Koski, T.A. See Stepanova, A. S. & Koski, T. A.

Koudal, Jens Henrik. *Rasmus Storms nodebog: En fynsk tjensekarls dansemelodier o. 1760.* Copenhagen, 1987.

Das Kralsche Geigenspielbuch = Kralowy husterski spęwnik. Eine Budissiner Liederhandschrift vom Ende des 18. Jahrhunderts. (With a foreword by Jan Raupp.) Facs. Bautzen, 1983.

Krause, Friedhilde. See *Serbische Volkslieder.*

Kresánek, Josef. see *Slovenské l'udové piesne.*

Kreutzwald, Friedrich Reinhold. See *Kalevipoeg.*

Krohn, IImari. *Über die Art und Entstehung der geistlichen Volksmelodien in Finnland.* Helsinki, 1899.

Krohn, IImari. See *Vanhoja pelimannisävelmiä*

Kruta, Beniamin. "Aperçus de la polyphonie albanaise et rapports de genèse" (*CPA*, 1981, p. 45–76).

Kruta, Beniamin. "Eléments musicaux convergents et divergents entre l'épopée albanaise" (*CPA* 4, 1984, p. 103–122).

Kruta, Beniamin. "Le chant polyphoniquè: deux voix de Toskeria" (*CPA*, 1984, p. 75 100).

Kumer, Zmaga. "Nachrichten zum Tanz im slowenischen Volkslied" (*Festschrift für Karl Horak*, 1980, p. 121–125).

Kumer, Zmaga. "Schriftzeugnisse und Bildquellen

von Instrumentalensembles in Slowenien" (*SIMP* 2, 1972, p. 165–172).

Kumer, Zmaga. "Volksmusikinstrumente in Slowenien" (*SIMP* 8, 1985, p. 144–146).

Kumer, Zmaga. *Die Volksmusikinstrumente in Slowenien.* Ljubljana, 1986 (Handbuch der europäische Volksmusikinstrumente Ser. 1 Bd 5).

Kunz, Ludvik. *Die Volksmusikinstrumente der Tschechoslowakei.* Leipzig, 1974 (Handbuch der europäischen Volksmusikinstrumente Ser. 1 Bd 2).

Kuusi, Matti & Honko, Lauri. *Sejd och saga. Den finsta forndiktens histona.* Trans. from Finnish. Stockholm, 1983.

Kvifte, Tellef. *Instruments and the Electronic Age: Toward a Terminology for the Unified Description of Playing Technique.* (Thesis, 1987).

Kvifte, Tellef. "Strøkfigurer–en side av bueteknikken i den norske hardingfele–og felemusikken" (*Sumlen*, 1986, p. 19–32).

Kvifte, Tellef. See Blom, Jan-Petter & Kvifte, Tellef.

Kvitka, K.V. *Izbrannye trudy v dvukh tomakh.* Ed. P. Bogatyrev. Moscow, 1971.

Kvitka, K.V. "Über die Verbreitung einiger Typen belorussicher Kalender und Hochzeitslieder" (*Sowjetische Volkslied- und Volksmusikforschung*, p. 309–328).

Laade, Wolfgang. "Musik in Süditalien" (*Die Karawane* 10:2, 1969, p. 82-92).

Laade, Wolfgang. *Die Struktur der korsischen Lamento-Melodik.* Thesis (Collection d'études musicologiques–Sammlung musikwissenschaftlicher Abhandlungen. 43), Baden-Baden and Strasbourg, 1962.

Laing, Dave Dallas, Karl, Denselow Robin, & Shelton, Robert. *The Electric Muse: The Story of Folk into Rock.* London, 1975.

Laitinen, Heikki. "Rune-Singing, the Musical Vernacular" (*Finnish Music Quarterly*, 1985 1–2, p. 36–41).

Landstad, Magnus B. See *Norske folkeviser*.

Landtmanson, Samuel. "'Menuetter och Polska Dantzar:' En fången karolins musikminnen" (*Svenska landsmål och svenskt folkliv*, 1912, p. 78–125).

Larsen, Holger. "Mellan magi och musikakustik: Något om vallhornets hantering" (*Musikmuseet Rapport*, 1986:2, Stockholm).

Larsen, Holger. "Bockhorn med påslående trätunga: En anmälan" (*STM* 59:2, 1977, p. 71–78).

Larsen, Holger. *Folkmusik i Europa: Fyra introducerande kapitel.* Stockholms universitet, Musikvetenskapliga institutionen, 1986.

Larsen, Holger. "Vallhornet i Sverige: Terminologi" (*STM* 61:2, 1979, p. 19–40).

Larsson, Gunnar. "Die estnisch-schwedische

Streichleier, ihre Spieltechnik und ihr Repertoire" (*SIMP* 6, 1979, p. 87–92).

Larsson, Sam. "De uppländska spelmanstävlingarna i Uppsala 7–8 maj 1909." (*Svenska landsmålen B* 5, p. 1–58.) Stockholm, 1909.

Launis, Armas. "Über die Notwendigkeit einer einheitlichen Untersuchungsmethode der Volksmelodien" (*Report of the 4th congress of the International Musical Society*, 1912, p. 185–86).

Leach, MacEdward. See *The Critics and the Ballad*.

Ledang, Ola Kai. "Aleatorik in der Volksmusik: Reflexionen über Spieltechnik und musikalische Eigenschaften der norwegischen Rindenflöte" (*SIMP* 7, 1981, p. 116–119).

Ledang, Ola Kai. "Fra gjetarinstrument til turistsuvenir. Seljefløyta i plast-alderen" (*Tvärspel* p. 44–53).

Ledang, Ola Kai. "Instrument–Player–Music on the Norwegian Langleik" (*SIMP* 3, 1974, p. 107–118).

Ledang, Ola Kai. *Norsk folkemusikk: Folkets musikk for og nå.* Oslo, 1979.

Ledang, Ola Kai. "Revival and Innovation: The Case of the Norwegian Seljefløyte" (*YTM* 18, 1986, p. 145–155).

Ledang, Ola Kai. "Seljefløyta–eit naturtoneinstrument?" (*Spelemannsbladet* 30, 1971, p. 8–10).

Leisiö, Timo. "Gedanken über die Beziehungen von finnischen und europäischen Trompeten, Flöten und Klarinetten in der Frühgeschichte" (*SIMP* 8, 1985, p. 147–156).

Leisiö, Timo. *Suomen ja Karjalan vanhakantaiset torvi- ja pillisoittimet.* Kaustinen, 1983 (Kansanmusiikkiinstituutin julkaisuja).

Leng, Ladislav. *Slovenské l'udové hudobné nástroje.* Bratislava, 1967.

Leydi, Roberto. See *I canti popolari italiani*.

Leydi, R. & Guizzi, F. See *Strumenti musicali . . .*

Leydi, Roberto & Mantovani, Sandra. *Dizionario della musica popolare Europea.* Milan, 1970.

Lindeman, Ludvig M. See *Ældre og nyere norske fjeldmelodier*.

Lindgren, Adolf. "Om polskemelodiernas härkomst" (*Svenska landsmålen* XII:5, p. 1–27). Stockholm, 1893.

Lindström, Anders. See *Folkliga koraler*.

Ling, Jan. *Europas musikhistoria–1730.* Uppsala, 1983.

Ling, Jan. "Folkmusik: En brygd" (*Fataburen*, 1979, p. 9–34).

Ling, Jan & Ramsten, Märta. "Gärdebylåten: En musikalisk ut- och invandrare" (*Sumlen*, 1984, p. 37–65).

Ling, Jan. *Levin Christian Wiedes vissamling. En studie i 1800-talets folkliga vissång.* Uppsala, 1965 (Studia Musicologica Upsaliensis 8).

Ling, Jan. *Nyckelharpan. Studie i ett folkligt musikinstrument.*

Stockholm, 1967 (Musikhistoriska museets skrifter 2).

Ling, Jan. "'O tysta ensamhet': Från känslosam stil till hembygdsnostalgi" (*Sumlen*, 1978, p. 10–58).

Ling, Jan. *Svensk folkmusik: Bondens musik i helg och söcken.* Stockholm, 1964.

Ling, Jan. See *Tvärspel*.

Liptov. Panorama l'udovej piešnovej a hudobnej kultúry. 4 phonograph records produced by Svetozar Stračina. 1982 Opus 9117 1211–14.

Lloyd, Albert Lancaster. *Folk Song in England.* London, 1967.

Lomax, Alan. *Cantometrics: An Approach to the Anthropology of Music.* Berkeley, 1976 (Cassettes and handbook).

Lomax, Alan. (Ed.) *Folk Song Style and Culture: A Staff Report on Cantometrics.* Washington, 1968.

López Chavarri, Eduardo. See Chavarri, Eduardo López.

Lopes-Graça, Fernando. See Giacometti, M. & Lopes-Graça, F.

Lord, Albert B. "History and Tradition in Balkan Oral Epic and Ballad" (*Western Folklore* 31:1, 1972, p. 53–60).

Lord, Albert B. See *Serbo-Croatian Folk Songs*.

Lord, Albert B. *The Singer of Tales.* Cambridge (Mass.), 1960 (Harvard studies in comparative literature 24).

Lounela, Pekka. "Finland's National Treasure–the Kalevala" (*Finnish Music Quarterly* 1–2., 1985, p. 4–11).

Lovatto, Alberto. *Primi appunti sulla ribeba in Valsesia.* Bologna, 1983.

Lönnrot, Elias. See *Kalewala*.

Lönnrot, Elias. See *Uusi Kalewala*.

Lönnroth, Lars. *Den dubbla scenen: Muntlig diktning från Eddan till Abba.* Stockholm, 1978.

Luchsinger, Richard. *Untersuchungen über die Klangfarbe der menschlichen Stimme.* Berlin, 1942.

Luihn, Astri. *Føroyskur dansur: Studier i sangdanstradisjonen på Færøyene.* MS, Oslo, 1979.

Lund, Cajsa. "Benflöjten i Västergötland–fynd och traditioner: En musikarkeologisk studie" (*Vi äro musikanter alltifrån Skaraborg.* Ed. Jan Ling, Skaraborgs länsmuseum, 1983, p. 13–40).

Lund, Cajsa. "Kinderklanggeräte und Musikarchäologie" (*SIMP* 8, 1985, p. 18–23).

Mačák, Ivan. "Die Kinderinstrumente in der Slowakei" (*SIMP* 8, 1985, p. 33–37).

Mačák, Ivan. "Streichinstrumentenensembles in der Slowakei" (*SIMP* 2, 1972, p. 137–145).

Mačák, Ivan. See *Musikethnologische Jahresbibliographie Europas*.

Macievsky, Igor V. "Zum Programmcharakter in instrumentaler Volksmusik" (*BzM* 14, 1972, p. 63–76).

Magnus, Olaus. *A Description of the Northern Peoples, 1555.* Ed. P. G. Foote. London: The Haklyut Society, 1996. (Original title: *Historia de gentibus septentrionalibus.*)

Maguin, Tom. *The Whistle Book.* Cork, 1985.

Magyar Népdalok. Ed. Béla Bartók & Zoltán Kodály. Budapest, 1906.

A magyar népzene tára: Corpus musicae popularins hungaricae. Ed. Béla Bartók & Zoltan Kodály . . . Vol. I–VI. Budapest 1951–73 (I. *Gyermekjátékok* 1951; II *Jeles napok* 1953; III *Lakodalom* 1955; IV *Párositók* 1959; V. *Siratók* 1966; VI. *Népdaltípusok* 1973).

Mahillon, Victor. *Catalogue descriptif et analytique du Musée instrumental du Conservatoire royal de musique de Bruxelles.* Ghent, 1880–1922.

Mahler, Elsa. *Die russischen dörflichen Hochzeitsbräuche.* Berlin, 1960 (Veröffentlichungen der Abteilung für slavische Sprachen und Litteraturen des Osteuropa-Instituts an der Freien Universität Berlin 20).

Mangård, Carl. *Richard Dybeck, romantikern och fornforskaren: En biografi.* Stockholm, 1937 (Västmanlands fornminnesförenings årsskrift 25).

Mankell, Abraham. *Musikens historia, i korta berättelser lättfattligt framställd.* Örebro, 1864.

Manker, Ernst. *Die lappische Zaubertrommel: Eine ethnologische Monographie.* Vol. 1–2. Stockholm, 1938–50 (Nordiska Museet; Acta lapponica 1; 6).

Mantovani, Sandra. See Leydi, R. & Mantovani, S.

Marcel-Dubois, Claudie. "The Type and Nature of French Instrumental Ensembles" (*SIMP* 2, 1972, p. 173–183).

Markl, Jaroslav. "Instrumental Ensembles in Böhmen" (*SIMP* 2, 1972, p. 146–151).

Markl, Jaroslav. "Zu einigen Fragen des folkloristischen Musik-Katalogs" (*Methoden der Klassifikation* . . . Bratislava, 1969).

Martin, György. *Hungarian Folk Dances.* Budapest, 1974 (trans. from Hungarian).

Martin, György. "Improvisation and regulation in Hungarian folk dances" (*Acta Ethnographica Academiae Scientiarum Hungaricae* 29:3–4, 1980, p. 391–425).

Matzner, Joachim. *Zur Systematik der Borduninstrumente.* Thesis, Baden-Baden, 1970 (Sammlung musikwissenschaftlicher Abhandlungen 53).

McCullough, Lawrence E. "Style in Traditional Irish Music" (*Ethnomusicology* 21:1, 1977, p. 85–97).

McDonald, Joseph. See A Collection of Highland Vocal Airs . . .

Meinert, Joseph George. *Alte deutsche Volkslieder in der Mundart des Kuhländchens.* Vienna, 1817.

Mersenne, Marin. *Harmonie universelle contenant la théorie et la pratique de la musique.* Cramoisy et Ballad, 1636–37/rptd. 1963.

Methoden der Klassifikation von Volksliedweisen. Symposia 2. Ed. Oskar Elschek & Doris Stockmann. Bratislava, 1969 (Slowakische Akademie der Wissenschaften. Institut für Musikwissenschaft.) (See Elschekova; Markl; Suppan.)

Miso, Pirro. "Le rôle et la fonction ethno-artistique de la lahouta" (*CPA*, 1985, p. 187–200).

Miso, Pirro. "Le sharkie (instrument cordophone) et ses fonctions musicales" (*CPA*, 1981, p. 133–152).

Moberg, Carl-Allan. "Bröllopsmusiken på Runö" (*Om visor och låtar. Studier tillägnade Sven Salén, den 7 november, 1960.* Stockholm, p. 96–111).

Moberg, Carl-Allan. "De folkliga koralvarianterna på Runö" (*STM*, 21, 1939, p. 9–47).

Moberg, Carl-Allan. "Två kapitel om svensk folkmusik: 1 Tonalitetsproblem i svensk folkmusik, 2 'Ro, ro till fiskeskär,'" (*STM* 32, 1950, p. 5–49).

Moberg, Carl-Allan. "Från kämpevisa till locklåt: En översikt över det folkmusikaliska uppteckningsarbetet i Sverige" (*STM* 33, 1951 p. 5–52).

Moberg, Carl-Allan. "Om vallåtar: En studie i de svenska fäbodarnas musikaliska organisation" (*STM* 37, 1955, p. 7–95).

Moberg, Carl-Allan. "Om vallåtar II: Musikaliska strukturproblem" (*STM* 41, 1959, p. 10–57).

Moeck, Hermann. "Typen europäischer Kernspaltflöten" (*SIMP* 1, 1969, p. 41–73).

The Morris Book. See Sharp, Cecil J.

Mosenko, Z.R. *Pesni Belorysskogo Polesj'a I–II.* Moscow, 1983–84.

Mozart, Wolfgang Amadeus. *Les influences étrangères dans l'oeuvre de W.A. Mozart. Etudes réunies et présentées par A. Verchaly.* Paris, 1958 (Colloques internationaux du Centre national de la recherche scientifique).

Munro, Ailie. *The Folk Music Revival in Scotland,* London, 1985.

Musical Instruments of the World. London, 1976. Swedish translation, 1979.

Musique corse de tradition orale. Recorded by Felix Quilici 1961–63. Phonograph record. 1982. Archives sonores de la Phonothèque nationale APN 82-1-3.

La musique des paysans de Grèce. Recorded by Wolf Dietrich. Phonograph record. 1979. SFPP AMP 2909 (Anthologie de la musique des peuples).

Nadel, Georg. *Georgische Gesänge.* Berlin, 1933.

Nagy, Béla C. "Typenprobleme in der ungarischen Volksmusik" (*SMASH* 2, 1962, p. 226–266).

Narodni pesni ot Samokov i Samokovsko. Ed. Elena Stoin. Sofia, 1975 (Publishers of the Bulgarian Academy (folk melodies collected by Vasil Stoin)).

Narodni tanzi ot Srednogorieto. Ed. Anna Ileva (Publishers of the Bulgarian Academy, 1978).

Nataletti, Giorgio. "Alcuni strumenti de musica popolari italiani" (*Les colloques de Wégimont* 4, 1958–60, p. 75–84).

Nazina, U.D. *Belorusskie narodnye muzykal'nye instrumenty.* Minsk, 1979.

När ja' va' en liten gutt. Folkliga barnvisor och ramsor från Bohusl n. Urval och kommentar Annika Norström. Folklig sång och musik i Västsverige. Musik i Väst. 3. Skriftserien. Göteborg, 1986.

Neal, John & William. *A Collection of the Most Celebrated Irish Tunes Proper for the Violin, German Flute or Hautboy.* Dublin, 1724/rptd. 1986.

Nenola, Kallio. *Aili: Studies in Ingrian Laments.* Suomalainen Tiedeakatemia. Academia scientiarum Fennica vol. C. no. 234. Helsinki, 1982.

Népdalok. Ed. Béla Bartók & Zoltan Kodály. Budapest, 1923.

Nielsen, Svend. *Stability in Musical Improvisation: A Repertoire of Icelandic Epic Songs (Rímur).* Copenhagen, 1982 (Dansk Folkemindesamling, Skrifter 4. Acta Ethnomusicologica Danica 3).

Nilsson, Helge. See *Visor och ramsor i Nordanstig.*

Nilsson, Martin P. *Årets folkliga fester.* Stockholm, 1936.

Norinder, Johan & Berg, Göran. "Som Kebnekajse fast mer arrangerat: Med bomber och bombarder i Bretagne" (*Musikens makt,* 1975:1, p. 4–5).

Norlind, Tobias. *Gamla bröllopsseder.* Stockholm, 1919.

Norlind, Tobias. *Studier i svensk folklore.* Lund, 1911.

Norsk folkemusikk. Ser. 1 Hardingfeleslåtter bd 7. Ed. Jan-Petter Blom, Reidar Sevåg & Sven Nyhus. Oslo, 1981.

Norske barnerim og leikar med tonar. Collected by Bernt Stöylen. Oslo, 1899.

Norske folkeviser. Ed. Magnus B. Landstad. Oslo, 1853.

Nyberg, Bo. *Namensläika: Om bröllopsmelodier från Rågöarna.* Uppsala, 1986 (Uppsats för 80 poäng i ämnet musikvetenskap vid Uppsala universitet).

Nyhus, Sven. See *Norsk folkemusikk.*

Nyhus, Sven. *Pols i Rørostraktom: Utgreiing om en gammel feletradisjon.* Oslo, 1973.

Obreschkoff, Christo. *Das bulgarische Volkslied.* Thesis, Bern & Leipzig, 1937.

O'Canainn, Tomas. *Traditional Music in Ireland.* London, Boston & Henley, 1978.

Ochlewski, Tadeusz. see *Dzieje muzyki polskiej . . .*

Oetke, Herbert. *Der deutsche Volkstanz: Mit einer Auswahlbibliographie und einem Notenanhang von Kurt Petermann.* Berlin, 1982.

Oinas, Felix J. *Studies in Finnic-Slavic Folklore Relations: Selected Papers.* Helsinki, 1969 (FF communications 205).

Old Jewish Folk Music: The Collections and Writings of Moshe Beregovski. Ed. Mark Slobin. Philadelphia, 1982.

Oliveira, Ernesto Veiga de. *Instrumentos musicais populares Portugueses*. Lisbon, 1966.

Ondrejka, K. m.fl. *Z pramenov krásy a proznania*. Smena, 1979.

O'Neill, Francis. See *The Dance Music of Ireland*.

O'Neill, Francis. See *Eighteen Hundred and Fifty Melodies*.

O'Neill, Francis. *Irish Minstrels and Musicians*. Chicago, 1913/rptd. 1987.

Ostenfeld, K. *Balmodikon i Danmark: dets tillkomst og anvendelse i musikpedagogisk sammanhaeng*. Copenhagen, 1976.

Övergaard, Einar. *Einar Övergaards folkmusiksamling*. Edited with comments by Märta Ramsten. Stockholm, 1982.

Pena, Paco. *Toques flamenco*. Bimport, 1976.

Pennant, Thomas. *A Tour in Scotland, and Voyage to the Hebrides, 1772*. Vol. 1–2. London, 1776.

Petermann, Kurt. "Die deutschsprachigen Tanzlehrbücher des 18. und 19. Jahrhunderts als Quelle für den Volkstanz" (*Festschrift für Karl Horak*, p. 35–54).

Petrides, Ted. *The Dance of the Rebets*. (*Rembetica . . .* p. 29–30).

Petrovič, Anca, *Ganga: A Form of Traditional Rural Singing in Yugoslavia*. (Ph.D. thesis, 1977).

Petrovič, Radmila. "The interrelationship of text and melody in Serbian lyric songs" (in *The Past of Yugoslav Music: Articles by Yugoslav Musicologists*. Moscow, 1970).

Petrovič, Radmila. "Some Aspects of Formal Expression in Serbian Folk Songs" (*YIFMC* 2, 1970).

Petrovič, Radmila. See *Serbian Folk Music*.

Piae cantiones ecclesiasticae et scholasticae . . . 1582/rptd. 1967. Ed. E. Marvia . . . Helsinki.

Pibroch, George Moss. Text & transcription: Peter Cooke. Edinburgh,1982. Tangent Cassette Series (Scottish tradition 6. School of Scottish Studies).

Picken, Laurence. *Folk Musical Instruments of Turkey*. London, 1975.

Playford, John. *The English Dancing Master or Plaine and Easie Rules for the Dancing of Country Dances with the Tune to Each Dance*. London, 1651/rptd. 1957.

Pohren, D.E. *The Art of Flamenco*. Madrid, 1962.

Pohren, D.E. *Lives and Legends of Flamenco: A Biographical History*. Seville, 1974.

Polskie Koledy i pastoralki. (Ed. Anna Szweykowska.) Polen, 1985.

Popova, Tat'jana Vasil'evna. *Russkoe narodnoe muzykal'noe tvorčestvo*. Moscow, 1955–1964.

Praetorius, Michael. *Syntagma musicum I–III*. 1616–1619/rptd. 1958–59.

Proca-Ciortea, Vera. "On Rhythm in Romanian Folk Dance" (YIFMC 1, 1969, p. 176–199).

Profeta, Guiseppe. "Canti nuziali nel folklore italiano." Florence, 1965 (Bibl. di Lares 22).

Propp, Vladimir. *Russkie agrarnye prazdniki*. Leningrad, 1963.

Putilov, B.N. *Russkij i juznoslavjanskij geroiceskij epos*. Moscow, 1971 (Akademia nauk SSR) (Institut etnografii im N.N. Miklucho-Maklaja).

Rabinovic, B. See Bacer, D. & Rabinovic, B.

Rajetzky, Benjamin. "Ost und West in der ungarischen Klageliedern" (*Festschrift für Walter Wiora . . .* p. 628–632).

Ramsay, Allan. *Scots Songs*. Edinburgh, 1719.

Ramsay, Allan. *Tea-table Miscellany*. Edinburgh, 1724.

Ramsten, Märta. See Dybeck, Richard.

Ramsten, Märta. "'Jag vet så dejlig en ros': Om folklig vissång" (*Folkmusikboken*, p. 104–157).

Ramsten, Märta. See Ling, Jan & Ramsten, Märta.

Ramsten, Märta. See Övergaard, Einar.

Ranger, Terence. See *The Invention of Tradition*.

Rapapallit ja Lakuttimet (Fornfinländska musikinstrument). Kauhava, 1985.

Rapport från herrgårdsseminarium och exkursion 2. Stencil, 1987.

Raupp, Jan. see *Das Kralsche Geigenspielbach . . .*

Raupp, Jan. "Der sorbische Dudelsack." *The Brussels Museum of Musical Instruments Bulletin*, Ed. René de Maeyer. Vol. VI–1/2, 1976, p. 32–36.

Recueil de chants et de danses populaires. Ed. "La Bourrée," société artistique des originaires du Massif Central. Paris n.d.

Rehnberg, Mats. *Folk: Kaleidoskopiska anteckningar kring ett ord, dess innebörd och användning under skilda tider*. Stockholm, 1977.

Rehnberg, Mats. see *Helg och söcken . . .*

Rehnberg, Mats. *Klackarna i taket. Om halling och jössehäradspolska*. Stockholm, 1966.

Rehnberg, Mats. *Säckpipan i Sverige*. Stockholm, 1943 (Nordiska museets handlingar 18).

Reimers, Lennart. *Alice Tegnérs barnvisor*. Thesis, Göteborg, 1983 (from Musikvetenskapliga institutionen, Göteborg, 8).

Rembetica: Songs from the Old Greek Underworld, Ed. Katherine Butterworth & Sara Schneider. New York, 1975.

Remmet, M. See Rüütel, I. & Remmet, M.

Rimmer, Joan. *Two Dance Collections from Friesland and Their Scotch, English, and Continental Connections*. Grins, 1978.

Rjujtel, I. See Rüütel, I.

Ronström, Owe. *Balalajkan: En instrumentstudie.* Stockholm, 1976 (Södra bergens balalajkors skriftserie 3). (60-poänguppsats Stockholms Univ. Musikvetenskapliga institutionen.)

Ronström, Owe. *Folkmusik i Europa, definitioner och begrepp.* MS 1987.

Ronström, Owe. *Säckpipan: Symbol för samtid och historia* (Föredrag vid säckpipefestivalen i Dala Järna. Edited version, 1986).

Rosenberg, Susanne. *Lisa Boudres sångliga och melodiska gestaltning i tre visor.* 60-poängsuppsats i musikvetenskap, Stockholms universitet, 1986.

Rouget, Gilbert. See Brăiloiu, Constantin.

Ruberto, Roberto. "Folk Poetry and Folk Music in Italy" (*Italian Quarterly* XIII/50, 1969, p. 33–49).

Rumanian Folk Music: Collected by Béla Bartók. Ed. Benjamin Suchoff. Haag, 1967 (The Bartók archives studies in musicology 24).

Rund um den Wein. Ed. Norbert Hauser, 1984, nr 5.

Runeberg, Johan Ludvig. *Älgskyttarne* (1832) (Samlade arbeten. Bd 2. Helsinki, 1921).

Runokoraler Folklig koralsång från svensk-Estland. Phonograph record 1985 (recorded 1938). Caprice CAP 1310 (Folkmusik i Sverige 26).

Ruong, Israel. See Arnberg, M., Ruong, I. & Unsgaard, H.

Rüütel, Ingrid & Remmet, M. "Några problem betrffande notation och analys av vespianska gråtsånger" (*Soome-ugrilaste rahvamuusika ja naaberkultuurid* Ed. I. Rüütel. Tallinn, 1980, p. 169–194).

Rüütel, Ingrid. See Stepanova, A.S. & Koski, T.A.

Rüütel, Ingrid. See *Finno-ugorskij muzykal'nyj* . . .

Salmen, Walter. "'Tyrolese favorite songs' des 19. Jahrhunderts in der Neuen Welt" (*Festschrift für Karl Horak,* p. 69–78).

Sandvik, Ole Mörk. *Ludv. M. Lindeman og folkemelodien.* Oslo, 1950.

Sandvik, Ole Mörk. *Setedalsmelodier.* Oslo, 1952.

Sandvik, Ole Mörk. *Springleiker i norske bygder.* Oslo, 1967.

Sárosi, Bálint. "Angaben über die instrumentale Volksmusik Ungarns in den Gedichten von József Gvadányi und János Arany" (*SIMP* 5, 1977, p. 114–120).

Sárosi, Bálint. "Gypsy Musicians and Hungarian Peasant Music" (*YIFMC* 2, 1970 (tr. 1971), p. 8–27).

Sárosi, Bálint. *Folk Music: Hungarian Musical Idiom.* Trans. from Hungarian. Budapest, 1986.

Sárosi, Bálint. "Geige und Zigeunermusikanten in Ungarn" (*Die Geige in der europäischen Volksmusik,* p. 60–70).

Sárosi, Bálint. "Instrumentalensembles in Ungarn" (*SIMP* 2, 1972, p. 116–136).

Sárosi, Bálint. *Die Volksmusikinstrumente Ungarns.* Leipzig, 1967 (Handbuch der europäischen Volksmusikinstrumente Ser. 1: 1).

Sárosi, Bálint. *Zigeunermusik.* Zürich, 1977 (original title: *Cigányzene*).

Sångboken, Vår gemensamma sångskatt: Visor, sånglekar och daner fram till 1950. Ed. Bertil Hallin. Malmö, 1984.

Sånglekar från Nääs. Ed. Otto Hellgren. Stockholm, 1905–28.

Scheurleer, D.F. "Welches ist die beste Methode, um Volks- und volksmässige Lieder nach ihrer melodischen (nicht textlichen) Beschaffenheit lexikalisch zu ordnen?" (*Zeitschrift der internationalen Musikgesellschaft* I 1899 f., p. 219).

Schindler, Kurt. See *Folk Music and Poetry of Spain and Portugal.*

Schiørring, Nils. See *Folkevisen i Danmark.*

Schiørring, Nils. *Det 16 og 17 århundredes verdslige danske visesang: En efterforskning efter det anvendte melodistofs kår og veje.* Thesis, Copenhagen, 1950.

Schiørring, Nils. "Omsyngning og inkonstans" (*DMT,* 1961:3, p. 74-78).

Schjelderup-Ebbe. Dag, see Benestad, Finn & Schjelderup-Ebbe, Dag.

Schmidt, Christian Martin. *Johannes Brahms und seine Zeit.* Regensburg, 1983.

Schmidt, Leopold. "Verwehte Volksmusikklänge bei Goethe und einigen seiner Zeitgenossen" (*Festschrift für Karl Horak,* 1980, p. 55–67).

Schneider, Manfred. See *Festschrift für Karl Horak.*

Schneider, Sara. see *Rembetica.*

Scotland and Scotsmen in the Eighteenth Century. Ed. A. Allardyce. Edinburgh & London, 1888.

The Scots Musical Museum (1787–1803). Ed. James Johnson in collaboration with Robert Burns.

Scots Song. Ed. Allan Ramsay. Edinburgh, 1719.

A Scottish Ballad Book. Ed. David Buchan. London & Boston, 1973 (The Scottish series).

Scottish Fiddle Music in the 18th Century. See Johnson, David.

The Scottish Psalter, 1929: Metrical Version and Scripture Paraphrases, with Tunes. London, 1929.

Scottish tradition cassette series. Tangent Records (School of Scottish studies. University of Edinburgh) (See *Pibroch*; *Waulking Songs from Barra*).

Seeger, Charles. *Studies in Musicology 1935-1975.* Berkeley, 1977.

Seide, J.G. *Tirol und Steiermark* 1841/rptd. Munich, 1980.

A Select Bibliography of European Folk Music. Ed. Karel Vetterl. Prague, 1966.

Serbian Folk Music. Ed. Radmila Petrovic. Phonograph record. Belgrade, 1981. RTB Records 25 10057.

Serbische Volkslieder Bd 1. Ed. Vuk Stefanovic Karadzic. Leipzig, 1824.

Serbische Volkslieder: Gesammelt und herausgeben von Vuk Stefanovic Karadzic, Ausgewählt und mit einem Nachwort versehet von Friedhilde Krause. Leipzig, 1980.

Serbo-Croatian Folk Songs: Texts and Translations of 75 Folk Songs from the Milman Parry Collection and a Morphology of Serbo-Croatian Folk Melodies. Ed. Béla Bartók & Albert B. Lord. New York, 1951 (Columbia University Studies in Musicology 7).

Sevåg, Reidar. *Det gjallar og det læt. Frå skremme- og lokkereiskapar til folkelege blaseinstrument.* Oslo, 1973 (Norsk kulturarv 10).

Sevåg, Reidar. "Geige und Geigenmusik in Norwegen" (*Die Geige in der europäischen Volksmusik*, 1971, p. 89–101).

Sevåg, Reidar. "Neutral Tones and the Problem of Mode in Norwegian Folk Music" (*SIMP* 3, 1974, p. 207–213).

Sevåg, Reidar. See *Norsk folkemusikk*.

Shanties from the Seven Seas: Shipboard Work-Songs and Songs Used as Work-Songs from the Great Days of Sail. Collected by Stan Hugill. London & New York, 1961.

Sharp, Cecil J. *English Folk Songs, Selected Edition.* London, 1921–23/rptd. 1959.

Sharp, Cecil J. *English Folksong: Some Conclusions.* Ed. Maud Karpeles. London, 1965 (Mercury books 61).

Sharp, Cecil J. *The Morris Book. A History of Morris Dancing with a Description of Dances as Performed by the Morris-Men of England.* London, 1907–13.

Sharp, Cecil J. *The Sword Dances of Northern England, Together with the Horn Dance of Abbots Bromley.* London, 1911–13.

Shaw-Smith, David. *Ireland's Traditional Crafts.* London, 1986.

Shepherd, John. See *Whose Music?* . . .

Shituni, Spiro. "Les traits originaux de la polyphonie de la Berie" (*CPA*, 1984, p. 101–114).

Shituni, Spiro. "A propos de l'échelle pentatonique dans la polyphonie de la Berie" (*CPA*, 1982, p. 69–80).

Siniveer, Kaarel. see Frey, Jürgen & Siniveer, Kaarel.

Siraták. See *A magyar népzene tára.*

Skjöldebrand, Anders Fredrik. *Voyage pittoresque au Cap Nord.* Stockholm, 1801.

Slaviūnas, Zenonas Jono. "Zur litauischen Vokalpolyphonie" (*DJbfVk* 13, 1967, p. 223–243).

Slavjanskij muzykal'nyj fol'klor. Ed. I. Zemtsovskij. Moscow, 1972.

Slobin, Mark. See *Old Jewish Folk Music.*

Slovenské l'udové piesne. Ed. Alica Elscheková, Oskár Elschek, & Josef Kresánek. Bratislava, 1959 (Slovenian Academy)(Slovakian folksongs, collected and organized by Béla Bartók).

Slovenské l'udové piesne a nástrojová hubda. Ed. Alica Elscheková & Oskár Elschek. Bratislava, 1982.

Sobieska, Jadwiga. See *Grajcie dudy, grajcie basy.*

Sobieska, Jadwiga. *Ze studiów nad folklorem muzycznym Wielkopolski.* Warszawa, 1972 (Polskie Wydawnictwo Muzyczne. Z Publikacji Folklorystycznych Polskiego wydanictwa muzycznego i institutu sztuki Polskiej).

Sobieska, Jadwiga & Sobieski. *Marian, Polska muzyka lodowa i jej problemy: Wybór prac.* Krakow, 1973.

Sokolova, V. K. "Ballady i istoriceskie pesni" (*Sovetskaya etnografija* 47:1, 1972, p. 52–57).

Soome-ugrilaste rahvamuusika ja naaberkultuurid. See *Finno-ugorskij muzykal'nyj fol'klor* . . .

Sowjetische Volkslied- und Volksmusikforschung: Ausgewählte Studien. Ed. Erik Stockmann & Hermann Strobach. Berlin, 1967 (Deutsche Akademie der Wissenschaften zu Berlin. Veröffentlichungen des Instituts für deutsche Volkskunde 37).

Sreer-Thacenko, A. Ja. See *Istorija ukrainskoj muzyki.*

Staatliche Museen: Preussischer Kulturbesitz. Museum für Deutsche Volkskunde. Berlin, 1980 (Kunst der Welt in den Berliner Museen).

Stamp, tramp och långkut: Kalle Almlöf. Phonograph record. Hurv KRLP2.

Stepanova, A. S. & Koski, T. A. "The Karelian Ejgi" (*Soome-ugri rahvaste muusikapärandist.* Ed. Ingrid Rüütel. Tallinn, 1977).

Stepanova, A. S. & Koski, T. A. *Karelskie Pricitanija.* Kaselija, 1976.

Stephan, Brigitte. *Studien zur russischen castuška und ihrerEntwicklung.* Munich, 1969 (Slavistische Beiträge 38). Thesis, Mainz, 1968.

Steszewski, Jan. "Geige und Geigenspiel in der polnischen Volksüberlieferung" (*Die Geige in der europäischen Volksmusik*, p. 16–37).

Steszewski, Jan. "Über die disharmonischen Funktionen eines staatlichen Tanz- und Musikensembles" (*Bidrag till musiksociologisk konferensrapport*, Göteborg, 1988).

Steszewski, Jan. "Z zagadnién wariabilnossci muzyki ludowej" (*Studia Hieronymo Feicht septuagenario dedicata.* Ed. Zofia Lissa. Krakow, 1967).

Stinnerbom, Leif. See *Groupa.*

Stockmann, Doris. *Der Volksgesang in der Altmark: Von der Mitte des 19, bis zur Mitte des 20, Jahrhunderts.* Berlin, 1962.

Stockmann, Doris. See *Albanische Volksmusik.*

Stockmann, Doris. See *Methoden der Klassifikation* . . .

Stockmann, Doris & Stockmann, Erich. "Die vokale Bordun-Mehrstimmigkeit in Südalbanien" (*Les colloques de Wégimont* 4, 1958–1960, p. 85–135).

Stockmann, Erich. See *Albanische Volksmusik.*

Stockmann, Erich. "Die Darstellung der Arbeit in der instrumentalen Hirtenmusik" (*SIMP* 3, 1974, p. 233-236).

Stockmann, Erich. See Emsheimer, E. & Stockmann, E.

Stockmann, Erich. "Die europäischen Volksmusikinstrumente: Möglichkeiten und Probleme ihrer Darstellung in einem Handbuch" (*DJbfVk* 10, 1964, p. 238–253).

Stockmann, Erich. See *Handbuch der europäischen Volksmusikinstrumente.*

Stockmann, Erich. See *Des Knaben Wunderhorn in den Weisen seiner Zeit.*

Stockmann, Erich. See *Musikethnologische Jahresbibliographie Europas.*

Stockmann, Erich. See *Swjetische Volkslied- und Volksmusikforschung.*

Stockmann, Erich. "Volksmusikinstrumente und Arbeit" (*DJbfVk* 11, 1965, p. 245–259).

Stockmann, Erich. "Zur Sammlung und Untersuchung albanischer Volksmusik" (*Acta musicologica* 32, 1960, p. 102–109).

Stockmann, Erich. See Stockmann, Doris & Stockmann, Erich.

Stoin, Elena. See *Narodni pesni ot Samokov* . . .

Stoin, Vasil. See *Narodni pesni ot Samokov* . . .

Stöylen, Bernt. See *Norske barnerim og leikar.*

Strajnar, Julijan. "Ein slowenisches Instrumentalensemble in Resia" (*SIMP* 2, 1972, p. 158–163).

Stratigraphische Probleme der Volksmusik in den Karpaten und auf dem Balkan. Ed. A. Elscheková. Bratislava, 1981.

Stravinsky, Igor. *Expositions and Developments.* London & New York, 1962.

Strobach, Erich. See *Sowjetische Volkslied- und Volksmusikforschung.*

Strumenti musicali popolari italiani. (Cassettes issued by the Italian national committee of ICTM, 1–3.) 1983.

Strumenti musicali e tradizioni popolari in Italia. Ed. R. Leydi & F. Guizzi. Rome, 1985 (Ethnomusicologia 5).

Studia instrumentorum musicae popularis. Stockholm: Musikhistoriskamuseet, 1969– (Musikhistoriska museets skrifter).

The Study of Folklore. Ed. Alan Dundes. Englewood Cliffs (NJ), 1965.

Subotić Dragutin P. *Yugoslav Popular Ballads: Their Origin and Development.* Folcroft, 1976.

Suliţeanu, Ghizela. "Kommandorufe bei der Forstararbeit. Ihre Bedeutung für die musikethnologische Forschung" (*DJbfVk* 15:1, 1969, p. 66–83).

Suliţeanu, Ghizela. "Antique South-European Elements in the Rumanian and Greek Contemporary Musical Folklore" (*Musikethnologische Sammelbande* 7 Graz, 1985, p. 181–208).

Sundin, Bertil. *Barns musikaliska utveckling.* Lund, 1978.

Suojanen, Päivikki. *Finnish Folk Hymn Singing: Study in Music Anthropology.* Tammerfors, 1984 (University of Tampere, Institute for folk tradition publications 11.) (Culture and language 3).

Suomalaista kansanmusiikkia 2. See *Arkkiveisuja* (Skillingtryck).

Suomalaista kansanmusiikia (Finnish Folk Music). Series of phonograph records with text booklets.

Suppan, Wolfgang. "Das Deutsche Volksliedarchiv und die Katalogisierung von Volksweisen" (*Methoden der Klassifikation* . . . Bratislava, 1969).

Suppan, Wolfgang. "Das geistliche Volkslied im Donauraum" (*Festschrift für Karl Horak*, p. 111–119).

Suppan, Wolfgang. "Melodiestrukturen im deutschsprachigen Brauchtumslied" (*DJbfVk* 10, 1964, p. 254-279).

Suppan, Wolfgang. "Über die Totenklage im deutschen Sprachraum" (*JIFMC* 15, 1963, p. 15-24).

Suppan, Wolfgang. "Volksgesang, Volkslied pflege und Chorwesen" (*Südtiroler Volkskultur* XXI/4–5, 1969, p. 59–62).

Suppan, Wolfgang. "Volksmusikforschung in Österreich" (*Volksmusik in Österreich*, p. 112–116).

Svea Jansson sjunger visor från Åbolands skärgård. Phonograph record (Caprice 1156).

Svenska låtar. By Nils Andersson. Stockholm & Lund, 1922–40/rptd. 1972–78.

Svenskt musikaliskt lexikon. See Envallsson, Carl Magnus.

Sveriges medeltida ballader. Ed. Svenskt visarkiv band 1–2, Uppsala, 1983, 1986.

Swartz, Anne. "The Polish Folk Mazurka" (*SMASH* 17, 1975, p. 249-255).

Szendrei, Janka. "Zur Frage der Verbreitung der Regös-Melodien" (*SMASH* 9:1–2, 1967, p. 33–53).

Szomjas-Schiffert, György. "Wiederkehrende Liedform in der ungarischen und in der tschechische-mährischen Volksmusik ('Neuer Stil')" (*SMASH* 20, 1979, p. 113–150).

Szövérffy, Joseph. "History and Folk Tradition in Eastern Europe: Matthias Corvinus in the Mirror of Hungarian and Slavic Folklore" (*Journal of the Folklore Institute* 5, 1968, p. 68–77).

Tampere, H. See *Eesti rahvalaule viisidega.*

Tampere, H. *Estonskja narodnaja pesnja.* Leningrad, 1983.

Tarasti, Eero. "The Kalevala in Finnish Music" (*Finnish Music Quarterly* 1-2, 1985, p. 12–23).

Tea-Table Miscellany. Ed. Allan Ramsay. Edinburgh, 1724.

Tegen, Martin. *Populär musik under 1800-talet.* Stockholm, 1986.

Tegnér, Alice. *Sjung med oss Mamma!* Stockholm, 1892 ff.

Ternhag, Gunnar. See *Folkliga koraler.*

Ternhag, Gunnar. "Spelmän i lag" (*Folkmusikvågen*, p. 19–40).

Thiel, Helga. "Quellen und Nachrichten zur volkstümlichen Geigenmusik in Österreich" (*Die Geige in der europäischen Volksmusik*, p. 102–123).

Thorsén, Stig-Magnus. *Ande skön kom till mej: En musiksociologisk analys av musiken i Götene filadelfiaförsamling.* Thesis, Göteborg, 1980 (Skrifter från Musikvetenskapliga institutionen, Göteborg 5).

Thorsén, Stig-Magnus. "Från spinnvisor till P3-musik. En historisk diskussion av arbetsmusikens funktioner" (*STM* 69, 1987, p. 7–36).

Thorsén, Stig-Magnus. See Bengtsson, Ingmar . . .

Thorsteinsson, Bjarni. *Islenzk thodlög.* Copenhagen, 1906–09.

Thuren, Hjalmar. *Folkesangen paa Færøerne.* Copenhagen, 1908.

Thuren, Hjalmar & Grüner-Nielsen, Hakon. *Færøsk melodier till danske kæmpeviser.* Copenhagen, 1923.

Tiersot, Julien. *Histoire de la chanson populaire en France.* Paris, 1889/rptd. 1978.

Tillhagen, Carl-Herman & Dencker, Nils. *Svenska folklåtar och danser.* Stockholm, 1949–50.

Tobler, Affred. *Kühreien oder Kühreigen: Jodel und Jodellied in Appenzell.* Leipzig & Zürich, 1890.

Todorov, Manol. "Instrumentalensembles in Bulgarien" (*SIMP* 2, 1972, p. 152–157).

Torp, Lisbet. *European Chain and Round Dances: A Comparative Study.* (MS 1987.)

Torp, Lisbet, *Danish Women's Dance in the 19th Century and in the Late 20th Century: Tradition and "Counter-Tradition."* (MS 1987.)

Torp, Lisbet, "'Hip hop dances': Their Adoption and Function among Boys in Denmark from 1983–84" (*YTM* 18, 1986, p. 29-36).

Tove, Per-Arne. See Bengtsson, Ingmar . . .

The Traditional Tunes of the Child Ballads with Their Texts . . ., vol 1. Ed. Bertrand Harris Bronson. Princeton, 1959.

Trautmann, Reinhold. *Der Volksdichtung der Grossrussen.* Heidelberg, 1935 (Sammlung slavischer Lehr- und Handbücher. Reihe 3:7).

Trojanowicz, Alicja. "Zur Spieltechnik der polnischen Sackpfeifen" (*SIMP* 6, 1979, p. 169–174).

Trutovskij, Vasilij. *Sobranie russkich prostikh pesen s notami.* St. Petersburg, 1776.

Trutovskij, Vasilij. *Vanacii na russkie pesni.* 1780.

Tschchikwadse. See Čikvadze.

Tvärspel: Trettioen artiklar om musik. Festskrift till Jan Ling. Göteborg, 1984 (Skrifter från Musikvetenskapliga institutionen, Göteborg 9).

Ujfalussy, József. see Bartók, Béla (1981).

Ungarische Volksliedtypen. Ed. Pál Járdányi . . . Trans. from Hungarian. Budapest, 1964 (*Volksmusikbibliothek*, Ed. Zoltán Kodály, 1).

Unsgaard, Håkan. See Arnberg, M., Ruong, I. & Unsgaard, H.

Uusi Kalevala. Ed. Elias Lönnrot. Helsinki, 1849.

Vanhoja pelimannisävelmi (Gamla spelmansmelodier). Ed. Ilmari Krohn. Helsinki, 1975.

Vargyas, Lajos. *Hungarian Ballads and the European Ballad Tradition.* Trans. from Hungarian. Budapest, 1983.

Vertkov, K.A. See *Atlas musikalnisch instrumentov narodov.*

Vertkov, K.A. "Beiträge zur Geschichtc der russischen Guslitypen" (*SIMP* 1, 1969, p. 134–141).

Vésteinn Ólason. *The Traditional Ballads of Iceland.* Thesis, Reykjavik, 1982.

Vig, Rudolf. "Gipsy Folk Songs from the Béla Bartók and Zoltan Kodály Collections" (*SMASH* 16:1–4, 1974, p. 89–131).

Visboken min nya skattkammare. Ed. Harriet Alfons. Stockholm, 1980.

Visor och ramsor i Nordanstig. Collected by Helge Nilsson. Malung, 1980.

Vītoliņš, Jēkabs. *Latviešu tautas mūsika, II: Kazu dziesmas.* Riga, 1968 (Latvijas PSR zinātnu akademja. Valodas un literatūras institūts).

Vītoliņš, Jēkabs. "Die lettischen Hirtenlieder" (*DJbfVk* 13, 1967, p. 213-222).

Volkov, Solomon. *Vittnesmål: Sjostakovitjs memoarer.* Trans. Nils L. Wallin. Stockholm, 1980.

Volks- und Hochkunst in Dichtung und Musik. Tagungsbericht eines Colloquiums. Saarbrücken, 19–22 October 1966.

"Das Volkslied in seinem Einfluss auf die gesammte Entwicklung dermodernen Musik" (article in *Die Gegenwart eine encyklopädische Darstellung der neuesten Zeitgeschichte für alle Stände.* Leipzig, 1849, bd 3, p. 667 ff).

Volksmusik in Österreich. Ed. Walter Deutsch. Vienna, 1984. (See Deutsch, Horak, Suppan, Wolfram.)

Vuk Karadžić. See Karadžić, Vuk Stefanović.

Wagner, Hermann. See *Das Erbe.*

Walin, Stig. *Die schwedische Hummel.* Stockholm, 1952.

Waulking Songs from Barra. Text booklet: Peter Cooke. Phonograph record. Edinburgh, 1972. Tangent Records TNGM 111 (Scottish tradition 3. School of Scottish Studies).

Wetter, Gustaf. "Uppsalastämman och folkmusiken" (*Hembygden*, 1954:4, p. 69–71).

Whose Music? A Sociology of Musical Languages. John Shepherd. London, 1977.

Wiora, Walter. "Concerning the Conception of Authentic Folk Music" (*JIFMC* 1, 1 949, p. 14–19).

Wiora, Walter. "Die Bedeutung der schriftlichen Quellen die Geschichte des europäischen Volksgesanges" (*SMASH* 13, 1971, p. 297-306).

Wiora, Walter. *Das echte Volkslied.* Heidelberg, 1950 (Musikalische Gegenwartsfragen 2).

Wiora, Walter. "Systematik der musikalischen Erscheinungen des Umsingens" (*Jb Volksliedf* 7, 1941, p. 128–195).

Wiora, Walter. *Europäische Volksmusik und abendländische Tonkunst.* Kassel, 1957 (Die Musik im alten und neuen Europa. Ed. Walter Wiora 1).

Wiora, Walter. See *Festschrift für Walter Wiora.*

Wolfram, Richard. "Das 'Gäurerlein' in Rothenthurm (Innerschweiz)" (*Festschrift für Karl Horak*, 1980, p. 87–94).

Wolfram, Richard. *Principien und Probleme der Brauchtumsforschung.* Vienna, 1972 (Österreichische Akademie der Wissenschaften. Philosophische-historische Klasse 278:2).

Wolfram, Richard. *Schwerttanz und Männerbund.* Kassel, 1936–38.

Wolfram, Richard. "Volkstänze" (*Volksmusik in Österreich*, p. 45–55).

Wolfram, Richard. *Die Volkstänzen in Österreich und verwandt Tänze in Europa.* Salzburg, 1951.

Wünsch, Walter. *Die Geigentechnik der südslawischen Guslaren.* Brno, Prague, Leipzig, & Vienna, 1934 (Veröffentlichungen des musikwissenschaftlichen Institutes der deutschen Universität Prague 5).

Wünsch, Walter. *Heldensanger in Südosteuropa.* Berlin, 1937 (Berlin Universität. Institut für Lautforschung. Arbeiten 4. Ed. D. Westermann).

Zemcovskij. See Zemtsovsky

Zemtsovsky, I. *Iskateli pesen.* Leningrad, 1967.

Zemtsovsky, I. *Melodika kalendarnych pesen.* Leningrad, 1975.

Zemtsovsky, I. "Russian Folk Music" (*NG* 19, p. 388–98).

Zemtsovsky, I. *Russkaja narodnaja pesnia.* Leningrad, 1964.

Zemtsovsky, I. *Russtaja protjažnaja pesnja.* Leningrad & Moscow, 1967.

Zemtsovsky, I. See *Slavjanskij muzykal'nyj fol'klor.*

Zilynakyj, Oret. "Ukrajinská lidová píse' v raných ņemeekých překladech a paraphrázích" (*Slavia* 37, 1968, p. 335–342).

Zimmermann, Georges-Denis. *Songs of the Irish Rebellion. Political Street Ballads and Rebel Songs 1780–1900.* Dublin, 1968.

Index

Accordion, 162
Albania: group singing, 119, 121; *gusle*, 139; *tambura*, 138, 140
Alpine romance, 112–113
Andersson, Otto, 55, 57
Art music, 1
Austria, 190–191, 192

Bagpipe, 140–148
Balkans: *gusle*, 8; heroic songs, 15, 86–90; "slavic melodies," 8; wedding music, 55
Ballads, 94–101; 111–114
Bartók, Béla, 19, 52, 202, 209–212, 213: folk music trascriptions 68, 71, 88; Hungarian songs, 107–110, 111; wedding music, 54
Basque country, 168–169
Beethoven, Ludvig van, 201–202, 203, 205
Beregovsky, Moshe, 216–217
Bilini, 15, 83–84, 85
Bjørkvold, Jon Roar, 46
Böhme, Frans Maghus, 18, 46, 200–201
Brahms, Johannes, 200–201, 202, 204
Break-dance, 194–197
Brentano, Clemens, 12–13
Broadsides, 103–104
Bulgaria: dance music, 182, 184; *gadulka*, 139–140; harvest songs, 38; *tambura*, 138, 140; wedding songs, 52, 58. *See also* Serbian songs

Carpathians, 119–120
Ceremonial music: calendar songs, 71–73; Christmas, 66–69, 71; harvest festivals, 35; seasons, 65–66, 69–71
Chastushka, 106–107, 212
Children's songs, 45–49
Chopin, Frédéric, 6, 206–207

Christmas songs, 66–69, 71
City music folklore. *See* Urban folk music
Clarinet, 163
Colinde, 68, 71
Competitions, song, 105–106, 174–175
Contredanse. *See* England: dance
Corsica, 63–64
Csárdás. See Hungary: dances
Czechoslovakia-Moravia, 15–16, 141
Czekanowska, Anna, 35–36

Dahlström, Greta, 118
Dance, folk. *See* Folk dances
Debussy, Claude, 209–210
Denmark: folk music, 13; May Day songs, 69–70; *Staffan* songs, 67, 68; violin, 155
Doina, 106, 107
Dulcimer, 136, 137
Duma, 85–86, 87
Dvorák, Antonín, 8, 9
Dybeck, Richard, 26–31

Elscheková, Alica, 111, 119–120
England: bagpipes, 143; Christmas carols, 68–69, 71; concertina, 162, 164; dance, 71, 182, 191–192, 193, 194; hurdy-gurdy, 148–149; lyrical songs, 106
Ensembles, folk music: duos, 168–170; festivals, 167; gypsy orchestra, 170–173; instrumental, 4; international, 176; revival groups, 217–218; unison/octave playing, 170
Epic songs, 35
Estonia, 14, 38, 60, 62. *See also Kalevala*

Fado, 215–216
Faeroe Islands, 98–99, 184
Feuilles volante, 103–104

Fiddle, 126, 154–161

Finland: domestic labor songs, 41; folk music performance, 118; herding music, 25; *jojk*, 74–78; *kantele*, 134–136; Karelian laments, 59–60, 61; lyrical songs, 106; popular hymns, 115; runic song, 7–8, 78–79, 106; violin, 155, 159; wedding music, 50, 53, 55

Flamenco, 214, 215

Flugblätter, 103–104

Flutes, 125–126, 127, 131–132

Folk dances: couples' 184, 187–193; definition, 1, 4, 179; group, 197; instruments, 180; line and ring, 180–186; music, 179–180; solo, 193–197

Folk melodies: as inspiration for composers, 4, 199–204, 206–212; variations on, 203–206

Folk music: classification, 108–109, 110–111; collections, 2–5, 6–21, 111, 113; definition, 1–3; diffusion, 5; methods of study, 21; performance, 8, 9, 19–20, 116–121; polyphonic, 118–121; popular arrangements, 200–203; publication, 2, 10–21; transformation, 3, 104, 206–219

Folk Music Coucil. *See* International Council for Traditional Music (ICTM)

Folk songs. *See* Folk music

Fortune telling songs, 69

France: *accordion musette*, 162; bagpipe, 145, 146; cattle drivers, songs of, 6; Christmas songs, 71; dances, 192–193; folk music collection, 16; *epinette*, 136, 137; hurdy-gurdy, 150–151; wedding songs, 52–53, 56, 57

Gammaldans, 215

Germany: dances, 179, 187, 191; *Des Knaben Wunderhorn*, 12–13; folk music collection, 18; group singing, 118; hurdy-gurdy, 150; recorder, 164; songs of work, 35, 41

Greece: *bouzouki*, 138, 141; ceremonial songs, 69; childrens' songs, 48, 50; laments, 64–65; *lira*, 139–140; *rebetiko*, 212–214; wedding songs, 52

Greni, Liv, 47, 48

Grieg, Edvard, 202–203, 207, 208, 210

Gusle, 84, 87–88

Gypsy music, 11, 55, 170–173, 214

Haeffner, Johann Christian Friedrich, 76–77

Halling dance, 194–197

Harmonica, 162

Harpu(*kantele*), 7–8

Harvest songs, 36–38

Haydn, Joseph, 200, 205, 206

Herding music, 23–36, 130–133

Heroic songs, 8, 15, 77–94, 101

Holst, Gail, 213–214

Hornpipe, 194, 195

Horns and trumpets, 130–131

Hungary: calendar song(*regös*), 72–73; Christmas songs, 71; *cimbalom*, 136; dances, 186–188, 190, 191; folk music, 10–11, 18–19; folk music orchestra, 171–173; laments(Siratók), 61–63, 64; lyrical songs, 107–110; performance, folk music, 117, 121–122; *tárogató*, 163; violin, 159; wedding songs, 52, 54

Hurdy-gurdy, 148–151

hymns, popular, 114–116

Iceland, 91–93, 120

Improvisation, 47, 105, 106, 108, 176, 179, 185–186

Instruments. *See* Musical instruments, folk

International Council for Traditional Music (ICTM), 19, 111

Ireland: bagpipes, 143–146; dance, 18, 194; Finn cycle(Fianaíocht), 15; folk music collection, 17–18; harp, 17, 152; nationalism in music, 90; performance, folk song, 118; *sean-nós*, 90–92; tin whistle, 129–130

Irish harp, 17, 152

Italy: bagpipes, 146–147; children's songs, 48, 49; folk music collection, 16; folk song competitions, 106; group singing, 48; harp, 152; heroic song(*storia*), 101; *lira*, 139–140; *ocarina*, 162–163, 164; songs of work, 39; violin, 159–160; wedding songs, 53, 55

Jewish folk music, 215–217

Jew's harp, 161–162

Jig, 18, 194–195

Jojk, 74–78

Kaden, Christian, 23, 24, 25

Kalevala, 14, 15, 79–83. *See also* Runic song

Kantele, 81–82

Kockim, T.A., 59, 61

Kodály, Zoltán, 18, 209, 210–212

Koledy, 67–68, 70

Kuhreihen, 6, 26, 28, 32, 33

Laments, 35, 51–52, 57–65

Ländeler. See Austria

Latvia, 52,53, 71, 73

Launeddas, 129

Lazarski, 70

Ledang, Ola Kai, 116–117

Lindeman, Ludvig Matthias, 12, 13, 115

Liszt, Franz, 10–11, 35, 51–52, 55, 57–65, 207–209

Lloyd, Albert, 1, 69, 106

Lönnrot, Elias, 3, 14, 59, 82–83, 134–135

Love songs, 50

Lubotjnaja, 103–104
Lullaby, 45–47
Lutes, 134–140, 151
Lyres, 134, 140, 151
Lyric song: ballads, 111–114; definition, 103; dissemination, 103–104

Martin, György, 186–187
Men and folk music: heroic songs, 8, 15, 77–94, 101; performance, 28, 60, 119, 120
Military music, 173
Minuet. *See* France: dances
Moberg, Carl-Allan, 26, 31, 33–34, 55, 57, 76, 114–115
Moral songs, 49
Morris dance. *See* England: dances
Mourning, songs of. *See* Laments
Mozart, Wolfgang Amadeus, 200, 204
Musical instruments, folk: bagpipe, 140–147; categorization, 124–127; definition, 123–124; fiddles, 126, 151, 154–161; flutes, 125–126, 127, 131–132; *gusle*, 136; horns and trumpets, 130–131; hurdy-gurdy, 148–151; *kantele*, 134–136; *launeddas* (triple clarinet), 129; reed pipe, 128–129; spontaneously created, 123–124, 126–128, 130; tin whistle, 129–130; tools and utensils, 22–23; "universal", 125–126; zithers and lutes, 134, 140, 151

Nationalism: and folk music, 12, 14, 15, 90, 143–144, 163, 190; in Irish music, 90; in lyrical ballads, 113–114; in Scottish music, 17, 113–114; in Slavic music, 8; in Swedish music, 9–11
Nielsen, Svend, 91–93
Norlind, Tobias, 110, 188–190
Norway: children's songs, 46–47, 48; dances, 105, 194–197; folk music collections, 12; Hardanger fiddle, 157–159; harp, 152; *jojk*, 74–78; *langeleik*, 136, 137; lullabies (*barnsuller*), 46–47; popular hymns, 115, 116; *sjöflöjt*, 164; *Staffan* songs, 66, 68

O'Canainn, Tomás, 90–91, 118

Pastoralki, 67–68, 70
Petrović, Radmila, 36–38
Poland, 67–68, 70, 149, 154, 159
Polska. See Sweden: dances
Popova, J.V., 52, 54, 60, 61
Popular music, 119, 200–203
Portugal, 39, 48, 49, 215–216

Rebetiko, 212–214
Reel, 18, 194, 195
Revival groups, 20
Rímur, 91–93

Romania: bagpipes, 141; children's songs, 48, 50; Christmas songs, 48, 50; *cobza*, 138, 139; dances, 70–71, 185–186; *doina*, 106, 107; folk music orchestras, 171, 172; laments, 64–65; violin, 159
Runic song, 78–79. *See also Kalevala*
Russia: *baja*, 162, 164; *bilini*, 15, 83–84, 85; *chastushka*, 106–107, 212; dances, 182, 183, 185; *dombra* and *balalaika*, 137, 138; folk music collections, 17, 18; folk music orchestras, 173–174; *gusle*, 136; hurdy-gurdy, 149; *jojk*, 74–78; laments, 58, 59, 60–61; New Year songs, 69; wedding music, 50, 51, 52

Sárósi, Bálant, 121–122, 140, 170, 171, 172
Scotland: bagpipe, 140, 143–146; ballads, 94–95; dance, 194, 195; folk music collections, 16–17; nationalism in music, 17, 113–114; popular hymns, 114, 115; songs of domestic labor, 41–43; violin, 155–156
Serbian songs, 36–38, 50
Shanty songs, 40–41
Slovakia, 52, 54, 70, 131–132, 171, 172
Society for Ethnomusicology, 19
Songs of work: domestic labor, 41–43; harvest, 35–39; pile-driving, 39; shanty, 40–41
Spain, 16, 35, 214, 215
Staffan songs, 66–67, 68
Stepanova, A.S., 59, 61
Stockman, Doris, 118–119
Stravinsky, Igor, 6, 52, 208–209, 211
Suppan, Wolfgang, 46, 47
Sweden: ceremonial songs, 71; children's songs, 48; criteria, folk music, 20; dances, 20, 184–185, 188–190, 194–197; ensembles, 173–176; folk music collections, 18; folk rock, 176–178; *gammaldans*, 215; herding music, 23–24, 26–27, 29–30; instruments, 20, 136, 137, 140–141, 142, 148, 150, 151, 154, 155, 157; *jojk*, 74–78; lyric song, 103; national anthem, 9–11; nationalism in music, 14; *Staffan* songs, 66–68; wedding music, 55–57; yodelling, 33, 34
Switzerland, 20, 33, 34, 120–121
Szendrei, Janka, 72–73

Telemann, George Philip, 199–200
Tyrolean songs, 112–113

Ukraine: *bandura*, 138, 140; *duma*, 84, 85–86, 87; folk music collection, 18; hurdy-gurdy, 149; laments, 60–61
Urban folk music, 1, 4, 14, 199, 212–218

Vargyas, Lajos, 99–101
Vaughan Williams, Ralph, 205, 206
Violin, 154–161
von Herder, Johann Gottfried, 2, 12

Wedding dances, 56–57

Wedding songs: "free marriage," 49–50, 51; instrumental, 53–55; singing weddings, 50, 52, 58; weeping weddings, 50, 51–52

Wiede, Levin Christian, 13, 111–112, 113

Women and folk music: accordion, 162; ballads, 94–95; hurdy-gurdy, 149–150; laments, 58, 60; lyrical songs, 8; performance, 28, 30, 36, 42–43, 51, 119

Work music. *See* Songs of work

Written music. *See* Lyric song

Yodelling, 33, 112

Zemtsovsky (Russian musicologist), 69, 71–72, 74

Zithers, 134, 140, 151